Negotiating Environmental Agreements in Europe

Negotiating Environmental Agreements in Europe: Critical Factors for Success

Edited by

Marc De Clercq

Centre for Environmental Economics and Environmental Management, Ghent, Belgium

Edward Elgar
Cheltenham, UK • Northampton, MA, USA

Published by
Edward Elgar Publishing Limited
Glensanda House
Montpellier Parade
Cheltenham
Glos GL50 1UA
UK

Edward Elgar Publishing, Inc.
136 West Street
Suite 202
Northampton
Massachusetts 01060
USA

A catalogue record for this book
is available from the British Library

Library of Congress Cataloguing in Publication Data
Negotiating environmental agreements in Europe : critical factors for success /
edited by Marc de Clerq.
        p. cm.
    Includes index.
    1.Environmental policy–Europe–Case studies.2.Environmental law,
    International. I.
    Clerq, Marc de, 1951-

GE190.E85 N44 2002
363.7'0526–dc21   2001056887

ISBN 1 84064 717 5

Printed and bound in Great Britain by MPG Books Ltd, Bodmin, Cornwall

Contents

Figures

Tables

Contributors

Josee J. Ligteringen, Hans Th. A. Bressers and Ellis Immerzeel of the Centre for Clean Technologies and Environmental Policy of the University of Twente (CSTM)

Giorgio Vicini, Jane Wallace-Jones of the Fondazione Eni Enrico Mattei of Milan and Venice (FEEM)

Franck Aggeri of the Ecole des Mines of Paris (CERNA-CGS)

Roger Salmons of the Centre for Social and Economic Research on the Global Environment of the University College London (CSERGE)

Helge Jörgens and Per-Olof Busch of the Forschungstelle für Umweltpolitik of the Free University of Berlin (FFU).

Marc De Clercq, André Suck, Steven Baeke, Akim Seyad, Bart Ameels, Centre for Environmental Economics and Environmental Management, Ghent University (CEEM)

Acknowledgements

As a general project co-ordinator of the NEAPOL project and editor of this book, I wish to express my sincere thanks also to Akim Seyad, Steven Baeke, André Suck, Bart Ameels and Roeland Bracke who subsequently assisted me in this task. Thanks also to all the project partner teams and their members, for the fruitful co-operation and the interesting discussions.

A sincere word of gratitude also to Liesbet Vanhollebeke who took excellent care of the book lay-out and of many practical aspects. Martine Veys assisted me in the financial aspects of the co-ordination of the project. I would also like to thank the European Commission and especially Katri Kosonen, who gave us the institutional support needed and who by her critical remarks always reminded us of our obligation to produce policy relevant research results.

PART ONE

Theoretical Reflections on Negotiated
Agreements

1. Introduction

Marc De Clercq

This book is the result of the European Commission sponsored NEAPOL project, which stands for 'Negotiated Environmental Agreements: Policy Lessons to be Learned from a Comparative Case Study'. The main goal of this project was to push the analysis on negotiated agreements further in a co-ordinated and multidisciplinary way. More precisely, the NEAPOL project focused on the use of negotiated agreements (NAs) as a policy instrument to deal with environmental problems.

This research project was financed by the European Commission and co-ordinated by the Centre for Environmental Economics and Environmental Management of Ghent University (CEEM), more particularly by Prof. dr. Marc De Clercq, Bart Ameels, Steven Baeke, Akim Seyad and André Suck. The partners of this research project were:

- Hans Bressers and Ellis Immerzeel of the Centre for Clean Technologies and Environmental Policy of the University of Twente (CSTM)
- Giorgio Vicini, Jane Wallace-Jones and Marialuisa Tamborra of the Fondazione Eni Enrico Mattei of Milan (FEEM)
- François Lévêque, Mathieu Glachant and Franck Aggeri of the Ecole des Mines of Paris (CERNA-CGS)
- Stephen Smith and Roger Salmons of the Centre for Social and Economic Research on the Global Environment of University College London (CSERGE)
- Martin Jänicke, Helge Jörgens and Per-Olof Busch of the Forschungsstelle für Umweltpolitik of the Free University of Berlin (FFU).

Negotiated agreements were defined in this research project as: 'agreements between public (national, federal or regional) authorities and industry, wherein both parties commit themselves to realise the environmental goals stated in the negotiated agreement'.

In plain words this definition of negotiated agreements boils down to a contract between two or more parties. However, while in some countries the term negotiated agreement is commonly used, in other countries the same or comparable initiatives by industry could never be called agreements in the traditional sense of two or more parties signing a contract with mutual obligations. Therefore, only few cases would have been available for study. Consequently this research also took into account unilateral commitments or initiatives by industry recognised by the government, as these can be considered to be factual agreements.

In recent years, several works have already been published on negotiated environmental agreements or NAs in Europe. This book however distinguishes itself from these, on the one hand through the multidisciplinary approach, on the other hand through the methodology used.

1. THE CENTRAL RESEARCH QUESTION

The central question of this research project was:
Which specific characteristics of negotiated agreements and which factors within the institutional-economic context wherein a negotiated agreement is used, influence the performance of negotiated agreements?

This central question can be broken down into the following research questions:

- Which theories with regard to negotiated agreements can justify the use of this instrument in combination with or as an alternative for traditional instruments of environmental policy?
- What are the characteristics of the negotiated agreements and of the sectors wherein they are used?
- How do the negotiated agreements perform?
- Which elements of the institutional-economic context had or have, an influence on the performance of these negotiated agreements?
- What policy options can be extrapolated out of the insights gained from the research questions above?

2. A MULTIDISCIPLINARY APPROACH

Due to the background of the different project partners, this book provides scientific reflections on NAs originating from different economic perspectives. Next to the obligatory literature analysis, the first part of the book contains scientific insights on NAs using:

- a policy science approach, which assessed negotiated agreements through the policy process focusing on the actors involved in the process and the interaction between the actors;
- a general economic approach, which focused on the role of market structure and on strategic interaction involved in the negotiation and/or the decision to negotiate an agreement. In this approach the number of firms entering the market and industry concentration is given and, by doing so, this approach concentrates on the influence of market structure on NAs;
- an innovational approach, which developed a knowledge-based perspective on negotiated agreements by investigating their dynamic properties in stimulating collective learning;
- an informational approach, which provided a stylised model of information processes at the implementation stage of negotiated agreements.

3. THE METHODOLOGY USED

As indicated already, the basic research strategy of the NEAPOL project is a comparative case study analysis. In the NEAPOL project twelve case studies on negotiated agreements spread over Belgium, France, Italy, The Netherlands and the United Kingdom were performed.

Because these case studies had to be cross-compared in the final stage, they had to be made up using a certain 'case study design'. This research design is the logic that links the data to be collected (and the conclusions to be drawn) to the initial questions of the NEAPOL project, it is the action plan to go from the research questions to the policy options.

Also for the cross-comparison, an unusual technique has been used: in order to be able to answer the central research question, a set of statements was drawn up. These statements could be scored for each of the NAs studied. Sub-aggregates of these scores, combined with a qualitative evaluation of each NA, then allowed the answering of the central question and the formulation of policy options.

4. THE DIFFERENT STAGES OF THE PROJECT

The NEAPOL project consisted out of three well-defined stages. The first stage could be called the 'theoretical stage'. This stage resulted in a more precise description of the central research question.

On the one hand the theoretical findings provided us with a more workable definition of 'performance'. According to us, the performance of a NA does not only depend on its application, but also on its environmental and economic impact, and on the development of the resource base it produced.

On the other hand, we got more insight in the specificity of the factors within the institutional-economic context that can play a role. More precisely, we expected the four following factors within the institutional-economic context to play a role in the performance of NAs:

- the policy tradition;
- the existence of an alternative legal instrument;
- the sector structure;
- the consumer pressure.

The influence of these factors was combined into four different hypotheses. Studying different NAs in Europe then allowed us to test these.

1. *A policy hypothesis*: The fact that public environmental policy evolves in a tradition and in a climate of consensus seeking, joint problem solving, mutual respect and trust is a crucial positive factor for the performance of negotiated agreements.
2. *An instrumental hypothesis*: The fact that public policy makers show readiness to use alternative policy instruments, as a stick behind the door to deal with the environmental problems, in case the negotiated agreement fails, is a crucial positive factor for the performance of negotiated agreements.
3. *A sectoral hypothesis:* The fact that the industry sector involved is homogeneous, has a small number of players and is dominated by one or two players, or has a powerful industry association that can speak for all its members, is a crucial positive factor for the performance of negotiated agreements.
4. *A competition hypothesis:* The fact that firms can gain competitive advantages by co-operating in the negotiation and by compliance with a negotiated agreement, is a crucial positive factor for the performance of negotiated agreements, due to the consumer pressure.

The second stage can be described as the empirical phase. In this phase, all case studies on the different NAs studied, were carried out. This was done using a common case study design, to allow for comparison between the cases. A shortened version of each case study can be found in the second part of the book. Here we give a brief overview of the studied agreements:

- Belgium
  — The negotiated agreement with respect to selective collection and processing of used batteries (BBAT);
  — The negotiated agreement with respect to emission reductions of SO_2 and NO_x from the electricity supply industry (BELE).
- United Kingdom
  — The negotiated agreement on energy efficiency in the chemical sector (EEFF);
  — The farm films recovery scheme (EFAR).
- France
  — The French household waste case: the Eco-Emballages consortium (FECO);
  — The French CFC conventions (FCFC).
- Italy
  — The 'Agip/Unione Petrolifera' negotiated agreements (IAGI);
  — The 'Vicenza' negotiated agreements (IVIC).
- The Netherlands
  — The negotiated agreement of the collaborative electricity producing companies on the reduction of SO_2 and NO_x emissions (DSO_2);
  — The negotiated agreement on the disposal of household appliances (DWHI).
- Germany:
  — The voluntary agreement on take back and disposal of batteries and accumulators (GBAT);
  — The self-commitment on environmental sound recycling of old cars (GELV).

The third stage of the project was the comparative and evaluation phase. All NAs studied were compared with respect to their performance and with respect to the institutional-economic context wherein they were created. This was done both qualitatively through discussion between the different project partners, and quantitatively through the setting up of an extensive checklist with regard to performance and context.

Once this was done, an evaluation could be made, and policy conclusions could be drawn. This is done in the third part of the book.

Different workshops between 1998 and 2000 were organised to provide for communication between the project partners and between the project partners and the European Commission, who financed this research, and to evaluate preliminary results. These workshops were organised in Venice, Twente, Paris, London and Ghent.

The final results were presented on a workshop organised at Ghent University, where respected scientists and practitioners were asked to comment upon the preliminary report. Their many relevant comments were taken into consideration when preparing this final research output.

Throughout the project, the CEEM team took care of the general administrative and scientific co-ordination. Although the research team was of an interdisciplinary nature, we were impressed by the effectiveness and efficiency of its collaboration.

2. Theoretical Reflections on the Proliferation of Negotiated Agreements[1]

Edited by Marc De Clercq and André Suck

1. INTRODUCTION

Negotiated agreements are a subset of the broader category of voluntary approaches. Voluntary approaches are commitments from polluting firms or industrial sectors to improve their environmental performance. The essential characteristic of a voluntary approach is of course voluntarism, meaning that the polluters who enter into this approach, do this on a voluntary basis without formal obligation put upon them by the government. Accordingly, they have a greater degree of freedom to act in comparison to other instruments of environmental policy (in most cases different forms of regulation). However, this statement has to be nuanced:

- First of all, in many cases the voluntary character of the action undertaken by the polluter is relative. Polluters make use of a 'voluntary' approach in order to prevent government intervention by other instruments (regulation or charges) that are deemed to be more damaging to their interest or in order to build up a positive relationship with certain stakeholders (consumers, associations, environmental NGOs, insurance companies, trade unions and so on), thus indirectly avoiding damaging action of those organisations to their interests.
- Second, the voluntary character relates to the decision whether or not to participate in the voluntary approach. However, not every action, in every case, can be freely chosen. Sometimes part of the action is determined by the government unilaterally, sometimes the terms of the action partly have to be negotiated with the government or other stakeholders.

Following Lévêque (1998), three groups of voluntary approaches can be distinguished: unilateral commitments, negotiated agreements and public voluntary programmes. The main criterion to differentiate between these three categories of voluntary approaches is probably the degree of public involvement in developing the contents of the agreement. It is lowest in the case of unilateral agreements: they are developed by the industry without any engagement of official bodies and governments. And it is highest in the case of public voluntary programmes: here, the contents of the agreement are mainly developed by the government; the industry and its enterprises are invited to participate in the arrangement voluntarily. Since negotiated agreements are the main subject of investigation in this project they are explained in detail more the following section.

1.1 Definition and Characteristics of Negotiated Agreements

Negotiated agreements are voluntary approaches between two parties: the contents and targets of this approach are neither the result of an purely industrial commitment nor of a purely governmental or administrative proposal. Instead they are the consensus result achieved after negotiations between the two parties. By this, negotiated agreements are arrangements between the public (national, federal or regional) authorities and industry. They are signed by the public authorities and either the single companies or an industrial association as the institution representing the single enterprises and firms of a branch or sector. Different contracting forms are possible, each effecting the cost-efficiency of the agreement in a special way. In most cases negotiated agreements include implicitly the affirmation of the government not to introduce a new piece of legislation (for example a compulsory environmental standard or an environmental tax) unless the voluntary action fails to meet the target (Lévêque, 1998). This legislative threat can be seen as typical characteristic of negotiated agreements in general.

Finally, some annotations are provided explaining the environmental topics adressed by negotiated agreements. In the study of EC DG III.B.5 (1996) a clear overview is given of the scope and the economic sectors in which negotiated agreements are most used. The most important environmental problems are emission reductions, waste, product recycling, energy use reduction/efficiency, product replacement, and input usage phase-out. NAs are used mostly in the following sectors: the chemical sector, the food sector, the transport, storage and communication sector, the metal sector, and the electricity, gas and water supply sector.

1.2 Reasons for the Increasing Use of Negotiated Agreements

Different surveys prove that negotiated agreements have become very popular as instruments of environmental policy, and that their use is growing over the years. This is very well illustrated by the conclusions of a study ordered by DG III.B.5 (see Figure 2.1) that made an inventory of 305 negotiated agreements in the European Union.

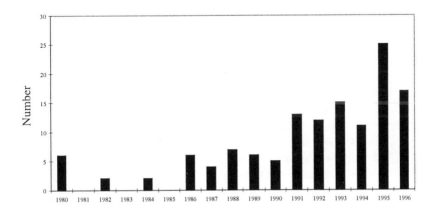

Source: EC DG III B.5, 1996

Figure 2.1   The growing use of negotiated agreements in the EU member states

This study indicates that every member state has, at least once, used negotiated agreements to deal with environmental problems. Further, it shows that The Netherlands and Germany account for 65 per cent of all the negotiated agreements signed in the European Union (see Table 2.1).

Table 2.1   Percentage share of each Member State in the use of negotiated agreements in the EU (until 1997)

A	B	D	DK	E	F	G	I	Ir	L	NL	P	S	Fin	UK	Total number
7	2	30	5	2	3	0	4	0,3	2	35	3	4	1	3	305

Source: EC DG III B.5 (1996)

In the literature, different authors come up with a huge diversity of the advantages, disadvantages, incentives and risks concerning negotiated agreements (for example Croci and Pesaro (1996), Ten Brinck and Morere (1998), EC (1997), Ingram (1996), Moffet and Bregha (1998), Imura (1998), Börkey and Glachant (1997), Seyad et al. (1996), Nilsson (1998). Table 2.2 provides for an overview of the most important advantages and disadvantages of negotiated agreements.

Table 2.2   Chances and risks of negotiated agreements

	Main advantages/incentives	Main disadvantages/costs/ risks
General	• Based on consensus and partnership • Reduced rule making time and potential to be implemented more quickly • Decreased litigation over a final agency rule • Integration of environmental improvement into business planning cycle: integration of sectoral industrial and environmental policies • Encouragement of innovationn	• Risk of free-riders • Distortion of competition • Postponement of regulation • Nothing more than business as usual • Uncertainty in the forecast of the results
For public authorities	• 'Information' disclosure by companies, in cases of information asymmetry • Higher efficacy and distribution efficiency of the environmental policy (cutting down times and common costs) • Promotion of proactive attitude of firms • Higher acceptability from industry • Incentives leading to innovation and technological transfer	• Risk of regulatory capture, although a means to reduce this problem is the design of mechanisms to review, update and improve the agreement • More costly to monitor compliance • Binding commitment on future governments and restrictions of governmental freedom • Danger of excessive bureaucracy

		• Dilemma: credibility depends on the setting of demanding requirements
For industry	• Possible influence on policy making: avoiding, affecting or delaying a coercive regulation • Flexibility in reaching the environmental goals (cutting down times and costs by keeping the same goals set by the regulation): quicker and smoother • Improvement of the image, which can lead to a better competition position • Finding out innovative technological solutions • Provision of cost-effective, tailor-made solutions • Motivating the staff	• Relative disadvantage for small and medium-sized companies (which cannot afford the necessary investments) • Costs: negotiation, implementation, monitoring and reporting costs • Better knowledge by public authorities increases the chance of sanctions in case of non-compliance • Loss of competitive advantage by means of publicly available information • Technological transfer to potential competitors, with the risk of free-riders as a consequence • Unpredictable effects on third-party groups
For third parties	• Increased influence on industry's behaviour	• More difficult and costly to participate and monitor

1.3 Theoretical Approaches

Different theoretical approaches are applied within the NEAPOL-project to explain the implementation and performance of negotiated agreements. The following section provides an overview of different approaches used to analyse the topic.

The first approach consists of *the public policy approach*. This approach forms part for a good introduction to the issue of negotiated agreements as it illustrates comprehensively the main features and aspects when this voluntary approach is implemented. In this regard, the methodological concept of the policy cycle will be used to take into account the dynamic implications of policy making. By applying this concept, negotiated agreements can be analysed throughout the whole policy process focusing on the actors involved and the interactions between them.

Another way to deal with negotiated agreements is the *general economic approach.* This theoretical approach examines the development and implementation of negotiated agreements from the perspective of individual actors. In this regard it is important to notice that scientifically, collective actors (enterprises, firms, institutions) can also be modelled as individual actors. This approach tries to explain the existence of negotiated agreements as a result of decision choices of individual rational actors. Besides, it also focuses on the role of market structure and on strategic interaction involved in the negotiation and/or the decision to negotiate an agreement. In this context the free-riding problem during the implementation of negotiated agreements becomes a relevant research topic. The public policy approach and the general economic approach are the main theories applied to analyse negotiated agreements in the NEAPOL project. However,   these   basic theories are supplemented by two other perspectives which seem to be specifically relevant in the context of negotiated agreements. Previous theoretical and empirical research on negotiated agreements stressed the innovational potential of negotiated agreements due to their capability to induce learning processes by the involved participants. For that reason, a *knowledge based perspective on negotiated agreements* will be developed by investigating their dynamic properties in stimulating collective learning.

Finally, a last paragraph analyses the *informational aspects of negotiated agreements.* Because of the fact that negotiated agreements are stipulated away from normal political institutions, different possible implementation structures affect their performance in specific ways.

2. THE PUBLIC POLICY APPROACH

Explaining the public policy approach is a good introduction to the issue of voluntary approaches as it illustrates comprehensively the main features and aspects of their implementation. By using the methodological concept of the policy cycle it takes into account the dynamic implications of policy making. By applying this concept, negotiated agreements can be analysed throughout the whole policy process focusing on the actors involved and the interactions between them.

The key elements of this approach are explained in the following text. In the beginning, *policy* will be defined as 'striving towards the achievement of particular goals by means of particular instruments in a particular timeframe.' In this sense, policy is the response to a problem (Hoogerwerf, 1985). Public policy analysis often starts with an analysis of the *problem.* A problem can be defined as a discrepancy between a standard or a desired situation on the one hand and the perception of the actual or expected situation on the other hand. Therefore, the experience of a situation as a problem situation depends on our standards as well as on our perception of the situation.

The basis of the public policy approach is the *policy process*. The policy process consists of several phases (see Figure 2.2) (note that the phases do not necessarily follow up on each other, in practice it is a much more diffuse process during which phases can take place at the same time).

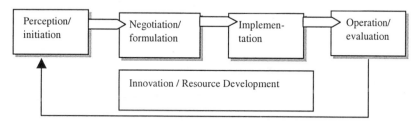

Figure 2.2   The different phases of the policy cycle

The concept of the policy cycle is applied to the development and implementation of negotiated agreements. As the central research question of the NEAPOL project deals with specific characteristics of negotiated agreements and factors within the institutional-economic context affecting their performance, the concept of the policy process can be succesfully combined with the examination of the preconditions of agreements. This will be achieved by relating the tested hypotheses to this concept. Before that, the concept of the public policy approach will be explained regarding its different characteristics.

2.1 Actors and Their Objectives

The focus chosen in the NEAPOL project is on the actors involved in the policy process. The role that the actors play in that process is – to large extent – determined by the actor's objectives and their resources. In order to complete the picture of the policy process further attention is paid to the interactions between the actors: the structure and character of interaction.

Different actors, individual or collective, public or private, participate in the negotiation process of the agreement. An actor is characterised by the ambition to realise specific objectives through the application of specific resources and instruments. In this context an actor can be an individual as well as a collective subject. The condition for defining a collective subject as an actor is (only) the internal homogeneity of its objectives. If this condition is not fulfilled, we can determine several actors within this single collective subject. In this case the collective subject wherein different actors play their part is called an 'arena'.

2.2 Actors and Their Resources

Every type of behaviour requires resources. The participation in a policy process implies the use of different resources by the actor in order to achieve the objectives. Different types of resources exist with no specific hierarchy between them: one actor, for instance, can balance the lack of one type of resource (such as economic resources) by using another type of resource (such as political or strategic resources), resulting in a win-constellation. The 'power' (weight) of an actor is therefore determined by the total amount of different resources, and by its ability (which is a resource in itself) to make use of them within the process. Four main types of resources can be identified: economic, political, legal and cognitive resources. Some resources may be exchangeable while others may not. 'Money' as an example of an economic resource is exchangeable while 'authority' as legal resource is not. The exchangeability of resources influences the power an actor derives from its resources.

2.3 The Interactions within the Policy Network

Finally, the interaction between the actors plays a major role in a public policy-oriented approach. The need to solve a collective problem leads to collective interaction between different stakeholders. Normally, this interaction results in the establishment of a network. This network again is characterised by specific patterns of interactions. Besides, a pattern of interaction involves the way in which actors approach each other and subsequently continue their interaction. Three main patterns of interaction can be identified: confrontation, bargaining and problem solving. Patterns of interaction can also be seen as strategies. Applying these strategies, the actors try to reach their objectives by influencing the decision-making process. The application of a specific pattern depends on the actors' perception concerning the distribution and quality of resources. A confrontation pattern is often the result of the concentration of crucial resources on few actors. In this pattern the actors perceive a high possibility for a win situation without any need for a compromise. In these cases, the crucial resources are often not exchangeable, or the remaining actors perceive them as not likely to be exchanged by the actors. For that reason bargaining is perceived as being out of the question.

The other two patterns (bargaining and problem solving) are the result of a broader distribution of resources. In the problem-solving pattern, resources are so diffused that the only way to achieve a solution is to co-operate. This presupposes that resources are exchangeable, because otherwise there is no need to bargain.

The pattern of interaction within a policy network can change during a decision-making process. Actually, once again, the strategy of the actors is determined by their perception of the situation in the process. The perception of resources (availability and exchangeability) is crucial for the way specific interaction patterns are chosen. In the context of the NEAPOL project it is assumed that the bargaining and the problem-solving pattern are of a specific concern as a precondition for successful negotiated agreements (policy hypothesis). In the following section the different hypotheses concerning the success factors of negotiated agreements postulated within the project will be analysed from the public-policy perspective.

2.4 Considerations Regarding the Formulated Hypotheses

As mentioned in the first chapter, four hypotheses have been formulated by the project partners. We will review each of them and consider their strength at first face by the (lack of) support they get from different authors and experiences.

2.4.1 Policy hypothesis
The fact that public environmental policy evolves in a tradition and climate of consensus seeking, joint problem solving, mutual respect and trust is a crucial positive factor for the performance of negotiated agreements.

In consensus-oriented policy the definition of objectives takes place within a context of complex dependency relations between different actors. The actors are mutually dependent in order to attain effective bargaining or problem solving. In a concept of public policy defined as 'consensual steering' a system of actors must be motivated to co-operative behaviour in order to solve an environmental problem. 'consensual steering' can be defined as some kind of bilateral communicative strategy. As Van de Peppel and Herweijer (1994) remark: this type of steering serves the goal of policy formation as well as getting support for public policy. In this context the implementation of negotiated agreements may provide for an efficient environmental policy in the following cases:

- the intended objective cannot be achieved adequately by means of regulation;

- in the exploratory phase of high uncertainty, agreements – possibly in anticipation of regulation – may result in an environmentally beneficial outcome providing for innovational benefits;
- an agreement can be signed in anticipation of regulation taking into account its contents;
- existing regulation is supplemented or tightened up in a covenant.

In the following, this public policy concept will be introduced in general terms. Glasbergen (1998) addresses five characteristics of this steering concept:

1. no single public actor is able to independently start a process of environmental renewal;
2. in order to attain problem solving a structured process of interaction and communication between public and private actors must be started;
3. in the interaction and communication process the environmental objectives must be set in a broad development perspective (socio-economic objectives) bearing in mind the different dimensions of sustainability (economic, social and environmental dimension);
4. the development perspective of public policy implies the creation of new opportunities for realising social interests; these social interests are forced for new reorientation by newly emerging environmental problems;
5. the development perspective results in a package deal offering each actor a win-situation in long-term perspective.

Within Dutch environmental policy the consensual steering concept became popular during the 1980s and 1990s. It fits perfectly with the general tendency towards a 'negotiating state' (Nelissen, 1994) and the internalisation of environmental objectives (Glasbergen, 1994). Consensual policy making can increase public support for policy measures.

2.4.2 Instrumental hypothesis
The fact that the public policy makers show readiness to use alternative policy instruments, as a stick behind the door to deal with the environmental problems, in case the negotiated agreement fails, is a crucial positive factor for the performance of negotiated agreements.

This hypothesis is acknowledged by different theoretical and empirical research. Van de Peppel and Herweijer (1994) recognise the importance of a stick behind the door, like the instrumental hypothesis does. If the policy maker does not keep sufficient power resources in reserve, for example if he cannot threaten the target group with direct regulation, often the agreement will not be achieved (Lindblom, 1980).

In this regard, 'speak softly and carry a big stick' is an old adage. A policy that aims at encouraging companies for the good and restricting them from the bad, calls for a delicate balance between external pressure and internal motivation. A policy approach on the basis of 'consensual' negotiations can only succeed if the realisation of the environmental objectives is ultimately perceived by all participants to be 'inevitable' and this perception can only be achieved by means of sufficient social and political pressure. In such a twin-track policy it is essential to achieve an optimal fine-tuning of legislation and enforcement on the one hand and consultation and self-regulation on the other.

The assumption that policy making is simply a free choice between different options has been discarded by policy sciences as empirically not tenable. As a consequence, the policy hypothesis as independent variable should be enhanced. The hypothesis should run as follows: 'The performance of a negotiated agreement is better when the public policy makers have alternative policy instruments as a realistic option at their disposal and show readiness to use them, as a stick behind the door to deal with the environmental problems, in case the negotiated agreement fails.'

2.4.3 Sectoral hypothesis
The fact that the industry sector involved is homogeneous, has a small number of players and is dominated by one or two players, or has a powerful industry association that can speak for all its members, is a crucial positive factor for the performance of negotiated agreements.

Glasbergen (1998) uses the sectoral hypothesis more as a requirement for concluding an agreement, than as a criterion for its effectiveness. He states that with regard to the issue or target of an agreement, it should be possible to distinguish well-organised parties. Representatives of those parties are supposed to represent their constituencies. The covenant can thus only be applied in an institutionalised field of actors in a social arena. 'An environmental covenant can be closed if it is possible to identify specific groups with a common interest. Those groups should also have an effective internal structure and a certain authority'. Glasbergen (1998) mentions this as one of the prerequisites for the conclusion of an agreement. In this regard, Klok and Kuks (1994) state that in a public-policy perspective, interest mediation must be realised by representitives, because without representation there would be too many actors involved.

One feature increasing the probability for the conclusion of negotiated agreements is a high degree of 'interconnectedness' of the policy network wherein the bargaining is taking place (Bressers, 1993). Interconnectedness includes a high intensity of interaction, multiple affiliations of persons to different network organisations and the existence of cross-functions between organisations. Under the assumption that the choice of policy instruments will tend to re-create the characteristics of the policy network involved, a high degree of interconnectedness is an important basis for the feasibility of negotiated agreements.

2.4.4 Competition hypothesis
The fact that industries are close to the final markets, is a crucial positive factor for the performance of negotiated agreements, due to the consumer pressure.

A high degree of closeness between final markets and consumers increases the risk of bad impacts for industries performing badly. Due to the salience of the produced brand, the chance of being criticised increases, with possible effects on both sales to consumers and on the 'toughness' of the provoked responses by authorities. It gives firms an additional incentive to keep a clear environmental record, both by accepting and complying with regulations and sometimes also by improving environmental performance on their own initiative. A second effect could be that the authorities feel extra stimulated to address the industry because of its high visibility to the public. Richard Andrews (1996) argues that the success of instruments like covenants (one type of self-regulation) depends highly on the motivations of the industry involved: if it is in the immediate economic interest of industry to achieve a better environmental performance, chances are high that the covenant is a success. Andrews distinguishes two types of business benefits: (1) reduced costs (of wasted materials and energy, of administrative costs of being regulated, etc.) and (2) maintaining or expanding markets (end-user consumer demand for green products and practices and customer demand for green products and so on). These argumentations will be reflected by applying the general-economic approach in the next section.

3. THE GENERAL ECONOMIC APPROACH

The general economic approach analyses negotiated agreements from the perspective of individual actors. In this regard, negotiated agreements can be seen as specific arrangement for collective action with different stakeholders participating. The general economic approach examines the decisions of single actors to participate and maintain such collective structures of action from an individual perspective. By that, it tries to explain the development, implementation and persistence of negotiated agreements from the perspective of individual rational actors and their choices to participate in such voluntary agreements. It also focuses on the role of market structure and on strategic interaction as important independent variables influencing the decision to participate. In this context the free-riding problem becomes relevant jeopardising an efficient implementation of negotiated agreements.

The theoretical analyses that will be developed basically share the following characteristics:

- *Perfect information.* In order to keep the topic easily manageable the lack of perfect or symmetric information will not be dealt as a problem.[2]
- *Oligopolistic framework.* Apart from the empirical importance of this industry structure, it will be apparent that an oligopolistic framework is particularly suitable for an assessment of the economic effectiveness of voluntary approaches as environmental policy tools.
- *Fixed number of actors.* The number of firms does not change due to the signature of a NA.
- *Non-cooperative Nash competition.* Firms act as 'singletons' by considering the strategies of other firms and public bodies as given. Therefore, the establishment of cartels during the implementation of a negotiated agreement is not possible. In short, the individual firm will be the main subject studied in the private sector (not the industrial organisation which can play the role of intermediary).

Given such a framework, NAs constitute an additional tool that firms can apply to improve their performance. Performance is typically measured in terms of profits. Therefore, eligible explanations for voluntary abatement must be translated into terms of greater profit levels. By that, the development, existence and persistence of negotiated agreements will be explained by the effects of their implementation on the production costs of the single enterprises. It does not try to explain, for example how non-economical interests of stakeholders like pressure groups and employees affect firms, behaviour. The general economic approach further analyses different welfare outcomes achieved by different policy solutions. By comparing them it looks for best policy solutions depending on the context in which the policy takes place.

In the individualistic economic approach the decision of single actors to participate in negotiated agreements can be explained by applying the following two considerations:

- *Reputation enhancing.* NAs would be an answer (in terms of quality enhancing and/or differentiation of products) to demand pressure for firm's environmental performance. If this would be the case, voluntary emission abatement would be rewarded by an increased demand and higher profits.

- *Regulatory gains.* The advantage from the signing of an NA would consist of the avoided costs of a public regulation aimed at addressing the environmental problem.[3]

3.1 The 'Green' Reputation - Enhancing-Explanation

The 'green' reputation-enhancing explanation stresses that the environmental utility of goods forms a central part of the utility function for consumers as well as for producers. If firms become aware of the fact that the environmental characteristics of goods form part of the utility functions for consumers they usually try to capture the implied additional demand. This will be achieved by ameliorating the environmental quality of their commodities and/or by differentiating their products with respect to their competitors. In this way, the consumers' sensitivity to the environmental quality of products affects the market demand. In the presence of 'green consumerism' firms do not only increase their potential market by enhancing their green reputation (demand shift), but also attain relatively higher prices and face lower demand reductions (slope variation) than in the standard case when this effect is not considered.

Brau, Jones, Tamborra and Vicini (1999) apply an economic model of Garvie (1997) who enhances the traditional Cournot model by integrating the effects of green consumerism into its considerations. In the traditional Cournot model the environmental externalities do not affect the firm's decision of activity. Garvie's model enhances the traditional Cournot model by integrating the 'green consumerism argument' into the firm's production decisions: If consumer behaviour is affected by the level of emissions, firms will start to internalise their pollutant externalities into their production decisions. In fact, if the emissions levels affect demand, enterprises must consider them when maximising profits. In a next step the oligopolistic framework is introduced to the model. Due to the presence of competitors, free-riding problems are expected to occur. A cleaner industry is in fact a sort of public good, in a sense that each firm entering a given market faces an increased demand due to 'green' preferences. The main results of the model applied are:

- The optimal firm's effort in reducing emissions is equal to zero only if consumers are not able to consider the environmental damage caused by the production of the good at all. If sensitivity to pollution is present to some extent (or if the standard is low enough for firms to over-comply with), then it is optimal for firms to abate voluntary.

- If consumers have partial awareness of environmental damage the result is, however, sub-optimal if compared with the social optimum.
- Industry output can be larger or lower than social optimum. In fact, imperfect competition tends to reduce the equilibrium output with respect to the socially efficient level,[4] while the externality effect acts in the opposite way. The lower the number of firms and the higher the degree of internalisation of the environmental damage, the more likely the output will be sub-optimal.
- Market structure affects social welfare. Due to the free-riding mechanism, a larger number of firms involves a lower level of total abatement effort.

The problem of free-riding may be reduced by establishing a co-ordinated solution. Garvie's co-ordinative solution exists of a two-stage game, where in a first stage an industrial association determines a voluntary abatement code knowing how, in the second stage, single firms chose their optimal supply level. The main results of this model are the following:

- The free-riding problem is, of course, solved: hence the new abatement level per firm is higher than in the uncoordinated case.
- Social welfare increases due to industry co-ordination. This result depends on the positive relationship between utility and abatement effort and the positive relationship between total quantity produced and abatement effort, that is consumers enjoy higher production levels of higher quality goods.

To summarise, Garvie's model shows how to insert green consumerism in an oligopolistic framework, and its co-ordinated equilibrium case can be closely identified with some NAs taking place in practice.

3.2 Regulatory Gains

A second explanation (consistent with the profit maximisation hypothesis) for the decision of firms to undertake voluntary action is to avoid future losses due to the intervention of a public body, whether a regulator or a legislative assembly. In this case, costs associated with the signing of the NA are lower than the costs that would have been caused by the introduction of a regulation. Public intervention can be in the form of an emission tax as well as a mandatory level of emissions. Also the degree and the extent of the intervention can be conceived to be fixed or dependent on firms' actions. In order to become workable, the regulatory gain hypothesis usually needs the introduction of some additional hypotheses (Borkey et al., 1998). In some cases it must be assumed that by reducing emissions through a voluntary action, firms can reach a given objective with lower costs than in the case when they are forced to satisfy a compulsory standard. Sometimes, it is also assumed that a well-chosen abatement level can pre-empt definitively a regulatory intervention that would impose a tighter standard, so that the environmental target is actually lower under the voluntary approach regime. In such a situation the implementation of a legislative solution is often very costly and the benefits offered by the agreement are always greater than the fixed costs implied by the legal intervention. In this case, the results in terms of effectiveness appear to be more problematic, given that even a small voluntary abatement effort can pre-empt a strict compulsory requirement.

Another argument jeopardising the effectiveness of negotiated agreements may consist in the existence of a private agenda on the side of the public authorities. This assumption describes the fact that the public institution charged with signing a NA acts in order to satisfy a private agent, which leads to sub-optimal solutions in terms of social welfare-solutions in general. The satisfaction of interests of the private agenda does not coincide with the objectives the institution is charged within aiming to address environmental problems.

3.3. An Assessment of the Main Implications Derived from the Models Surveyed

Within the general economic approach the models presented in the previous sections differ considerably in terms of their basic hypotheses. As a consequence, it is difficult to be more or less confident with respect to a given study and its main conclusions. Of course, some models are very general and use just a few acceptable presumptions, while the results obtained in others can be contingent to very restricted circumstances.

However, it is possible to check for the assumptions which are used to come to the stronger conclusions, in order to detect those prescriptions which hold even with a limited number of presumptions or with contrasting hypotheses. As a final assessment, we therefore present a list of main results so far encountered and of the main hypothesis they are based on. Here is a list of more important conclusions that have emerged.

- Firms' actions are strategic complements with respect to abatement effort.
- Voluntary abatement always occurs when there is consumer sensitivity.
- Greater consumer sensitivity to environmental problems usually implies higher abatement levels.

- A larger number of firms involve lower voluntary abatement.
- Co-ordination enhances welfare and environmental results.
- Policy mix indication (a): good policy mix between NAs and standards.
- Policy mix indication (b): good policy mix between NAs and subsidies (while it is negative when combined with taxes).
- The existence of a threat usually implies a positive equilibrium level of voluntary abatement.
- A more severe threat implies a better social result.
- Rivalry between regulator and legislator produces more negotiated agreements.
- Rivalry between interest groups produces weaker pollution regulation.

This is a list of the main assumptions which have been used until now:

Assumption A: consumers are sensitive to the pollution consequences of goods (green reputation enhancing assumption).

Assumption B: environmental sensitivity is directly related to income levels.

Assumption C: there is market segmentation on the demand side.

Assumption D: firms compete in terms of quantity.

Assumption E: firms compete in terms of prices.

Assumption F: an industrial association or co-ordination, which does not behave as a monopolist, exists.

Assumption G: a legislative threat exists and it can be pre-empted by signing a NA (the regulatory gain assumption).

Assumption H: pre-emption through negotiated agreements is automatic.

Assumption I: transaction and production costs under the voluntary regime are lower.

Assumption J: the regulator has a private agenda.

Assumption K: regulatory capture is possible.

Assumption L: decreasing returns in abatement levels for consumers' utility.

Assumption M: increasing returns in abatement levels for consumers' utility.

Assumption N: increasing marginal costs in abatement levels for firms.

Assumption O: constant marginal costs in abatement levels for firms.

In Table 2.3 we summarise both by connecting possible assumptions with adequate solutions. It is indicated if a special assumption is needed to result in a special conclusion. It will also be illustrated under what circumstances a given conclusion is predicted by different models with contrasting hypotheses (which become sufficient conditions). To distinguish these two cases, we use respectively the symbol **+** and the symbol **★**. Hence a great number of **★** indicates that the statement is contingent to a large number of ad hoc hypotheses, while a large number of ✦ indicates that the statement holds in different cases.

For example, in the presence of 'green consumerism', conclusion 1 (the more a firm voluntary abates, the more its competitors do the same) holds when firms compete in quantities as well as when they compete in prices and without particular assumptions regarding the marginal effects of pollution on consumers' utility. Conversely, the statement that the presence of a regulatory threat is sufficient to ensure a positive level of voluntary reduction of emissions is dependent on the assumption that both the firm and the regulator face lower cost under the negotiated regime.

Table 2.3   A summary of the main implications of the literature and of the hypotheses on which they are based.

Main Implications	Assumptions needed														
	A	B	C	D	E	F	G	H	I	J	K	L	M	N	O
Statement 1			✦	✦	✦						✦	✦	★		
Statement 2	★												★	★	
Statement 3							★				★	★		★	
Statement 4	✦			✦	✦		✦				✦	✦	✦	★	
Statement 5	✦			★		★	✦	✦			✦	✦	✦	✦	✦
Statement 6	★		★		★								★		
Statement 7	✦		★				✦	✦						✦	✦
Statement 8							★	★	★				★		★
Statement 9							★	★	★				★		★
Statement 10							★	★		★			★		
Statement 11							★				★	★		★	

Note: The ★ indicates that the assumption is absolutely necessary. The ✦ shows that the assumption indicated or its alternative is required. For example a ✦ both for hypothesis D and E means that the hypothesis is valid whether firms compete in quantities or in prices.

On the whole, it can be seen that the results which have a higher degree of generality are the number 4, 5, and 7, that is:
* A larger number of firms (more competition) involves lower voluntary abatement, given that this result is obtained
    a.   whether the reputation enhancing or the regulatory gain hypothesis is used;

    b.   whether firms compete in prices or in quantities and;

    c.   whether the marginal effects of abatement effort on consumers' utility are increasing or decreasing.

- Co-ordination among firms improves welfare and environmental effectiveness, given that it is predicted
  a.   whether the reputation enhancing or the regulatory gain hypothesis is used;
  b.   whether the marginal effects of abatement effort on consumers' utility are increasing or decreasing;
  c.   whether firms' marginal costs of abatement are constant or increasing.

- The association of a subsidy to the use of NAs is recommended, given that it holds
  a.   whether the reputation enhancing or the regulatory gain hypothesis is used;
  b.   whether firms' marginal costs of abatement are constant or increasing.

3.4 Considerations Regarding the Formulated NEAPOL Hypotheses

3.4.1 The policy hypothesis

The fact that the public environmental policy evolves in a tradition and in a climate of consensus seeking, joint problem solving, mutual respect and trust, is a crucial positive factor for the performance of negotiated agreements.

The theoretical analyses developed in the previous sections allow us to positively assess the policy hypothesis, but only indirectly. This conclusion emerges when studying the free-riding problem.

It is well known that in the presence of positive externalities related to a non-excludable good, its supply is sub-optimal and can even become zero if its unitary cost is sufficiently high. Conversely, it is also known that the reality is more complex and that the implications of a perfectly egoistic behaviour are often violated in the real world (and also in experimental economics). When individual behaviour is not exclusively egoistic, individual supply of the non-excludable good is greater than expected.

With specific attention paid to the hypothesis of a joint problem-solving climate, Garvie (1997) and Maxwell et al. (1998)'s models clearly prove that a greater degree of environmental performance and social welfare can be reached through co-operation between firms. In addition, in most of the models, firms are strategic complements in abatement efforts, that is they find it optimal to increase their own effort provided that the other competitors are doing the same. Expressed in terms of environmental protection levels and of social welfare, these outcomes justify the recommendation concerning the limitation of antitrust policy when firms are engaged in the negotiation of an environmental agreement (Maxwell et al., 1998).

With respect to the aspect of trust between actors, we can highlight its importance if we consider the transaction costs as inversely related to the degree of trust existent in the social environment.[5] Segerson and Miceli (1998) and Hansen (1997) show how a reduction in transaction costs is able to increase the period for which the firm and the regulator find it convenient to sign an agreement.

As a final caveat with regard to this policy hypothesis, caution should be paid when a private agenda of the regulator seems to be possible. If that is the case, a climate of consensus seeking, mutual respect and trust could simply facilitate the signature of socially harmful agreements (signed very quickly without allowing for the stakeholders to become aware of the real contents of the agreement). This is in fact the argument by which Hansen (1997) explains his prudent judgement with respect to the use of NAs.

3.4.2 The instrumental hypothesis

The fact that the public policy makers show readiness to use alternative policy instruments, as a stick behind the door to deal with the environmental problems, in case the negotiated agreement fails, is a crucial positive factor for the performance of negotiated agreements.

In general this hypothesis is proved by the theory, in particular through Segerson and Micelli's (1998) model which specifically deals with the role of legislative threat and its influence on social-optimal welfare solutions. In their work they proved that under certain circumstances an increase of this threat brings the result towards the social optimum. When there is a stick behind the door the voluntary abatements periods acceptable for firms and the regulator is wider. The wider scope of the abatement period increases the probability that the social optimum will be within this interval.

There are, however, two caveats. As shown by Hansen (1997), if alternative policy instruments are in the hands of other institutions, the regulator has the incentive to sign the agreement even if it is socially damaging. In addition, Maxwell et al. (1998) basically indicate that if the stick is too near the door, that is a regulatory intervention takes place even if the NA outcome only slightly differs from consumers' expectations, firms do not abate and wait instead for the stick to be used. In other words, regulation is perceived as inevitable.

3.4.3 The sectoral hypothesis

The fact that the industry sector involved is homogeneous, has a small number of players and is dominated by one or two players, or has a powerful industry association that can speak for all its members, is a crucial positive factor for the performance of negotiated agreements.

Here we interpret the term 'homogeneous' as referring to the good causing the emissions during its production. Applying this interpretation, the initial part of this hypothesis referring to the homogeneity of the sector, is in fact not supported by any green reputation enhancement models as they need product differentiation. In these models, firms are strategic complements. Therefore if a firm differentiates its product according to some characteristic of environmental performance, then the other firm(s) will find it optimal to improve their environmental performance by differentiation of the product.

All of the models support the hypothesis that a small number of players is socially beneficial: Garvie (1997) and Maxwell et al. (1998) through the free-riding mechanism; Segerson and Miceli (1997) provided that the dispersion of the cost distribution is positively related to the number of firms. The free-riding problem is, in fact, always inversely related to the number of players; the same is true for the possibility of reaching a co-operative equilibrium.

Our analysis does not allow the assessment of the statements concerning the preference of having one or more dominant players. To be able to do so we would need a leader/follower model.

Finally, Garvie (1997) supports the element of having an industrial organisation. This is particularly true in the model if an industrial organisation is seen as a tool for co-operation.

3.4.4 The competition hypothesis

The fact that industries are close to the final markets, is a crucial positive factor for the performance of negotiated agreements, due to the consumer pressure.

This statement is indirectly supported by Garvie (1997) and Arora and Gangopahdyay (1995), providing the reasonable hypothesis that consumers are more aware of the environmental consequences of products that they directly consume as opposed to intermediate outputs.

The assertion is not, however, supported by Maxwell et al. (1998), because a very strong consumer pressure would result in regulatory intervention and not in a voluntary abatement. This outcome is shown to be socially undesirable.

3.5 Conclusion

The crosscheck we made between the main results of our theoretical approach and the hypotheses posed by the NEAPOL project, has confirmed their validity. The few caveats, which were made, had emerged around the possibility of a regulator's private agenda and the threat of regulatory capture. In these cases, it is prudent not to generalise the validity of the 'instrumental' and 'competition' hypothesis (too strong threats or stakeholder pressure can discourage voluntary actions).

4. NEGOTIATED AGREEMENTS AND INNOVATION

4.1 Introduction: Critical Assessment of Traditional Public Policy Concepts with Regard to their Integration of Innovation

The following section investigates the dynamic properties of negotiated agreements in stimulating efficient collective learning and information processes. In this context a knowledge-based perspective will be developed pointing to the fact that an efficient monitoring of innovation is essential for a succesful implementation.

A knowledge-based perspective on voluntary approaches aims to extend the traditional framework for evaluating public policy. In more traditional concepts of public policy as in the institutional rational choice models, policy outcomes are the result of pressure and negotiations, between defined actors or interest groups with clearly defined strategies. Such concepts consider the political process as mainly driven by power relations between public authorities and firms[6]. Beyond other differences, at least four common assumptions can be identified that characterise such models:

1. The actors (authorities, elected representatives, interest groups) are regarded as homogenous categories whose influence is in line with the size and homogeneity of the group (Olson, 1965).
2. Each group of actors has information, which they attempt to hide from the others (assumptions of asymmetry of information and strategic behaviour).
3. The actors have a strategic overview of the process in which they are involved, that is they are presumed to have relevant information that enables them to establish preferences and pinpoint risks and opportunities.

4. The analysis focuses on the processes in the political arena, i.e. on the arguments traded and compromises reached between the authorities and company representatives.

These basic assumptions in many current examinations of voluntary approaches must be put into question – especially, when a knowledge-based analysis of this approach is taken into consideration. For that reason, the following two criticisms of the previous assumptions[7] are made:

1. They tend to over-estimate the cognitive and strategic capabilities of organisations – firms in particular. However, these organisations are characterised by contradictory debates and conflicts. As a consequence, the emergence of shared beliefs is never taken for granted.
2. They focus too much on power relations between public authorities and firms, but pay no attention to the current state of knowledge, which is the vivid starting point of a knowledge-based perspective. In fact, the forms of public intervention will be different, depending on the nature of problems to be dealt with and the knowledge available at different points in the negotiation process.

In this regard, the knowledge-based perspective of negotiated agreements is founded on a dynamic, interactive view of public policy. In order to achieve ambitious environmental targets, the authorities are forced to abandon their traditional role of unilaterally imposing a regulatory framework because they lack the necessary knowledge. Therefore, the issue of public intervention is no longer one of defining, implementing and controlling measures, but rather one of co-ordinating innovation. It is an active form of co-ordination seeking to identify obstacles that could threaten the innovation process.

In a knowledge-based approach this traditional viewpoint of public policy is unsuitable for evaluating situations of great uncertainty, involving long periods of time, a wide range of actors and controversial issues as it proves to be typical for contemporary environmental problems. It will be illustrated that an improvement of co-operation and collective learning needs a more dynamic and interactive view of public policy. This new and innovative view will result in a new definition of the tasks and the role of the state. In particular, once collective innovation is regarded as the chief means of achieving ambitious environmental targets, and no longer solely the issue of defining, implementing and controlling measures, the function of co-ordinating and managing innovation becomes more and more relevant.

4.2 New Co-operative Approaches: from Implementation-Oriented NAs to Innovation-Oriented NAs

The transition from the passively negotiating, regulating and controlling state to the more actively coordinating and innovation managing state is empirically accompanied by a change of nature of the negotiated agreements implemented. The early generation of agreements fits with the traditional view of governmental tasks and duties. In the following this generation is defined as '*implementation-oriented agreements*'. These agreements were implemented in a context of newly emerging and established administrative structures for environmental policy. They adhered to a 'hygienistic perspective': they aimed to combat localised pollution and identifiable polluters, where urgent intervention was required. Mostly, these agreements are characterised by a small local scope because of localised pollution. Furthermore, a feature of them is their low degree of uncertainty: the environmental problems to be dealt with are characterised by clear causal relations.

During recent years a new generation of negotiated agreements emerged reflecting a qualitative change. This qualitative change relates directly to a fundamental change of the problems this instrument tries to deal with. This new kind of problem is formed around the expression 'sustainability'. The imperative of realising sustainable targets implies an integration of social, economic and environmental objects. The need for reconciling the different dimensions of sustainability increases the complexity of adequate solutions to environmental problems. Furthermore, the concrete nature of environmental problems changed with a growing relevance of their global and transnational dimension. This increasing complexity led to new challenges for negotiated agreements themselves: they now have to deal with diffuse pollution, with controversial scopes and effects and with an increasing number of relevant participants and intermediaries (experts, government bodies, professional organisations). This new kind of challenge sets specific tasks for negotiated agreements: it requires an increase of the potential for innovation, which can only be achieved by a new understanding and definition of the instrument itself. It starts with the consideration that the setting of individual targets does not make much sense in such a context because the key issue is not only to diffuse technologies already available within an industrial sector, but rather to co-ordinate complementary efforts to invent new technologies and organizations in an open process. Furthermore, shortsighted 'corrective' policies are no longer enough. Forward planning is also required, coupled with long-term preventive measures aimed at definitive change in the behaviour of economic actors. Whereas in the past, state intervention took place in a stable setting where uncertainty and controversy were limited, it increasingly occurs in 'controversial universes' (Hourcade et al., 1992) characterised by enormous confusion about the nature and scope of pollution, the identity of the polluters, the validity of scientific knowledge and therefore about the solutions that should be implemented. The solution of these controversies cannot be envisaged without co-operation between various actors (scientists, manufacturers and representatives of civil society)[8] over long periods of time (often several decades), and at the cost of considerable effort regarding innovation.

All these developments led to a new understanding of negotiated agreements that resulted in a new definition of their characteristics and targets. This new generation of agreements is defined as *'innovation-oriented agreements'*. They are characterised by diffuse pollution, complex interdependencies between causes and effects, a high degree of uncertainty and innovation as a central challenge run on.

Table 2.4 summarizes the most significant differences between both types.

Table 2.4   Innovation-oriented NAs vs. implementation-oriented NAs

	Implementation-oriented NAs	Innovation-oriented Nas
Nature of the environmental problem	Localised pollution	Diffuse pollution
Level of uncertainty	Low	High
Key issue	Diffusion of BAT	Innovation at the source
Nature of monitoring	Control	Co-ordination

4.3 Innovation-Oriented NAs and Collective Learning Processes

In a knowledge-based perspective of negotiated agreements the motivation of innovation processes forms the main challenge for this approach nowadays. This applies in particular to innovations at the source[9] (cleaner technologies, recycling channels, green products and so on; contrasted to the *end-of-pipe innovations*: new depollution techniques for plants, catalytic converters for cars, waste water plants, etc. aiming to solve localised pollutions without changing the core process technology) – these demand specific efforts in order to be successful. *Innovations at the source* aim at reducing pollution by re-engineering the whole technology or product. Here, the change is much more important and may concern a wide range of actors, organisations and technologies since many problems are tackled on an international scale and require an extensive co-operation between heterogeneous actors. In such circumstances, monitoring focusing on co-ordination is necessary to stimulate co-operation, and to prevent opportunistic behaviour from threatening the whole process[10]. For adequate sustainable solutions – *innovations at the source* – we assume that an increasing number and heterogeneity of actors including a growing number of transformation stages and a higher level of uncertainty, result in a stronger need for efficient co-ordination schemes. Economic instruments, however, produce strong incentives but provide no indications for the technological paths to be explored. By contrast, voluntary agreements – at least innovation-oriented ones – include a stronger co-ordination scheme (quantitative objectives, designation of responsibilities, know-how transfer rules, monitoring schemes) and they therefore seem *a priori* well adapted to this situation. Moreover, their implementation may be complemented by economic instruments if efficient incentives are missing.

Subsequently, the application of innovation-oriented agreements will be illustrated by the example of waste management policy in the European Union. This policy subject was regarded as a priority issue from the beginning of the 1990s. In the early phase, the challenging task consisted in defining the general interest for this policy field. This subject could be broken down into several areas (household waste, hospital waste, building industry waste, used vehicles and so on). For that reason, pinpointing the general interest was not self-evident. Of course, there was general agreement on the fact that dumping had to be reduced, but the debate on waste valorisation suggested that not all methods are good ones: was it better to promote recycling or incineration with energy recovery? At what level should targets be set, and what form should they take? Was it advisable to set different targets for different materials? At the start of the 1990s, no one could reply to those questions because of a lack of scientific information: there were no recycling networks, no organised waste sorting and collection; further, virulent arguments divided the supporters of incineration, dumping and recycling. In other words, defining the general interest required the conduction of further investigations, which gave rise to learning processes.

In such circumstances a flexible negotiated approach in the form of an innovation-oriented agreement may be justified when schemes are devised from the start as those for learning and for monitoring innovation, and not as an inviolable contract. *'Innovation-oriented voluntary agreements'* take over this dynamic perspective: the agreement is defined not as an end in itself, but as a mean for acquiring new knowledge and organising the monitoring of a joint innovation process.

4.4 An Innovation Perspective on Different Aspects of Monitoring

In order to evaluate the new form of innovation-oriented agreements as co-operative approach strategy, different notions of the monitoring task will be examined. This will be done for the following reasons. The question of monitoring is connected with the problem of co-ordination. It is assumed that without active and co-ordinated monitoring, the innovation process will have less chance of achieving its goals: it will be eroded between incompatible worldviews. When the degree of uncertainty is significant, incentives are not enough to guide action, and learning is not merely the fruit of mutual contacts. In fact, collective learning works because monitoring schemes make it possible to pool knowledge, providing points of reference and enabling action to be oriented. In this section different aspects of a knowledge-based perspective related to monitoring and coordination will be contrasted with the traditional view of public policy in order to substitute them. They represent critics of the traditional approach in order to improve compliance with the newly emerging challenges (sustainability). The contrasting perspectives are illustrated in Table 2.5.

Table 2.5 The dialectics of environmental innovation

Traditional perspective	Innovation perspective
Competition	Learning, co-operation
Free-riders	Fast learners
Information asymmetries	Shared uncertainties
Best available technologies	Technological progress
Implementation	Innovation
Control	Co-ordination
Static efficiency	Procedural efficiency

Subsequently, the different notions of the most important features (shared uncertainties, fast learners, procedural efficiency) will be explained by comparing them with the traditional view of public policy.

4.4.1 The notion of shared uncertainties

The idea of asymmetries of information refers to the fact that the knowledge possessed by certain actors is not available to the others. In particular, industrial stakeholders are supposed to possess information about technologies and costs of environmental measures which the authorities do not own. In a knowledge-based perspective this assumption, which forms the core of agency theory, proves to be short-sighted with respect to the potential for innovation in such situations of uncertainty. Asymmetries of information only exist in a field of action, which has already been explored. In other words, asymmetries do not matter when the challenge of policy is the motivation and stimulation of innovation.

In the case of recycling, *'shared uncertainties'* (Aggeri and Hatchuel, 1997) existed at the start of the process because it was not possible to clearly identify opportunities and threats of this new policy. Each party took the risk of co-operation in order to find out new strategies and solutions in this policy field. Indeed, the innovation process provided an opportunity to gradually lift those uncertainties. But later, as information emerges and leads to the development of technologies, new opportunity problems arise. Naturally, manufacturers who have identified those new sources of income will tend to want to protect them by failing to reveal certain information. Thus, asymmetries of information will gradually be built up, not merely between manufacturers and the authorities, but also among manufacturers. From then on, the initial co-operation process will be reshaped and groups in competition with one another may emerge.

It can be concluded that information asymmetries are not a problem of innovation-oriented agreements in the beginning of their implementation due to their object to explore new information and strategies not discovered before. In this perspective innovation-oriented agreements are not jeopardised by the problem of information asymmetries. This only becomes true after first information has been discovered and developed. But in that moment, the agreement might already have achieved some of its targets.

4.4.2 The notion of the fast learner

The knowledge-based perspective of policy further criticises the bias of traditional policy and economic theory to treat the existence of free-riders as a problem in realising collective solutions. In these theories free-riders are reflected in the negative way that their strategic behaviour jeopardises the general interest. By this, their existence leads to sub-optimal policy results. Instead of reflecting and reasoning too much on the role of free-riders, an knowledge-based perspective of public policy tends to concentrate more on the notion of 'fast learners'. Instead of narrowing the public policy debate on the question how free-riders prevent innovation processes, more interest should be invested in fast learners, who are willing to take the risk of experimenting with new strategies in order to attain a better competitive position on the market. An innovation-based theory points to the fact that an understanding of *both* types (free-riders and fast learners) is necessary to understand the development and existence of strategies and the choice of alliances. Only by doing so will it enable us to understand the relative speed of learning as a central criterion in the innovation process.

4.4.3 The notion of procedural efficiency

This dynamic perspective of environmental policy has significant drawbacks on the way environmental policies can be considered. In a context of radical uncertainties and controversies, there is growing consensus that the question is not a matter of determining optimal solutions but rather of a sequential process of decision-making to provide framing while avoiding irreversible options (Hourcade, 1998). Consequently, as soon as monitoring is considered a key issue, having a great influence on the trajectories that can be taken by firms and on further public decisions, procedural efficiency is considered most appropriate. That does not mean that the initial characteristics of the problem do not have any influence on the final result. On the contrary, depending on the initial level of uncertainty, on the existence of credible threats, on the nature of the relationships within an industrial sector, and on the ease with which polluters can be identified and sanctioned, we may assume that voluntary agreements will have greater or lesser chances of stimulating innovation and co-operation processes among firms. But this initial context is not sufficient to predict the success or failure of this kind of approach.

To summarize, the dynamic quality of effectiveness depends not only on the initial circumstances but also on the monitoring methods put into practice by all parties, and in particular by the authorities. However, scientific efforts should concentrate on more effective forms of monitoring and co-operation mechanisms in the future.

4.5 Conclusion

In this section, we have tried to highlight the interests and limits of a new form of co-operative approach shaped by instruments and doctrines. It fits to the new kind of environmental problems emerging around the term of 'sustainable development'. In this context, the state does not have sufficient knowledge to lead the innovation process. As a consequence, its tasks change: it should create conditions that encourage co-operation between firms. In this regard, authorities and manufacturers have an interest to apply innovation-oriented agreements in situations of shared uncertainty and unidentifiable polluters. Such agreements serve as co-ordination mechanisms, encouraging co-ordinated learning and experimental action in companies. In addition – and this is more paradoxical – the introduction of these agreements could gradually increase the state's leeway to gain new knowledge.

5. THE INFORMATIONAL EFFICIENCY OF NEGOTIATED AGREEMENTS

This section is primarily concerned with the informational phenomena occurring at the implementation stage of negotiated agreements. It is analysed how different negotiation forms are affecting the informational efficiency and cost-effectiveness of agreements. In the model applied, two independent variables are set as given: asymmetries of information and shared uncertainties. Three burden-sharing schemes – translating a collective target into individual commitments and resulting in different cost-efficiencies – will be distinguished and their information efficiency assessed. The result derived from the examination will be that in a context of shared uncertainties, negotiated agreements lead to better results than regulation, while in a context of asymmetries of information only agreements with a strong industrial association may lead to a similar result as a regulation scheme.

In the following section the relationships between burden-sharing shemes, informational efficiency and cost-effectiveness will be discussed. Subsequently, the results will be summarised. The summary leads to a model of three burden-sharing schemes which can be found in the European Union. The section concludes with a discussion of the results and the implication for the NEAPOL project.

5.1 The Problem: Burden Sharing, Inter-Firm Bargaining and Transaction Costs

In the beginning, the influence of burden-sharing schemes on the cost-efficiency of negotiated agreements will be explained. By this, it can be concluded that the informational efficiency of these schemes provides for an indirect indicator to evaluate the cost-efficiency of negotiated agreements.

The degree of cost-efficiency (that is pollution abatement cost minimisation) is decided in the implementation stage of negotiated agreements. After concluding the collective agreement, firms have to split the collective target into single pollution abatement efforts in order to achieve it. In analytical terms, the issue is to efficiently allocate private pollution abatement objectives through inter firm bargaining. Cost minimisation will be reached if the allocation leads to the equalisation of private marginal abatement costs. This requires individual firms' pollution abatement objectives to be differentiated according to their cost performances. Firms with high pollution abatement costs have to get lower targets than the targets of low cost firms. Is it possible in the case of NA? The answer is: it could be but it is hindered by the existence of information/transaction costs.

5.1.1 It could be . . .

Theoretically, cost minimisation would be possible, because the industry as whole has an incentive to select an allocation of pollution abatement efforts which minimises the sum of these costs. But the most cost-efficient solution is a collective one and does not necessarily coincide with the interest of individual firms. They are interested in their own (private) cost and not in the aggregate pollution abatement costs. In particular the interests of low-cost firms contradict the collective interest since they have to complete higher objectives. A solution to this problem may be monetary transfers between firms allowing solution of the distributive conflict.

5.1.2 . . . but it is hindered by the existence of information/transaction costs

One general lesson of bargaining theory is that, the total exploitation of the 'gain from trade' is hindered by high information/transaction costs. The allocative efficiency of bargaining is threatened by high transaction costs. These transaction costs are mainly caused by the fact of strategic behaviour of the single actors. The information on preferences and costs is mainly private (that is only owned by the concerned firms). This leads to a high risk of manipulation of information in order to achieve own surpluses. In the end, costs and delays prevent the realisation of the best cost-efficient solution. This is why a large part of the economic profession is a priori doubtful about the cost-effectiveness of these collective negotiated agreements.

5.2 The Informational Efficiency as an Indirect Way to Assess Cost-efficiency

In the following we focus the analysis on the factors that impede the achievement of cost minimisation: the transaction/information costs. The evaluation of these costs will then provide with an indirect assessment of (pollution abatement) cost-efficiency. This approach is in line with Coase's insights on the efficiency of environmental policy (Coase, 1960). In this part, we try to develop this second option. For that, transaction costs will be restricted to information collection and processing costs.

5.3 Meta Study Results: The Different NA Burden-Sharing Schemes

Before the evaluation of information cost, we need to characterise NA burden-sharing processes. Besides the very rare case where individual obligations are already included in the agreement it is usual that the agreement only contains a collective target. This collective target must be translated into individual obligations in subsequent negotiations during the following implementation process. Three translation methods or burden-sharing schemes are possible (see Figure 2.3). One is the definition of individual obligations between firms themselves, another that by firms and an industrial association. Finally, direct bargainings between each firm and the regulator are another possibility. In this regard the following burden-sharing schemes between firms and an industrial association are possible.

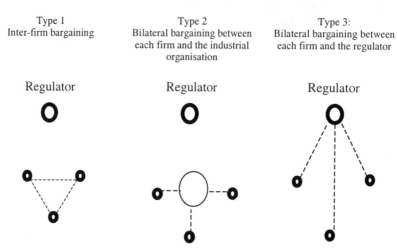

| Type 1
Inter-firm bargaining | Type 2
Bilateral bargaining between each firm and the industrial organisation | Type 3:
Bilateral bargaining between each firm and the regulator |

Figure 2.3   Three stylised burden-sharing schemes

These different models of burden-sharing schemes can be evaluated in terms of occurring *information costs* and the *ability of each scheme to minimise* them. When comparing the schemes in each informational context, the results are different. The ranking in terms of information costs is the following:

- Asymmetric information: Type 2 = Type 3 < Type *1*
- Shared uncertainty: Type 2 < Type 1 < Type 3

A powerful industrial association is always efficient (the type 2 scheme) because it provides two advantages: (i) it saves communication costs through the polarisation of communication structure and (ii) saves enquiry costs through the monopolistic completion of enquiry by the industrial organisation.

If no active industrial organisation is available (for cultural and/or historical reasons), a strong involvement of the regulator (type 3 scheme) is efficient in a context of asymmetric information because of savings in communication costs. However, in a context of shared uncertainty it prevents collective learning and the type 1 scheme is preferred. When, the number of firms in the agreement (which reflects the concentration in the sector) increases, this trend is reinforced.

The theoretical approach we have carried out in this section is very different from the standard economic approach. We have not investigated the cost-effectiveness but the cause for cost-effectiveness: the cost of information processing about pollution abatement techniques undertaken by the agents (the regulator or the firms). In this regard, good performances of NAs in an uncertain context are mainly due to collective learning. When using NAs, intense collective learning improves information of the firms and allows them to implement their private pollution abatement objectives at a lower cost. However, our approach remains exploratory. In particular, it is very sensitive to the assumptions which are made about the nature of information which is processed and the nature of the different information processing systems. More empirical work remains to be done about informational aspects in NAs to improve these assumptions.

6. EVALUATION FRAMEWORK AND PERFORMANCE INDICATORS

6.1 Introduction

Interest in the use of voluntary approaches as an alternative to regulatory and economic instruments has grown rapidly since the publication of the Fifth Environmental Action Programme (5EAP) in 1992, which advocated broadening the range of policy instruments that should be considered for the implementation of environmental policy, including '*the encouragement, in appropriate circumstances, of voluntary agreements and other forms of self-regulation*'.[11]   This view was reinforced in 1996 by the Commission's proposal for a review of the 5EAP[12],which highlighted (*inter alia*) voluntary agreements for special attention.

Within the broad range of voluntary approaches, particular attention has focused on the use of negotiated agreements (or environmental agreements), and in 1996 the Commission produced a Communication on the use of such agreements[13] which included a number of general guidelines that were intended to ensure their effectiveness, credibility and transparency. However, little attention has been paid to the evaluation of environmental agreements, either in terms of developing a coherent evaluation framework, or in terms of performing *ex post* analyses of actual agreements.[14]

In 1997, the OECD published a report on the evaluation of economic instruments (OECD, 1997), which identified a number of criteria for assessing their environmental and economic impacts. However, this report considered only the evaluation of charges and taxes, subsidies, tradable emissions permits, and deposit refund schemes; and it did not cover environmental agreements. Furthermore, the report adopted a narrow 'open loop' perspective of evaluation, focusing on the 'hard' impacts arising from the operation of an instrument. While it did discuss how the prevailing institutional framework may affect the feasibility and performance of an instrument, no consideration was given to how the process of formulating and implementing an instrument might change the institutional framework.

The objective of this chapter is to broaden the evaluation framework, and to develop specific evaluation criteria that can be applied to environmental agreements. In particular, a 'closed-loop' perspective is adopted, with explicit consideration given to the feedback that can arise during the formulation, implementation and operation of an instrument. As such, a policy instrument is regarded as an ongoing and adaptive process, rather than a one-time action.

In section 6.2, a general evaluation framework is outlined, which can be applied to a wide range of different policy instruments (that is emissions charges, permit-trading schemes, and environmental agreements). In section 6.3, the general framework is tailored to the particular case of environmental agreements, and a number of specific evaluation criteria are identified.

6.2 General Evaluation Framework

In this section a general evaluation framework is outlined, which can be applied to a wide range of different policy instruments (that is emissions charges, permit trading schemes, or environmental agreements). The framework is developed in the context of a 'policy cycle', which encapsulates the process by which a policy instrument is adopted, implemented, and amended (see Figure 2.4).

The policy cycle comprises four sequential stages: initiation, formulation, implementation, and operation. The cycle starts with the definition of a policy objective (or multiple objectives), and the selection of a preferred policy instrument (or set of instruments). For example, an air quality standard may be set for a particular pollutant (that is the target environmental variable $(TEV)^{15}$), with a tradable permit scheme proposed as the preferred implementation mechanism. The initiative may be driven by a number of different factors, including (*inter alia*): the discovery of new information about a particular environmental problem (or of the possible solutions); a coalescence of interests of certain actors in the policy process; or external forces such as a requirement to implement a particular EU Directive. In addition to the explicit policy objectives that are defined, there may be additional implicit objectives that can be inferred. For example, while it may not be stated as a policy objective, cost-efficiency can be inferred as an implicit objective from the preference for an economic instrument over direct regulation.

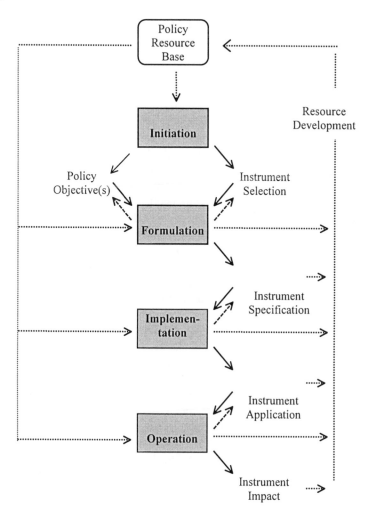

Figure 2.4   The policy cycle

In the second stage, the detailed specification of the instrument is developed. The nature of this process will depend on the choice of instrument. In the case of a charge, or a permit trading system, the authorities may undertake consultation exercises (either formally or informally) to get input from interested parties, and relevant experts, regarding the detailed design.[16] In the case of an environmental agreement, this stage represents the negotiations that take place between the parties regarding the detailed provisions of the agreement. In either case, it is possible that the process may lead to the rejection of the original choice of instrument (for example negotiations may fail to yield an agreement), or to an amendment of the policy objectives.

A distinction is made between the implementation of the instrument (that is the translation of the specification into an operational form) and its ongoing operation, although in reality there is a degree of overlap between the two. Again, the exact nature of the implementation process will vary between the different instrument types. It may require the setting up of new systems, and/or organisational structures (both for the authorities and those subject to the instrument), or even new markets. The original specification may require legal clarification and interpretation. In the case of an environmental agreement that has been negotiated by an industry association (or other representative body) it might include the drawing up of subsidiary agreements with individual firms. Consequently, there may be a divergence between the original specification of the instrument and its application in practice. To the extent that this is unintended (and undesirable),[17] the more care that is exercised over the specification of the instrument during its formulation, the less scope there is for discretion over its implementation.

The instrument may have a finite operational life, or it may be open-ended. The former is more likely to be applicable to an environmental agreement, the latter to an emissions charge. In the case of an open-ended instrument, provision may be made for review and/or revision after a specified period of time (see below). In addition it is possible that operational experience of the instrument may lead to some fine-tuning of the instrument without resorting to a full-scale re-formulation.

An important feature of the policy cycle is the concept of a 'policy resource base' which comprises: the prevailing *institutional network* (both formal and informal); the economic, political, legal, and cognitive *resources* of the various actors involved in the policy process (either directly or indirectly); the state of *relations* between these actors; and the actors' *perceptions* of the scale of the problem, the need for action, and the validity of different policy instruments. In particular, the resource base includes the state of knowledge of the actors (both collectively and individually), encapsulating both the total 'quantum' of knowledge, and also the 'distribution' of knowledge amongst the various actors. As such, it can accommodate the important informational concepts of 'shared uncertainties' (a low state of knowledge on the part of all actors in the process) and 'information asymmetries' (a discrepancy in the existing state of knowledge between actors) (see Aggeri 1999).

It is clear that the resource base may exert an influence on all stages of the policy cycle.[18] However, the various processes in the policy cycle (together with their outcomes) may in turn have an impact on the resource base. Potential positive feedback,[19] or 'resource development', would include (*inter alia*): the improvement of relations between actors resulting from increased mutual respect and trust; the generation of new and innovative information about the problem and potential solutions; the dissemination of knowledge amongst the actors. As such, resource development can reflect either an increase in the total quantum of resources (for example a reduction in shared uncertainties), or a decrease in the inequality of existing resource distribution between actors (for example a reduction in information asymmetries).

The dynamic nature of the policy cycle (with the inclusion of the 'resource development' feedback) allows it to accommodate the related concepts of learning and adaptation. During the course of its life, an instrument may pass through several phases, being amended as circumstances change and/or new information comes to light. Each phase can be thought of as a fresh policy initiative. Thus, any learning that occurs in the early phases of the instrument's life will change the resource base that shapes the later phases. This change could lead to a revision of instrument specification (for example an increase in the level of an emissions charge; a reduction in the number of permits allocated by the authorities; a renegotiation of the target in an environmental agreement). Alternatively, it might lead to the adoption of an alternative instrument altogether (for example the replacement of an environmental agreement with an emissions charge or a technology standard).

Within the context of this policy cycle, there are two issues that an evaluation might address. First, an evaluation could be undertaken to assess the desirability of the policy objective itself (that is a cost-benefit analysis). Second, an evaluation could be undertaken to assess the desirability of the selected instrument as the means of implementing the policy objective. Clearly, these two issues are interdependent – the choice of instrument will affect the cost of achieving the policy objective and hence (possibly) its desirability. Notwithstanding this however, the evaluation framework developed below addresses the second of these issues in isolation.

In relation to the desirability of a particular instrument, there are a number of 'policy relevant' questions that an evaluation might seek to answer. In particular, four generic questions have been identified that are of general relevance to a range of different instruments. Associated with each is a particular 'evaluation dimension'.

- Is the instrument type administratively, legally and politically feasible? ('feasibility')
- Is the specified/applied instrument capable of achieving the (explicit and implicit) policy objectives? ('capability')
- What are the expected/actual environmental, economic and social impacts of the instrument? ('impact')
- Has the formulation/implementation/operation of the instrument enhanced the policy resource base? ('resource development')

Ultimately, it is only the last two dimensions – the impact of the instrument and the development of the resource base – that are of intrinsic (or direct) interest. However, the 'capability' of an instrument may be expected to provide a good instrumental (or indirect) indicator of its eventual performance. While this remains an unproven hypothesis, it has an intuitive rationale. For example, the exemption of energy intensive industries from a carbon or energy tax, would be expected to undermine either the environmental effectiveness, or the cost-effectiveness, of the tax (or both).

While it is possible to evaluate an instrument at any stage of the policy cycle, in practice there are three points in the cycle where evaluation is likely to be particularly relevant. The first is prior to the initiation of the instrument; the second is shortly after its implementation; the third is after it has been in operation for a longer period of time. Different evaluation dimensions will be relevant at each of the three points (see Table 2.6), reflecting the differing underlying objectives.

Table 2.6   The evaluation framework

Evaluation Dimension	*Ex ante* evaluation	*Ex post* evaluation (short term)	*Ex post* evaluation (long term)
Feasibility	√	√	
Capability		√	?
Impact	√	?	√
Resource development		√	√

Prior to initiation, an *ex ante* evaluation may be undertaken to determine whether the instrument should be submitted to the formulation process. Empirical models may be used to predict the impact on the target environmental variable; to estimate the cost burden arising under the instrument and its distributional incidence; to assess any wider economic impacts such as changes in prices, employment and competitiveness. An assessment can be made of the extent to which the instrument harmonises with the interests of the key actors in the policy process, and whether it is compatible with the prevailing institutional framework within which it will have to operate (in particular, whether existing national and international laws prohibit its use, or would prevent it from operating effectively). Of course, these issues are not necessarily independent. The political feasibility of a particular instrument will (to a certain extent) depend on its expected impact on different interest groups, while its compatibility with national and international law will often rest on the detailed specification.

The second evaluation point arises after the instrument has been in operation for a relative short period of time (that is 1–2 years). There are three potential objectives for an *ex post* evaluation undertaken at this stage in the policy cycle. First, an evaluation might seek to identify those factors, which were critical to the acceptance, or rejection, of the proposed instrument. Second, an evaluation could assess the effect of the formulation and implementation processes on the policy resource base. For example, have new communication channels been created; have relations between actors improved? Both of these objectives relate to 'learning' about the instrument type (for example the feasibility and desirability of a charge, or an environmental agreement and so on), in order to inform future policy initiatives. In contrast, the final objective relates more to the 'control' of the specific instrument under consideration. An evaluation at this early stage could assess whether the implemented instrument is likely to achieve the policy objectives, and identify the need for any fine-tuning. While some early impacts of the instrument may be observable, it is highly unlikely that the full effects would have fed through. Consequently, an evaluation at this stage would focus on the credibility of the instrument as a predictor of future performance.

Given the inertia of behavioural responses,[20] an instrument may have to be in operation for a relatively long period of time (for example 5–10 years) before an evaluation of the full impacts can be undertaken. Unfortunately, this delay compounds the methodological problems associated with this type of analysis (OECD, 1997). In particular, as time passes it may become increasingly difficult to disentangle the effects of the instrument under consideration from other, related, policy initiatives that have been undertaken in the intervening period. Linked to this, is the problem of determining the appropriate counter-factual for the evaluation (that is what would have happened otherwise?). Again, the longer the timescale, the more difficult it is to establish a valid baseline.

Despite the fact that the full impacts of the instrument are unlikely to have worked through, there are a number of advantages in conducting an *ex post* evaluation after a relatively short period of operation. First, the actors involved in the formulation and implementation of the instrument are more likely to be available to survey or interview; memories are less likely to be distorted by the passage of time; and relevant information is less likely to have been destroyed or mislaid. Second, it is likely to be easier to collect good information relating to the capability of an instrument (albeit that some of this information is qualitative) than it is to uncover its long-run impacts. Third, to the extent that there have been any short-run impacts, the problems of disentangling other policy measures, and of determining a valid counter-factual, will be less significant. Fourth, the identification of any deficiencies in the specification and/or implementation of the instrument, allows early corrective action to be taken. Finally, any learning about the factors affecting the feasibility of the instrument type, and the impact of the formulation process on resource development, may in themselves be extremely beneficial in directing future policy initiatives.

6.3 Evaluation Criteria for Environmental Agreements

In this section, the general evaluation framework is tailored to the particular instrument type of environmental agreements. With the exception of the first evaluation dimension (feasibility) which is binary, the evaluation dimensions highlighted in section 6.2 are themselves multidimensional, and in some cases qualitative. Consequently, in order to facilitate an assessment of the performance of an environmental agreement along each of the dimensions, a number of specific 'evaluation criteria' have been identified. Many of these criteria reflect the guidelines proposed by the European Commission in their 1996 communication on environmental agreements (European Commission, 1996). Others – particularly those relating to its impact – are derived from the OECD report on the evaluation of economic instruments (OECD, 1997).

The evaluation criteria are intended to provide guidance in assessing the performance of an environmental agreement along each of the identified dimensions. As such they highlight the issues that are relevant for a prototypical agreement. However, it is not intended that every evaluation exercise should consider every criterion. Certain criteria will be more, or less, relevant for particular agreements, and (as noted in section 6.2) the particular dimensions covered will depend on the timing and objectives of the evaluation.

When evaluating the performance of an environmental agreement, it is important to recognise that this broad term covers a wide range of different types of agreement. An agreement may be negotiated 'collectively' with a representative body (for example the relevant industry association), or there may be a series of *individual agreements* with specific firms. In the case of a *collective agreement*, the number of firms covered may be pre-determined (that is a *closed agreement*),[21] or firms may be free to decide whether they wish to join (that is an *open agreement*).

In addition to these administrative classifications, it is also possible to position agreements on a spectrum according to the underlying policy objectives that they support. While the explicit policy objectives for different agreements may appear similar (for example, the achievement of an improvement in the value of a target environmental variable), the implicit objectives that underlie the agreements may be very different.[22] At one extreme, *an 'implementation oriented' agreement* (IMOA) may be used to achieve an efficient diffusion of an existing technology base to meet an established target; while at the other, the emphasis of an *'innovation oriented' agreement* (INOA) is on learning about the problem and the identification of new technologies.[23]

The orientation of an agreement determines the relevant design issues for the agreement, and hence the relative importance of different evaluation criteria. For an IMOA the emphasis is on control, efficiency, and reducing information asymmetries. Hence the key evaluation (and design) issues are burden sharing mechanisms, monitoring and enforcement, and dissemination of 'best practice'. In contrast, for an INOA the emphasis is on co-operation and learning, and hence the key evaluation issues are co-ordination mechanisms, and collective incentives.

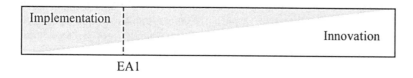

EA1

Figure 2.5   The spectrum of environmental agreements

In practice most environmental agreements will lie in a middle range of the spectrum, and the distinction will be one of relative emphasis. For example in Figure 2.5, while the focus of agreement EA1 is on implementation, it is also intended to encourage some effort on innovation. Consequently, for evaluation purposes, a decision rule will be required to classify an agreement as either an IMOA or an INOA. A simple approach for determining the relative orientation would be to consider whether the target can be achieved by the diffusion of existing best available technology (BAT), even if this is currently not cost-effective. If this is the case then the relative emphasis of the agreement should be considered as being implementation.

6.3.1 Feasibility

Is an environmental agreement administratively, legally and politically feasible?

This evaluation dimension addresses the question of whether the negotiation process will/did result in the signing of an agreement? As such, it is binary (that is, yes or no). It addresses only the ability to conclude an agreement, and it does not consider the 'quality' of the resultant agreement (which is covered under the other dimensions). However, there may be a relationship between the two issues. For example, it may be that the more stringent the provisions of the agreement (that is, the more credible), the less likely it is to be acceptable to all actors.

6.3.2 Capability

Is the environmental agreement capable of achieving the (explicit and implicit) policy objectives?

The capability of an environmental agreement has two aspects. The first relates to the *specification* of the agreement in terms of its consistency (or 'fit') with the underlying policy objectives, and its compatibility with national and international law on trade and competition. The second relates to the *application* of the agreement in practice, and the extent to which this reinforces, or erodes, the original agreement. Of course, there is a degree of overlap between the two aspects. For example, a loosely specified 'gentlemen's agreement' may be more prone to erosion during implementation than a precisely defined legal contract.

Specification The guidelines proposed by the European Commission (European Commission, 1996) provide a good starting point for the development of evaluation criteria in relation to the specification of an environmental agreement. However these must be augmented, as they are not complete (excluding the important issue of burden sharing), and they make no distinction between different types of agreement. The evaluation criteria identified below provide a 'theoretical ideal'. In practice, it may not be feasible for an agreement to compare well against all of the criteria (see section 6.3.1 above). However, they provide a useful benchmark against which to assess the capability of a particular agreement.

a.   Target
The inclusion of a clearly defined and quantified target is crucial for the success of an environmental agreement.[24] Where the target is expressed as a percentage change, the base year and reference value should be indicated.

Ideally, intermediate targets (or milestones) should be identified to allow the monitoring of progress during the course of the agreement.

Clearly, a quantified target is essential in the case of an IMOA which focuses on control. However, it can also play an important role in the case of an INOA, providing a focal point around which actions can be co-ordinated (see Aggeri, 1999). Although in the latter case it may prove necessary to revise the target in the light of subsequent learning.

While the inclusion of a quantified target is a necessary condition for success, it is not sufficient. It is also important that the target represents a real improvement on 'business-as-usual', and that it makes a 'proportionate' contribution to the achievement of the overall policy objective. For example, if the agreement is one of a number of instruments that are being used in pursuance of a particular policy objective, the reduction implied by the target should represent a realistic contribution to the overall burden.

b.   Burden sharing (IMOAs)

Where an IMOA relies on individual actions by firms to meet a collective target (for example energy efficiency agreements), it is more likely to be successful when accountability is devolved to individual firms. This is best achieved by the inclusion of an explicit 'burden-sharing' rule, or a mechanism, for apportioning the collective target.[25] However, the *cost efficiency* of the agreement will depend crucially on the design of this rule or mechanism. Consequently, it is important that it should take account of cost differences between firms, or alternatively that some flexibility mechanism should be included to allow subsequent adjustments. One possibility would be for the agreement to call for the setting up of an 'internal' permit-trading scheme. However, where the agreement comprises only a relatively small number of large firms, there is a danger of strategic behaviour in the permit market, particularly if the firms operate in the same output market.

Alternatively, the agreement may require collective action (for example collective recycling schemes), with the total cost of the action being shared by the constituent companies. However, if the cost of the scheme is affected by the actions of individual firms (for example where the recycling target is expressed as a percentage of collective output), then it is important that the design of the burden-sharing rule should encourage efficient responses.

Burden sharing is less appropriate for an INOA, where the intention is to encourage co-operation and joint-ownership of the problem. In this situation, it is likely to be more desirable to have collective accountability.[26]

c.   Monitoring mechanisms

The inclusion of adequate monitoring mechanisms is important for all types of environmental agreement. However, the nature of these mechanisms depends on the orientation of the agreement. For an IMOA, monitoring is concerned with *control*, that is, measuring performance against the target (or milestones) and identifying the need for any corrective action to be undertaken. As such, it is important that the mechanism that is put in place should provide accurate, timely and actionable information. In this context, monitoring is closely related to the issues of burden sharing and sanctions for non-compliance.

Ideally, the performance of an agreement would be monitored using information collected and collated by an independent body. Unfortunately, in most cases this is unlikely to be possible, and monitoring of performance will rely on self-reporting by firms. In this situation, the credibility of the information will be enhanced by the appointment of an independent auditor (for example a consultancy, or an expert committee) to verify the accuracy of a sample of the returns.

In contrast, for an INOA the focus is on *co-ordination*, that is, ensuring the compatibility of individual actions, and enhancing the potential for collective learning (see Aggeri, 1999). As such, it is important that the monitoring mechanism is sufficiently flexible to be able to collect, process and disseminate a diverse range of 'soft' information. In this context, monitoring is closely related to learning.

d.   Additional guarantees or sanctions

The inclusion of additional guarantees regarding the achievement of targets will considerably enhance the credibility of an agreement. Explicit provision might be made for sanctions to be imposed on individual firms that fail to comply with their obligations under the agreement. There are a variety of different sanctions which could be imposed, ranging in severity from a simple fine, to expulsion from the agreement and/or retrospective taxation.[27] Of course, individual sanctions of this type rely on accountability for the overall target being devolved to individual companies. Where this is not the case, it is only possible to impose some form of collective sanction. In particular, the agreement might provide for a periodic review of progress with the (explicit) threat that failure to achieve intermediate 'milestone' targets would lead to the revocation of the agreement, and the introduction of an alternative instrument such as a tax.

e.   Contractual form

The EC Guidelines (European Commission, 1996) recommend the use of legally binding agreements (that is, contracts). While, their use to date has been limited, experience suggests that these may be more likely to achieve their environmental objectives. By providing a clear legal framework, that is enforceable through court decisions, a binding contract adds considerable force to an environmental agreement.

f.   Legal compliance

In addition to complying with the provisions of the national law under which it falls, an agreement must also comply with the requirements of the *EC Treaty* and its derived legislation. In particular, the agreement should have been notified to the European Commission, and been granted an exemption under Article 85(3) of the EC Treaty. It is also important that an agreement complies with the rules of the World Trade Organization (WTO) relating to free trade, and technical barriers to trade. In particular, GATT article III requires that an agreement should not discriminate against foreign companies.

g.   General provisions

In order to avoid potential confusion and disputes during the operation of the agreement, it is important that a number of basic issues are clarified. All of the parties to the agreement should be identified, and their respective obligations clearly specified. Any important terms should be clearly and unambiguously defined. The duration of the agreement should be stipulated, as should the conditions under which it can be revised or terminated. In the case of a contractual agreement it should specify whether the agreement is under civil or public law, and also designate the competent jurisdiction.

Application

a.   Integrity

It is possible that some of the detailed provisions of an agreement will have to be interpreted, or adapted, when it is put into practice. In doing so, the original force of the agreement may be eroded, reducing its credibility as a mechanism for delivering the policy objectives. For example, if the specified reporting requirements prove to be impractical, there is a danger that an alternative arrangement might compromise the ability of the authorities to monitor the performance of the agreement.

b.   Extent

The extent of application refers to the *lifespan* of the agreement (that is, the length of time that it remains in force), and the *coverage* of the target sector(s) that it achieves. In general, the longer an agreement remains in force, and the wider the coverage that it achieves, the more likely it is to be successful.[28] An agreement that collapses prematurely is unlikely to be effective in promoting the policy objectives.

For a closed agreement, the coverage of the sector is predetermined. However, in the case of an open agreement, where eligible firms can choose whether to join, there is a danger that *free-riding* will occur and that coverage will remain low. This problem may be particularly significant if there is no alternative instrument (for example, a tax) to provide an incentive for firms to join. There is likely to be a high degree of correlation between the coverage achieved by an open agreement and its lifespan. In particular, high levels of free-riding may be a significant factor leading to the collapse of an agreement.

c.   Compliance

The degree of compliance with the terms and conditions of the agreement during the course of its operation will have a significant bearing on its capability as a policy instrument. A failure to show demonstrable progress towards meeting the stated target, and/or a poor level of compliance by firms in relation to their individual obligations, will severely undermine confidence in the ability of an agreement to deliver the desired environmental improvement. At the aggregate level, progress towards the collective target can be assessed by comparing actual performance with any milestones that are specified in the agreement. Where explicit milestones have not been identified, reference values may be (linearly) interpolated from the base year and target values.

At the individual level, compliance may be assessed in relation to a firm's obligations under the terms of the agreement (for example provision of information, participation in specified initiatives and so on). In addition, where the aggregate target has been broken down, it may be possible to assess progress towards the individual targets.[29] Where a firm has failed to comply with its obligations, the credibility of the agreement requires that appropriate corrective action be taken. In particular, where the agreement provides for the imposition of sanctions, it is important that these are actually applied.

6.3.3 Impact

What are the actual environmental, economic and social impacts of the negotiated agreement?

For most environmental agreements, it is unlikely that there will be any significant social impacts, and the evaluation will therefore concentrate on the environmental and economic effects. However within these two areas, the evaluation should consider a wide range of potential impacts, and should not be confined only to those variables that are related to the explicit and implicit policy objectives.

Environmental effectiveness As with any instrument, the *environmental effectiveness* of an agreement has several components. The main concern relates to its aggregate impact on the target environmental variable (TEV), which – as noted previously – may not be explicitly identified as a policy objective. To this end, it is important that the 'boundaries' for the evaluation (and the associated policy question) are clearly defined. For example, there is a difference between assessing whether an agreement on energy efficiency with sector X has reduced the emissions of CO_2 for sector X, or whether it has reduced total emissions of CO_2 for the economy as a whole. In most cases, the first question is more relevant,[30] in which case the appropriate definition of the TEV for the purposes of the evaluation is 'emissions of CO_2 by sector X'.

However, as was highlighted in section 6.2, there are two potentially significant problems which must be addressed when calculating the magnitude of this impact. First, the impact of the agreement must be disentangled from that of any other policy measures that have been introduced. However, since in many cases environmental agreements specifically preclude the introduction of other instruments, this may not be a significant problem – particularly if the agreement has only been in operation for a relatively short period. Second, a realistic 'business-as-usual' counter-factual must be established, which provides an estimate of the outcome that would have occurred in the absence of any policy initiative. It is possible that such a scenario may have been produced at the time of the negotiations, in which case this might be used (although it will need adjusting to reflect any differences between expected and actual macroeconomic conditions).

If it is not possible to determine a realistic counter-factual then one possible approach proposed by the European Environment Agency (EEA, 1997) is to measure the *environmental improvement* that has occurred since the introduction of the agreement. Unfortunately, it is not possible to say *a priori* whether this represents an upper bound, or a lower bound, on the *environmental effectiveness* of the agreement. An alternative approach might be to establish (through interviews and/or surveys) the percentage of firms introducing new technology, or changing production processes/management practices, etc., explicitly as a result of the agreement. This could provide a good indication of whether the actual outcome represents a significant difference versus 'business-as-usual'.

In some instances, it may also be necessary to assess the spatial distribution of the impact. For example even though the aggregate impact on the TEV may be positive, there may be some particular locations (that is 'hotspots') where it is negative. However, since in most cases, an agreement will require some level of reduction (or at least no increase) by all constituent firms, this is unlikely to be a significant issue. Finally, consideration should be given to any major secondary environmental impacts that may have arisen as a result of the agreement. For example, an agreement to reduce CO_2 emissions may also lead to reductions in SO_2 and NO_x. These secondary impacts may be positive or negative, depending on whether the variable in question is a complement or a substitute for the TEV.

Economic efficiency   There are two aspects of *economic efficiency* that an evaluation should address. The first relates to the direct economic costs arising under the environmental agreement; the second relates to the indirect costs incurred by its operation. Ideally, an agreement would minimize direct costs, while imposing low 'overhead' costs.

The *direct economic costs* of the agreement for an individual firm reflect the reduction in its profit (relative to the counter-factual scenario), arising from the annualised cost of investment in new equipment; any increase in operating costs; and any decrease in revenues. However, obtaining direct measures of cost-efficiency is highly problematic. First, there is the issue of the counter-factual – that is, what would the profit have been in the absence of the agreement. Second, in order to assess whether the outcome is efficient one needs to consider the variance of the marginal costs (that is marginal reductions in profit) across all the firms. In practice, such an analysis will not be possible. The specification of the agreement may give an indication whether cost-efficiency is possible. As a proxy measure, one could consider the relative contributions of the individual firms/plants to the overall reduction, and the types of solutions adopted. Heterogeneity of responses may suggest a cost efficient outcome,[31] although this would have to be judged in the context of other information about the agreement and the resources available to individual firms.

The *indirect costs* of the agreement relate to the administration and compliance costs incurred by its operation. Administration costs relate primarily to the costs incurred by the body responsible for managing the agreement (for example, the industry association). They might include incremental personnel costs, information processing costs, and other support costs (such as publicity). In addition, the Government (or its agencies) may incur auditing costs, and/or they may have certain financial obligations under the terms of the agreement. Compliance costs relate to the administration costs incurred by the individual firms – for example, management time (or incremental personnel), data collection and processing costs.

While the additional activities associated with the agreement may be straightforward to identify, it may not be so easy to calculate their cost. For example, it is unlikely, that firms' accounting systems will be able to separate out the necessary incremental cost data. However, by considering factors such as the type and amount of information that is required; the complexity and rigour of monitoring and enforcement mechanism; and the synergy with existing activities; it may be possible to obtain a qualitative proxy measure for the scale of the administrative burden.

Wider economic impacts   The potential for wider economic impacts will depend to a large extent on the scale of the environmental agreement. For example, a cross-sector agreement on packaging waste is more likely to have an impact on the general level of consumer prices, than a single-sector agreement to reduce emissions of a particular pollutant.

There is a broad range of impacts that might be considered under this heading, and it is difficult to judge a priori which (if any) are likely to be relevant to a particular agreement. However, given the co-operative nature of environmental agreements, there is the potential for *distortion of competition*. In particular, there is a danger that an agreement may encourage collusion among some (or all) of the signatories. It is also possible that an agreement may put non-signatories at a competitive disadvantage, particularly if there are barriers to joining the agreement. However, this is less likely to be a problem if the agreement has been registered with the appropriate competition authorities.

6.3.4 Resource development
Has the negotiation/implementation/operation of the environmental agreement enhanced the policy resource base?

Due to the nebulous character of the policy resource base, it is difficult to identify general evaluation criteria for resource development. To a certain extent the nature of any feedback will be specific to the circumstances of a particular agreement. Nonetheless, there are three aspects of resource development that may be expected to have general relevance – learning, relations between actors, and general awareness and attitudes. It is likely that there will be a degree of overlap between the three criteria. For example, the process of collective learning may itself help improve relations between actors. Conversely, an improvement in relations may open the way for more effective collective learning.

Learning   Learning is potentially an important outcome for all types of environmental agreement. However, it will differ in nature depending on the orientation of the agreement. In the case of an INOA, learning relates primarily to a reduction of the 'shared uncertainties' of all actors regarding the scale of the problem, the appropriate responses, and the potential solutions that might be adopted. As such the focus is on innovation. In contrast, the focus of learning in an IMOA is on the dissemination of knowledge in order to reduce the level of 'information asymmetries' between actors   (principally   between   firms)   regarding   existing technological/managerial possibilities.

In both cases learning can lead to a reduction in the overall cost of achieving the target set in the agreement. However, whereas with innovation this is achieved by reducing the level of costs for all firms through the introduction of new technology, with dissemination it is achieved by reducing the spread of costs between firms through the wider application of current 'best practice'.

Relations between actors   One of the major advantages that is claimed for environmental agreements over other instruments is that the process of negotiation can lead to an improvement in relations between actors. In particular, the EC Communication (European Commission, 1996) claims that the process can lead to a common understanding of environmental problems and mutual responsibilities. The improvement in relations – which may be between the Government and the sector as a whole, or between individual firms within the sector (that is, intra-sector), or both – may be brought about by a range of different factors, including the development of new channels of *communication*, an improved *understanding* of respective perceptions, and the strengthening of mutual *respect and trust*.

General attitudes and awareness   In addition to any changes in the relations between firms, it is possible that the active involvement of industry in the negotiation and implementation of an environmental agreement may also lead to changes within individual firms. In particular, it might lead to an increased level of *awareness* of environmental problems in general on the part of senior management, and a change in their *attitudes* towards these problems. Such changes may be subtle, and difficult to identify. However, it may be possible to make some inferences from any changes to management structures and practices (for example the introduction of environmental reporting), or from increased participation in public voluntary schemes (for example EMAS, ISO14001), and/or other voluntary initiatives.

It is also possible that there may be changed *perceptions* regarding the validity of the environmental agreement (and agreements in general) as a means of implementing the policy objective. This would include both the perceptions of those actors directly involved in the agreement, and also other significant interest groups (for example environmental NGOs) within the wider policy process. Perceptions may be affected both by the outcomes at the various stages of the policy cycle (for example, the specification, application, and impact of the agreement), and also by the processes themselves (see Figure 2.4). Thus for example, a transparent negotiation process, which allowed the participation of all interested groups, might be expected to improve the credibility of the agreement. Of course, this would depend on the extent to which outside views were taken into account in the final specification of the agreement (for example in the setting of meaningful targets).

NOTES

1. This is a summary of the theoretical part of the NEAPOL project. It is based upon the contributions of the different partners. Each contribution (in full) is available as a monograph.
2. This case would require the elaboration of a theoretical analysis with one principal and many interdependent agents which would complicate considerably our framework (as a basic reference, see Demski and Sappington, 1983; Laffont and Tirole, 1993).
3. Studies refer to these aspects in various ways, for example 'green consumerism' or 'pre-emption of public regulation'. Here we follow Börkey et al. (1998)
4. Through this expression we mean the perfect competition equilibrium in the absence of externalities.
5. In the presence of high transactions costs, the more likely outcome is the creation of a 'hierarchy' or 'government structure' (Williamson, 1975). However, in addition to the fact that the constitution of a hierarchy could not be feasible (for example it could be a nationalisation), it is argued that a market structure can be preserved, provided that in the society there is a sufficient degree of 'embeddedness' (trust?) of the actors in a society (Granovetter, 1985).
6. This representation refers, among other works, to the *institutional rational choice* models.
7. This point of view is in line with recent works which aim at developing a dynamic and interactive view of public policies. Among these works, the Advocacy Coalition Framework (Sabatier and Jenkins-Smith, 1993) propose a very stimulating framework putting forward the cognitive limitations of actors and explaining the dynamics of public policies through the progressive construction of coalitions shaped by belief systems. However, as we will see, there are differences between this approach and the one we propose in this part. In particular, we suggest focusing much more on monitoring devices and collective learning processes, also paying more attention to internal relationships inside the firm.
8. Callon and Rip (1991) have shown how situations where there is extreme confusion over the facts and a large number of conflicting values (mad cow disease, the hole in the ozone layer and so on) exist. The best way to resolve the controversies is to involve as many of the parties concerned as possible.
9. Most of the normative economic works refer implicitly to end-of-pipe innovation, modelling situations in which innovation is seen as an individual process in which each firm is setting its own strategy independently from the others.

10. In some cases, both types of innovation may be required. Nevertheless, one type is often dominant.
11. COM(92) 23 of 3.4.1992, point 31.
12. OJ C 140 of 11.5.1996, page 5.
13. Communication from the Commission to the Council and the European Parliament on Environmental Agreements, COM (96) 561 Final.
14. The European Environment Agency attempted to evaluate the environmental effectiveness of a sample of six agreements across different European countries (EEA (1997)). However, they found that it was not possible to make a quantitative assessment of their performance due to the lack of reliable monitoring data and consistent reporting.
15. A distinction should be made between the stated policy objective for the instrument, and the underlying target environmental variable (TEV). While it is possible that the objective will relate directly to the TEV, this need not necessarily be the case. Consequently, the TEV may have to be inferred from the stated objective and the policy context. For example, where an objective has been set for recycling/recovery rates, the underlying TEV might be the amount waste disposed to landfill.
16. An example of this is the extensive consultation exercise undertaken by the UK Government regarding the design of the UK Landfill Tax. As a result of this exercise, a weight-based tax was adopted rather than the original intention of an ad valorem tax.
17. This need not necessarily be the case. For example, in the United Kingdom the regulatory agency has traditionally been given a high degree of flexibility in how they interpret BATNEEC regulations for individual plants.
18. The OECD report on the evaluation of economic instruments (OECD (1997)) considers how institutional factors can affect the feasibility, implementation and operation of an instrument.
19. Negative feedback is also possible. For example, the process may lead to a deterioration of relations between actors, or to an increase in the degree of 'information asymmetries'.
20. This inertia may reflect a number of different factors. Information deficiencies may mean that decision-makers are unaware of the true costs of the instrument. Even when these are known, the speed of response may be determined by investment cycles, etc.
21. Acceptance of the terms of the agreement might be made a condition of membership of the industry association. In which case, a firm wishing to opt out of the agreement would have to leave the industry association. Similarly, a firm wishing to sign up to the agreement would have to join the association.
22. Of course, it may be the case that the explicit policy objectives of the two agreements make the distinction clear.
23. Note that this classification is slightly different to that proposed by Aggeri (1999).
24. The EC Communication cites the lack of quantified targets as a significant factor in the weakness and bad reputation of past agreements.
25. For example, a burden-sharing rule might specify that all firms covered by the agreement are required to achieve the same percentage reduction/improvement. Alternatively, there are a number of burden-sharing mechanisms that could be defined. These could include the use of auctions, or some form of bargaining (see Glachant, 1999) between firms leading to the signing of subsidiary agreements.
26. In some cases it may be necessary to define the allocation of tasks (for example research activities) between firms.
27. Expulsion, and/or retrospective taxation is particularly relevant when the agreement allows the signatories to opt-out of a parallel environmental tax. A good example of this is the Danish agreement on energy efficiency, under which signatories are exempted from the energy tax.
28. This need not necessarily be the case. For example, if an INOA is intended only to generate information about a problem, and potential solutions, as a forerunner to another form of regulation, a short lifespan may be an indication of success.

29. Assessing progress at the individual firm level may be problematic. Whereas it is reasonable to expect a relatively smooth progression towards the target at the aggregate level, it is more likely that an individual firm will make a single step change at some point during the life of the agreement. The timing of this change will vary between firms (due to different investment cycles and so on), and hence it is quite likely that some firms will show no apparent progress during the early years of the agreement.
30. Unless, of course, the agreement with sector X was the only policy initiative undertaken by the Government in pursuance of its policy objective.
31. Homogeneous responses and solutions would only be consistent with cost efficiency in the unlikely event of all firms having identical compliance cost curves.

BIBLIOGRAPHY

Aggeri, F. and Hatchuel, E. (1997), 'A Dynamic Model of Environmental Policy. The Case of Innovation-Oriented Agreements'. *Nota di Lavoro*, FEEM Fondazione Eni Enrico Mattei, Milan, pp. 24–97.

Aggeri, F. (1999), 'Negotiated Agreements and Innovation: A Knowledge-Based Perspective on Environmental Policies'. In CEEM, *Neapol project: Theoretical Report*, Ghent University, pp. 73–96.

Andrews, R. (1996), 'Regulation and Self-Regulation of Business.' Paper prepared for the second conference on the *'Ecological State: Towards a new Generation of Environmental Policy and Institutions'*. Seville, Spain, November 1996.

Arora, S. and Gangopadhyay, S. (1995), 'Toward a Theoretical Model of Voluntary Overcompliance'. *Journal of Economic Behaviour and Organisation*, **28**, 289–309.

Börkey, P. and Glachant, M. (1997), *Les engagements volontaires de l'industrie dans le domaine de l'environnement: nature et diversité*, CERNA, 135 p.

Börkey P., Glachant, M. and Lévêque, F. (1998), *Voluntary Approaches for environmental Policy in OECD Countries*, OECD, Paris.

Brau, R., Jones, J.W., Tamborra, M.L. and Vicini, G. (1999), 'General Economic Approach in an Oligopolistic Framework'. In CEEM, *Neapol project: Theoretical Report*, Ghent University, pp. 47–73.

Bressers, H. Th.A. (1993), 'Beleidsnetwerken en instrumentenkeuze'. in *Beleidswetenschap*, Vol. 7, No. 4, 309-30. (Also published in English: The Choice of Policy Instruments in Policy Networks. In: B.G.Peters and F.K.M. van Nispen (eds), *Public Policy Instruments*, Cheltenham: Edward Elgar, pp. 85–105.

Callon, M. and Rip, A. (1991), 'Forums hybrides et négociations des normes socio-techniques dans le domaine de l'environnement'. Environnement Collectif (ed) *Science et Politique*, 227–38.

Coase, R. (1960), 'The Problem of the Social Cost'. *The Journal of Law and Economics*, **3**, 1-44.

Croci, E. and Pesaro, G. (1996), 'Voluntary Agreements and Negotiations: Evolution at Italian and European Level'. paper for a workshop in Venice on 18-19 November, 25 pp.

Demski, J. and Sappington, D. (1983), 'Multi-Agent Control in Perfectly Correlated Environments'. *Economic Letters*. **13** (4), 325-30.

EC, European Commission (1996), 'Communication from the Commission to the Council and the European Parliament on Environmental Agreements'. COM (96) 561.final, November 27.

EC, European Commission, Brussels, Directorate General III.01 (1997), 'Industry: Study on Voluntary Agreements concluded between Industry and Public Authorities in the Field of the Environment'. Final Report, Brussels.

EEA, European Environment Agency (1997), 'Environmental Agreements: Environmental Effectiveness'. *Environmental Issues Series*, 1&2 (3), Copenhagen.

Garvie, D. (1997), 'Self-Regulation of Pollution: The Role of Market Structure and Consumer Information', *Nota di Lavoro*, FEEM Fondazione Eni Enrico Mattei, Milan, pp. 59.97.

Glachant, M. (1999), ' The Cost Efficiency of Voluntary Agreements for Regulating Industrial Pollution: a Coasean Approach'. In Carraro, C. and Lévèque, F. (Eds.) (1999), *Voluntary Approaches in Environmental Policy*, Kluwer Academic Publishers.

Glachant, M. and Whiston, G. (1996), 'Voluntary Agreements between Industry and Government – The Case of Recycling Regulations'. in F. Lévèque (ed.), *Environmental Policy in Europe – Industry, Competition and the Policy Process* ,Cheltenham: Edward Elgar.

Glasbergen, P. (1994), 'Milieuproblemen als beleidsvraagstuk' [Environmental Problems As Policy Question]. In: P. Glasbergen (ed.), *Milieubeleid: een beleidswetenschappelijke inleiding*, The Hague: VUGA, pp. 341–58.

Glasbergen, P. (1998), 'Partnership As Learning Process – Environmental Agreements in the Netherlands'. In Glasbergen, P. (ed.), *Co-operative Environmental Governance, Public-Private Agreements as a Policy Strategy*, Dordrecht: Kluwer Academic Publishers, pp. 133-56.

Godard, O. (1998), 'Concertation et incitations efficases, deux dispositifs incompatibles? Une analyse à partir du dispositif de gestion des déchets d'emballages en France', *Journées de l'Associations Français de Sciences Economiques* (AFSE). Toulouse, France.

Granovetter, M. (1985), 'Economic Action and Social Structure: The Problem of Embeddedness', *American Journal of Sociology*, **91** (3), 481–510.

Hansen, L.G. (1997), 'Environmental Regulation Through Voluntary Agreements', *Nota di Lavoro*, FEEM Fondazioni Eni Enrico Mattei, Milan, pp. 23.97.

Hoogeerwerf, A. (1985), '*Overheidsbeleid* [Public Policy]'. Alphen aan den Rijn: Samsom Uitgeverij.

Hourcade, J.C. (1998), 'Analyse économique, modélisation perspective et développement durable ou comment faire remonter des informations de futur?', *Economies et sociétés*, Série F., nr. 36, pp. 175 –98.

Hourcade, J.C., Salles, J.M. and Théry, D. (1992), 'Ecological Economics and Scientific Controversies: Lessons from some Recent Policy Making in the EEC'. *Ecological Economics*, **6**, 211–33.

Imura, H. (1998), 'The Use of Voluntary Approaches in Japan, An Initial Survey'. paper for an informal workshop at the OECD on the use of voluntary approaches in environmental policy, Paris, 1-2 Juy.

Imura, H. (1998), '*The Use of Unilateral Agreements in Japan, Voluntary Action Plans of Industries Against Global Warming*'. ENV/EPOC/GEEI(98)26, 29 p.

Imura H. and Sugiyama R. (1998), 'Voluntary Approaches in Japan'. paper for the CAVA workshop, Ghent, 26-27 November.

Ingram, V. (1996), 'The Economics and Law of Voluntary Approaches in Environmental Policy'. paper for a FEEM workshop in Venice on 18–19 November.

Ingram V. (1998), 'An Environment for Consensus?'. paper for the CAVA workshop, Ghent, 26-27 November.

Ingram, V. (1998), 'Joint Environmental Policy Making in the EU. The Packaging'. Wageningen University.

Klok, P.J. and Kuks, S.M.M. (1994), 'Het doelgroepenbeleid [The Target Group Policy]'. in P. Glasbergen (ed.), *Milieubeleid: een beleidswetenschappelijke inleiding*, The Hague: VUGA, pp. 79–96.

Laffont, J.J. and Tirole, J. (1993), *A Theory of Incentives in Procurement and Regulation.* Cambridge, MIT Press, 705 p.

Lévêque, F. (1998), 'Voluntary Approaches'. *Environmental Policy Research Briefs*, nr. 1, CERNA, Paris, 13 p.

Lindblom; C.E. (1980), *'The Policy Making Process'.* Englewood Cliffs, NJ: Prentice Hall.

Maxwell, J. and Lyon, T. (1998), 'An Overview and Investigation of the EPAs'. pp. 33–50 Program, preliminary draft.

Maxwell, J, Lyon, T. and Hackett, C. (1998), 'Self-Regulation and Social Welfare: The Political Economy of Corporate Environmentalism'. *Nota di Lavoro*, FEEM Fondazioni Eni Enrico Mattei, Milan, pp. 55-98.

Moffet J. and Bregha F. (1998), 'An Overview of Issues With Respect to Voluntary Environmental Agreements'. paper for the CAVA workshop in Ghent, 26-27 November, 26 p.

Nelissen, N.J.M. (1994), 'Het themagericht milieubeleid [The environmental policy by themes]'. in P. Glasbergen (ed.), *Milieubeleid: een beleidswetenschappelijke inleiding*, The Hague: VUGA, pp. 59–77.

Nilsson, B. (1998) 'Improving Environmental Performance through Voluntary Agreements'. Mimeo, Lund University, 31 p.

OECD (1997), *Evaluating Economic Instruments for Environmental Policy.* Paris.

Olson, M. (1965), *The Logic of Collective Action. Public Goods and the Theory of Groups,* Cambridge, MA: Harvard University Press.

Peppel, R.A. van de and Herweijer, M. (1994), 'Het communicatieve sturingsmodel [The communivative steering model]'. in: P. Glasbergen (ed.), *Milieubeleid: een beleidswetenschappelijke inleiding*, The Hague: VUGA, pp. 189–207.

Sabatier, P. and Jenkins-Smith H. (ed.) (1993), *'Policy Change and Learning. An Advocacy Coalition Framework'.* Boulder, Co: Westview Press.

Segerson, K. and Miceli, T. (1997), 'Voluntary Approaches to Environmental Protection: The Role of Legislative Threats', *Nota di Lavoro*, FEEM Fondazioni Eni Enrico Mattei, Milan, pp. 21–97.

Segerson, K. and Miceli, T. (1998), 'Voluntary Environmental Agreements: Good or Bad News for Environmental Protection?', *Journal of Environmental Economics and Management*, **36**, 109 –30.

Serré, Y. (1998), 'Accord volontaires et dynamique de changement structurel. Eclairage de la relation à partir de la politique française de gestion des VHU'. *Revue d'économie industrielle*, n°83 – 1er trim., pp. 225–38.

Seyad, A., De Clercq, M. and Senesael, F. (1996), 'Milieubeleidsovereenkomsten als instrument van milieubeleid: bespreking en stand van zaken voor België (Vlaanderen)'. *Energie en Milieu*, Gent, pp. 95-102.
Ten Brinck P. and Morere M. (1998) 'Voluntary Initiatives to Address Climate Change'. paper for the CAVA workshop, Ghent, 26-27 November.
Williamson, O.E. (1975), *'Market and Hierarchies, Analysis and Antitrust* Implications: *A Study in the Economics of Internal Organisation'*. New York: Free Press.

PART TWO

Twelve Case Studies on European Negotiated
Agreements

3. Self-Commitment on the Collection and Recovery of Spent Batteries and the Reduction of Mercury Content in Batteries

Per-Olof Busch and Helge Jörgens

1. INTRODUCTION

In 1988 a voluntary agreement (VA) was concluded which committed producers and importers of household batteries in Germany to reduce the heavy metals content of their products. Furthermore, certain types of batteries containing harmful substances were to be labelled, taken back by retailers and recycled and/or disposed of separately in order to reach the overall goal of the VA: to reduce the uncontrolled dispersion of heavy metals stemming from household batteries.

This VA led to some relevant success in the substitution of lead, mercury and cadmium in batteries. However, the scheme for take-back and separate recycling and disposal was less successful and a large quantity of batteries containing harmful substances continued to be disposed of with household waste.

From 1989 on the German *Ministry for the Environment* (BMU) presented various drafts for a federal batteries ordinance, which had become necessary in order to transpose the EC Council Directive 91/157 on batteries and accumulators containing harmful substances and its amendment through the Commission Directive 93/86 into national law. However, it was not until 1998 that a batteries ordinance was finally adopted. By taking into account the shortcomings of the VA of 1988 the ordinance reveals a certain learning process by the involved actors.

2. CONTEXT

2.1 The Environmental Problem

In general, batteries can be differentiated into non-rechargeable primary batteries and rechargeable accumulators or secondary batteries. Primary batteries containing a low level of harmful substances today make up the largest part (87 per cent). The greatest environmental threat is posed by the remaining 13 per cent of batteries and accumulators containing high levels of harmful substances, especially mercury, cadmium and lead (see Table 3.1).

Table 3.1   Batteries put in circulation in Germany by type in 1999

Battery	Form	Type	Dry batteries	
			Number	% of total weight
Primary batteries	Cylinder	Alkali-manganese	416 038 664	48.58
		Zinc-oxygen	14 551	0.12
		Zinc-carbon	282 128 699	36.791
		Lithium	14 603 571	1.053
		Mercury oxide	2 548 740	0.026
		Silver oxide	24 795 357	0.216
		Alkali-manganese	12 684 407	0.126
		Zinc-oxygen	31 798 514	0.181
		Lithium	26 962 610	0.366
Total primary batteries			**811 575 113**	**87.459**
Accumulators	Cylinder	Nickel-cadmium	49 209 719	7.352
		Nickel-hydride	16 829 602	2.686
		Lithium-ion	4 403 297	1.29
		Lead	345 348	1.16
		Alkali-manganese	165 458	0.026
	Button	Nickel-cadmium	622 967	0.006
		Nickel-hydride	59 519	0.018
		Lithium-ion	199 794	0.002
Total accumulators			**71 835 704**	**12.541**
Total			**883 410 817**	**100**

Source: GRS, 2000

The total quantity of batteries sold in Germany increased about 96 per cent between 1986 and 1999. In 1986 450 million batteries were put into circulation with a total weight of 15 500 tons. In 1999 approximately 883.5 million batteries and accumulators for electronic appliances were sold in Germany (see Table 3.1) with a total weight of nearly 25 023 tons.

The main environmental problems related to the production, use and disposal of batteries and accumulators are:

- the release of heavy metals, especially cadmium, mercury and lead, into the environment after disposal of batteries with the household waste; and
- the relatively low energy output: energy input for batteries is up to 50 times higher than energy output (Scholl, 1995a).

While the latter aspect has not yet received much political attention and has not led to the formulation of political programmes, the environmental problems related to the disposal of batteries found their way onto the political agenda in the beginning of the 1980s. At this time especially, the mercury content of batteries was perceived as a severe environmental problem. Today, after a far-reaching elimination of mercury in the production of batteries, nickel-cadmium (NiCd) accumulators, which have been increasingly used in mobile appliances during the 1990s, pose the most significant threat to the environment.

The disposal of used batteries can follow three different paths: landfill, incineration and recycling. The batteries landfilled with household waste gain importance because improper landfill conditions may lead to the leaching out of the chemical substances contained in batteries and thereby to a contamination of the environment, especially the soil and the groundwater (Scholl, 1995a). About two-thirds of all batteries are disposed of together with household waste (Hiller, 1998; Jülich, 1998). Batteries are responsible for about 85 per cent of all cadmium and 11 per cent for mercury in household waste (Jülich, 1998).

Although only 30 per cent of all batteries are incinerated, this way of disposal has received attention due to generation of hazardous residues which have to be disposed of properly in order to prevent any negative impact on the environment (Hiller, 1998; Jülich, 1998). Depending on the assumptions about the recycling quotas, the contribution of batteries to the overall heavy metal load of waste scheduled for incineration differs widely. Assuming that no batteries are recycled, cadmium contributes to the heavy metal content in incinerated waste with 38 tons and mercury with 3.6 tons (see Table 3.2).

Table 3.2   Estimated contribution from batteries to the heavy metal load from incinerated domestic waste

Metal	Metal content in waste in tons	Input in tons (recycling quota = 0)	Input in tons (recycling quota assumes life span of 5 years)	Input in tons (recycling quota assumes life span of 7 years)
Cadmium	171.5	38.3	13.2	29.0
Mercury	32.1	3.6	1.36	2.42
Nickel	865.00	38.5	13.3	29.3

Source: UBA, 1993b

As an alternative to landfill and incineration batteries can be recycled. The possible recycling paths for the sorted battery fractions concentrate on recovering materials such as cadmium, lead, mercury, silver, iron, nickel and copper. Before recycling, the used batteries must be collected separately. However, battery mixes, as can be found usually in collection boxes, are difficult to recycle, because they require several preparatory processes to separate the different metals and other contents of the batteries (UBA, 1992). Attempts to recycle a mix of different battery types have proven very expensive and highly energy and waste intensive.

3. NEGOTIATION PROCESS

3.1 Structure of the Economic Actors Involved

Concrete numbers about the structure of German battery producers and importers are hardly available. In 1998 the whole batteries industry employed approximately 8600 people. In 1997, the total turnover amounted to 1.9 billion DM (ZVEI, 1998b). All large international battery producers Duracell, Ralston, Rayovac, Philips and Panasonic have affiliated companies in Germany (Scholl, 1995a). The only domestic producer is VARTA AG. Official government estimates count 13 market leaders in the batteries sector which together have a market share of 90 to 92 per cent in the field of primary batteries and 78 per cent in the field of accumulators. About 85 per cent of primary batteries are produced by only four companies: VARTA, Duracell, Philips and Ralston (Bundesregierung, 1997).

With a share of about 70 per cent of primary batteries and about 84 per cent of accumulators, most batteries sold in Germany are imported (Bundesregierung, 1997).

Besides the battery producers, the producers of electronic consumer applications (for example laptops, personal computers, mobile telephones) play an important role in the so-called OEM-market (Original Equipment Manufacturing). These companies buy about 65 per cent of the accumulators sold by the producers (Nathanie and Reger, 1998). According to Nathanie and Reger the influence of the OEM-companies cannot be underestimated, especially if one considers possible innovation incentives resulting from their economic or environmental goals (Nathanie and Reger, 1998).

The retail sector, the third largest sector in Germany, employs about 3.3 million people and its turnover amounts to DM 964 billion (HDE, 1999). Its structure is very heterogeneous, ranging from internationally operating companies to family-owned retail shops. There are 25 different retail trade associations representing about 470 000 enterprises, organised at the federal level in the umbrella organisation *Federal Association of German Retail Trade* (Hauptverband des Deutschen Einzelhandels – HDE).

3.2 The Development of the Voluntary Agreement

Already in 1980 a first VA between the *Ministry of the Interior* and the batteries industry was signed. The batteries industry agreed to separately collect mercury oxide batteries and recover the mercury content. In 1985 the batteries industry additionally started a programme for the reduction of mercury in household batteries (Kiehne, 1998a). However, the agreement of 1980 did not succeed in taking the batteries issue off the political agenda.

With the adoption of the Waste Management Act (Abfallgesetz – AbfG) in 1986, government's competencies for passing product-related regulations were significantly enlarged. At the same time this law paved the way for a more co-operative approach in German waste policy, enabling government to set concrete targets for the avoidance, reuse or recovery of specific types of waste while at the same time leaving it up to the target groups how to reach these goals. In the case that the goals are not reached or sincere efforts are not made within a given time, the Minister of the Environment is entitled to rule this area by means of an ordinance (SRU, 1991).

The adoption of the AbfG was perceived by the batteries industry as posing a serious threat, especially because the BMU had signalled to the responsible sector that batteries were one of the priority waste areas where regulation could be expected. The BMU considered the content of harmful substances in batteries as the most significant environmental problem and aimed to reduce it. Among the regulatory options brought into the debate by various actors were (Jülich, 1998):

- a mandatory deposit on batteries containing harmful substances (Council of Environmental Experts);
- the prohibition of appliances with permanently built-in batteries;
- the separate collection of all batteries regardless of their harmfulness (UBA and BMU);
- the introduction of a legal take-back and return obligation for industry and consumers respectively; and
- the introduction of mandatory take-back and recycling quotas.

On 9 September 1988 – following intensive negotiations with government – the producers and importers of batteries organised in the German Association of Electrical Appliances Producers (Zentralverband der Elektroindustrie – ZVEI) together with the federal retail association (HDE) presented the Self-Commitment on the Collection and Recovery of Spent Batteries and the Reduction of Mercury Content in Batteries to the Federal Minister of the Environment (see section 3.3). According to the BMU, the negotiations which led to the VA had concentrated mainly on the reduction of harmful substances in batteries whereas the separate collection of batteries had not been controversial.

The decision of the batteries industry to propose a VA was clearly 'influenced by the changed priorities and new regulatory possibilities which had been offered by the modified waste legislation' (Scholl, 1995a). In the perception of the batteries industry, the seriousness of the former Minister for the Environment Klaus Töpfer in particular in putting into practice the concept of extended producer responsibility, had significantly increased the probability of regulatory measures in the area of batteries.

By proposing a VA, the batteries industry intended to anticipate possible regulatory measures and thereby retain some influence on the regulatory development in this issue area (Scholl, 1995a). Compared to alternative measures such as a total ban on batteries containing harmful substances, the introduction of a deposit-refund system and/or the mandatory recollection of all, harmful and non-harmful, batteries, the measures proposed in the VA could clearly be regarded as the minor evil.

Another factor which influenced the offer of the VA was a previous decision of the European, North American and Japanese battery producers to gradually eliminate the mercury content in alkali-manganese batteries (Scholl, 1995a). The underlying motives for this decision were, among environmental, also purely economic considerations. In Germany, the use of mercury in the production of batteries led to continually rising costs because the battery producers had to fulfil ambitious health and safety as well as environmental standards due to the classification of mercury as hazardous substance in 1990 (Nathanie and Reger, 1998).

The main goal of the HDE and the participating large retail companies during the negotiations and also during the later developments was to prevent a take-back obligation exclusively for retailers. The HDE considered the continuation of collection by municipal authorities as essential in order not to confuse the consumer. Retailers saw no reasons to take back the batteries exclusively because product responsibility did not lie with them.

Although the state did not assume any formal obligations, the environment ministry accepted the self-commitment and announced that it would refrain from any legal regulation on the issue if the goals were met. The BMU had no explicit preference either for an ordinance or for a VA. At the time the agreement was concluded, the BMU considered the targets as sufficient (Jülich, 1998), although it would have preferred the inclusion of concrete reduction targets for additional harmful substances into the VA. Because of the lack of quantified targets with respect to the recycling and take-back quotas (see below) it remained unclear at which level the BMU would consider the goal attainment as sufficient and renounce from any further regulatory measures.

An additional factor which kept the ministry for the environment from using direct regulation at that point in time was the debate beginning on a European directive and the resultant uncertainties for national policy making in this issue area (Jülich, 1998).

3.3 Content

The self-commitment's overall goal was to reduce the uncontrolled dispersion of heavy metals from household batteries. The main targets and measures formulated in the VA, which came into force on 1 April 1989, were (see also UBA, 1988; SRU, 1991):

- for producers to give preference to the development and production of battery systems without or with only a reduced content of hazardous substances, and to develop battery systems which are substitutes for those containing hazardous substances;
- to reduce the mercury content of alkali-manganese batteries in three steps from approximately 0.2 per cent to less than 0.1 per cent by weight; by the end of 1988, mercury content was to be reduced to 0.15 per cent, by the end of 1990, to 0.1 per cent and by the end of 1993, to less than 0.1 per cent;
- for retailers to take back from the second quarter of 1989, small accumulators, NiCd-accumulators, car batteries, button cells containing mercury, and alkali-manganese batteries with a mercury content of 0.1 per cent or more; these batteries were to be labelled with

the recycling symbol (ISO: 7000-Reg.No. 1135) and the label was to be explained to the consumer on the package; and

• for producers to accept all labelled batteries from retailers and to recover hazardous substances from the returned batteries according to the recycling principle of the AbfG.

The goal of reducing harmful substances in batteries concentrated on mercury, cadmium and lead. However, only with regard to mercury did the agreement formulate concrete and quantified reduction targets. Other heavy metals were either considered as being less environmentally harmful (Jülich, 1998) or – as in the case of lead – functioning recycling schemes had already been developed.

Finally, in order to guarantee the functioning of the collection system, which to an important degree would depend upon the participation of consumers, the agreement aimed at informing consumers about the difference between low-emission and environmentally harmful batteries and the possibilities of returning harmful batteries.

4. ANALYSIS

4.1 Performance

4.1.1 Target relevance
The reduction targets for mercury formulated in the VA were not very far-reaching if one takes into account the technical options already available at that time. A number of studies, therefore, have argued that it is rather questionable, whether the technological developments which could be observed after the coming into force of the VA actually exceeded the 'business-as-usual' development (Jülich, 1998; Scholl, 1995a).[1] On the one hand, reduction targets did not go beyond the announcement made in 1984 by leading international battery producers to reduce the mercury content of alkali-manganese batteries by at least 85 per cent by the year 1989. On the other hand, already in 1987 a mercury content of 0.025 per cent had been reached by leading producers and 0.015 per cent were seen as technically feasible (SRU, 1991).

Besides environmental considerations, the reductions of mercury, cadmium and lead in existing battery systems and the substitution of harmful substances through the development of new battery types were also motivated by economic considerations – for example the above mentioned high costs caused by the use of mercury in the battery production and/or the prospect of competitive advantages for innovative producers (Jülich, 1998). A survey carried out by the German Institute for Ecological Economics Research partly confirms this assumption: different actors attached a minor importance to the VA with respect to its incentive function and stated that competition with other manufacturers and a change in the areas of application had been the most significant motives to develop innovative battery systems (Scholl, 1995a).

According to Nathanie and Reger the major incentives for battery producers to start substituting NiCd-accumulators by nickel-metal-hydride (NiMH) and lithium-ion (Li-ion) accumulators were set by market developments. The producers of consumer applications on the OEM-market forced the development of new accumulators because in the course of the increased use of mobile consumer appliances they demanded the development of improved accumulators with respect to their size, durability or stand-by times and power. NiMH- and Li-ion accumulators were clearly more appropriate to fulfil these new requirements than NiCd-accumulators (Nathanie and Reger, 1998).

On a more general basis it can be argued that concrete targets were set only for the most easily solvable problem. On the one hand, while targets for the reduction of mercury were set, this did not happen with regard to other environmentally harmful heavy metals (especially cadmium). On the other hand, the existing mercury reduction targets only referred to alkali-manganese batteries, not to the environmentally relevant group of button cells containing mercury. Although in both cases the lack of concrete goals was mainly due to the fact that substitution within the existing battery systems was considered not to be feasible, an overall goal on the reduction of cadmium and lead in accumulators and mercury in button cells could have served as an incentive for producers to develop altogether different battery systems (Jülich, 1998).

In sum, it can be seen as the merit of the VA to have given a clear signal that the feasible reduction potentials should be realised by all German producers and importers. However, in particular as well as general environmental considerations by the batteries industry the VA was only one of several factors contributing to the efforts in reducing the harmful substances in batteries.

With regard to the take-back of spent batteries, no concrete quotas for collection and recycling of batteries have been set. However, the existence of such quotas has been considered an important element for the relative success of similar waste management schemes such as the German Packaging Ordinance of 1991. It could be argued that also in the area of batteries, the formulation of concrete quotas could have been an important element in order to increase the relevance of the targets and subsequently reduce the disposal of spent batteries together with normal household waste. Finally, those batteries which were directly built into consumer appliances, were not included in the VA at all.

4.1.2 Goal attainment

Since the VA contained few quantifiable targets, it is difficult to evaluate its goal attainment precisely. However, different studies and evaluations of the VA show that while the quantified targets for the reduction of harmful substances in batteries have been reached quickly and have generally been exceeded, there is an astonishingly clear failure in setting up a functioning take-back system for labelled batteries. Although concrete quotas were missing, it is clear that the collection quotas, which were actually attained, could not be interpreted as a success and led to a failure with respect to the goal of reducing the contents of heavy metals (mainly cadmium and nickel) from batteries in household waste.

Reduction of harmful substances in batteries Chemical analysis of different types of batteries showed that the goals concerning the reduction of heavy metals, especially mercury, were reached and even exceeded. Alkali-manganese batteries with reduced mercury content contained less than 0.025 per cent of mercury. Lead and cadmium contents were below measurability. With zinc-carbon batteries, mercury as well as lead and cadmium contents were below measurability (for example $Hg < 0.005\%$, $Cd < 0.001\%$, $Pb < 0.01\%$) (UBA, 1991). Already in 1993 most alkali-manganese and zinc-carbon cylinder batteries were free of cadmium and mercury. Taking into account that these two types of batteries account for about 80 per cent of all batteries, this has clearly been an environmental success (UBA, 1993; Jülich, 1998).

In sum the mercury content of batteries decreased from 19.8 tons in 1986 to 4.2 tons in 1997 (see Table 3.3). In contrast to this reduction the cadmium content of batteries increased from 198.3 tons in 1986 to 442.8 tons in 1997 (see Table 3.3).

Table 3.3   Total amount of selected metal in batteries in 1986 to 1997 (Germany) (tons)

	1986	1991	1993	1994	1995	1996	1997
Nickel	198.5	604.2	647.9	642.7	921	1 105.3	1 334.2
Cadmium	198.3	604	647	619	528.4	466.8	442.8
Mercury	19.8	16.1	16.2	6.8	5.3	5.5	4.2

Source: UBA, 1999

The development of new battery systems can be observed in areas where harmful substances cannot be substituted in existing battery types. Mercury-oxide button cells, for example, have been substituted to some extent by the less harmful zinc-air cells. Between 1988 and 1997 the amount of zinc-air cells sold had risen from 6.6 to 33 tons while the number of mercury oxide cells decreased from 55.9 to 11 tons (see Table 3.4). Low emission lithium cells and NiMH-accumulators have increasingly substituted the environmentally more harmful NiCd-accumulators since they were developed and put on the market. In 1988 only 3 tons of lithium batteries were sold, but in 1997 this amount increased to 344 tons. In 1997, 2 259 tons of NiMH-accumulators were sold; two years after their introduction (see Table 3.4).

Table 3.4   Tons of sold batteries in Germany and market share

			1988*		1993		1997	
			Tons	% of total	Tons	% of total	Tons	% of total
Primary Batteries	Cylinder	Alkali-manganese	6 229.5	31.67	8 815	35.07	10 946	39.79
		Zinc-carbon	12 331.8	62.69	13 185	52.46	11 636	42.3
	Button-cells	Mercury-oxide	55.9	0.28	43.8	0.17	11	0.04
		Silver-oxide	52.1	0.26	41.1	0.16	45	0.16
		Alkali-mang.	n.a.	n.a.	11.8	0.05	23	0.08
		Zinc-air	6.6	0.03	6.8	0.03	33	0.12
Total primary batteries			**18 675.9**	**94.93**	**22 103.5**	**87.94**	**22 694**	**82.49**
Lithium-batteries		*Cylinder*	n.a.	n.a.	0	0	300	1.09
		Button-cells	3.8	0.02	10	0.04	44	0.16
Total lithium-batteries			**3.8**	**0.02**	**10**	**0.04**	**344**	**1.25**
Accumulators	Cylinder	Nickel-cadmium	921.7	4.69	2 925	11.64	2 205	8.01
		Nickel-hydride	n.a.	n.a.	0	0	2 210	8.03
	Button-cells	Nickel-cadmium	69.9	0.36	95	0.38	9	0.03
		Nickel-hydride	n.a.	n.a.	0	0	49	0.18
Total accumulat.			**991.6**	**5.05**	**3 020**	**12.02**	**4 473**	**16.25**
Total			**19 671.3**	**100**	**25 133.5**	**100**	**27 511**	**100**

Note: *: estimated numbers for 82 million inhabitants in the Old Länder

Source: ZVEI, 1998b

However, in spite of the increasing use of Li-ion and NiMH-accumulators, NiCd-accumulators are still sold in great quantity. Their amount decreased gradually from 3 020 tons (1993) to 2 214 tons (1997) (see Table 3.4).

Recollection and Recycling Several studies have analysed the collection and recycling scheme and revealed that in particular the take-back scheme did not work successfully. According to a study of the Bavarian Trade Agency (Landesgewerbeanstalt Bayern) only 60 per cent of the retailers were informed about the take-back obligation, although 88 per cent had generally been in favour of the goal to take back used batteries and treat them in an environmentally sound way (UBA, 1992). Additionally, maybe as a result of insufficient information given to retailers, 83 per cent of the retailers participating in the collection took back all types of batteries and did not distinguish between labelled and non-labelled batteries (Jülich, 1998; Baumann and Muth, 1997).

Estimates on the number of returned batteries differ from source to source.[2] The Institute for Environmental Protection at the University of Dortmund found in 1992 that only 42 per cent of all button cells containing mercury and only 22 to 36 per cent of NiCd-accumulators were returned. The rest continued to be disposed of mainly with household waste. Similarly, Jülich (1998) estimates a collection quota for NiCd-accumulators of 17 per cent to a maximum of one third. In 1996 a study carried out by the Technical University of Berlin confirmed these results (Bundesregierung, 1997). The retail trade estimated that only 25 per cent of all batteries sold were returned and the UBA estimated the actual return to be even lower (UBA, 1991). Similarly, the Council of Environmental Experts estimated take-back quotas, dependent on the type of battery, to be less than one third. These numbers differed enormously from those given by the batteries industry: 82 per cent for button cells and 50 per cent for accumulators (UBA, 1993) and thereby indicated that monitoring may not have been taken very seriously by the parties who signed the VA.

The apparent failure of the collection system led to a failure with respect to the goal of reducing the contents of heavy metals (mainly cadmium and nickel) from batteries in household waste.

The main reasons for this failure were assumed to be:

- a general reluctance of the retail sector to inform consumers about their possibilities for returning used batteries (in around 63 per cent of the retail shops information was given only if explicitly requested by the customer, additionally the HDE quickly refrained from an initially planned information campaign) (Jülich, 1998);

- the refusal of many retail shops and supermarkets to put collection boxes in central and highly visible places; and
- a lack of participation on the side of consumers who obviously had difficulties in distinguishing batteries containing harmful substances from those that could be disposed of with household waste.

In sum, Scholl concludes 'that the trade is one of the major bottlenecks within the recollection chain' (Scholl, 1995a). The BMU points out, that one reason for this failure might have been the HDE's lacking the potential of sanctions in order to implement the obligations resulting from the VA in every single retail shop.

Finally, with regard to the target of recycling labelled batteries, evaluation studies indicate a relative failure of the VA. Based on diverging assumptions (for example on the life span of NiCd-accumulators), the actual recycling quotas for NiCd-accumulators have been calculated to range between 24 and 51 per cent in 1993 and between 17 and 33 per cent in 1996 (Jülich, 1998; Baumann and Muth, 1997). For mercury button cells the Institute for Environmental Research (Institut für Umweltforschung) estimated a recycling quota of 35.7 per cent in 1994 (Baumann and Muth, 1997).

Generally, a study commissioned by the Bavarian State Agency for Environment found that a majority of 56 per cent of all labelled batteries containing harmful substances continued to be disposed of with normal household waste while only 44 per cent were recycled (see Table 3.5) (Scholl, 1995a). Although, due to methodological difficulties, the accuracy of these studies should not be overestimated, they clearly indicate that recycling efforts in the area of batteries have not been successful.

Table 3.5 Batteries and their disposal in 1994

Used batteries	Disposal alternatives		
	Disposal as domestic waste (%)	Disposal as hazardous waste (%)	Recycled (%)
Labelled	36	20	44
Non-labelled	82.2	17.8	0
Labelled and non-labelled	80.8	17.8	1.4

Source: Scholl, 1995a

In sum, these numbers show that the overall goal of significantly reducing the disposal of batteries containing harmful substances in normal household waste was missed.

Concerning the innovative impact of the VA in the area of batteries recycling, no significant technological developments occurred. According to the UBA, little progress was made in the recycling of NiCd-accumulators.

4.2 Cost Efficiency

As agreed in the VA, battery producers established the collection scheme and were to bear the entire costs for collection, disposal and recovery or recycling. Therefore a Battery Consortium (ARGE Bat) with three employees was founded, of which 29 battery producers were members. The turnover of the *ARGE Bat* developed from DM 480 000 in 1990 to 4.1 million in 1998 (ZVEI, 1998b).

The distribution of costs for the collection and recycling scheme was informally negotiated between the participating battery producers based on their estimated market shares (Benzler et. al, 1995).

Additional costs arose from developing new battery systems with reduced or substituted harmful substances. However, about these costs no information was available. Costs concerning the labelling of batteries were only marginal according to information from the batteries industry (Jülich, 1998). The major cost factors for the batteries industry were the fees for the parcels with spent batteries which were sent from retail shops without postage, the provision of the logistic material for collection (boxes for the retailers, which had to fulfil certain technical standards) and the storage of collected materials (Jülich, 1998). Additionally, the insufficient differentiation between less harmful (that is non-labelled) and environmentally harmful (that is labelled) batteries during collection and take-back – both by consumers and retailers – led to unexpected and rising costs for the batteries industry.

The ARGE Bat carried these additional costs sorting and the disposal of less harmful batteries, although the VA did not oblige it to do so. In general, the batteries industry raised the prices of batteries in order to compensate for their additional costs. Depending on their competitive situation the retailers passed it on to the consumer.

According to the batteries industry and the UBA one significant problem, a collection and recycle scheme of batteries has to cope with, is the plagiarism of batteries and grey imports. Because of these practices the free-rider problem becomes evident and increases the costs for those battery producers and importers who participate in the collection and recycling scheme. Compared to the estimated number of about 500 battery producers and importers operating in Germany, the 29 members participating in ARGE Bat do represent only a small share of the total number of battery companies. Taking into account this share, one could assume that the problem of free-riders might have been evident during the implementation of the VA.

However, the participating companies are those with the largest market share. Concrete numbers for assessing the free-rider problem, which usually leads to rising costs for the participating firms, are not available. The batteries industry estimated the share of overall collected NiCd-accumulators from non-participating battery importers at about 25 per cent (Kiehne, 1997). The BMU, in principle, recognised the free-rider problem, but saw no immediate need for corrective measures.

4.3 Monitoring, Participation and Transparency

As with many other VAs, participation and transparency were rather low as neither environmental nor consumer organisations were involved in the negotiations leading to the VA (Jülich, 1998).

In order to asses the performance of the VA, yearly reports by the producers' and retailers' associations were to be submitted to the BMU. However, the VA did not foresee any sanctions in the case where the formulated goals were not reached. Rather, it stated that if take-back of labelled batteries proved not to be practicable, the respective provisions in the VA would be reformulated (Jülich, 1998).

The required data for the monitoring originates from the battery producers and they are also responsible for the monitoring. An independent monitoring was not foreseen in the VA. Additionally, no numbers were available from other actors, which could have been compared to the provided data of the battery producers. However, as has been shown above, there were several studies in order to assess goal attainment. The quantity of batteries, which were built-into consumer applications, has not been taking into account by the battery producers or other organisations or institutions.

4.4 Further Development: The German Batteries Ordinance of 1998

In 1992 and in 1994 the BMU presented further proposals for a federal ordinance on recycling and disposal of used batteries and accumulators which were designed to overcome the already visible shortcomings of the VA and to transpose into national law the EC Council Directive 91/157 on batteries and accumulators containing harmful substances and its amendment through the Commission Directive 93/86. The legal basis for these drafts was the Closed Substance Cycle and Waste Management Act (Krw/AbfG) which was adopted by parliament in 1994 and came into force two years later on 7 October 1996. This new waste management act depicts the legal basis for product regulations concerning, for example, end-of-life-vehicles, packaging, or batteries. On this legal basis, government is entitled to develop ordinances with detailed product requirements such as:

- restrictions regarding the composition/characteristics or destined uses of certain products;
- product bans;
- labelling obligations;
- return or take-back obligations.

The batteries industry perceived the EC directive, the subsequent drafts for a batteries ordinance and the Krw/AbfG as serious threats and tried once again to anticipate these measures. Additionally, the experiences with the VA of 1988 played an important role in their considerations.

Consequently, producers, importers and retailers presented in 1995 a proposal for a second VA, which took into account the provisions of the EC Directive. Among other elements it included a take-back and recycling/disposal scheme for all household batteries (including batteries without harmful substances). Furthermore, the sale of batteries containing mercury-oxide was to be phased out by the end of 1997, labelling should be improved, producers and importers were to commit themselves to participate in the development of technologies for sorting and recycling of batteries, and regular reports on the implementation of the VA should be provided to the BMU.

In spite of this proposal for an improved VA, government chose to pass an ordinance on batteries and accumulators in March 1998 which came into force in October 1998. Since a self-commitment by the batteries industry would not have been sufficient to transpose the EC Directive into national law, this ordinance had become necessary. It was drafted in informal co-operation with the HDE and the ZVEI. The ordinance generally follows the proposal for a VA of 1995, adding an obligation for consumers to return used batteries to the selling point or to special municipal collection posts. The main elements of the ordinance are:

- a general obligation for retailers to take back all spent batteries and leave them to the producers for recycling or disposal;
- an obligation for retailers to inform customers about the possibilities of returning spent batteries free of charge;
- an obligation for customers to bring back spent batteries to retailers or special return stations;
- a prohibition on bringing into circulation alkali-manganese batteries containing more than 0.025 per cent of mercury or appliances with built-in batteries containing hazardous substances which cannot be removed by the customer after use;
- a deposit of DM 15 for car batteries.

According to the BMU the ordinance was designed to overcome the shortcomings of the voluntary take-back scheme. The BMU judged the VA of 1988 as only partially successful because of its failure to separately collect all labelled batteries. However, in spite of considering it as an effective instrument, the ministry refrained from introducing a deposit-refund system for household batteries. Due to the strong opposition by the Ministry for Economic Affairs the BMU judged a deposit-refund system as politically not feasible.

Although, a first draft of the batteries ordinance had limited the take-back and return obligation to batteries containing harmful substances (*Abfallwirtschaftlicher Informationsdienst*, 1997), the BMU later decided to expand this obligation to all batteries. As mentioned above, the experiences with the VA had revealed significant difficulties on the part of consumers in separating labelled and non-labelled batteries. In order to further reduce the disposal of batteries containing hazardous substances together with normal household waste government chose the instrument of a general take-back obligation for all types of batteries (Scholl, 1995a). This position was strongly backed by the retail sector, but initially opposed by the batteries industry. In the end, however, taking into account the failure of the former collection system and after informal discussions with government and the HDE, the batteries industry agreed to a general take-back obligation.

5. CONCLUSION

Considering the reduction or substitution of heavy metals in batteries, the VA of 1988 was only partially successful. Only for mercury did the VA contain well-specified and quantified targets. Subsequently, the mercury content of batteries was reduced successfully. However, the same could not be observed with regard to other heavy metals, especially the equally hazardous cadmium. While the total mercury content in batteries steadily decreased (from nearly 20 tons in 1986 to little more than four tons in 1997), the overall use of cadmium more than doubled in the same period (from nearly 200 tons in 1986 to 440 tons in 1997). So, in spite of the significant success in banning mercury from the production of batteries, other heavy metals, especially cadmium, continue to impose an environmental threat. The development of new battery systems has alleviated this trend, but not yet solved the problem.

Furthermore, it needs to be pointed out that the observable reduction in the heavy metal content of batteries has not exclusively been the result of the VA. Rather, market developments and economic considerations of the battery producers contributed to the significant reduction of mercury and especially the more recent reduction of cadmium.

With regard to the overall environmental goal of reducing or eliminating heavy metal contamination of household waste resulting from the disposal of batteries, which was neither well specified nor quantified, the VA has not been successful. Besides the failure in reducing the cadmium content of batteries, this is due to the inadequate functioning of the collection and recycling scheme. Retailers' participation in the separate collection of used batteries was generally low. Additionally, and in spite of the public sensitivity towards the problem, consumers were reluctant to return spent batteries to the dealers and did not differentiate between harmful and less harmful batteries. Finally, at least part of the failure of the agreement can be seen in the structure of the underlying problem. The type of product to be regulated explains to some degree the various failed attempts to implement some form of producer responsibility on a voluntary basis. Contrary to large, long-lived and individually registered products such as cars, batteries are small, cheap and short-lived items over which producers or public authorities have little control after they are sold. In cases characterised by such an unfavourable problem structure, voluntary measures seem to function only if policymakers can credibly threaten to use an alternative instrument in the case that targets are not met. While in the Belgian batteries case (in this book) the pending eco-tax served as such a 'stick behind the door', the German ministry for the environment did not have at its disposal a comparable threat.

For the reasons mentioned above, it is unclear whether alternative measures – which had been discussed at the time the VA was drafted – would have been significantly more successful. It can be assumed that the introduction of a general take-back and return obligation for *all* types of batteries would have reduced uncertainties on the part of the consumers as to which types of batteries were to be returned and therefore might have led to increased collection quotas for those batteries containing harmful substances. But – as first evaluations of the new Batteries Ordinance show – even in this case, a significant quantity of batteries would probably have continued to be disposed of with household waste. From a purely environmental point of view the introduction of a mandatory deposit for harmful batteries would have been a promising alternative. However, this option has always been criticised, among other reasons, for its lack of economic feasibility and was strongly opposed by important actors such as the Ministry for Economic Affairs.

In general, the VA and especially its further development reveals a learning process by the different actors. Taking into account the failure of the VA in collecting harmful batteries, the batteries industry finally agreed on an ordinance, which was mainly designed to cope with the problems related with the former collection scheme, and abandoned its opposition to the collection of all batteries, irrespective of their harmfulness. Similarly the BMU, considering the failure of the voluntary collection scheme, rejected any kind of differentiation between harmful and less harmful batteries and introduced an ordinance, which obliged the consumer to return and the retail and batteries industry to take back all types of batteries. Whether this ordinance will succeed in reducing the amount of batteries disposed of with the household waste remains to be seen.

NOTES

1. In retrospective, the BMU confirms this assumption.
2. One of the major reason for these differences are diverging assumptions about the lifespan of batteries which lead to diverging reference years. In general, the return quotas are calculated on the basis of the returned batteries as well as the batteries sold in the reference year and depending on the assumed life span of batteries. The ZVEI assumes a lifespan for NiCd-accumulators of seven years, whereas the University of Dortmund calculates the return quotas assuming a lifespan of five years for the same battery type pointing out that the lifespan of seven years is a very optimistic assumption.

REFERENCES

Abfallwirtschaftlicher Informationsdienst (1997), No. 4, 30 June.
Baumann, Werner and Muth, Anneliese (1997), *Batterien. Daten und Fakten zum Umweltschutz*, Berlin: Springer-Verlag.
Benzler, Guido, Halstrick-Schwenk, Marianne et al. (1995), *Wettbewerbskonformität von Rücknahmeverpflichtungen im Abfallbereich*, Untersuchungen des Rheinisch-Westfälischen Instituts für Wirtschaftsforschung Heft 17. Essen: RWI.
Bundesregierung (1997), *Zustimmungsbedürftige Verordnung über die Rücknahme und Entsorgung gebrauchter Batterien und Akkumulatoren*, Drucksache 13/9516, 18 December 1997.
GRS (Stiftung gemeinsames Rücknahmesystem Batterien) (2000), *Jahresbericht 1999*, (http://www.GRS-Batterien.de/intro.htm).
HDE (1999), *Wer wir sind*, (http://www.einzelhandel.de/rech0001.htm).
Hiller, Fritz (1998), 'Maßnahmen zur Entsorgung von Gerätebatterien', in Fritz Hiller, Ralf Gierke and Heinz-Albert Kiehne (eds), *Entsorgung von Gerätebatterien. Primärbatterien und Kleinakkumulatoren*, 3rd edition. Renningen-Malmsheim: Expert-Verlag.
Jülich, Ralf (1998), 'The Battery Agreement', in ELNI (ed.), *Environmental Agreements – The Role and Effect of Environmental Agreements in Environmental Policies*, Cameron May.
Kiehne, Heinz-Albert (1997), 'Collection and Recycling of NiCd-Batteries in Germany'. State of the Art, Paper presented at the OECD Workshop, Lyon, 23–25 September.
Kiehne, Heinz-Albert (1998a), 'Freiwillige Vereinbarung vom 9.9.1988 zur Batterieentsorgung', in: Fritz Hiller, Ralf Gierke and Heinz-Albert Kiehne (eds), *Entsorgung von Gerätebatterien. Primärbatterien und Kleinakkumulatoren*, 3rd edition. Renningen-Malmsheim: Expert-Verlag, pp. 9-14.

Kiehne, Heinz-Albert (1998b), 'Die Rolle der Batteriehersteller. Schadstoffminderung, Kennzeichnung, Mengen', *ARGE Bat*, Paper presented at the ZVEI Tagung zur Batterieverordnung 1 April 1998, Frankfurt am Main.

Nathanie, Carsten and Guido Reger (1998), 'Cadmiumfreie und wiederaufladbare Batterien', in Kathleen Spielok and Horst Pohle (eds), *Entwicklung und Anwendung innovativer Umwelttechnologien*, Berlin: UBA, pp. 292–351.

SRU *(German Council of Environmental Advisors)* (1991), *Sondergutachten Abfallwirtschaft*, Stuttgart: Metzler-Poeschel, 1991.

Scholl, Gerd (1995a), Product policy and the environment: The example of batteries, 'Schriftenreihe des IÖW 87/95'. Berlin.

Scholl, Gerd (1995b), 'Instrumente des produktbezogenen Umweltschutzes – Das Beispiel Gerätebatterien', in *IÖW/VÖW Informationsdienst*, **10** (2), 11–13.

UBA *(Federal Environmental Agency)* (1988), *Jahresbericht 1988*, Berlin: UBA.

UBA (1991), *Jahresbericht 1991*, Berlin: UBA.

UBA (1992), *Untersuchungen über die Auswirkungen gesetzlicher Beschränkungen auf die Verwendung, Verbreitung und Substitution von Cadmium in Produkten*, Berlin: UBA

UBA (1993a), *Jahresbericht 1993*, Berlin: UBA.

UBA (1993b), *Abfallverhalten neuartiger Batterien. Mengen, Inhaltsstoffe, Verwertungs- und Behandlungsmethoden von Batterien*, Berlin: UBA.

UBA (1999), *Rückführung von Gerätebatterien in Deutschland – Ein Blick auf die Batterieverordnung ein halbes Jahr nach Ihrem Inkrafttreten*, unpublished report.

ZVEI (Zentralverband der Elektroindustrie) (1998a), *Hersteller organisieren gemeinsames Rücknahmesystem für verbrauchte Battereien*, Pressemitteilung Pr – 61/98 (http://www.zvei.de/news/Presseinformation/ Pressearchiv/ne_pr_rei_pr61_98.html).

ZVEI (Zentralverband der Elektroindustrie) (1998b), *Protokoll der ordentlichen Mitgliederversammlung*, 3 September 1998.

INTERVIEWS

Mrs Böttcher-Thiedemann, Federal Environment Agency
Mrs Boettcher, Federal Association of German Retail Trade
Mr Blickwedel, Federal Minstry for Environment, Nature Protection and Nuclear Safety
Mr Eichler, German Council of Environmental Experts
Mr Kiehne, former chairman of the Battery Consortium

4. The Voluntary Pledge Regarding the Environmentally Sound Management of End-of-Life Vehicles

Helge Jörgens and Per-Olof Busch

1. INTRODUCTION

The disposal of end-of-life vehicles (ELVs) became an important environmental issue in Germany in the late 1980s. First national goals in the area of ELV-management were set in 1990 by the German government. This was the starting point of an intensive debate on regulatory measures for the reorganisation of the national system of ELV-management. In the following years several draft ordinances regarding the disposal of ELVs were developed by the Ministry for the Environment (BMU) and discussed with the relevant actors. In February 1996, after lengthy informal negotiations and the repeated threat of passing an ELV-Ordinance, 16 branch organisations of the automotive, recycling and supply sector submitted the Voluntary Pledge Regarding the Environmentally Sound Management of End-Of-Life Vehicles (Passenger Cars) Within the Framework of the Closed Substance Cycle and Waste Management Act which was informally accepted by the BMU.

As a reaction to the voluntary pledge, the German government refrained from a comprehensive regulation, but presented a 'lean ordinance' to supplement the voluntary solution. The ELV-Ordinance was adopted by parliament in June 1997. Both, the voluntary agreement (VA) and the parallel ELV-Ordinance came into force in April 1998.

2. CONTEXT

2.1 The Environmental Problem

When assessing the environmental impacts of car traffic most attention has been paid to problems related to the use of automobiles, for example air pollution, noise, fuel consumption and climate relevant emissions (Enquête–Kommission, 1994). Environmental problems related to the disposal of ELVs have received less attention. However, significant environmental problems occur during recovery and disposal of ELVs (SRU, 1991; Benzler and Löbbe, 1995; Schenk, 1998; Zoboli, 1999; SRU, 2000):

- direct pollution during the dismantling of ELVs (for example soil or groundwater contamination caused by the leaking of operating fluids);
- generation of shredder waste (automotive shredder residue – ASR) which is contaminated with heavy metals, polyvinyl chloride (PVC), polychlorinated biphenyl (PCB) and so on and which traditionally has to a large extent been landfilled together with normal household waste;
- the irregular ('wild') disposal of ELVs.

In Germany the number of deregistered motor vehicles, and thus the potential amount of ELVs to be disposed, has continually increased during the 1990s. Since 1991, when nearly 2.26 million cars were deregistered, the number increased by 34.5% to nearly 3.05 million units in 1999. In the same time, the number of registered cars increased from nearly 32.1 million by 31.9% to nearly 42.3 million in 1999 (see Table 4.1). However, the number of deregistered cars is not identical with the number of ELVs to be disposed. As the official statistics do not distinguish between the different causes for deregistration (ARGE-Altauto, 2000), it is difficult to assess the actual annual number of ELVs to be disposed of in Germany. An important number of cars deregistered in Germany are being exported to other countries either as second-hand cars or as ELVs. Additionally, a small number of deregistered cars are stored temporarily on private property. Between 1997 and 1999, the Consortium End-of-Life Vehicles, ARGE-Altauto, estimates the annual number of ELVs to be disposed of in Germany between 1.1 to 1.7 million (ARGE-Altauto, 2000).

Table 4.1   Registered and deregistered cars in Germany 1995-99

Year	Number of registered cars	Number of deregistered cars
1991	32 087 560	2 265 291*
1993	38 772 493	2 252 601
1995	40 404 294	2 949 704
1997	41 371 992	3 392 358
1999	42 323 672	3 045 903
Change from 1991	+ 31.9%	+ 34.46%

*Old Länder

Source: KBA 2000; KBA, 2001; ARGE-Altauto, 2000

Traditionally, the system for recycling of ELVs has been oriented towards the recovery of steel and metals, which has relatively early led the automobile to be one of the most extensively recycled long-lasting consumer items (Schenk, 1998). Estimates assume that prior to the VA approximately 75 per cent in weight of ELVs – mainly metal and steel components – had already been reused or recycled (Institut der Wirtschaft, 1998).

The remaining 25 per cent in weight most of it being ASR, constitute a significant environmental problem. ASR consists of a conglomerate of plastics and rubber, glass, textiles and wood fibre materials which shows significant contamination with heavy metals, PVC, oils and cancerous substances like PCB (Rennings et al. 1996). When landfilled, the contaminated ASR poses a threat to the environment, especially to the ground water (UBA, 1997). Several factors contribute to or aggravate the environmental problems related with ASR:

- increased use of plastics in the construction of vehicles – from around 2 per cent in the 1960s to more than 14 per cent in 1995 (Rennings et al., 1996; Schenk, 1998);
- recycling of plastics and other materials from ELVs and especially from ASR is still technically difficult and economically impracticable (Schenk, 1998);
- estimates assume that prior to the adoption of the VA only around 20 to 30 per cent of all 5 000 dismantlers kept the existing environmental standards and often significant quantities of operating fluids remained within the vehicles which were passed on to shredders, leading to an increased contamination of shredder waste (Kremer, 1998; Schenk, 1999).

Estimates as to the total amount of ASR from ELVs in Germany ranged from 300 000 to 600 000 tons.[1] In the medium term, the BMU expected a significant increase of this amount (Rennings et al., 1996). The generation of ASR has been the main reason for regulatory measures in the field of ELV-management. Already in the 1991 *Technical Guideline on Waste* ASR had been classified as hazardous waste to be disposed in special landfills or incinerators.[2]

Besides the generation of ASR, the uncontrolled disposal of old cars estimated very roughly at 100 000 vehicles annually and which often results in leakage of oils and other liquids, constitutes an additional environmental problem (Sacksofsky, 1996).

2.2 The Main Actors in the Area of ELV Management

2.2.1 Automobile producers, importers and suppliers

The automobile industry is one of the key sectors in Germany. In 1999 the total turnover of the automobile producers amounted to nearly DM 338 billion (VDA, 2000). The German automobile industry has an oligopolistic structure with few producers operating on a large scale and international or global scope (Zoboli, 1999). In 1999 5.3 million cars were produced in Germany and 727 529 people were directly employed in the automotive industry (VDA, 2000).

Suppliers, which are mostly medium-size enterprises, play an important role as they produce about 77 per cent of the components used in an automobile. To some extent they are responsible for the design and development of new components, but their influence is limited by the requirements set by automobile producers. In 1999 their turnover amounted to nearly DM 89 billion (VDA, 2000). When taking into account the secondary employment (for example supply of materials, components, and services) the number of employees in the automotive industry increases to 1.72 million in 1999 (VDA, 2000).

The automotive producers' decisions at the stage of automobile production – for example design, material composition and durability of new cars – significantly affect the environmental impact and the scope and profitability of the actions of other actors at the later stage of ELV-management (Lucas, 2000). Until recently, recycling and disposal of ELVs played an inferior role in strategic decisions of the automotive industry. A survey among automobile producers conducted in 1997 showed that the principal motive for taking action in the area of recycling and dismantling of old cars has been to proactively influence the policy development and to be prepared for possible political actions in the issue area (Schenk, 1998).

Economic incentives to consider environmental aspects such as waste avoidance and recyclability at the development stage have traditionally been rather weak. This is mainly due to the distance between automobile producers and consumers which is high compared to most other consumer goods or services. Automobiles are among the most long-lasting consumer goods. The total time span from the development of a car to its disposal ranges from 15 to 25 years (Schenk, 1998). Taking into account this long time span between development and disposal as well as the changing ownership during a car's product life, it is rather unlikely that variances in the cost of disposal between different car types will significantly influence the customer's decision when purchasing a new car. Furthermore, if environmental aspects play any role at all, factors like fuel consumption or emissions into the air have traditionally received much more attention by consumers than waste and recycling characteristics of automobiles (Benzler and Löbbe, 1995). These facts provide little ground for expectations that competition among producers emerging from consumers' demand could directly lead to a significant incorporation of recycling aspects into the development and construction of cars.

Additionally, the goal of minimising the environmental impact resulting from the management of ELVs conflicts with a number of other goals such as passenger security, fuel consumption, comfort, variability, production costs, styling, or durability (Schenk, 1998). For example, reducing the fuel consumption of the vehicle fleet provides a much more effective and perceptible way of improving a brand's environmental image. However, since reductions in fuel consumption can be reached mainly by decreasing a car's weight and thus by a greater use of lightweight plastic components or composite materials which are difficult to recycle and which increase the generation of environmentally problematic ASR, a conflict arises between the goals of fuel efficiency and recyclability. This conflict shows that a one-sided orientation towards recycling and disposal on the part of producers may not be feasible.

2.2.2 Automobile dealers and repair stations

As dealers in spare parts, repair stations buy or take back used components and sell used or refurbished parts to car owners. Both dealers and repair stations can buy or take back ELVs either for reconstruction or in order to recover spare parts. When purchasing a new or used car, customers can usually give their old car as a trade-in. Trade-in has become an important service and marketing instrument for car dealers. Automobile dealers and repair stations then either resell the cars or pass them on for disposal.

Economically, automobile dealers are mainly interested in taking back old cars from customers who buy a new or second-hand car. Furthermore, many dealers are reluctant to hold ELVs on their premises as this could create a negative image (Schenk, 1998). Repair stations are not interested in improvements in the dismantling of cars, because this would also lead to reduced repair costs and, therefore, threaten one of their major sources of income.

2.2.3 Dismantlers

The market for ELV-dismantling has a polipolistic structure. Traditionally, most dismantlers have been small businesses with two to five, rarely more than ten employees, with generally low qualifications. There were no official statistics as to the total of dismantlers in Germany prior to the coming in force of the VA and its supplementing ELV-Ordinance. Based on a review of the literature, Schenk estimated a total of 3 500 to 6 000 dismantlers in Germany. Other sources speak of approximately 4 500 to 5 000 (Wöhrl, 1998; Kremer, 1998; Holzhauer, 1998). The number of employees has been estimated at 10000 to 15000 (Schenk, 1998). In 1993 the turnover of the dismantling industry in Germany was roughly estimated at DM 6 billion. According to interviews carried out by the Institute of Marketing in Münster their main source of income is the sale of spare parts (up to 80 per cent of their income). Less important for their income is the recycling of materials (about 10 to 20 per cent of their income) (Meffert and Kirchgeorg, 1998).

The dismantling businesses constitute the first important stage in the process of automobile recycling and have a pivotal role in the ELV management for reaching substantial increases of recycling rates and reducing the environmental problem of ASR (Zoboli, 1999). The main steps in the dismantling process are draining (extraction of oil, gasoline, brake fluids and so on), recovery of spare parts, materials–oriented recovery of components (such as batteries, catalytic converters or heat exchangers), storage, and finally delivery to a shredder company (Schenk, 1998). Due to their weak organisation (at least three branch organisations claim to represent dismantlers at the national level), the small number of employees, the relatively bad public image and weak lobbying, the specific interests of dismantlers have generally been weakly considered in the political process (Schenk, 1998).

Considering the incentives at the stage of the dismantlers to increase the recycling and recovery rates and thus to reduce the environmental problems related to the generation and composition of ASR, Schenk observes a market failure which contributes to and aggravates the environmental problem of ASR (Schenk, 1998). The amount of hazardous waste in shredder waste depends largely on the quality of the dismantling process (the amount of recovered parts as well as the draining of operating fluids). For economic reasons, dismantlers only recover those materials, which are suitable for reuse, recycling or sale. There is no positive incentive for them to recover other materials, for example for ecological reasons. Additionally, the price calculation of shredder companies to whom the dismantled car wrecks are sold (which is based on weight rather than quality of car wrecks) sets a negative incentive. If dismantlers recover more materials than they can expect to sell at a positive market price, they would have to pay the additional costs for the work and the storage, and at the same time earn less money by selling the car to the shredder company because of its reduced weight. Without outlets for recycled and recovered components or materials, which render dismantling under conditions of cost-efficiency possible, dismantlers have no incentive to increase their recovery and recycling rates (Zoboli, 1999). However, a more recycling oriented design of cars by the responsible automobile producers could ease the dismantling and recovering of parts, consequently reduce the dismantling costs and thus contribute to a reduction of ASR generation at the dismantling stage.

2.2.4 Scrap processors (shredders) and scrap dealers
In the late 1980s approximately 40 shredders were operating in Germany (SRU, 1991). In April 1999, one year after the enactment of the ELV-Ordinance and the VA, a total of 49 shredder companies were registered in Germany, most of them owned by large steel companies (ARGE-Altauto, n.d.; Schenk, 1998). In 1997 they produced about 1.3 million tons of steel shredder.

ELVs are the most important source of income for shredders. They reduce the ELV to small pieces and extract the different metals from the residue. While metals are reused, the remaining ASR is disposed mainly in normal landfills together with household waste.

Being the ultimate stage in the processing of ELVs, shredder companies have little influence on the composition of the car wrecks which are delivered to them. Additionally, they have so far not been able (or have had no strong incentive) to pass on the cost of an environmentally sound disposal of ASR to the other actors in the chain of ELV-management. Although, shredders are ultimately responsible for the environmental damage resulting from the dumping of contaminated ASR, in general, their strategies are highly constrained by developments occurring at earlier stages of the ELV chain.

2.2.5 Car owners
Beside his role as consumer (see above), the car owner plays another role in the actor network of ELV management as he decides how the ELV is disposed of. In general, his decision about the way of disposal is influenced by the costs of the different alternatives which depend among other factors on the disposal charge to be paid to the dismantler or return station and the costs of transportation (Schenk, 1998), but also on the time and effort needed to

dispose of an old car. If the last owner judges these costs as being too high he might consider selling the car to an exporter or dispose of the ELV illegally. Most cases of uncontrolled disposal occur in regions with a low density of population and long distances to the nearest dismantle company or return station for ELVs (Schenk, 1998).

3. NEGOTIATION PROCESS

3.1 Negotiations

Two major developments have placed the regulation of ELV management on the political agenda. At the international level, the inclusion of ELVs in the group of priority waste streams by the European Commission influenced German environmental policy in this issue area (Zoboli, 1999; UBA, 1993). At the national level, ELV policy was initiated when prognoses indicated rapidly increasing waste volumes combined with an increasing scarcity of disposal capacities. In this light, waste management became a priority area within environmental policy. Besides the traditional goal of environmentally sound waste disposal, emphasis was increasingly placed on waste avoidance, reuse and recycling of products and materials (Jörgens and Jörgensen, 1998). In the second half of the 1980s and early 1990s, one result of this development was the preparation or adoption of a number of product–related ordinances in the areas of waste resulting from beverage containers, plastic packaging, paper or construction rubble (UBA, 1989: 189).

A first governmental proposal for a set of national objectives in the area of ELV management was presented by the BMU in August 1990. Informal negotiations mainly between the Association of the German Automotive Industry (VDA) and the BMU began in September 1990 and were characterised by serious conflicts about the distribution of costs, whereas the views about the environmental problems related to ELV-management differed only marginally between the involved actors.

The draft ELV-Ordinance of 1990 as well as successive drafts presented by the BMU intended to:

- set quantified recycling targets and quotas for certain materials;
- introduce a general take-back obligation free of charge for automobile producers irrespective of the car's age;
- establish a nationwide take-back and recycling network by the automobile producers;
- introduce a general return obligation for the car owners;

- set labelling obligations for plastics;
- call for the extraction and separate disposal of certain components.

The idea of a cost-free take-back of ELV followed the original concept of extended producer responsibility (OECD, 1998) and was intended to stimulate innovations in the recycling oriented construction of new cars.

During the negotiations the opposition of the automotive industry concentrated on the avoidance of the general take-back obligation free of charge for automobile producers irrespective of the car's age. Instead, car owners should bear the costs for the disposal of ELV. Apart from this central claim, the various alternative concepts of the automotive industry, finally leading to the offer of a VA, proposed:

- the introduction of new environmental standards for dismantlers; especially for the extraction of operating fluids, the dismantling and recycling of parts and materials;
- the establishment of a monitoring system for dismantlers based on certification by independent experts;
- the introduction of a proof of disposal which the car owner would receive from the dismantler and which would be a necessary precondition for de-registration of the car in order to guarantee proper disposal;
- the establishment of a nationwide take-back and recycling system for cars of their brands in co-operation with selected dismantlers;
- the establishment of an agency whose task it would be to co-ordinate the actions of the different actors in the course of ELV-management (Sacksofsky, 1996).

In February 1996, after lengthy informal negotiations and the repeated threat of passing an ELV-Ordinance, *the Voluntary Pledge Regarding the Environmentally Sound Management of End-Of-Life Vehicles (Passenger Cars)* was given by 16 branch organisations of the automotive, recycling and supply sector.

As a reaction to the voluntary pledge, the BMU refrained from a comprehensive regulation, but presented a 'lean ordinance' to supplement the voluntary solution which was adopted by parliament in June 1997. This supplementing ELV-Ordinance had been asked for by the signatories of the VA as a central precondition for its enactment. The VA and the parallel ELV-Ordinance came into force in April 1998; almost ten years after the issue had first been placed on the political agenda.

3.2 Contents

3.2.1 Voluntary agreement
The main goals of the VA on the environmentally sound management of
ELVs are:

- the recycling–oriented design of cars and their components;
- the environmentally sound treatment of ELVs, especially with regard
  to the removal of operating fluids and the dismantling of vehicles;
- the development, setting-up and optimisation of closed material cycles
  and facilities for recovery, especially with regard to the ASR in order
  to ease the strain on landfill capacities and natural resources.

This shall be reached by:

- setting up a nationwide infrastructure for take-back and recycling of
  ELVs no later than two years after the creation of the necessary
  regulatory framework (that is a 'lean' ELV-ordinance to be designed
  by government);
- reducing the amount of ASR for disposal from 25 per cent by weight
  to an average of maximum 15 per cent by the year 2002, and a
  maximum of 5 per cent by 2015;
- manufacturers taking back any ELVs of their production at market
  conditions and taking back, free of charge, cars which have been
  registered after the coming into force of the supporting ELV-
  Ordinance and which are not older than 12 years.

Additionally, in order for producers to take back their cars free of charge,
these must have been registered in Germany for at least six months prior to
return in the name of the last owner, be complete and movable, free of waste,
and without serious damage. Finally parts and accessories of these cars have
to comply with relevant statutory requirements.
Implementation of the VA shall be monitored through:

- ARGE-Altauto, a committee appointed at the VDA in order to co-
  ordinate the fulfilment of the VA and to verify the level of progress
  achieved;
- a monitoring report delivered every second year to the BMU and the
  Ministry of Economic Affairs (BMWi);
- the establishment of an advisory board including consumer
  organisations.

The key actors for implementing the VA are:

- automobile producers and suppliers who are required to continuously optimise the recyclability of their products and – in the case of automobile producers – set up a nationwide[3] system of return points and dismantlers;
- ARGE-Altauto which is responsible for supervising the implementation of the VA and for organising the monitoring process;
- car owners, who have to return their old car to a certified return point or dismantler in order to receive a proof of recycling necessary for de-registration and – in the case of cars registered before 1 April 1998 or older than 12 years – have to bear the costs of recycling and disposal;
- operators of return stations and dismantling facilities, who can either be part of one of the automobile producer's networks or act as independent competitors, and who have to implement the environmental standards and follow the instructions laid down in the *ELV-Ordinance* in order to receive certification (additionally, dismantlers have to attain the targets for re-use and recycling);
- certified shredders;
- independent experts who are appointed in order to issue certification.

Finally, the official text states that the VA will take effect with the creation of a regulatory framework introducing a mandatory certificate of disposal for owners of ELVs as well as legal requirements for return stations and dismantlers.

3.2.2 The *ELV-Ordinance*

This regulatory framework was created by the ELV-Ordinance of 4 July 1997 which regulates the process of ELV management and the relationship between ELV owners, operators of return stations, dismantlers, and shredders. It aims to guarantee the effective implementation of the VA and to ensure the competitive structure of the ELV-management market (Bundesregierung, 1996). It does so by:

- introducing a legal obligation for final owners to return ELVs to a certified return station or dismantler;
- requiring a proof of disposal issued by a certified dismantler in order for the last owner to deregister his or her car;
- establishing detailed organisational, technical and operative requirements for return stations, dismantlers and shredders or similar installations as preconditions for certification of these installations.

The certification of return stations, dismantlers and shredders is done by independent experts. The ELV-Ordinance sets up environmental standards for return stations, dismantlers and shredder companies. These standards should guarantee the environmentally sound treatment of ELVs and are set every year by independent experts. The environmental standards include detailed requirements concerning:

- adequate facilities which guarantee an environmentally sound storage, dismantling and recycling of ELVs;
- individual stages of dismantling (pre-treatment, recovery and recycling, disposal of remaining materials);
- the (contractual) agreement between the return station and the dismantler about adequate co-operation to prevent environmental damage caused by long-term storage of ELVs at the return station;
- the documentation of the entire dismantling process including the number of dismantled ELVs, the amount of recycled or recovered material, the process of recycling and the disposal of remaining materials.

The certification of the independent experts who control the environmental standards and certify the return stations, dismantlers and shredder companies shall be conducted by the Chambers of Industry and Commerce (Industrie- und Handelskamer - IHK) and other expert organisations (Bundesregierung 1996).

Finally, dismantlers are required to extract spare parts and materials amounting to at least 15 per cent by weight from the wreck by the year 2002 and ensure their reuse or recycling. Both shredders and dismantlers are required to reduce the average generation of waste for disposal to a maximum of 15 per cent by weight until the year 2002. By 2015 the generation of waste for disposal from all stages of ELV management shall be further reduced to a maximum of 5 per cent.

Summing up the negotiation process, it can be concluded that while the BMU succeeded in placing the issue on the political agenda and eventually in finding a political solution, it was less successful in pushing through its regulatory concept as it was presented in the ministry's first draft ordinances. This was mainly due to the unwillingness of the automotive industry to carry the costs of ELV-management and to accept detailed recycling quotas for different materials which would limit its choice of possible strategies for ELV-management. Within the cabinet, the strong opposition by the BMWi had blocked the enactment of an ELV-Ordinance against the interests of the automotive industry. Several draft ordinances were criticised and eventually vetoed by the BMWi, which favoured a voluntary solution and aimed at reducing the economic and competitive impacts resulting from regulations in the area of the ELV management.

4. ANALYSIS

4.1 Target Relevance

Less than three years after its enactment, it is still too early for a comprehensive and conclusive evaluation of the performance of the VA and a thorough assessment of its environmental impact. Critical appraisals, therefore, refer mostly to the relevance of the goals and measures formulated in the VA and the parallel ELV-Ordinance as well as to their impact on the behaviour of the relevant actors. In general terms it has been criticised that:

- the formulated goals and measures are not adequate to effectively solve the environmental problems caused by ELV-disposal;
- priority is placed on waste management instead of waste prevention (end-of-pipe policy);
- strong incentives for automobile manufacturers to increase the recyclability of their products are lacking.

More concrete and with regard to the goal of setting up a nationwide system for return and recycling of ELVs, critics have argued that such an infrastructure had already existed prior to the development of the VA (Rennings et al., 1996). However, if one takes into account the detailed and rather strict environmental standards for dismantlers, shredders and return-stations which are laid down in the ELV-Ordinance and which shall be enforced by means of independent certification and the exclusion of non-certified businesses from ELV-management, this goal seems to be a promising attempt to overcome the previously prevailing implementation deficit in this field.

With regard to the general recycling quotas laid down in the VA and the subsequent reduction of ASR for disposal, a twofold picture emerges. The short-term goal of reducing ASR for disposal to a maximum of 15 per cent in weight by the year 2002 can probably be reached relatively easily by merely extracting the operating fluids, tyres and spare parts prior to the shredding phase (SRU, 1998, 2000). However, the medium-term goal of reducing waste for disposal from ELV-management to 5 per cent by the year 2015 cannot be reached by improving the operations of dismantlers and shredders alone. Especially if one takes into account the increasing use of synthetic materials in the construction of new cars, this goal appears to be very ambitious.

While the third main goal in the VA, the recycling oriented design of new automobiles could, in principle, provide an effective and sustainable way of reducing environmental impacts of ELV-management, this goal remains rather vague and unspecified ('continuously optimise the recycling oriented construction of vehicles', 'continuously improve the recyclability'). Quantified targets and concrete time frames for reaching this goal are completely missing. Thus, a general lack of direct pressure on the automotive industry to increase the recyclability of their products can be stated. Furthermore, it remains unclear whether and how the related measures can indirectly induce a significant shift towards greater recyclability of automobiles. On the one hand, the recycling target for the year 2015 may provide an incentive. However, there is no direct causal link between the attainment of the recycling target and the goal of recycling oriented design. On the other hand, the measure of cost-free take-back of cars not older than 12 years may set an incentive for automobile producers to develop more recycling oriented cars, but the effectiveness of this measure – compared to the option of a cost-free take-back of all cars irrespective of their age – has been questioned (Rennings et al., 1997). In the light of an average automobile life-span of more than 12 years, it has been argued that vehicles fulfilling the conditions set out in the VA will almost certainly obtain a positive price on the market and therefore not be returned to the producer (SRU, 1998; Mikulla-Liegert, 1998).

The goal of reducing uncontrolled disposal of ELVs should be reached mainly by means of introducing a mandatory proof of disposal to be issued by certified dismantlers and which will be needed by the final owner for de-registration of his car. However, other possibilities for de-registration remain available such as presenting a sales contract or a declaration of whereabouts, which are hard to control effectively by the administration. It has been argued, that a general cost-free take-back obligation would provide a more effective measure to reduce uncontrolled disposal (Schrader, 1998). In addition, neither the ELV-Ordinance nor the VA have taken into account the geographical shift of the environmental impacts of ELVs caused by the increasing export of cars to other, mainly Central and Eastern European countries.

Generally, it has been criticised that additional (or alternative) regulatory options have not been taken into account. On the one hand, there are no targets related to the control of hazardous substances such as lead, cadmium or mercury. A ban on heavy metals in the construction of automobiles could be an important contribution to the decontamination of ASR. Furthermore, as has been argued above, the introduction of a general cost-free take-back of ELV irrespective of their age and condition could strengthen producer responsibility in this area and thus set a stronger incentive for automobile producers to improve the recyclability of their products. Finally, the option of reducing the environmental impact of ASR by systematically treating it as hazardous waste and thus applying stricter environmental standards for its disposal has not been followed through (SRU, 2000).

4.2 Target Realisation

4.2.1 ELV management processes

According to first evaluations and data provided by the ARGE-Altauto, the goal of setting up a nationwide infrastructure for take-back, recycling and disposal of ELVs consisting of independently certified companies has clearly been reached (ARGE-Altauto, 2000; SRU, 2000). Already in April of 1998, when the VA and the parallel ELV-Ordinance came into force, 2 800 return stations, 250 dismantlers, and 40 shredder-plants had been certified. Additionally, 50 independent experts had been appointed to pass certification (BMU press release of 31 March 1998).[4]

Although the successful creation of a nationwide infrastructure for the take-back of ELVs comes as no real surprise because a sufficient number of return stations, dismantlers and shredders already existed prior to the enactment of the VA, a significant qualitative improvement can be observed. A great number of the facilities which were functioning prior to the enactment of the ELV-Ordinance have not applied for or have not received certification under the new regulations. Consequently, the number of businesses operating in the sector has decreased considerably compared to the time before 1998. Especially the number of dismantlers underwent a marked decline by at least 50 per cent from an estimated 3 000 to 5 000 facilities to approximately 1 132 certified businesses in the year 2000 (ARGE-Altauto, 2000). This fact is commonly interpreted as an indication for an increasing professionalisation of dismantlers and other actors in the area of ELV-management and for a significant overall rise of environmental standards in the sector (Schenk, 1999; ARGE-Altauto, 2000). Furthermore, in September 1998, an inquiry by the German Federation for Motor Trades and Repairs (ZDK) in 130 certified return stations found that almost 74 percent had already concluded a contract of co-operation with dismantlers, which is required by the ELV-Ordinance (ZDK, 1998).

However, in spite of these apparent improvements some loopholes and implementation deficits remain. First evaluations show that a significant number of certified operators still do not fully meet the environmental standards laid down in the ELV-Ordinance. On the one hand, the independent experts have not been supervised sufficiently. Sometimes their qualification was poor. Additionally, public authorities have practically no means for penalising incorrect certification (ARGE-Altauto, 2000). On the other hand, this is due to the fact that certification practices vary considerably among the different federal states (Bundesregierung, 1999). According to an inquiry carried out at 600 certified dismantlers in September 1998, public authorities at the local or state level often continue to tolerate dismantlers which do not fulfil the required environmental standards (Abfallwirtschaftliche*r* Informationsdienst, 1998).[5]

Besides these apparent shortcomings found in the certification of ELV-management facilities, a major implementation deficit can be observed with regard to the newly introduced proof of disposal for the car owner in order to deregister his car. In practice, effective control by local and state authorities is lacking and alternative ways of deregistering a car continue to exist. Apart from submitting a proof of disposal, a final owner can deregister his car by presenting a sales contract or by declaring that for a limited time the car is stored on private grounds (declaration of whereabouts). In both cases the public authorities are not capable of verifying the correctness of these declarations. In cases where the final owner declares to have sold his car to a buyer in a non-EU country, it is virtually impossible for public authorities to confirm the authenticity of the sales contract (Schrader, 1998). Declarations of whereabouts given to the local registration offices often cannot be passed on to the authorities responsible for implementing the *ELV-Ordinance* because in many cases these authorities have not yet been designated (ARGE-Altauto, 2000). Even if the declaration of whereabouts is passed on to the responsible agency, control is limited to spot checks (Bundesregierung, 1999).

4.2.2 Recycling-oriented car development and recovery of ASR

In general, the automotive industry claims in its first monitoring report that criteria for recycling have been integrated into the process of developing new automobiles, that the number of materials used in the automobile construction has been reduced and the amount of recyclable materials in cars has been increased, and that disassembly of old automobiles has been facilitated (ARGE-Altauto, 2000). Additionally, ARGE-Altauto declares that draining of operating fluids has been eased, plastic components are marked with regard to their material composition, automobile producers are supplying disassembly information to the recycling industry, and recycled plastic materials are used in the production of new automobiles. However, apart from singular examples given in the monitoring report, no general figures are available to confirm these improvements. So far, singular pilot projects are mentioned by individual companies or by the ARGE-Altauto (ARGE-Altauto, 2000; see Table 4.2), some of which had already been initiated as early as 1988, mainly as a reaction to early signals at the German and European level indicating an increasing regulatory activity in the area of ELV-management (for a detailed account of recycling initiatives by German producers see Zoboli et al., 2000).

While dismantling technologies are already available and an increase in their use can be observed, the BMU expects innovations in the area of sorting, decontamination and recycling technologies for ASR as a result of the implementation of the VA and the ELV-Ordinance.

Table 4.2   Projects for recycling-oriented car design and recovery of ASR

Name of project (responsible organisation)	Content/ Aim
DaimlerChrysler	Increasing the share of recyclable and recoverable materials Development of recycling systems
Several automobile producers	Special recycling departments, examining the recyclability of the whole car as well as single components and developing quality standards and guidelines for recycling which are to be considered by their construction and purchasing departments as well as by suppliers
Several automobile producers	Co-operation structures between automobile producers, suppliers, dismantlers and shredders
Several automobile producers	Developing concrete measures for recycling oriented design of cars in order to improve the possibilities of recovering and recycling materials, the use of recyclable materials and spare parts
PRAVDA (VDA in co-operation with raw material suppliers, dismantlers, plastic-reprocessing companies and moulders)	Examining technically feasible recycling options, especially for plastics, and elaborating guidelines for recycling and dismantling
International Dismantling Information System (several automobile producers)	Software program providing information about different materials and their location in cars of ten different automobile producers in order to improve the recycling of cars
ARGE-Altauto, BMU, Federal Environmental Agency, State Consortium Waste	Pilot plant for sorting and decontaminating ASR Thermal recovery of ASR in the power generation plant Schwarze Pumpe Incineration of ASR together with household waste while the heat from incineration is transformed into energy

4.3 Transparency and Third Party Participation

As with most VAs, third-party participation has been rather low in the course of the negotiation process. Environmental or consumer organisations did not directly participate in the formulation of the VA. They had no formal possibilities to influence the policy development with respect to ELV management. At present it is not clear whether the advisory board foreseen in the VA (ARGE-Altauto, 2000) in which consumer and environmental organisations should be represented, is functioning adequately.

However, the ARGE-Altauto has been very active in fostering the information exchange between the different actors in the ELV chain by initiating workshops, conferences, meetings and other internal events. Furthermore, the ARGE-Altauto provides comprehensive information about the progress in the implementation of the VA (for example the first monitoring report), such as regularly updated numbers of certified dismantling and shredder companies, third-party evaluations of the VA, official documents, and information on the further policy development in this field on its Internet web site.

4.4 Costs

It is difficult to assess the VA's costs as official numbers are not available. However, some rough estimates on the costs have been given.

An inquiry conducted by the Association of German Car Dismantlers (IGA) in 249 dismantling facilities estimates an average investment of DM 360 000 for these facilities in order to comply with the environmental standards of the ELV-Ordinance (IGA, 1999). While these investments were made by individual dismantlers under the assumption that material flows would considerably increase as a consequence of the ELV-Ordinance and the VA, today most dismantlers face a decrease of the ELVs delivered to them due to the high export rates to France, Belgium and especially to Central and Eastern European countries. At present, it can be assumed that the income of dismantlers has decreased rather than increased after the coming into force of the ELV-Ordinance and the VA. For return stations investment costs in order to obtain a certification were much lower. An inquiry by the ZDK estimates the average costs for return stations at about DM 1 900 (ZDK, 1999). The general costs for setting up an adequate disposal infrastructure for old cars are estimated to be high, especially in the light of increasing recycling quotas, but concrete numbers are not available.

As a consequence of the new legal framework, higher administrative expenses and increased investment costs, the *General German Automobile Club* (ADAC) had expected an increase in prices for ELV-disposal to around DM 800 per car (Mikulla-Liegert, 1998). However, one year after the coming into force of the VA and the ELV-Ordinance, disposal prices to be paid by the last owner of an ELV are unexpectedly low. Due to rapidly rising export rates for old cars and the subsequent shortage of ELVs to be recycled in Germany, prices have decreased rather than increased. In 1999 the government estimated the average costs for recycling and disposal of an ELV at around DM 100 to 150, ranging between cost-free and DM 200 for an ELV (Bundesregierung, 1999; ZDK, 1998).

4.5 Competition

While it has been argued that a general take-back obligation could lead to a process of market concentration and domination by the automotive industry in the recycling sector (Rennings et al., 1997; Schrader, 1998), this has not occurred so far. Under the present regulations, automobile producers see little reason for getting involved in this market and have limited their engagement to smaller pilot projects.

As early as 1994, *Volkswagen* in co-operation with PREUSSAG Recycling GmbH established a cost-free take-back and recycling network for selected cars of its production (Benzler and Löbbe, 1995). (Zoboli, 1999). BMW, Ford and Opel have established an independent car dismantler network associated to their companies. The dismantling companies are bound by individual contracts, which lay down the technical requirements and the control system (Zoboli, 1999).

Considering the competitive situation of dismantlers, one must differentiate between independent and producer-owned or producer-related dismantlers as well as between two distinct markets created by the ordinance and the VA:

- cars which are registered before 1 April 1998 or are older than 12 years and which are taken back to fair market value;
- cars which are registered after 1 April 1998 and are no older than 12 years and have to be taken back free of charge by their producers.

Concerning cars which are registered before 1 April 1998 the market is open to independent and producer-related dismantlers, whereas for cars which are registered after 1 April 1998 the producer-related dismantlers have a competitive advantage, because cars will be exclusively given back to them, unless the independent dismantlers can afford to take them back free of charge, too (Giesberts and Hilf, 1998).

Finally, critics argue that the above mentioned diverging practices of the independent experts and the continued tolerance of dismantlers not fulfilling the environmental standards has led to unjustified competitive advantages for dismantlers in regions where the certification standards are not implemented as rigorously as in other regions (*Abfallwirtschaftlicher Informationsdienst*, 1998).

4.6 Monitoring

Monitoring reports have to be prepared every two years. This task is performed by the ARGE-Altauto in co-operation with the IGA and the Federal Association of the German Steel Recyclers. The first monitoring report was submitted in April 2000 to the BMU and BMWi and was published in October 2000 on the web site of ARGE-Altauto (ARGE-Altauto, 2000).

Although the monitoring report is very detailed and comprehensive, it necessarily remains rather vague as to the attainment of the goal of reducing ASR for disposal to 15 per cent by 2002 and to 5 per cent by 2015. On the one hand, a first assessment cannot realistically be done before the deadline of the intermediate goal in 2002. On the other hand, most initiatives for reducing the amount of ASR for disposal (see above) have not yet gone beyond their pilot stage. Clear assessments of their potential for reducing ASR for disposal cannot be made at this early point in time.

However, based on the goals and measures formulated in the VA, a number of general assumptions on the possibility of monitoring can be made. In a study commissioned by the Federal Environmental Agency (UBA), the Institute for Ecology and Policy has pointed out that necessary preconditions for an effective monitoring of the VA and the ELV-Ordinance are lacking (Institut für Ökologie und Politik, 1999). Based on the monitoring system outlined in the ELV-Ordinance and the officially available data it will not be possible to check:

- whether a car after deregistration is actually recycled by a certified business or is disposed of in another way because a central institution responsible for collecting and processing all deregistration forms has not been designated or created;
- the number of ELVs taken back by return stations and recycled by dismantlers;
- the number of exported ELVs,
- the actual level of the achieved recycling quotas, because neither the dismantlers nor the shredder companies are obliged to provide any information about the mass flows in their companies;
- the extent of improvements in the recycling oriented design of new automobiles, because quantified targets are lacking and cause-to-effect relationships are difficult to establish.

The first monitoring report in principle seems to confirm these concerns. On the one hand, ARGE-Altauto itself acknowledges the lack of reliable data and the insufficient control of deregistration forms (ARGE-Altauto, 2000).

On the other hand, with regard the integration of criteria for recycling into the production process, the monitoring report largely limits itself to singular examples while general assessments of the scale of changes in the development and production of automobiles are missing.

5. CONCLUSION

During the 1980s the environmental problems related to the disposal and recovery of ELVs increasingly received public and political attention. However, only in 1998 and after lengthy negotiations, have specific environmental regulations in this area come into force, whose goals, however, clearly go beyond any business-as-usual-scenario. Implementation of the VA of 1998 and the supplementing *ELV-Ordinance* were influenced by a number of factors:

- a relatively homogeneous producing sector with common interests and a powerful industry association who was able to fight off a stronger responsibility for car producers;
- a heterogeneous and weakly organised dismantling sector which has not been able to obstruct or influence the formulation of the actual measures;
- diverging views within and between the BMU and the BMWi which impeded the consensual passing of an ELV-Ordinance which would bring about a different distribution of costs for ELV-management,
- the resulting lack of a credible threat of an alternative regulation (stick behind the door) in the case that negotiations on the VA fail;
- the long distance between car producers (especially regarding the design of new automobiles) and the final owners of ELVs, which practically excludes recycling characteristics from being an important element in the consumers' decisions to buy a certain automobile.

Generally, it can be argued that the major responsibility for reaching the more immediate goals and costs are carried by dismantlers and shredders. The combination of the VA and the ELV-Ordinance leaves a great leeway for automobile producers and importers as to the concrete measures for reaching their goals, but introduces rather strict, detailed and cost-intensive regulations for dismantlers and return stations. A clear responsibility of automobile producers is either postponed and even partly excluded (for example the temporal and qualitative limitations on cost-free take-back) or formulated in very vague terms (for example the goal of recycling oriented car design). It is questionable whether this will be sufficient for leading automobile producers to effectively assume an extended responsibility for their products. Additionally, due to its vagueness, attainment of the goal of recycling oriented design will be rather difficult to monitor and control. Finally, the BMU foresees no clear and credible sanctions for the automotive industry in the case that the goals of the VA are not reached ('stick behind the door'). The introduction of a general cost-free take-back for ELVs could have strengthened the need for the automotive industry to more strongly assume their producer responsibility. Although, with regard to the environmental problem, it seems reasonable to impose strict environmental standards on the operations of recycling facilities, it has to be pointed out that this approach to some extent stands in contrast to the basic concept of extended producer responsibility. At least in the short run, the voluntary and regulatory measures, therefore, can be characterised as being mainly end-of-pipe oriented rather than preventive.

In sum, the automotive industry as a very homogenous, well organised and powerful actor, succeeded during the lengthy negotiations in anticipating and avoiding far-reaching regulatory measures and the implementation of quantified goals as well as in shifting much of the responsibility towards other, less powerful, weakly organised and more heterogeneous actors. Especially the support of the BMWi helped the automotive industry to fight off the adoption of an early ELV-Ordinance and the formulation of more far-reaching measures and has weakened the threatening potential of an alternative ELV-Ordinance in the case the goals of the VA not being reached.

In contrast, the shredder and the dismantling businesses did not succeed in avoiding regulatory measures in their area. This 'failure' might be explained by their weak organisation and political influence, compared to the automotive industry, but also by the general acceptance of the immediate necessity of improving environmental performance at this stage of ELV management and their more or less direct responsibility for the environmental pollution occurring during the dismantling and shredder processes. In contrast, to this immediate and directly visible pollution at the dismantling stage, the responsibility of the automotive industry for environmental problems related to the disposal of ELV is less visible and has been perceived as being rather indirect due to the time lag between the production of a car and its disposal, as well as the distance of the automotive industry from the ELV management.

In conclusion, from an environmental point of view the combination of the VA and the ELV-Ordinance differentiates in an appropriate manner between the immediate and the long-term solutions of the environmental problems related to ELV management. The policy approach first concentrates on the most relevant or urgent problems by pursuing a regulatory end-of-pipe policy and then pursues in a long-term perspective a preventive policy corresponding with the principle of producer responsibility aimed at improving the recycling oriented design of cars. In practice, the general concept of the new measures is aimed at the environmentally sound recovery and disposal of ELVs rather than at the avoidance or minimisation of potentially hazardous waste. However, taking into account the above mentioned lack of a sufficiently large market for recycled materials and the weakness of price incentives for the automobile producers to design recycling oriented cars, it has to be questioned whether voluntary measures in this area can be sufficient. Nevertheless the co-operative ties between the different actors in the ELV chain, especially between the automotive industry and the dismantling companies, that resulted from the VA might contribute to an intensive information exchange, which could contribute to innovations and improvements in the recycling oriented design of cars. The introduction of a cost-free take-back of all ELVs through the recently adopted European ELV-Directive could certainly help to strengthen producer responsibility and thereby lead to a greater involvement of the automotive industry in the process of ELV management.

NOTES

1. While the BMU speaks of approximately 500 000 tons (BMU press release of 12 June 1997), Kremer (1998) estimates an amount of 540 000 tons per year and the *Federal Environmental Agency* (UBA) speaks of approximately 600 000 tons (UBA, 1997). Some sources argue that shredder waste from refrigerators and other household products has to be deduced from these numbers and thus expect the total amount of ASR originating from ELVs to be less than 400 000 tons (Wöhrl, 1998). If one takes into account the ELVs exported from Germany, the BMU has estimated the amount of ASR generated at German shredders to be as low as 300 000 tons.
2. Despite this regulation, however, in practice shredder waste has mainly been landfilled together with normal household waste. This was possible because state agencies have granted vast exceptions to the shredder companies responsible for disposal, due to the comparatively high costs of hazardous waste disposal which would economically threaten the operations of shredder companies.
3. Nationwide means at least one return station in every district (Sacksofsky, 1996).
4. By mid-2000 the ARGE-Altauto estimated a total of 14 000 return stations. 91 independent experts were appointed, 1 132 certified dismantlers were registered with ARGE-Altauto, 49 shredders were certified in Germany and another 16 certified shredders were operating in other European countries (ARGE-Altauto, n.d.).
5. The Association of Automobile Recyclers estimates that almost 3 300 dismantlers, of which less than half are certified, continue to operate (Schmitz, 1999).

REFERENCES

Abfallwirtschaftlicher Informationsdienst (1998), No. 5, 16 September.

ARGE-Altauto (n. d.), Internet site of the ELV-Working Group ARGE-Altauto at the Association of the German Automotive Industry – VDA (http://209.182.11.149/shredder.htm).

ARGE-Altauto (2000), *1. Monitoringbericht gemäß Punkt 3.6 der Freiwilligen Selbstverpflichtung zur umweltgerechten Entsorgung von Altfahrzeugen (PKW) im Rahmen des Kreislaufwirtschafts-/Abfallgesetzes.* Der Bundesregierung vorgelegt am 31. März 2000. Berichtszeitraum: 1. April 1998 bis 31. März 2000, Frankfurt: ARGE-Altauto.

Benzler, Guido and Klaus Löbbe (1995), 'Rücknahme von Altautos – Eine kritische Würdigung der Konzepte', *RWI-Papiere Nr. 40.* Essen: RWI (Rhine-Westphalia Institute for Economic Research).

Bundesregierung (1996), *Verordnung der Bundesregierung über die Entsorgung von Altautos und die Anpassung straßenverkehrsrechtlicher Vorschriften*, 07.11.96, 13/5998.

Bundesregierung (1999), *Unterrichtung durch die Bundesregierung. Entsorgung von Altautos*, 14.06.1999: Bonn.

Enquete-Kommission (1994), 'Schutz des Menschen und der Umwelt' des Deutschen Bundestages (ed.), *Die Industriegesellschaft gestalten. Perspektiven für einen nachhaltigen Umgang mit Stoff- und Materialströmen*, Bonn: Economica Verlag.

Giesberts, Ludger and Juliane Hilf (1998), *Kreislaufwirtschaft Altaut: Altautoverordnung und freiwllige Selbstverpflichtung. Rechtsfragen und praktische Umsetzung*, Berlin: Erich Schmidt Verlag.

Holzhauer, Ralf (1998), 'Die Altauto-Verordnung – Entwicklung und Umsetzung', in Jürgen Beudt and Stefan Gessenich (eds), *Die Altautoverordnung. Branchenwandel durch neue Marktstrukturen. Chancen und Grenzen für die Abfallwirtschaft*, Berlin, Heidelberg and New York: Springer, pp. 1–7.

IGA (Interessengemeinschaft der deutschen Autoverwerter) (1999), 'Infrastruktur zur Annahme und Verwertung von Pkw in Deutschland. Zu Verwertungsbetrieben', Paper presented at the Symposium 'Ein Jahr Altauto-Verordnung und Freiwillige Selbstverpflichtung in Deutschland' on 15 April 1999, Schloß Waldthausen, Mainz.

Institut der Wirtschaft (1998), 'Automobiler Stoffkreislauf', IW-Umwelt-Service No.1 (http://www.iwkoeln.de/Umwelt/U1-98-4.htm)

Institut für Ökologie und Politik (1999), *General requirements for monitoring the recycling of long-lived, technally complex products with an in-depth-analysis of end-of-life vehicles.* Summary.
(http://www. Oekopol.de/Archiv/Stoffstrom/Autoeng.htm).

Jörgens, Helge and Kirsten Jörgensen (1998), 'Abfallpolitik in der Bundesrepublik Deutschland', in Gotthard Breit (ed.), *Neue Wege in der Umweltpolitik*, Schwalbach: Wochenschau Verlag, pp. 40–52.

KBA (Federal Motor Transport Authority) (2000), *Statistische Mitteilungen. Löschung von Kraftfahrzeugen und Kraftfahrzeuganhängern nach Fahrzeugarten in den alten Bundesländern einschl. Berlin (West) und in Deutschland 1965-1999.*
(http://www.kba.de/Abt3/KraftfahrzeugStatistiken/Loeschungen/Loe_Kfz_Deutsch land.pdf)

KBA (Federal Motor Transport Authority) (2001), *Statistische Mitteilungen. Bestand Kraftfahrzeugen und Kraftfahrzeuganhängern in Deutschland 1965-2000.* (http://www.kba.de/Abt3/KraftfahrzeugStatistiken/Bestand/Bestand_an_Kfz_in_De utschland.pdf)

Kremer, Hans-Peter (1998), 'Das bisherige Verfahren der Lizenzierung und das zukünftige der Zertifizierung gemäß Altauto-Verordnung', in Jürgen Beudt and Stefan Gessenich (eds), *Die Altautoverordnung. Branchenwandel durch neue Marktstrukturen. Chancen und Grenzen für die Abfallwirtschaft*, Berlin, Heidelberg and New York: Springer, pp. 77–86.

Lucas, Rainer (2000), 'Altautoverwertung zwischen Staat und Markt. Bedingungen und Potentiale zur Modernisierung von Lagerhaltung und Marketing gebrauchter Autoteile', *Wuppertal Papers* No. 104. Wuppertal: Wuppertal Institut für Klima, Umwelt, Energie.

Meffert, H., Kirchgeorg, M., (1998), *Gutachterliche Stellungnahme zur Gestaltung von Rücknahmemodalitäten für Altautomobile*, Münster: Handelshochschule Leipzig (http://209.182.11.149/mef.htm).

Mikulla-Liegert (1998), 'Probleme und Möglichkeiten des Letztbesitzers durch die Altauto-Verordnung', in Jürgen Beudt and Stefan Gessenich (eds), *Die Altautoverordnung. Branchenwandel durch neue Marktstrukturen. Chancen und Grenzen für die Abfallwirtschaft*, Berlin, Heidelberg and New York: Springer, pp. 37–52.

OECD (1998), *Extended and Shared Producer Responsibility. Phase 2. Executive Summary*, Paris: OECD.

Rennings, Klaus, Karl Ludwig Brockmann, Henrike Koschel, Heidi Bergmann and Isabel Kühn (1996), *Nachhaltigkeit, Ordnungspolitik und freiwillige Selbstverpflichtung. Ordnungspolitische Grundregeln für eine Politik der Nachhaltigkeit und das Instrument der freiwilligen Selbstverpflichtung im Umweltschutz*, Heidelberg: Physica-Verlag.

Rennings, Klaus, Karl Ludwig Brockmann and Heidi Bergmann (1997), *Voluntary Agreements in Environmental Protection – Experiences in Germany and Future Perspectives*, Mannheim: Zentrum für Europäische Wirtschaftsforschung.

Sacksofsky, Eike (1996), 'Anmerkungen zu verschiedenen Konzepten einer Neuregelung der Altautoentsorgung', in *Zeitschrift für Umweltpolitik und Umweltrecht*, **19** (1), 99-108.

Schenk, Martin (1998), *Altautomobilrecycling. Technisch-ökonomische Zusammenhänge und wirtschaftspolitische Implikationen*, Wiesbaden: Deutscher Universitäts Verlag.

Schenk, Martin (1999), 'AltautoV und FSV: Eine Zwischenbilanz', paper presented at the symposium 'Ein Jahr Altauto-Verordnung und Freiwillige Selbstverpflichtung in Deutschland' on 15 April 1999, Schloß Waldthausen, Mainz.

Schmitz, Hans Joachim (1999), 'Verwertung von Altautos – Schlupflöcher höhlen Umweltschutz aus', *WLB Wasser Luft und Boden*, **5**, 72–74.

Schrader, Christian (1998), 'Die deutsche und die europäische Altauto-Regelung aus ökologischer Sicht', in Jürgen Beudt and Stefan Gessenich (eds), *Die Altautoverordnung. Branchenwandel durch neue Marktstrukturen. Chancen und Grenzen für die Abfallwirtschaft*, Berlin, Heidelberg and New York: Springer, pp. 53–66.

SRU (Rat von Sachverständigen für Umweltfragen) (1991), *Abfallwirtschaft. Sondergutachten September 1990*, Stuttgart: Metzler-Poeschel.

SRU (Rat von Sachverständigen für Umweltfragen) (1998), *Umweltgutachten 1998. Umweltschutz: Erreichtes sichern – neue Wege gehen*, Stuttgart: Metzler-Poeschel.

SRU (Rat von Sachverständigen für Umweltfragen) (2000), *Umweltgutachten 2000. Schritte ins nächste Jahrtausend*, Stuttgart: Metzler-Poeschel.

UBA (Umweltbundesamt) (1989), *Jahresbericht 1989*, Berlin: UBA.

UBA (Umweltbundesamt) (1993), *Jahresbericht 1993*, Berlin: UBA.

UBA (Umweltbundesamt) (1997), *Daten zur Umwelt. Der Zustand der Umwelt in Deutschland. Ausgabe 1997*, Berlin: Erich Schmidt Verlag.

VDA (Verband der Automobilindustrie e.V.) (2000), *Zahlen aus der Automobilwirtschaft* (http://www.vda.de/zahlen/).

Wöhrl, Stefan (1998), 'Die Freiwillige Selbstverpflichtung zur umweltgerechten Altautoverwertung (PKW) – Ausblick auf die EU-Altautorichtlinie', in Jürgen Beudt and Stefan Gessenich (eds), *Die Altautoverordnung. Branchenwandel durch neue Marktstrukturen. Chancen und Grenzen für die Abfallwirtschaft*, Berlin, Heidelberg and New York: Springer, pp. 15–23.

ZDK (Zentralverband Deutsches Kraftfahrzeuggewerbe e.V) (1998), *Blitzumfrage bei anerkannten Annahmestellen im Kfz-Gewerbe.*
(http://209.182.33.320.umfr.htm).

ZDK (Zentralverband Deutsches Kraftfahrzeuggewerbe e.V) (1999), 'Infrastruktur zur Annahme von Pkw in Deutschland: Annahmestellen', paper presented at the symposium 'Ein Jahr Altauto-Verordnung und Freiwillige Selbstverpflichtung in Deutschland' on 15 April 1999, Schloß Waldthausen, Mainz.

Zoboli, Roberto (1999), 'Environmental Regulation and Innovation in the End-of-Life-Vehicle Sector', paper presented at the International Conference 'Innovation-Oriented Environmental Regulation – Theoretical Approaches and Empirical Analysis', Potsdam, 27–29 May 1999.

Zoboli, Roberto, Giancarlo Barbiroli, Riccardo Leoncini, Massimiliano Mazzanti and Sandro Montresor (2000), *Regulation and Innovation in the Area of End-of-life Vehicles*. Seville: Institute for Prospective Technological Studies (IPTS).

INTERVIEWS

Dr Kopp, *Federal Ministry for the Environment, Nature Protection and Nuclear Safety*

Mrs Schnepel, *Federal Environmental Agency*

Dr Schenk, *End-of-Life Vehicles Consortium*

Mr Cohrs, Mr.Leuning, *Federal Association of the German Steel Recyclers*

Mr Fried, *BMW*

Dr Schäper, *Audi*

Mr Zumbroich, *Opel*

Mr Menzel, *Volkswagen*

5. The Belgian Agreement upon the Collection and Recycling of Batteries

Marc De Clercq and Bart Ameels

1. INTRODUCTION

In Belgium, as in other countries, there has been a legal debate on how to regulate the use, collection and recycling of batteries in a way that minimises the polluting effects of their use. Already in 1988 and 1990, the Belgian battery industry made a voluntary agreement with the Belgian state to set up a mercury reduction or elimination programme. As a result, the percentage of batteries free from mercury and cadmium, the main polluting materials, rose to 95 per cent.

One year later, a directive of the European Union of 18 March 1991 stated that member countries had to take measures to mark and collect some batteries separately, in order to eliminate the harmful effects of batteries containing dangerous materials.

In Belgium, the government imposed a tax on all sold batteries (16 July 1993), which would come into effect on 1 January 1994. This tax was an implementation of the general ecotax law, which determined a whole range of products that had to be taxed, with the primary goal of discouraging the use of these products in favour of less polluting substitutes. An ecotax commission was set up to determine which products would fall under this ecotax and to elaborate an appropriate regulation for each of them.

According to the battery industry, this law was neither necessary nor efficient in the case of batteries, for several reasons: economical, environmental and technical, which will be discussed later. The battery industry therefore started negotiations with the ecotax commission in 1993, trying to find a more appropriate solution for the separate collection of batteries. In short, the industry tried to avoid the ecotax, first by minimising the application field of the ecotax, later on by proposing a voluntary collection scheme organised by the industry.

Eventually, the ecotax commission agreed with a voluntary collection scheme. In order to make this 'voluntary agreement' executable, the ecotax law for batteries was changed on 7 March 1996, stating that batteries were exempted from the ecotax when a voluntary collection and recycling scheme was set up. Certain conditions had to be met:

- the system had to be financed by the industry itself;
- until the year 2000, certain collection percentages had to be met (1996: 40 per cent of all batteries sold in Belgium, 1997: 50 per cent, 1998: 60 per cent, 1999: 67.5 per cent, 2000: 75 per cent). After 2000, further negotiations would be held to set new collection percentages.

If these conditions were not met, the ecotax on batteries would be levied on all household batteries sold in Belgium.

The battery industry set up a non-profit organisation called BEBAT, which coordinates the collection and recycling of batteries, and sees to it that the prescribed collection percentages are reached, amongst others by setting up media campaigns. The voluntary agreement itself was signed on 16 June 1997.

On 22 December 2000 the national government agreed to pass the arrangements on to 2001, but the collection percentage is lowered to 60%. With this decision, the battery sector was definitely exempted from the ecotaxes until 2000. The prescribed collection percentages were always reached or nearly reached and so the amount of collected batteries rose every year. The reached collection percentages are quite high, comparing them with the collection percentages before and with present collection percentages abroad.

2. CONTEXT

2.1 The Legal Framework Concerning Batteries

The legal framework concerning batteries, can be divided in three levels: a European level, a federal level and a regional level.

At the European level, two directives concern the use of batteries. The first directive of 18 March 1991 (91/157/CEE) concerns only the most harmful batteries, that is batteries containing more than 25 mg of mercury (except alkaline-manganese batteries) or more than 0.025 per cent of their weight in cadmium, or containing more than 0.4 per cent of their weight in lead and alkaline-manganese batteries containing more than 0.025 per cent of their weight in mercury. The directive states that the member states have to ban the commercialisation of alkaline-manganese batteries containing more than 0.025 per cent of their weight in mercury (except the alkaline-manganese batteries in button-form). The member states also have to take measures in order to ensure the separate collection of used batteries. Therefore all sold batteries have to be marked, containing information on the separate collection, the recycling and the content of heavy metals. The member states have to set up programmes in order to reach the reduction of heavy metals in batteries, the promotion of batteries containing less dangerous materials, the progressive reduction of the amount of batteries in common household waste, the promotion of research concerning the reduction of dangerous materials in batteries and the separate elimination of batteries.

The second directive of 4 October 1993 (93/86/EEG) states that all batteries that are subject to the directive of 18 March 1991, need to have a mark on them as of 1 January 1996. The mark in question is an image of a waste container that is crossed, indicating that these batteries need to be collected separately.

At the Belgian level, environmental policy is mainly dealt with by the three regional governments of Flanders, Brussels and the Walloon region. The national government is left with only limited powers in this field: mainly related to product standards, nuclear waste and to the negotiation and the implementation of the international engagements of the country (for example the introduction of EC directives in Belgian environmental law). Concerning batteries, the federal ecotax however plays a crucial role. This tax is federal because it is a consumption tax. Laws concerning the separate collection and the recycling of batteries are of a regional nature (see below). The implementation of the ecotax in the field of battery consumption, is expressed in the law of 18 July 1993. This law states that all sold batteries are subject to an ecotax of BEF 20 per battery, except batteries which are difficult or dangerous to be removed, for example in medical appliances. Batteries can also be exempted from the tax when they are subject to a deposit-refund system. The deposit has to be at least BEF 10 a battery, and the batteries subject to this system need to have a mark on them, indicating that they are subject to a deposit-refund system.

Apart from this regulation, the Belgian battery industry (represented by FEE and Fabrimetal) signed two codes of good conduct (in January 1988 and April 1990) with the Federal Ministry of Economic Affairs and the Federal Secretary of the Environment. These codes were in fact an engagement of the industry to replace the mercuric oxide batteries by zinc-air batteries before the end of 1990 and to reduce the content of mercury in alkaline batteries.

At the regional level, each region has its own environmental law and its own regulations concerning the treatment of waste, including batteries. Each of the three regions treats batteries as being 'small chemical waste'. This means they have to be collected separately. In order to do this, each region has municipal fixed collection sites at which the inhabitants can dump their waste in prescribed containers. Also, public or private collection and recycling companies periodically raise this waste. For each waste unit, these companies deliver a certificate of destruction or recycling, showing that the waste is being treated in accordance with the regional legislature.

Moreover, in the Flemish region, legislature obliges sellers to take back any used battery they sold.

2.2 Environmental Policy of the Battery Industry

Looking at the earlier voluntary actions by the battery producing companies, that is reducing the amount of mercury in batteries on a voluntary basis, one could say the environmental policy of the companies consists of making batteries as clean as possible. However, these voluntary actions are primarily the result of anticipating future law or/and technological and economic possibilities.

Since there are only a few big producers of batteries worldwide, Belgian producers and distributors are relatively dependent of them, so they cannot follow an independent environmental policy.

In their 'environmental commitment', Duracell, the world leader in this industry, claims they have carried out mercury elimination efforts after concerns had been raised about the presence of mercury in solid waste. They also advise consumers to collect batteries that still contain mercury or lead separately. Another leading company, Panasonic-Matshushita, informs only the American consumers through their website how to dispose of different types of batteries.

This, among other things, shows that the environmental policy of these multinational companies is global and not country-specific. The Belgian market only represents a small part of their global market, and these companies will probably not act locally as long as their competitors don't.

At the federal policy level, the Belgian battery industry signed two codes of good conduct, in which the Belgian battery industry voluntarily promised to reduce the content of mercury in batteries. This led to an actual decrease of mercury in batteries. The decrease of mercury use however was a global trend and was primarily the result of technological innovation.

2.3 Public Policy in Belgium

2.3.1 Environmental policy in Belgium: the ecotaxes

In Belgium environmental policy is mainly dealt with by the three regional governments, the national government is left with only limited powers. In this respect it is important to note that there is no hierarchy of legal systems in Belgium. Hence the national government cannot impose its will on regional governments in environmental matters. In cases where they are all stakeholders, the national government and the regional governments have to consult with each other. They then arrive at a common position by – sometimes lengthy – negotiations.

In contrast to environmental matters that are mostly within the realm of regional competence, with respect to consumption taxes competence rests with national authorities. Therefore, the integration of environmental considerations into the tax system, like the introduction of the ecotax, is the task of the federal government.

Belgian federal ecotaxes are product taxes. Their main aim is to change the structure of relative prices in the Belgian economy, thus confronting Belgian consumers with a clean incentive to change their consumption pattern in a more environmentally friendly way. Underlying this approach is the idea that as the change in consumer behaviour would feed back into the economic system, producer behaviour would also change since producers have a clear interest in offering more attractive goods to the consumers in order to protect and expand their market shares.

Belgian ecotaxes are not of the Pigouvian type. Their tax rate is not related in a precise way to the environmental damage that the products on which they are levied, are causing. They are more of the Baumol-type, the level of the tax rate is rather high and set explicitly to put pressure upon the producers and the consumers to adapt to the alternative behaviour that is stipulated in the exemptions. In some instances the maximum price-raising effect however is rather uncertain.

A crucial variable in this respect is the elasticity of demand. Product taxes being indirect taxes, a low elasticity of demand means trouble: a high price increase and a small decrease in the consumption of the targeted goods. Therefore the law departs from the principle that ecotaxes are only installed when the consumers or the users of the goods they are levied upon, have an alternative – economically acceptable and ecologically desirable – by which they can avoid the payment of the ecotax. This is however not the case for batteries. Subsitutes for batteries, like solar cells, mostly cannot be used in everyday life.

Belgium is a small open economy, completely integrated in the European Union, based on the free movement of goods and services. Accordingly it has a high propensity to import and to export. Factors of production as well as consumers are very mobile. Due to its geographical situation in the centre of the Union, the country is also the heart of many distribution networks within the European Union. In order to protect the vital economic interests of the country a second principle was followed: exports have to be exempted from the ecotaxes, while imports have to be taxed in the same way as home-produced goods.

A follow-up commission was installed within the services of the Prime Minister. This commission has to aim for optimal ecological efficiency for the ecotaxes within the context of sustainable development. For this purpose the tasks of the commission are to be described as follows: evaluation of the ecotaxes considering the ecological efficiency as well as the micro- and macroeconomical consequences; making propositions on adaptations of the tax levels, on modifications of the conditions, on the deletion or addition of new ecotaxes.

2.3.2 The use of NAs in Belgium
Although voluntary agreements are recognised as an instrument of environmental policy in Belgium, they were not used systematically as they were in the Netherlands until recently. Their use depended highly upon the goodwill of the ministers of environment. Since 1994, there has been a growing interest in negotiated agreements between the government and the private sector. Up till now however there is still no alternative for environmental legislation, but these agreements serve instead as a supplement to the existing legislation.

Until now, approximately 24 voluntary agreements were signed with different industry federations. Nine of them however are not in force any more, since they were outdated or replaced by legislation. Nine of them were closed on a federal basis, twelve of them were closed between industry and the Flemish region, and three of them were signed in cooperation with the three regions and industry.

Not all of these agreements are however subject to the legal framework that was enacted for voluntary agreements in the Flemish region on 15 June 1994. This legal framework was instated to create an atmosphere wherein the use of voluntary agreements would be more successful, because in many policy plans, the closing of an agreement was announced, but not realised.

The framework describes negotiated agreements as 'agreements between the Flemish government and one or more industry organisations in order to prevent environmental pollution, to limit its consequences or to promote an efficient environmental management'. The agreement cannot replace legislation, nor be less severe than it. On the other hand, the Flemish government cannot issue more severe legislation during the existence of the agreement. The government however can turn the contents of the agreement into legislation. The decree further states that the agreement is binding for all parties and provides a start and ending procedure. Up to December 2001, seven agreements have been closed under this Flemish act: the collection of old medicines, the public storage of oil, the take-back and recycling of old paper, end-of-life vehicles, tyres, electric and electronic appliances.

Next to these agreements with industry organisations, the Flemish government also made an agreement with one company (BASF), with the Flemish communities and with the Flemish provinces.

At the federal level, article six of the law of 12 December 1998 concerning product norms for stimulating sustainable production and consumption patterns, enables the closing of sectoral agreements concerning the marketing of products. Voluntary agreements closed at the federal level would be subject to this law when they regulate the marketing of products.

3. NEGOTIATION PROCESS

3.1 How the VA Came on the Agenda

Already in 1988 and 1990, the Belgian battery industry made a voluntary agreement with the Belgian federal government to set up a mercury reduction or elimination programme. By doing this, the battery industry anticipated the European directive of 18 March 1991, stating that member countries had to take measures to mark and collect some batteries separately, in order to eliminate the use of batteries containing dangerous materials. Member countries also had to take action to accomplish the following objectives:

- reduction of the amount of heavy metals in batteries;
- stimulation of the use of batteries containing less dangerous and polluting materials;
- reduction in the quantity of batteries in household waste;
- stimulation of research to invent batteries with less dangerous materials and to recycle them.

As we have already seen, the percentage of batteries free from mercury and cadmium, rose to 95 per cent.

Although there was already a European law concerning batteries, the Belgian government also imposed the ecotax mentioned earlier on batteries (16 July 1993), which would start on 1 January 1994. All household batteries sold would become subject to an environmental tax of BEF 20, unless a deposit-refund system was set up (with a minimum deposit of BEF 10). The rationale behind the ecotax law was to stimulate the use of alternative, more environmental friendly substitutes by imposing a tax on polluting goods. We can ask ourselves if this general ecotax principle also applies in this case, since there are no practical substitutes for batteries. As mentioned in the introduction, political pressure was the main cause of this situation.

The national battery industry was strongly opposed to this tax, for quite a few reasons. We can divide those reasons into two categories: the economically founded reasons and the environmentally founded reasons. One can expect that it were mainly the economically founded reasons that caused the battery industry to react. The environmentally founded reasons could however help the battery industry in achieving its goal: escaping from the ecotax.

Economically founded arguments

- Since there is no substitute for batteries, the consumers would be the main victims of an ecotax. According to the industry, an ecotax on batteries would lead to an increase of annual household expenditure in amount of 1.5 billion Belgian francs.
- A higher price and less sales would lead to a fall in employment in the industry, who currently employs 2 000 employees in Belgium. Also the distribution sector would be hit.
- It would be technically impossible to set up a deposit-refund system since every battery, also the various types of button cells, would have to be marked in order to avoid fraud.
- A deposit-refund system would require an expensive administration, at the sales point as well as at the co-ordinating level.
- The European Directive of 8 March 1991 asked the member countries to use the necessary 'economic' instruments without jeopardising competition. An ecotax in Belgium alone would on the contrary lead to a competitive disadvantage for the Belgian producers and distributors.

Ecologically founded arguments

- The industry had already, in 1988 made, a voluntary agreement concerning the reduction of mercury in batteries. Since then, 95 per cent of the batteries sold were mercury and cadmium free, and introducing the ecotax here would be environmentally inefficient.
- The ecotax not only taxes the batteries that are defined as 'dangerous' by the European Union, but all batteries sold, also, again according to the industry, the harmless ones.
- Setting up a deposit-refund system would not be environmentally efficient in the first years, since only the newly marked (and least polluting) batteries would fall under this system. The older (and more

harmful) batteries would not have this mark and as a consequence would not be returned.

- Neither a deposit-refund system nor an ecotax puts requirements on the recycling of the used batteries, so there is no guarantee that the collected batteries are recycled. The voluntary collection system proposed by the industry would also take care of recycling the collected batteries.

3.2 The Negotiation Process

Therefore, the industry started negotiations with the ecotax commission, in order to formulate their objections to this law, and to propose some other solutions for this problem. The ecotax commission is an advisory body of the federal government that was set up to advise the government on the implementation of the ecotax law for the different product categories.

In the ecotax commission itself there was no unanimity on how to deal with this problem, certainly at the beginning of the negotiations. Several of its members made propositions as did the battery industry experts.

Since the European Commission made a difference between 'harmful' and 'harmless' batteries (91/157/CEE), the proposition was made to take into account this difference and hence to tax only the batteries the European Commission considered harmful. Only 5.5 per cent of all batteries would then fall under the ecotax. The other batteries wouldn't be taxed and could be thrown away with the common household waste.

The battery industry agreed with this difference, but proposed to tax only the mercury-containing batteries, since these batteries were in fact the 'harmful' batteries. The industry also proposed to add a paragraph to the law stating that the dangerous batteries wouldn't be taxed when they were collected by a voluntary collection system financed by the industry.

Another proposal was made to tax all the harmful batteries and to set up a voluntary collection system for the harmless ones. The environmental organisations however thought that a voluntary collection system could never achieve collection percentages that were as high as those that could be achieved with a deposit-refund system. In the latter case, consumers have an incentive to bring the batteries back after use. To back their arguments, they referred to the German voluntary collection system of nickel-cadmium batteries: this system collected merely 10 per cent of the batteries. These organisations also stated that the fraud possibilities of a deposit-refund system were fairly small.

The industry noted that a distinction between harmful and harmless batteries was impossible to maintain, because there was too much objection from the commission and from the green movements. The last two stated that each battery was harmful for the environment, whether or not it contained mercury, cadmium, lead.

The industry consequently proposed to set up a voluntary collection system for all batteries, harmful or not. This system would, according to them, have the following advantages:

- an immediate effect on the environment;
- a general collection of all batteries;
- an active participation of the industry;
- a limitation of import and fraud.

The system could, again according to the industry, be administered by a non-profit organisation. The results of this organisation could then be evaluated on a yearly basis by the ecotax commission and the Ministry of Economic Affairs. Financing could happen through a 'collection and recycling contribution' paid by the members of the organisation (that is battery producers and distributors). This contribution would be passed on to the consumers through a price increase. This price increase would be far lower then the current ecotax of BEF 20 (BEF 4 or BEF 5 per battery).

A minority of the ecotax commission however opposed to this idea for several reasons:

- a deposit-refund system is the best solution in order to achieve a high collection percentage;
- the changing of the law would again lead to a delay of this law, jeopardising the credibility of the ecotax commission;
- this modification in favour of the industry would lead to taking steps in the future in order to get more favourable treatment;
- in case of a voluntary collection system, the consumers would be confronted with an arbitrary collection and recycling contribution imposed by the industry.

This minority was backed by green movements, which participated in the negotiations during hearings. The 'Bond Beter Leefmilieu' (League for a Better Environment), which combines and represents more than 150 environmental organisations, had the following remarks:

- the so-called 'green batteries', that is the batteries that are not subject to the European directive, and which constitute about 95 per cent of the market, are not harmless at all. They also contain polluting materials and should be collected separately;
- solar cells can be a substitute for batteries;

- experience shows that a deposit-refund system yields far better results than a voluntary collection scheme: In the Netherlands, the deposit-refund system for bottles results in a 95 per cent collection, while the Belgian system of bottle containers only collects 73 per cent. In Germany, the government switched from a voluntary collection scheme for Ni-Cd batteries to a deposit-refund system, because the first only collected 10 per cent of the used Ni-Cd batteries.

The ecotax commission argued that, if a voluntary collection system was allowed, the prescribed collection percentages would be of a crucial importance with regard to the feasibility of the system.

An independent study had been ordered by the battery industry to compare the performance of a voluntary collection system with a deposit-refund system and to determine an achievable collection percentage (De Caevel, 1995). This study came to the following conclusions:

- cruising speed of collection can, in both systems, be attained within two years;
- in the first two years however, more batteries will be collected with a voluntary collection system, since in that case also old batteries can be collected. After the first two years, the number of batteries collected yearly using the different systems will be more or less the same. The cumulative amount however will be greater in case of a voluntary collection system.

Following the results of this study, a majority of the ecotax commission finally agreed with the introduction in the law of a paragraph stating that batteries are not subject to the ecotax when a voluntary collection scheme for all batteries is set up. The law in fact was altered on 7 March 1996.

The battery industry set up a non-profit organisation (BEBAT), that would be responsible for the collection and recycling of batteries in Belgium. This organisation would be financed by a 'collection and recycling contribution' born by the consumers through a price increase, as proposed by the industry. To make sure that the price increase would not be set arbitrarily by each producer, the amount had to be determined by Royal Decree.

3.3 Final Content of the NA

The voluntary agreement itself is an agreement between the federal government, the regional governments of Flanders, Walloon and Brussels, and the Belgian battery industry, represented by BEBAT. BEBAT, standing for 'Belgian Batteries' is a non-profit organisation founded by the battery industry for the sole purpose of this voluntary agreement. In legal terms, the agreement states that BEBAT is responsible for collecting and recycling used batteries that were sold on Belgian territory. Since BEBAT only consists of battery producers and distributors, and since non-compliance of the voluntary agreement has the same effect on members of BEBAT and non-members, we can equate BEBAT with the battery industry.

In short, the voluntary agreement deals with the several aspects of collecting and recycling a fixed percentage of used batteries in Belgium. BEBAT has to reach certain collection percentages, which are identical to those mentioned in the ecotax law, when a deposit-refund system would be set up: 40 per cent in 1996, 50 per cent in 1997, 60 per cent in 1998, 67.5 per cent in 1999 and 75 per cent in 2000. These percentages are calculated as follows:

$$\frac{\text{Weight of the collected amount of batteries during year t}}{\text{Weight of the sold amount of batteries during year t}}$$

The collected amount of batteries, used in the above calculation, includes not only the batteries collected by BEBAT, but also the batteries collected by the interurban waste companies of the regions, through the public collection sites.

Next to the collection of batteries, BEBAT is also responsible for the recycling of the batteries: the collected batteries have to be recycled according to the prevailing regional waste management legislature. To avoid misunderstandings about this, BEBAT has signed an agreement with the three regions, where the recycling method of each battery type is determined.

To make monitoring possible, BEBAT has to provide information to the ecotax commission, the administration of the regional governments and to the federal government at fixed intervals. After the yearly control, the ecotax commission can advise the government to allow the voluntary collection system for the following year. If the prescribed collection percentage isn't reached however, all sold batteries become subject to the ecotax law the following year. In addition to this, BEBAT has to pay a fine that equals the ecotax multiplied by the additional number of batteries that should have been collected.

The agreement started at the moment of signing, and ends on 31 December 2000. The agreement continues to exist as long as no new regional legislature, conflicting with the regulation of the VA, comes into force. Each party however has the right to end this agreement unilaterally, when one of the parties no longer complies with the regulations of the agreement.

The 'collection and recycling contribution' was determined by the Royal Decree of 16 April1996 to be BEF 4 per battery.

4. ANALYSIS

4.1 Organisational Structure

BEBAT has a board of directors which consists of three persons: one of them represents a major battery company (Duracell or Energizer for example), another works for a medium size company (for example, Panasonic), and the third one represents a small company (for example a local battery shop).

In 1998, 24 persons were working permanently for BEBAT. In order to increase the flexibility, BEBAT makes an appeal to exterior organisations for administrative and logistic work.

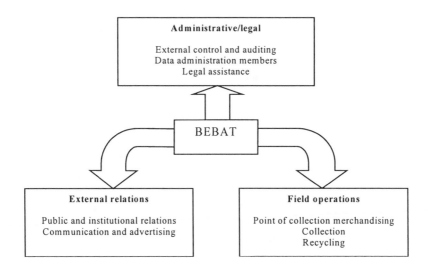

Source: BEBAT, 2001

Figure 5.1 The external relations of BEBAT

At the end of 1998, 286 companies were member of BEBAT. 13 500 retail sellers, 400 wholesalers and 4 000 schools co-operated with the system, that is placed collection boxes and campaign material in their infrastructure. In reality, this means that up to 90 per cent of all battery producers and distributors in Belgium pay the required contribution and are as a result represented by BEBAT. Expressed as the percentage of sold batteries, 95 to 98 per cent of all sold batteries in Belgium are sold by BEBAT-members. The low percentage of free-riders is probably the result of the monopolistic structure of the Belgian battery market.

4.2 Collection and Recycling of the Batteries

Today BEBAT places collection boxes at approximately 20 000 collection points (market stores, photo shops, jewellers, schools, public places and so on). At these collection points, BEBAT also offers equipment to enhance the collection of batteries for the consumers (plastic bags and boxes). This all happens at zero cost for the owners of the collection points.

During the first year of operation, BEBAT started an awareness campaign of eight months (March – October 1996) to inform the consumers and the distributors about the new collection system. By means of advertisements in papers and magazines, television and radio spots, newsletters, brochures, stickers and so on, consumers and distributors were informed about the new collection system.

Today, BEBAT still uses publicity campaigns to keep in touch with the consumers and to persuade them to collect used batteries separately. In 1998, BEF 120 million was spent on publicity. Media campaigns through television, radio and press account for BEF 38 million, house-to-house deliveries for BEF 58 million and school activities for BEF 17 million.

Schools turn out to be important battery collectors. Therefore, children are reached through an educational programme in which battery use, collection and recycling are explained. By collecting more batteries, schools can earn educational material and sports equipment.

In order to see whether further encouragement is necessary, BEBAT interviews 1 000 consumers each six months. These interviews show a significant evolution (Dimarso, 1997):

- approximately 70 per cent of the consumers claim to collect batteries separately from the common household waste;
- the conscience that batteries should be collected separately is growing;
- 90 per cent of the consumers find the BEBAT concept positive;
- 78 per cent have the intention of using the BEBAT collection boxes;
- the use of the collection boxes becomes a habit when it is once used;
- approximately 30 per cent of the consumers still throw away their used batteries with the common household waste, but this percentage is decreasing.

At fixed intervals, the locally collected batteries are gathered up by specialised firms: WATCO for the Flemish and Walloon region, NET BRUSSEL for the Brussels region. The batteries are then sorted in three categories: button cells, rechargeable Ni-Cd batteries, and others). Recycling of the batteries is done by INDAVER (button cells – Antwerp), SNAM (rechargeable – France) and REVATECH (others – Liège).

In order to reach the prescribed collection percentages, BEBAT uses not only the retail network of batteries, but also the industry and other large-scale consumers (for example, schools). Also the batteries collected by the regions (through the public collection sites) are part of the total amount of collected batteries, and can be passed through to BEBAT for recycling. This is not necessary however: if the regions can prove to BEBAT that they have had the collected batteries recycled following the requirements included in the agreement of 17 June 1997, BEBAT compensates the regions for this. Rumours that the regions would dump the larger part of the batteries they collected, urged BEBAT to collect these batteries itself at the public collection sites, so that all collected batteries are offered directly for recycling. These rumours would indeed be bad publicity for BEBAT.

In 1996, the regions still collected 460 tonnes of the total collected amount of 1 264 tonnes, through their public waste collection sites. In 1997, this was only 295 tonnes of a total of 1 354 tonnes. From 1998 on, the share of batteries collected by the regions becomes very small (see table 5.1).

In 1995, that is before the BEBAT system was installed, the Flemish public waste company OVAM collected 337 tonnes of household batteries. Estimating that 60 per cent of the battery sales took place in the Flemish region (since 60 per cent of the Belgian population lives in this region), we can estimate that OVAM collected only 22 per cent of the batteries sold.

By looking at Table 5.1, one can notice that the prescribed collection percentage of 60 per cent for 1998, 67.5 per cent for 1999 and 75 per cent for 2000 is not reached. Since it became difficult to reach these high percentages, BEBAT has asked the ecotax commission whether it would be possible to change the calculation method of the collection percentage of batteries. The initial calculation method treats all batteries in the same way, whereas in practice, there are quite some differences between rechargeable and non-rechargeable batteries that affect the result of the initial collection percentage calculation negatively:

- rechargeable batteries have a much longer lifetime than non-rechargeable ones;
- the sale of rechargeable batteries soared in the recent years, thanks to the emergence of for example, mobile phones, cordless appliances, etc.;

- certain consumers do not dispose of these rechargeable batteries, even when their power has decreased significantly.

These differences lead to the fact that the reported collection percentage is not a good approximation of the *actual* collection percentage: the denominator increases, since more and more rechargeable batteries are sold, while the nominator only reflects the collected rechargeable batteries that are sold in previous years, which are less in quantity.

The commission acknowledged this problem, and tried to find an alternative calculation method for the rechargeable batteries, together with the industry. From 1998 on an alternative calculation method was used to take into account the different properties of rechargeable batteries.

Table 5.1 Collected vs. sold batteries (tons) (Belgium)

	1996	1997	1998	1999	2000
Sold batteries available for collection*	2 768.5	2 676	2 659	3 138	3 200
Batteries collected					
by BEBAT	327	1 060	1 522	1 755	2 090
by the regions	460	295	40	80	15
stock**	477	0	0	0	0
Total	1 264	1 354	1562	1 835	2 105
Collection target (%)	40	50	60	68.5	75
Collection percentage (%)	45.7	50.6	58.7	58.5	65.8

Note: *: total batteries sold minus a part of the rechargeable batteries
           **: estimated amount of batteries in BEBAT collection boxes on 31 December, not yet collected by BEBAT that year.

Source   BEBAT, 2001

As stipulated, the agreement would end on 31 December 2000. On 22 December 2000, the national government reached an agreement about the future role of the ecotaxes. It was decided that they would renew the ecotax law by the end of 2001. Meanwhile, the current arrangements are passed on to the next year. For batteries in particular, it has been decided to keep the ecotax law in force, but the collection percentage is brought down from 75 to 60 per cent. This collection percentage could rise again to 65 per cent in 2004 after negotiations with BEBAT.

With this decision, the agreement that lasted until 31 December 2000 was positively evaluated. Although BEBAT has not always reached the prescribed collection percentages exactly, the amount of collected batteries rose every year. The reached collection percentages are quite high, comparing them with the collection percentages before and with present collection percentages abroad. As a result, batteries have been exempted from the ecotax between 1996 and 2000.

5. CONCLUSION

This agreement can be considered to be very successful. The sector was able to avoid the ecotaxes, and due to the agreement, the percentage of collected batteries rose more than significantly.

One very important determinant of this success was clearly the existence of an alternative instrument in the form of the ecotax. This instrument was already in place and could come into effect immediately if the prescribed collection percentages were not met.

Also the fact that the battery industry spoke with one voice during the negotiations, accelerated these negotiations.

The agreement itself was very precise and detailed concerning the targets to be achieved and the obligations of both parties. This also attributed to the good performance of this agreement.

BIBLIOGRAPHY

Amman, P. (1994), 'Le traitement des piles, néons et autres déchets contenant des métaux lourds', Report, Recymet.

Battery Manufacturers Association of Europe, USA and Japan, (1994), 'Study into recycling portable household batteries: a status report'.

BEBAT (2001), *Annual Report 2000,* St-Stevens-Woluwe.

Christopher, A. (1994), *Etude de la problématique déchet des piles 'grand public' en région de Bruxelles-Capitale,* Institut Supérieur de Commerce Saint-Louis.

De Caevel, B. (1995), *Ophaalsystemen voor gebruikte batterijen in België: gevoeligheidsanalyse,* FEE.

De Clercq, M. (1996), *Opvolgingscommissie betreffende de milieutaksen, jaarverslag 1995.*

De Clercq, M. (1997), *Opvolgingscommissie betreffende de milieutaksen, jaarverslag 1996.*

De Clercq, M. (1998), *Opvolgingscommissie betreffende de milieutaksen, jaarverslag 1997.*

De Clercq, M. (1999), *Opvolgingscommissie betreffende de milieutaksen, jaarverslag 1998.*

Dimarso, (1995), 'Ecotaks op batterijen: prijsverhoging en omruilgedrag'. Conjoint-analyse bij de Belgische bevolking, Brussels:Dimarso.

Europile, (1992), 'Batterijen en het milieu: de feiten.'

Fabrimetal (1994), Dossier Ecotaks batterijen, report, Brussels.

I.C.D.I., (1992), *Cahier technique* nr. 4, Les piles: composition, pollutions, traitements, recyclage.

Institut Bruxellois sur la gestion de l'environnement, (1994), 'L'essentiel de ce qu'il faut savoir à propos des piles grand public: de leur achat à leur traitement après utilisation', *report*, Brussels.

Lavrysen, L. (2000), 'Legal framework for the conclusion of environmental covenants in Belgium at the federal level and at the level of the Flemish region', *paper*, Ghent University.

Lentzen, L. (1993), 'La gestion des déchets. Application: les piles.'

Misonne, D. (2000), 'Legal frameworks of Environmental agreements in Belgium', *CAVA working paper*.

Pauwels, I. (1994), *Onderzoek zware metalen in 'groene' batterijen*, Bond Beter Leefmilieu.

SERV. (1997), *Rapport Milieubeleidsovereenkomsten*, Brussels, 145p.

SERVECO. (1995), 'Collecte et traitement des piles usagées.'

Wille, D. (2000), 'The integration of voluntary approaches into existing legal systems: an important instrument in the Flemish waste management', *CAVA working paper*.

INTERVIEWS

Mr Aeby, *General Manager of BEBAT and president of group 6 of the Federation of Electrics and Electronics (FEE)*

Mr D. Wille, *Openbare Vlaamse Afvalstoffenmaatschappij van het Vlaamse Gewest*

Mr P. Binnemans, *Federatie van de Electriciteit en de Electronica, jurist*

Mr C. Hermans, *Federatie van de Electriciteit en de Electronica, chairman*

Mr Dewulf, *Ministerie van Economische Zaken, Bestuur Kwaliteit en Veiligheid, Afdeling Concurrentievermogen*

6. Agreements on the Use of CFCs in France

Franck Aggeri

1. INTRODUCTION

The CFC (chlorofluorocarbon) case is interesting because it is the first time that international co-operation led to a concerted policy at the international level. It can be seen as the first attempt to consolidate the idea of 'sustainable development'. This is a case which was the subject of several studies (see Roan, 1989, Bensédrine, 1998, Gabel, 1995). As we are going to see later, the French case cannot be isolated from the debates that have taken place at the European and international levels during the past twenty years. First, French regulation has often followed the European regulation rather than preceded it. Second, French companies, in particular in the chemical industry, are international ones, with plants and markets all over the world. Third, negotiated agreements (NAs) which were signed in France in 1989 between the ministry for the Environment and different industrial sectors using CFCs, were deeply influenced by the regulatory and competition game, which had been taking place at the international level since 1987.

Although an important reduction in CFC production and use has been observed, it can hardly be seen as a direct consequence of the NAs, but rather as the direct consequence of European and international regulations. In fact, these NAs, with limited ambitions, were aimed at completing the existing regulations. More precisely, they were focusing on CFC use, looking for a good allocation of abatement efforts taking into account each sector's characteristics. Their lifespan was short, since from 1994 new regulations came into force, banning the production of CFCs, and therefore accelerating the search for substitutes on the users' side.

After presenting the case context in the next section, we will recall the main steps of the international regulatory process before describing the emergence of NAs in France in section 3. In section 4, we will undertake the evaluation of the

NAs pointing out the difficulties to separate the performance that can be attributed to NAs from the performance that can be attributed to regulations.

2. CONTEXT

2.1 The Environmental Problem

The substances considered here, CFCs, are complex chemical products which are made of carbon, fluorine and chlorine. These substances were used in a wide range of applications: first in aerosols, later also in refrigerants, air-conditioning systems, solvents, pharmaceutical products, foam, etc. They were known since the 1930s for their properties and qualities (odourless, low price), and their sales were rising 15 per cent per year until the beginnings of the 1970s.

2.2 Producers and Users

In the 1970s, the production of CFCs was concentrated in the hands of approximately 20 companies, mostly large Anglo-Saxon multinationals (Du Pont Nemours, ICI, Allied-Signal, Hoechst). DuPont was the leader with approximately 25 per cent of the world market. French producers (Rhône Poulenc and Ugine Kuhlman) still had a marginal position, but the merger of their CFC activities into one single company in 1987, Atochem, gave birth to the second largest world producer in the 1980s. On the French side, Atochem was the only private negotiating partner during the negotiations with the public authorities, which gave it a strong capacity of influence. At the international level, these multinationals had many contacts before the issue of CFCs arose but their co-operation on CFCs became stronger during the negotiation phase in order to influence it. In particular, several working groups and lobbies were created to this purpose.

Industrial users were found in diverse areas such as the cosmetic, automobile, packaging, pharmaceutical, refrigeration industries, etc. In France, these different users, represented by professional unions in regulatory negotiations, have different levels of concentration.[1.] The aerosol industry which was the major CFC user (60 per cent) is very concentrated (L'Oreal, the leader represents 50 per cent of the production). The automobile industry, which used CFCs for cool-air systems, is also concentrated. On the contrary, the refrigeration industry is much more fragmented. At the top of the system, there are distributors of fluids. In France, two major distributors share the market: Primagaz and Dehon service. They sell fluids to equipment manufacturers. There are a wide range of manufacturers from those who manufacture large equipment for the food industry (cold rooms, storage, supermarkets, and so on), domestic refrigerators, the refrigeration transport industry to the automobile industry (air-conditioning suppliers). For industrial applications, equipment is sold to fitters who are in direct contact with customers. Finally, at the bottom level, there is a large variety of users: domestic refrigeration, industrial refrigeration, air-conditioning in transport (automobile, aeroplanes, trains, and so on).

Table 6.1   The actors in the French refrigeration sector

Producers	Chemical industry (Atochem, DuPont and so on)
Distributors	Dehon service, Primagaz, ...
Equipment manufacturers	Industrial refrigeration: Multinational companies: Trane, York, Carrier,...
	Middle size firms : Ciat, Airwell,...
	Refrigerator manufacturers : Brandt, Arthur Martin,...
	cooling transport systems : Thermoking, Frigikind,...
Fitters	Individual firms, medium size
Users	Domestic refrigeration (refrigerators, individual air-conditioning), air-conditioning in transport, industrial refrigeration (storage, food industry), cooling transport

This variety of firms refers to the complexity of the refrigeration industry. In contrast to the aerosol industry, which was using CFCs, the refrigeration industry used a wide range of fluids depending on specific applications and depending on the kind of refrigeration technical system.

3. NEGOTIATON PROCESS

3.1 The International Negotiation Phase

3.1.1 First suspicions vis-à-vis CFCs
The context vis-à-vis CFCs changed radically from 1974, when new scientific evidence and technical progress (new ozone measurement systems in the atmosphere) made it possible to show that CFCs were not biodegradable. Two researchers, Rowland and Molina, published a paper in *Nature* (Molina and Rowland, 1974) where they stated that CFCs would downgrade the ozone layer, and consequently would cause serious damage to human health and the environment. Although several assumptions could not be proven, this article received a large echo in the press and the public opinion. Therefore, several

countries, like United States, Canada and Germany, from the mid 1970s envisaged regulating the use of CFCs in the aerosol industry which represented 60 per cent of emissions.

3.1.2 A virulent reaction of industrialists

From the beginning, there was a unanimous scepticism of industrialists towards the Rowland and Molina theory they qualified as 'absurd' and 'proofless' (Roan, 1989). They saw in this article an attempt by ecologist pressure groups to stop CFC production and use. Since 1972, CFC producers had created the PAFT (Program for Alternative Fluorocarbon Toxicity Testing) to study the ecology and toxicity of their products. Numerous scientific studies were financed by the PAFT. Most of these studies did not deny the Rowland and Molina theory but they indicated the uncertainties and the need for further research which justified the financing of new studies and the postponement of regulation. The PAFT presented the results to the American Congress, and regularly they provided reports to the Co-ordinating Committee on the Ozone Layer (CCOL) established by the United Nations to monitor scientific knowledge. Other structures like the COAS (Council of Atmospheric Sciences) were created in 1975 by producers and users of CFCs 'to collect every technical data necessary to found legislative or executive decisions and transmit them to public authorities'. Intensive communication campaigns were also organised, in particular by DuPont, towards citizens and politicians. In 1980, Du Pont de Nemours led the creation of the Alliance for Responsible CFC Policy (ARCFCP) with a stated aim of preventing any further regulatory threat to CFC business.

On the other side, public authorities and the United Nations organised a better understanding of the environmental problem through the establishment of several technical bodies and scientific committees with the most recognised experts in charge of studying the impacts of CFCs on the ozone layer, the conditions of substitution and so on.

Despite the constant efforts of CFC firms, they did not succeed in preventing a first regulatory phase in the most ecologically aware countries. In 1978, the use of aerosols was banned in the USA and strongly reduced in Germany. These decisions provoked very negative reactions from the producers who denounced the irresponsibility of policy makers and the effects of these decisions on industry, trade and employment.

A change occurred in the US administration when Ronald Reagan became president. From this moment, every regulatory project had to be submitted to a cost-advantage evaluation. At that time, scientific uncertainties about CFCs environmental effects were still very high. Therefore the Congress opposed an EPAs regulatory project on CFCs arguing that it was not possible to regulate such a vital product without greater certainties about environmental damage.

3.1.3 New scientific evidences about pollution

From 1985, new discoveries changed the scientific context. In May 1985, thanks to new measurement systems, British scientists in the Antarctic found the first evidence of ozone depletion. During the next two years, the depletion, also known as the 'ozone hole', grew constantly and the responsibility of CFCs in this phenomenon seemed more and more probable.

In 1986, a major event occurred: DuPont changed drastically its strategy by announcing it would unilaterally phase-out CFCs over a ten-year period. It was actually an argument for a proactive policy of regulatory restrictions on CFC production. Why did Du Pont reversed its strategy although it was very active in the coalition of CFC producers? A deep analysis of Du Pont's strategy is given by L. Gabel (1995). Several explanations could be invoked but maybe the most consistent is that Du Pont believed that it was ahead of its competitors in developing new CFC substitutes. Although DuPont and the other producers were collaborating to prevent a regulation, all the producers were, at the same time, involved in individual R&D efforts to find new substitutes in case a regulation appeared. Substitutes were more (twice as)costly to produce and less effective than CFCs. Therefore DuPont had no opportunity to sell these products without a regulation prohibiting CFCs. Even if substitutes were still some years away from market availability,[2] two major reasons could be used to explain Du Pont's announcement: on the one hand, CFC business was too small for Du Pont (2 per cent of its sales) to take the risk of damaging its public image by remaining passive, on the other hand, rents were expected to increase[3] with the shift towards substitutes combined with a tradable CFC permits system in the USA (see Gabel,1995). Within this underground competition, DuPont believed it would be possible to gain a competitive advantage and tried to benefit from this 'fast learner strategy' (Aggeri and Hatchuel, 1999) by influencing the forthcoming regulation.

3.1.4 The signing of the protocol of Montreal

It is proved that Du Pont's announcement did accelerate the signing of the protocol of Montreal in 1987. The EPA (Environmental Protection Agency in the USA) used the argument to convince other countries that phasing out CFCs was possible as substitutes were to come. Du Pont's strategy was denounced by several competitors (like the French company Elf-Atochem) as well as Friends of the Earth which accused Du Pont of manipulating regulatory policy and holding up CFC prices.

Can this story be considered as a classical 'regulatory capture' scenario? According to the regulatory capture theory (Stigler, 1971), there is a capture when public authorities choose a solution that is contrary to the general interest and favour deliberately private interests. As Gabel (1995) points out in this case: 'there is no implied generalisation that the regulatory body's idea of public interest is perverted. On the contrary, it may be facilitated, and one concern of the policy maker is to use the competitive game between firms to its advantage.' Interestingly, the EPA administration organised the competition between firms long before, announcing that if a producer proved there were substitutes for CFCs, this information would be used for regulation. This was a clear signal to encourage 'fast learning' strategies. In this dynamic process, as Gabel (1995) points out: 'compliance with the law is one of the least significant issues. The strategies we observed were anticipatory and involved thinking several steps ahead of both the regulation and one's competitors' (op. cit. p. 343).

As a result of new scientific evidence on the effects of CFCs on ozone depletion, discovery of substitutes for CFCs, and pressure from several countries and lobbies, the situation was mature for an international regulation. The Montreal protocol was signed by 93 countries in September 1987. This protocol defined a timetable for the reduction of the production of CFCs[4] (by 50 per cent by 1999). After the Protocol was signed, a first regulation was ratified in the European Community in 1988 taking over the same objectives and including a restriction of imports and trade of CFCs. This regulation was directly applicable to all member states.

3.2 A Continuous Regulatory Activity at the International Level

Whereas the initial phase of the negotiation mobilised the attention of researchers in social sciences, the implementation phase and its consequences mobilised researchers very little. This can be explained by the fact that the objectives of the protocol have not only been reached, but even exceeded. Thus, whereas the worldwide production of CFCs amounted to 1.2 million tons in 1987, it did not exceed 350 000 tons in 1994. Since the end of 1995, CFC production has ceased in the European Union and CFCs are manufactured only in certain developing countries that obtained derogation.[5] Therefore, why be interested in it? Because this process reveals intrinsic collective learning and regulatory processes which are worth being studied.

From the public intervention point of view, it is striking to note the strength and the duration of the regulatory activity: at the international level, since 1987, nearly ten international meetings were held on the subject, leading to four amendments with the protocol of Montreal. At the European level, a regulatory management committee on CFCs is held regularly, having produced over the period, four European regulations, without counting the multitude of national regulations. It is also necessary to stress the permanent scientific and technical groups, which have given support to this bureaucratic machinery for more than ten years (technical and scientific options committees working for the United Nations).

This continuous activity is fundamental: regulations go much further in the variation of the objectives by type of product: they specify the methods of assessment, they identify the exceptions (for example: the equipment to produce pharmaceutical products, in which CFC are still used for safety reasons), and they also regulate the conditions of use and recovery in the various sectors and the trade of these substances. In this continuous process, trying to separate negotiation, formulation and implementation phases would not make much sense. On the other hand, it is worth studying in tandem regulatory and industrial dynamics. In effect, these regulatory dynamics cannot be understood without stressing the industrial and competition dynamics that made them possible.

3.3 The Drawbacks of Regulation on Innovation, Trade and Competition

These different regulations had important consequences on the industry, on the production sector in particular. From 1986, the main producers knew that they had no means of escaping from regulations. They had a bad public image. Moreover, the protocol of Montreal being signed by 93 countries, and DuPont having announced, in March 1988, its commitment of withdrawing itself from the CFC market, it was necessary for them to develop new substitutes to remain competitive. From March to September 1988, one after another, every CFC producer announced its phase-out schedule for the next decade. In June 1990 the CFC phase-out was formalised with a revision of the original Montreal protocol to ban all CFCs by the year 2000.

3.3.1 The impacts on innovation

The development of substitutes is a very long and costly activity. The average development process takes about six years: approximately two years for R&D, two years for carrying out tests of toxicology and implementation, one year for tests of feasibility and one year for the building of new equipment. It is important to stress that the development of these substances takes place primarily within the same firm with industrial co-operation limited to the tests of toxicology. The investment generated by a new product are also very high (several hundreds of millions of dollars). The payback period on investment is rarely lower than ten to twelve years according to experts of the sector.

Since 1986, two generations of substitutes have been developed by the chemical industry. A first generation appeared at the end of the 1980s called HCFCs. These were products having a ozone-depleting potential much lower than CFC (from ten times to 50 times less). Thus quickly appeared a dilemma for CFC producers. Should they develop HCFCs of which the chemical structure is close to that of CFCs (still including chlorine atoms in their molecules), and which are thus more simple to develop, but which present the disadvantage of still having an impact on the ozone layer, and therefore, which were likely to be prohibited one day in their turn, or should they try to switch directly to another generation of substitutes containing no chlorine, without any impact on the ozone layer (HFC), but which are more difficult to finalise.

DuPont decided to invest in a large range of both HCFCs and HFCs in order to produce a full product line and to reduce its market and regulatory risks. Atochem followed the same strategy, investing to develop a whole range of HCFCs, considering that its 'chemical road'[6] was compatible with this strategy and could provide a good profitability. Developed as from 1986 by Atochem, the first HCFCs were marketed at the beginning of the 1990s. In 1994, Atochem had become the first world-wide producer of HCFCs. Although they were more costly to produce than CFCs (about twice as much), HCFCs had the advantage of being less expensive than HFCs (30 per cent less approximately). That made it possible for Atochem to get a significant market share. Other firms chose different strategies. For instance, ICI decided to by-pass HCFCs and jump directly from CFCs to HFCs. According to Gabel (1995), this decision is due to the fact that ICI had limited financial resources and chose to focus its limited investments on HFCs. But, as a second-mover in the game, ICI asked for new regulations, which prohibit the use of HCFCs in order to promote HFCs. On the contrary, Du Pont advocated for unrestricted use of HCFCs until 2030.

This competition among firms, characterised by contradictory announcements and the diffusion of information, served the interests of those (green lobbies and public bodies) who wanted to accelerate the regulatory process. The protocol of London (1990), reinforced by the European regulations of 1991, 1992 and 1994 defined a timetable for the progressive elimination of HCFCs. This was obviously a severe blow for HCFC producers whose the return on investment was threatened in the long term. On the contrary, this decision created new business opportunities for producers that had jumped directly to the HFC generation.

Now a new regulatory threat is profiled at the horizon for the producers. Indeed, within the framework of the protocol of Kyoto, CFCs and their substitutes (HFCFs and HFCs) get the attention of public authorities as greenhouse gases. Thus, at the European level, the non-producing countries (north-European countries) and NGOs militate for the progressive prohibition of the HFCs as well. They assert that solutions of substitution exist for almost every application. In particular they argue that there are substitutes based on hydrocarbon (known as 'natural products') for refrigeration applications. This new regulatory process is still another source of uncertainty for chemical firms whose investments in HCFCs and HFCs plants are threatened.

3.3.2 The impacts on trade and competition

The impact of these various regulations was considerable on the CFC market in the OECD countries (see Figure 6.1 and Figure 6.2). The production and consumption declined rapidly between 1986 and 1996. During the meantime, the production of substitutes (HCFCs and HFCs) has increased, but the global production (CFC, HFCF and HFC) in 1996 is half the CFC production of 1986.[7] How can it be explained? First, the new substitutes are much more complex to develop and produce than CFCs. Therefore, HFCFs are 30 per cent more expensive than CFCs on average, and HFCs are three times more expensive than CFCs. The elasticity of demand has proved actually to be higher than foreseen as users searched for cheaper alternative solutions. Thus, the use of fluorocarbons has almost disappeared in the aerosol industry where it has been replaced by butane or propane solutions, and it is losing market shares in the refrigeration and air conditioning industry where hydrocarbons and ammonia technologies have been developed. This contraction of the market has contributed to a concentration of the production sector, certain producers like Hoechst preferring to withdraw from a market in regression and threatened by regulatory risks.

On the demand side (users), efforts for reducing CFC consumption have been different from one sector to another (see Figure 6.2). In the aerosol industry, the decline of CFC use came very rapid after regulations came into force as substitutes existed (propane, butane) and were quite easy to implement. On the contrary, due to a combination of factors (the complexity of the sector, technical difficulties to redesign refrigeration systems using substitutes while reaching the same performance, and so on) the decline has been much slower and CFCs are still used today in old refrigeration equipment. For that purpose, recovery and recycling CFC schemes have been encouraged to provide fluids for older equipment, waiting for their replacement by new equipment.

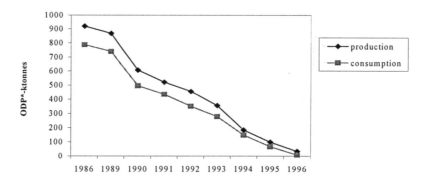

* ODP : Ozone Depletion Potential,
UNEP : United Nations Environmental Program

Source: UNEP, 1999

Figure 6.1   CFC market in OECD countries 1986-96

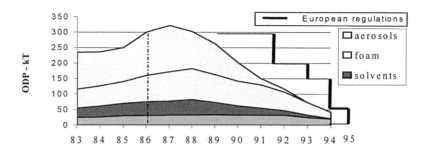

Source: European Chemical Industry Council, 1996

Figure 6.2   CFC use in the European Union by sectors

3.4 The Process in France

3.4.1 The situation before 1987

The French administration and French firms were not very active during the negotiations which preceded the Montreal protocol compared to the USA or Germany. On the administration side, only one representative from the ministry for the environment and representatives from the ministry of agriculture participated. On the industry side, Atochem – the second largest world producer – was present in the producer associations but engaged later than DuPont in the development of substitutes. French experts and specialists were very few in the technical and scientific committees. For example, the French refrigeration industry, through the 'Institut international du froid', was not represented in the United Nations technical committee whereas the American users (through the ASHRAE) were very active. How to explain this low involvement of French actors? First, it has to be remembered that France was the European leader for CFC production, and therefore, Atochem as well as the largest users had a strong influence on French authorities, the ministry for the industry in particular. Second, at that time, the ministry for the environment had still a weak legitimacy with limited means and capacity of influence and no clear doctrine on this issue. Third, ecological pressure groups and the public opinion were not mobilised on this issue as much as they were in northern European countries. On the contrary, a famous scientific personality, A. Tazieff, put into doubt the effects of CFCs on ozone depletion in 1989, creating debates and confusion in public opinion. Fourth, it was the first time that an environmental issue was tackled at the international level. French authorities as well as French firms were not prepared for the negotiations and they probably did not believe an international consensus could be reached on this issue.

3.4.2 The negotiations of the agreements

Once the Montreal protocol had been signed it was no longer possible for French authorities to postpone the regulatory process. It was then decided to accommodate it. The production (supply) had been regulated since 1988 at the European level, and there was no reason to add national regulations to it. But this was not the case for the use of CFCs (the demand) and the recycling of end-of-life products. Although the production sector was the object of international regulations, the risk was that users would not be prepared for using substitutes. Furthermore, it was not possible to consider uniform pollution abatement efforts for industrial users, since the different industrial sector users were facing different contexts (see Figure 6.2). For instance, in the aerosol industry, the substitution of CFCs (CFC11, 12, 114) was quite easy because it was possible to go back to the old technical solutions with butane or propane (which were used before the discovery of CFCs) which are a less secure but cheaper solution. Banned in the USA since 1978, aerosol producers had already developed substitutes for CFCs that could be easily put into practice in Europe. On the other hand, the situation in the refrigeration industry was much more complex with a wide range of specific applications using a large variety of CFCs (11, 12, 113, 115, HFCF 22). In most cases, substituting the fluids required, for technical reasons, a modification of all the refrigeration systems to get the same technical performance. This technical change was not easy to implement because it required the development of new efficient technologies and the involvement of a large number of actors (see Table 6.1) intervening all along the life cycle of refrigerant fluids. According to the United Nations Environmental Program (1999), three out of four old CFC refrigeration systems are still in operation in industrialised countries. A priori, nothing prevented the ministry for the environment from adopting a regulation but it was not in a position to impose a solution firms could have rejected. When we interviewed civil servants in charge of the issue, three arguments were put forward to explain why a negotiated agreement was preferred. First, the means of the ministry – the number of agents in the administration in particular – was, according to them, too small taking into account the number of industrial sites. Second, the co-operation of industrialists was preferable to define more adequate and acceptable targets. But the main reason put forward was to initiate a dialogue with industrialists – which did not pre-exist – and to guide them towards a more proactive attitude vis-à-vis CFCs. The ministry hoped that, through the negotiation process, the co-operation of industrialists would be obtained without requiring a command-and-control approach. Beyond all these explanations, it can be seen that the protection of industrial interests and competitiveness in the international market was probably more important than the protection of the environment itself. Another important issue was to build trust relationships with firms and to avoid free-riding attitudes, which could have led to illegal imports of CFCs. Surprisingly, firms' attitude towards NAs was positive. At that time, producers were in favour of agreements with users since they tried to promote their new substitutes (HCFCs). On the users' side, they did not have much information on the consequences of the Montreal protocol and European regulations and they were asking for a clarification of the regulatory context they would have to face. They were worrying about competition effects of CFC regulations in their sectors. Furthermore, it appeared, during the negotiation, that the objective of these agreements was not to go beyond the requirements of the Montreal protocol but rather to define sector targets taking into account the ability of each sector to reach them.

3.4.3 The 1989 agreements

Although the Montreal protocol and the European regulation nr. 3322/88 of October 1988 imposed a reduction of CFC production and consumption by 1998–99 of 50 per cent on a 1986 production basis, with an intermediate step in 1994 with 20 per cent reduction, there was no sectoral target for CFC users. The aim of the agreements signed in France with the major CFC user sectors (cosmetic industry for aerosols, foam industry, refrigeration industry and so on) was to introduce differentiated targets according to sector characteristics and abatement costs (burden-sharing). Thus, in the aerosol sector the target was to reach a 90 per cent reduction of CFC consumption by 1991 on a 1976 basis. In the foam industry, the target was to reach a stabilisation of consumption in 1993 and a 20 per cent reduction in 1999 on a 1986 basis. In the refrigeration industry, the target was to reach a stabilisation in 1993 and a 20 per cent reduction in 1999 on a 1986 basis Moreover, in the refrigeration agreement specific objectives for recuperation of fluids and their recycling were mentioned. Besides, each sector committed itself to give, through an independent intermediary organisation, data on the use of all CFCs aimed by the agreement. Concerning the monitoring of these agreements, no steering committee was envisaged to check their implementation. This series of agreements was supposed to run until 1999. In fact, they became ineffective from 1994 when the regulatory agenda accelerated. In effect, after the European regulation of 1988 (nr. 3322/88), a new one was adopted in 1991 (nr. 594/91) imposing, on a 1986 reference level, a reduction of CFC production of 50 per cent by the end of 1993 and a complete end to production by June 1997 and a timetable for HFCFs. The next year, a new European regulation (nr. 3952/92) was adopted, imposing a complete end of CFC production by 31 December 1994. In 1994, another European regulation (nr. 3093/94) was adopted confirming the total end for CFC production by 31 December 1994 and imposing stricter targets for substitutes. Consequently, from 1994, the French agreements had no significance since European targets had become more stringent than those defined in the agreements, and since CFC consumption had almost stopped in France except for specific applications (pharmaceutical products which had derogations) and for the refrigeration industry where old equipment still required CFC. It could be argued that, from 1994, these NAs could have been replaced by new ones focusing on the use of substitutes (HCFCs and HFCs). But, according to the civil servants we have interviewed, this did not prove to be necessary for two reasons: on the one hand, dialogue and co-operation was already effective with industrial users and did not require to be supported, on the other hand, the speed-up of the international agenda was so fast that there was no guarantee on the period of validity of the agreement.

3.4.4 The agreement of February 1993

The only sector which still had problems with CFCs was the refrigeration industry. The key-reason was that many installations were old and used to work with CFCs. The idea of the French authorities was to organise the recuperation and recycling of the old fluids when maintenance was necessary or for end-of-life products. This idea was extended to all refrigerant fluids having a potential effect on the ozone depletion, that is, CFC and their substitutes. A measure concerning recycling of old fluids was included in the agreement of 1989 with the refrigeration industry but it was vague about the financial responsibility and the organisation of collection and recycling. Therefore, a decree was signed in France with respect to this question in December 1992 (nr. 92-1271). It imposed on fluids' distributors, the recovery of old CFCs, HCFCs and HFCs and a principle of certification for recyclers, in order to ensure their professional capability. The key issue with respect to the decree's implementation was financial: who would support the economic cost of recuperation and recycling? The idea of a tax on new products to finance the collection and recycling of old fluids was proposed by the ministry for the environment. But it was rejected by the ministry for economy and finance which refused to consider any measure which would contribute to increasing the fiscal burden. To get round this problem, the solution envisaged was to sign a agreement with all representatives of the refrigeration sector, where firms would propose an economic scheme on a voluntary basis. In the agreement of February 1993, signed with different sectors (distributors, CFC producers and users (Association Française du Froid)), the distributors made a commitment that the collection of old fluids, their take-back and recycling would be financed by them. But in counterpart, they could freely pass on these extra costs in the price of new products. To monitor the implementation of this agreement, the text created an orientation committee, where all partners and public authorities were represented.[8] This text is still in application today but certainly for a limited period of time. In effect, a new European regulation is in preparation for 2001 which proposes the complete interdiction of CFCs, including their recycling, which concretely means that old equipment using CFCs will have to be replaced.

4. ANALYSIS

What evaluation can be made of these different NAs? What is their specific contribution in the reduction of the CFC problem? A cost/benefit analysis of the NAs is difficult to undertake. On the one hand, we have shown that negotiated agreements and regulations are so interwoven that it is impossible to evaluate the respective contribution of each instrument. On the other hand, there are no official data in France on the use of CFCs in the different industrial sectors covered by the agreements. Yet, according to the French ministry for the environment, data on the use of CFC have been collected by firms and transmitted to public authorities – at least during the first years –,but the latter did not publish them (except for recovery and recycling data), considering that these were private data without any guarantee on their validity. This lack of transparency is of course very prejudicial to the credibility of such agreements. In other words, we do not know whether the NAs have been properly enforced or not. The only data we have collected have been provided by the chemical industry association for the European Union. These data must be taken cautiously but apparently most sectors have succeeded in substituting CFCs by other substances. This information is confirmed by a more official one coming from the UNEP and based on independent audits. According to the UNEP report, the global consumption for CFCs in the OECD countries did not exceed 8 000 ODP-tonnes which represent less than 1 per cent of the 1986 level basis. Taking into account that French NA environmental targets were not ambitious,[9] and that the 1986 reference level in France for CFC consumption was more than 60 000 ODP-tonnes, it can be assumed that French sectors – as their European colleagues – have had no problems meeting these targets. Concerning the recovery of refrigerants fluids (CFC + HCFCs), data are collected and published by the ministry for the environment. In 1992, without any regulation, 250 metric tonnes of recovered refrigerant were reclaimed. Between 1992 and 1996, after making recovery mandatory and carrying out a deposit-refund scheme, the quantity rose from 250 to 550 tonnes and the number of refrigeration companies concerned doubled from 200 to 400 out of 2 500 (see table 6.2). Since then, the quantities have increased. Nevertheless, the rate of recovery for refrigerants in France was estimated in 1996 to 18 per cent (according to the Ministry for the Environment) which is still quite low compared to the estimates of the UNEP recovery potential (32 per cent). To go further and evaluate the indirect impacts of the NAs we shall refer to the four criteria proposed in the evaluation framework.

Table 6.2   Recovery volumes for refrigerants in France (CFCs and HCFCs)
            (tonnes)

Reclaimed	1989	1990	1991	1992	1993	1994	1995	1996
	120	150	260	250	300	420	500	550

Source: Ministry for the Environment, France

4.1 Feasibility

The environmental issue (CFC use) of these NAs was not strategic for public authorities. It is interesting to note that in other European countries they did not feel the need to regulate the demand for CFC products. Therefore, if NAs were signed in France, it is because they were 'feasible' at low cost (low administrative costs), due to their flexibility and easy setting. In other words, they were seen, from the ministry for the environment point of view, as a convenient and complementary instrument to implement beside the regulations. Politically and administratively, these NAs had the support of all ministries as well as industrialists as far as they allowed the clarification of how the burden would be shared between users.

4.2 Capability

4.2.1 Specification
Specification refers to the consistency of the agreement with the underlying policy objectives and its compatibility with national and international law on trade and competition. In this case, the specification of the agreements was far from the European commission's guidelines. Indeed, there were quantitative targets, but these targets were not more ambitious than those indicated in the regulations. These agreements were incomplete: they envisaged neither a monitoring scheme nor sanctions (a fortiori a burden-sharing scheme). Furthermore, the control of implementation was deficient and driven without any transparency. Concerning learning, no specific objective was included except reporting obligations, and concerning competition nothing was said to prevent free-riding. Besides, as we pointed out earlier, it can be wondered if the agreement on recycling was compatible with laws on trade and competition since there was no guarantee that the financial system put into place would not lead to a dominant position of distributors who had the capacity to pass on recycling costs in the price of new products.

4.2.2 Application

Application refers to the compliance of parties with respect to the targets and obligations specified in the agreements. Knowing whether the agreements on CFC have been applied or not is impossible to state for the simple reason that data are missing. This incredible lack of public monitoring reveals the low interest these agreements had for public authorities. On the one hand, the only civil servant in charge of the CFC issue was more concerned by the European and international regulatory process; on the other hand, except in the refrigeration sector which faced problems, other sectors apparently complied quite easily with the environmental targets.

4.3 Impact

The impact refers to the environmental effectiveness and the economic impacts of the agreements. In this case, there are real doubts about the actual impact of these NAs on pollution abatement (decrease of CFC use) as well as their social or economic impacts. It seems that this decrease should be attributed to the European and international regulations (Montreal protocol and European regulations) and had little to do with the NAs. In other words, it is probable that substitution would have occurred anyway, with or without the agreements. The clearest impact relates to the implementation of a recycling scheme based on a voluntary basis. This scheme did not change economic and social relations in the refrigeration sector because it rests on existing firms (the distributors). Furthermore, its efficiency and equity is questionable since there is a great opacity on the real cost of the operation (which is passed on in the price of new fluids). Regarding the economic efficiency, there are no arguments or data which could be used to say if NAs have contributed to lower or increased compliance costs compared to the baseline scenario (without NAs). As Glachant (1999), pointed out, NAs are often used to improve the dissemination of information, and therefore reduce information inquiry costs as well as administrative costs. But, in this case, as there were no specific measures or committees to disseminate information, there is no reason to consider that information asymmetries and information costs have been reduced. Nevertheless, if the results were limited, the administrative costs were very low too. In other words, it did not cost much to prepare, sign, implement and monitor these agreements.

4.4 Resource development

Resource development refers to improvements in the policy resource base resulting from negotiating and implementing the agreement. Taking into account the difficulty for public authorities of controlling every CFC user, NAs have, according to public authorities, favoured an easier collection of information at low cost. Another argument put forward was to say that these agreements have accelerated in sectors with small firms, like the refrigeration industry, the awareness vis-à-vis the CFCs. Prevention was also one of the ambitions of these agreements but, according to the industrialists, the reduction of CFC at the source and the substitution of CFCs is due more to the general regulatory pressure than to these specific agreements. According to the people we have interviewed, resource development seems to be a central issue. But for what purpose? To what extent have these 'so-called' better relations really improved the policy resource base since contacts became rare from 1991 and since the CFC problem almost disappeared from 1994?

5. CONCLUSION

French NAs on CFC use took place in a long and complex international regulatory process. Compared to the considerable impact the Montreal protocol had on public opinion, on the market structure as well as on industrial dynamics in the chemical sector, these NAs represent an epi-phenomenon. They have never been envisaged as a substitute to regulation but rather as a complement. From the beginning, the ambition of these NAs was limited, that is facilitating the implementation of international regulations on the users' side and preparing, along the way, firms to the substitution of CFCs. The difficulties of tracing back the story and consequences of these NAs reveal precisely the low interest and impacts they have produced in France. From the moment regulations made it possible to reach the environmental targets (baseline scenario) like in other European countries, why would it have been necessary to sign negotiated agreements? From the elements we have collected, the environmental impact and efficiency of these NAs is clearly questionable. Nevertheless, it should be noticed that the administrative costs to enforce the agreements have remained very low. Apart from NAs environmental performance, another issue is to wonder why public authorities designed agreements so deviating from the European Commission's recommendations (transparency, sanctions, information, monitoring)? A first explanation is to recall that the lack of formalisation and opacity was a constant characteristic of French NAs in the 1970s and 1980s (see Lascoumes, 1994). It reflects a traditional way of governing, based on informal relationships between the French administration and firms, soft and incomplete contractual forms. In our opinion, this explanation is not sufficient since we observe a decline of this for the benefit of more formal and monitored contracts in more recent agreements where issues are considered important (see the packaging waste case). If the

French administration did not design properly these agreements, two reasons can be invoked:

1. The issue (CFC use) was not very strategic for the ministry for the environment (less than CFC production issues for instance), since the process was already framed by European regulations. Furthermore, this limited interest declined rapidly when the acceleration of the regulatory agenda took up all the attention of the French administration.

2. The sectors' commitment would have been much more difficult to obtain if targets and obligations had been tougher. In other words, designing a 'good' agreement would have required means and willingness that were actually lacking. Furthermore, the interest of both parties (public and private) was to reach a rapid (even if it was incomplete) agreement, that could be put forward to prove the French commitment towards reducing ozone depletion.

NOTES

1. The level of concentration within an industry has a direct impact on their capacity of influence (see Olson, 1965).
2. In fact, substitutes were available only at the laboratory level and needed four to five years of further development before they could be put in the market.
3. (a) Rents for CFCs were very low because of a price war between producers (b) Du Pont thought demand was quite inelastic and hoped that the scarcity of CFC created by regulation would increase prices for CFC and substitutes.
4. More precisely the protocol define a list of substances, with their effects on the ozone layer, and the objective of 50 per cent is global and results from a weighing of the different substances (CFC11, 12, 113, 114, 115).
5. The last international meetings on ozone depletion in Montreal (1997) defined a schedule for developing countries on a 1995-97 reference level where CFC production should cease by year 2010.
6. By 'chemical road', experts mean the different industrial steps which are necessary to get a family of chemical substances. Chemical roads are different from one producer to another. In order to lower industrial investments and R&D expenses, the interest of producers is to limit the changes in the chemical road when passing from CFCs to substitutes. Therefore, taking into account the characteristics of their 'chemical roads', each producer did not have the opportunity to develop all kinds of substitutes at low costs.
7. The global production of fluorocarbons (CFC + HFCF + HFC) in the world reached 556 ODP-kilotons in 1996 (435 for HCFCs + 85 for HFCs + 36 for CFCs) against 1071 ODP-kilotons for CFCs in 1986 in the world (1 071 ODP-kilotons in the OECD countries) (source UNEP, 1999).
8. The agreement is quite surprising since it gives a dominant position to distributors, which have an interest to overestimate the costs they face as far as they can pass them on in the price of products. In this perspective, it can be asked whether such an agreement meets the necessary transparency conditions to avoid competition distortion.
9. Minus 20 per cent CFC use by 1 January 1999 for the refrigeration and foam sector on a 1986 reference level, minus 90 per cent by January 1991, for the aerosol industry.

REFERENCES

Aggeri, F. (1999), 'Voluntary agreements and innovation', *NEAPOL Project,* Theoretical report, June.

Aggeri, F. and Hatchuel, A. (1999), 'A dynamic model of environmental policy. The case of innovation oriented voluntary agreements'. Carraro C. and Lévèque F. (Ed.). In: *Voluntary approaches in Environmental Policy,* Dordrecht: Kluwer Academic Publishers, pp. 151-185.

Bensédrine, D. (1998), 'Les entreprises face aux controverses politico-scientifiques', *Revue Française de Gestion* n°119, pp. 91-106.

Clodic, D., Chang, Y.S. and Pougin, A.M. (1999), *'Evaluation des fluides frigorigènes à faible GWP',* report to the Ministry for the Environment.

European Chemical Industry Council. (1996), 'Report on CFC production and comsumption in Europe', *European Chemical Industry Council publication.*

Gabel L. (1995), 'Environmental management as a competitive strategy: the case of CFCs'. In H. Folmer, L. Gabel and H. Opschoor (eds), *Principle of Environmental and Resource Economics,* Cheltenham: Edward Elgar; pp. 56-80.

Glachant, M. (1999), 'The informational efficiency of negotiated agreements'. *NEAPOL Project,* Theoretical report, June.

Lascoumes P. (1994), *L'éco-pouvoir – Environnements et décisions,* Editions la Découverte. Paris.

Olson, M. (1965). *The Logic of Collective Action,* Cambridge, MA: Harvard University Press.

Roan, S.L. (1989), *Ozone Crisis.* New York: John Wiley Science Editions.

Rowland and Molina (1974). ?

Salmons R. (1999), 'Evaluation framework and performance indicators'. *NEAPOL project,* Theoretical report, June.

Stigler, G.J. (1971), 'The economic theory of regulation', *Bell Journal of Economic and Management Science,* **2**, 3-21.

UNEP (1999). 'Report on the refrigeration, air-conditioning and heat pumps technical option committee'. *United Nations publication.*

7. The Agreement on the Quality of Gasoline in Italy

Giorgio Vicini and Jane Wallace-Jones

1. INTRODUCTION

In the late 1980s, increased urban atmospheric pollution and the consequent pressure from public opinion stimulated the Italian government to tackle the problem of the environmental quality of gasoline through a series of negotiated agreements.

The European Community has regulated the content of benzene in gasoline since the end of the 1980s, fixing the maximum level of benzene in gasoline as 5 per cent volume. This limit was also imposed on Italian gasoline until 1989.

The three negotiated agreements regarding the improvement in the quality of gasoline were signed between 1989 and 1992 by the Unione Petrolifera (the Italian Oil Companies Association), the Ministry of the Environment, the Ministry of Industry and AgipPetroli, the leading Italian oil company.

The application of these instruments in the case studied signalled the adoption of a new approach in dealing with environmental problems by the Italian regulator, responding to the relevance of the problem and the urgent need for its solution. Moreover, the fact that the oil and gas sector in Italy is able to place certain pressure on public institutions seems, in this case, to have rendered resorting to a command and control policy less effective than concerted action.

The negotiated agreements here described emerge in this analysis, conducted in accordance with the NEAPOL methodology, as successful. In spite of the success of the negotiated agreements, and more precisely, due to the revelation of the technical feasibility of standards through the respect of the negotiated agreements targets, in 1996, the Italian regulator posed stricter emissions limits. The draft law (*Disegno di Legge*) nr. 2760 foresaw that the level of benzene in gasoline was to be reduced to 1.4 per cent of volume before 1 July 1997 and to 1 per cent before 1 July 1999. It was converted into law in 1997.

2. CONTEXT

2.1 The Content of Benzene in Gasoline: the Problem

At the end of the 1980s, in response to the repeated registering of emissions at levels above the limits in various urban areas in Italy, the Italian Government was forced to adopt alternative measures in order to bring about an improvement in the quality of gasoline and therefore reduce emission levels in an efficient and effective manner. A key element of these measures is the negotiated agreements for the reduction of the content of benzene in gasoline and, thus, in the emissions generated by these products. Benzene is a chemical that is part of the aromatics group. It is contained in crude oil and also, after the refining process, in gasoline. Benzene is not an additive compound, but is in the extracted raw material. The international research community has recognised that benzene is carcinogenic and its emissions are detrimental to health. International research institutions[1] classify benzene as class A1, as a certain carcinogenic agent for humans.

2.2 Environmental Policy in Italy: Moving Towards New Instruments

The evolution of environmental policy in Italy is said to have begun with the issue of Law 615, the 'anti-smog' law, in 1966 and, in this first phase, steps were taken to limit emission, mainly in response to apparent harm to human health.

The second phase (1976–85) is heralded by the Legge Merli for waste water control in 1976. A series of environmental statutes were then issued in the early 1980s concerning air and water pollution, industrial and urban waste and nuclear energy. In 1989, the local health units (USLs) were given responsibility for environmental monitoring and protection, though with a distinct bias in the interpretation of environment as those issues relating to health and sanitation. The phase was characterised by growing environmental awareness, not least because of the Seveso disaster in 1976. There were an increased number of environmental associations that added a greater dimension of conflict with industry. However, Pesaro (1999) notes that in this period, the weight of public opinion was still low, the opposition from industry to environmental policy was still very high and the implementation and enforcement of laws was slow and difficult. In addition, the statutes were often the result of European Community directive transposition. The available policy instruments in this phase were mainly command and control instruments while the proposed solutions for pollution control were almost exclusively end of pipe (Pesaro, 1999) though there were indeed signs that policy should address environmental problems in an integrated manner and, moreover, encourage the development of new cleaner technology.

The Ministry of the Environment was instituted in 1986. In its first years of existence, it issued a variety of norms regarding waste disposal, the institution of new national parks, dangerous substances and the limit to noise pollution (Lewanski, 1997). Though the Ministry of the Environment was not starting from scratch (existing policy measures were abundant), the first years of the Ministry's activity up till the early 1990s were to a large extent absorbed by the need to respond to recurring emergencies and disasters, while trying to catch up with the policy capacity of the other similarly developed Western nations by completing the legislative 'tool box', obtaining and spending financial resources, and developing an administrative structure (Ramieri et al., 1999). Politicians and thus central Government were placed under pressure due to the growing increase in domestic concern over environmental issues and, more importantly, the need to implement European Directives. National environmental policy thus became known as the 'politics of emergency' and resulted in being largely fragmentary and incomplete, 'often elaborated through a patchwork of measures in other sectors but never integrated in a comprehensive way' (Marchetti, 1996).

Ramieri et al. (1999) note that institutional capacity has been gradually upgraded through a strengthening of the Ministry itself in terms of the power it has and the finances and resources it controls, but also thanks to the creation of new technical agencies – such as ANPA, the Italian National Environment Agency. This was set up in 1994 in response to the outcome of a popular referendum which determined that an environmental control and monitoring system should operate in autonomy from that of the health service. Each region also has to set up its own branch (ARPA), though not all regions have yet done so.

However, it is only in recent years that there has been a progressive and perceivable move from basic environmental protection to an approach which somewhat embraces broader concepts such as sustainable development. This is mirrored by the use of new instruments such as taxes (the most notable example is the recent CO_2 tax (L. 448/1998)), eco-labels, eco-audits and negotiated agreements. There is now great emphasis on Italian commitments deriving from the Kyoto protocol and the 'Climate Pact' (November 1998), which is an agreement between the Government, NGOs and industry, according to which negotiated agreements are to be the favoured policy tool to address climate change in Italy (Ramieri et al., 1999). However, Pesaro (1999) notes that the first obstacle to an adequate use of these kinds of instruments in Italy is still the actors' difficulty to interact in this new way and to understand the conditions and constraints of such a system. Even if a significant improvement in the quality of the agreements can be seen, the effectiveness of the agreement still appears to be strictly tied to actors capability and willingness to create new and wider policy networks and ways of interaction.

2.3 The Legal and Administrative Framework for NAs in Italy

Croci (1998) highlights that the diffusion of negotiated agreements as environmental policy instruments in Italy can only come about through the reform of public administration and administrative procedures. In this regard, Law 241/90 on the administrative system ('Nuove norme in materia di procedimento amministrativo e di diritto di accesso ai documenti amministrativi') introduces agreements and planning contracts. Art. 11 provides that within an administrative process, private subjects can conclude an agreement with a public authority. This agreement can either better specify the contents of the final measure (supplementary agreement) or it can substitute the final measure itself (substitutive agreement). Croci (1998) notes that these possibilities have been little exploited in practice, mainly because of the lack of preparation on the part of the public administration to manage this new instrument and, also, the lack of stimulus from private actors.

There are two other sources of law which define forms of negotiation between public authorities and private parties. Art. 203 of the 1996 national financial law and the Intergovernmental Board of Economic Planning (CIPE) resolution of March 1997 provide for new types of co-operative planning instruments which tend, however, to give the public body the dominant role. These forms of negotiation are listed below:

1. negotiated planning *(programmazione negoziata)*: an agreed regulation between public and private subjects;
2. legal understanding *(intesa istituzionale)*: an agreement concerning long-term planning;
3. planning framework agreement *(accordo di programma quadro)*: an agreement between local authorities and private parties to implement that which is planned under item 2;
4. territorial agreement *(patto territoriale)*: an agreement between local authorities and other public or private subjects to implement local development projects; both public and private subjects can promote these agreements;
5. programme contract *(contratto di programma)*: a contract amongst competent public authorities, industries, unions and representative bodies

to promote projects in conformity with negotiated planning as under item 1;

6.   area contract *(contratto d'area)*: a contract amongst administrative parties and workers and employers representatives to promote development projects in less developed areas.

Out of the above agreements, those considered most similar to environmental agreements as defined by the European Commission are the planning framework agreement and the territorial agreement. More recent studies however have suggested that territorial agreements are even closer as they allow for public or private actors to promote the agreements. Although binding, the legal procedure does not foresee the use of sanctions, which are thus included if those party to the agreement choose to do so. For area contracts or territorial pacts, however, if the monitoring process shows discrepancies between the project agreed to be carried out and what is actually taking place, the funds can eventually be withdrawn.

The first provision for a 'voluntary agreement' to be used specifically as an environmental policy instrument appeared in the 'Decreto Ronchi', or rather, decree nr.22/97 on waste disposal. This decree implements the European Directives 91/156/EEC on waste, 91/689/EEC on special waste and 94/62/EC on packaging and packaging waste. Here, a voluntary agreement is defined as:

An official agreement concluded between the competent public authorities and the interested economic sectors, open to all actors who wish to take part; which discipline the means, the instruments and the actions for reaching the objectives in Art. 37.

The decree also specifies the conditions in which authorisation can be given, the context and application of agreements and the way in which agreements are to be drawn up. The decree also provides for the creation of a new obligatory Consortium (CONAI) that has the promotion of agreements on programmes with the regions and local bodies as part of its duties (these, however, are agreements between public partners, with the notable absence of a private partner). The Ministry of Environment and the Ministry of Industry, Commerce and Artisans have certain other duties and can promote agreements on programmes between the companies involved in the life cycle of durable domestic goods. These agreements can be concluded at regional, provincial and municipal levels (Article 22). Their objectives are to improve the management of waste, packaging and special waste with the contribution of the public authorities.

More recently, Article 28 in the legislative decree on water (no. 152, 1999) foresees that the competent authorities can promote and underwrite programme agreements and contracts with private subjects, with the aim of reducing the pollution of water and also its use.

2.4 Tackling the Problem

The European and Italian regulators have issued a number of laws and recommendations to reduce the level of emissions resulting from gasoline which we report below.

- European Regulation 441/87/CEE on the quality of gasoline;
- DPCM *(Decreto Presidente del Consiglio dei Ministri)* 240/88 on the sulphur content in oil products. The maximum level of sulphur in oil products is fixed at 0.3 per cent of weight;
- Decreto Legislativo 27/1/1992 Nr.97;
- European Regulation 93/12 on the level of sulphur in oil products;
- *Decreto Ministeriale* 152/94, that regulates the control of benzene in oil products;
- Law no. 413 of 4 November 1997, which concerns the benzene content in gasoline sold in Italy.

The negotiated agreements represent the first step in regulating the emission of benzene, which was then superseded by command and control regulation once the pertinent firms were capable of complying with the obligations foreseen by Law nr.413 of 4 November 1997 which regulates the maximum level of benzene in gasoline and the level of air emissions in Italy. In addition to law nr. 413/1997, the responsibility of monitoring gasoline quality passed from the Ministry of Industry's monitoring agency to ANPA (National Environmental Protection Agency): refineries and terminals (about 60 plants) today send on all their data on benzene and aromatics levels in gasoline to ANPA.

Regarding the technical solutions for this particular problem, in recent years, the oil industry in Italy has played a crucial role in the reduction of the benzene content in gasoline. There are four main solutions that have been identified for the improvement of gasoline environmental quality, solutions that were well known at the time of the agreements;

- the first is the reduction of benzene in the refining process, by extracting the carcinogenic product after the reforming process;
- the second solution is given by a special selection of crude oils to be refined; for instance, the raw materials that are extracted in Middle

Eastern countries have, in general, a lower benzene content. This solution is however, only considered theoretical because of logistic problems related to the optimal refining cycle;

- the third solution is an increase in the level of hydrogen in the refining process. This solution will decrease the level of benzene, but increase the hydrogen demand and therefore its production, which has consequences in terms of other higher pollutant emissions from the refining processes;

- other solutions are related to end-of-pipe processes: in particular low benzene gasoline, if associated with the use of vehicles with catalytic converters can significantly reduce the level of benzene emitted.

The optimal solution is probably a mix of the solutions described above.

2.5 The Downstream Industry in Italy

The following description of the Italian filling distribution market examines the efficiency of the market and the environmental quality of gasoline in Italy, drawing on comparisons with other member states. It allows a better understanding of the conditions under which, and the motivations for which, the agreements were signed.

If we consider the oil market in Italy we find that AgipPetroli, the market leader, has a market share of almost 20 per cent and is followed by Esso at 10 per cent. Other operators constitute 31 per cent of the market with a single market share of less than 3 per cent.

In recent years the Italian oil distribution sector has remained relatively stable in terms of the operators' relative market shares. The share of companies owned by the State and Italian private companies was 39 per cent in 1972 and 50 per cent in 1999. This has permitted the companies to remain rather static and to cover their inefficiency through their high market share and therefore through high operating profits. However, there have been some developments that have affected the organisation and operative structure of the sector during the course of 1997 and 1998.

2.6 The Italian Motor Fuels Distribution Network

In 1975 the motor-fuels distribution network in Italy reached almost 40 000 sales points. This was the result of a wide expansion which took place in the 1950s and 1960s, on the one hand, because of the related developments in motorization and on the other hand, as a consequence of the authorisation system that was in force from 1950 until 1970 and has been once again adopted instead of the concession system.

The Italian distribution network at year end 1997 comprised 27 100 sales points, 98 per cent of these providing unleaded petrol. Total petrol sales in 1997 were 23 900 000 m^3, of which 23 650 000 m^3 were sold through the sales point network; 51 per cent of petrol sold was unleaded.

The efficiency of the Italian distribution network can be understood by situating it in a European context. In fact, the development of the Italian motor-fuels distribution network can be seen as significantly lagging when placed in such a profile. There are an excessive number of sales points: Italy has 50 per cent more sales points than other European countries which are comparable with Italy (namely, France, the United Kingdom, and Germany). Furthermore, the number of vehicles for each sales point is almost 50 per cent of the average proportion for European countries such as France, Germany, the United Kingdom and Spain.

Of the motor-fuel distribution points, 43 per cent can be classified as small stations located in out-of-the-way places while 28 per cent are mere filling stations. Finally, as a consequence of the large number of sales points the Italian average throughput is one of the lowest in Europe.

Thus, the oil distribution market in Italy is characterised by a high market concentration (oligopolistic market), and in addition, by high industrial and distribution costs and inefficiencies. There are an excessive number of service stations that, in most cases, are small, a low level of average throughput, a low level of non-oil products sold and a low level of automated services such as self-service on payment.

Today the aim is to remove the source of these delays. With Legislative Decree nr. 32 of 11 February 1998 effective as of 20 March 1998, the Government sought to give a strong impulse to the restructuring of the Italian motor-fuels network. In particular, the Decree orders an immediate transfer of the retail distribution network from the concession system to a system based on authorisation; it also orders the streamlining of procedures required to obtain authorisation (a task assigned to the public administrations), and the acceleration of the process of restructuring through the closure of incompatible outlets in order to adjust the Italian network dimension to the European average both in terms of vehicles per sales points and average throughput. In order to comply with what is set out in the legislative decree, the oil companies prepared a detailed voluntary closing plan for 1998. The impact of this plan can be appreciated by looking at the sales point numbers at the end of 1998. During 1998, 2 025 sales points were closed while the number of closures during 1997 was 670.

Regarding the market leader, the Eni (AgipPetroli and IP) motor-fuels distribution network in Italy fell from 10 615 in 1997 to 9 828 sales points in 1998. This down-trend should lead to 8 000 sales points in 2002, and, at the same time, the average throughput of each outlet should rise from 1.47 million litres in 1998 to 1.9 million litres in 2002.

2.7 Taxation

Since the 1950s, the presence of public authorities in the Italian oil market has been reflected in the heavy taxation on oil products as well as in the determination of prices. In 1998 (Unione Petrolifera, 1999b) total fiscal revenue from oil products reached 62 300 billion lire, of which 46 500 billion came from excise taxes and the remaining 15 800 from VAT. Over the last two years the Government has not raised excise taxes on oil products in order to help bring inflation down while on 1 October 1997 VAT was raised from 19 to 21 per cent. In 1998, the main contributor to excise tax revenue was petrol, which made up 54 per cent of total revenues deriving from oil products. In 1998 estimated revenues from the sole source of excise duty on energy products (excluding VAT) totalled 56 100 billion lire (1.5 percent with respect to 1997): 47 000 billion came from mineral oils, 3 400 from electrical energy, and 5 700 from methane gas.

The Italian tax regulations appear muddled and penalising for the oil industry. They are characterised by a large number of rates of taxation which reflect different tax concessions depending on the destined use of the petroleum products, thus causing high operating costs and bureaucratic difficulty. Moreover, the fiscal burden is shared out in an unbalanced way over different alternative products (for example, gasoline in comparison with diesel gas-oil, and heating gas-oil compared with methane gas).

It is hoped that the Community harmonisation process could contribute to a profound reorganisation and rationalisation of Italian taxation. It began in 1993 and has resulted in bringing Italian legislation in this field up to date. These changes have, however, yet to be fully applied to those procedures, which are designed to guarantee that Italian operators enjoy the same competitive conditions, as do operators in the main member states.

In the 1990s, with the increase in environmental concern, taxation on energy products should provide consumers with signals on those more polluting products, but only partial interventions have been chosen. Law nr. 449 of 27 December 1997 introduced a taxation system on emissions of SO_2 and NO_x from large-scale combustion plants as of 1 January 1998, while the Government, with Article 8 of law no. 448 of 23 December 1998 determined the carbon tax rates which will come into effect by 1 January 2005. However, the criteria adopted to fix the excise entity among the different products, do not reflect the *real* contribution of each product to the CO_2 emissions. In addition, the steps were not taken with a view to a necessary harmonisation at the European level: the oil industry has pointed out the need to co-ordinate the environmental tax system within the European Community so as not to alter the conditions of fair competitiveness.

2.8   The Price System

The transition from a system of control to a market system regarding prices has been a long one. The price system in Italy fell under the authority's control in 1944 with the founding of the CIP (Comitato Interministeriale Prezzi). After the events of 1973, the system was rendered inadequate in terms of reflecting changes in the international market (the high variability in the price of raw materials). However, it was only in 1982 that a first step was taken; the beginning of a surveillance system which fixed the maximum price of diesel, heating oil and fuel oil to the average prices in five EEC countries (Germany, France, the United Kingdom, Belgium and the Netherlands).

The process of price liberalisation was started on 16 September 1991 and completed only in 1994.

Deficiencies in the Italian motor-fuels distribution network have been reflected in distribution costs and prices above all. If we regard the price of fuel oil, this appears higher than the European average.

This section has highlighted the peculiarity of the Italian distribution market: the management costs are high for companies and its efficiency is very low. If, however, we consider the quality of gasoline in terms of its environmental characteristics, the situation in Italy emerges as better than in other European countries. This is the result of the negotiated agreements signed between 1989 and 1992 aimed at improving the environmental quality of gasoline.

3.   NEGOTIATION PROCESS

3.1   The Evolution of the Negotiated Agreements

The principle actors involved in negotiating and signing the agreements are the Ministry of Environment, the Ministry of Industry, the Unione Petrolifera and AgipPetroli, the Italian oil company holding the largest market share.

The Unione Petrolifera represents 37 companies, though only eight of these are involved in the specific issue of petrol quality as they carry out refining activities.

At the time of the agreements, AgipPetroli was a publicly owned company. AgipPetroli, is part of the Eni Group and deals with the oil downstream sector, i.e. the refining and distribution market sectors. It operates in Italy with six refineries and about 30 per cent of the overall market share if the controlled company IP (Italiana Petroli) is included. Since 1994, with the transformation of Eni into a para-state company, AgipPetroli has entered the Unione Petrolifera and has been represented since that time in its dealings with other institutional actors. It has, since 1993 and, therefore, after the agreement period, pursued its own policy on questions of health, safety and the environment (HSE).

The relationship between these actors before the agreements was dictated largely by the nature of command and control; the authorities issued the laws and checked that they were respected while the oil sector was passively subject to the laws. Dialogue consisted of the Unione Petrolifera supplying information to the authorities aimed at guaranteeing that the laws were realistic.

Prior to 1989, the large companies showed little sensitivity to environmental matters unless they were urgent in nature. The attitude of the sector was one of seeking to have influence and thus protect its interests following the evolution of the law while ensuring it did not actively demonstrate its willingness to undertake action.

The period in which the agreements were stipulated is characterised by pollution levels in the main Italian urban areas increasing significantly, with emission limits being exceeded many times, thus creating an increase in the level of environmental concern and pressure from stakeholders. When discussions began concerning the problem, there was intense public pressure for a drastic limit to benzene and aromatic compounds in gasoline. Positions were taken by important bodies such as the national Psychological Consultative Committee which recommended a limit to the benzene content to less than 1 per cent and a limit to aromatics of less than 25 per cent. There were, therefore, a series of indications that political intervention concerning the limitation of benzene and aromatic compounds in gasoline was called for.

This is the point at which the Unione Petrolifera (UP) intervened by preparing a dossier for a meeting with the ministries. It recognised that the issue of benzene was a valid one and that, moreover, it was an issue that the sector could tackle. In addition, it affirmed that the aromatic compound problem was a less important one in that focusing on it would make a relatively small contribution to the air quality problem as a whole, while creating enormous problems to the national petrol industry should strict limits be imposed. In this meeting, the Unione Petrolifera showed what the effects of imposing legislation stricter than in other countries on the sector would be. It is said that the Ministers that the UP talked to, were able to understand that what public opinion was demanding was not completely feasible. It was also at this point that the Unione Petrolifera made it clear that they were, however, willing to reach certain targets before the rest of Europe and that they were willing to negotiate. In retrospect, the UP believes that they managed to avoid a law which did little for the environment and potentially damaged part of the industry (Unione Petrolifera, 1999c). In the Unione Petrolifera, there is a 'consultation committee' which makes decisions concerning the sector's strategy. This committee generated the idea of using a programme agreement. The practical in-house approach to the agreements was as follows. Once the problems were perceived on the political level, solutions were sought from the technical groups and from the various refinery technicians. The possible solutions were then approved within the Unione Petrolifera with the companies concerned before negotiations took place at the political level between the executives and the administration of the Unione Petrolifera with the support of this technical information. The meetings took place in the ministries according to an agreed agenda. The Ministry of Industry often sought to co-ordinate or at least, to mediate between the Unione Petrolifera and the Ministry of the Environment.

The 'programme agreements' emerged principally from the sector's intention to avoid the imposition of much stricter legislation which was to include obligations concerning a specified 'maximum' with sanctions in the case that these 'maximum' values were not respected; presenting serious implications for the sector as a whole. Instead, the agreements were created with indications concerning average quality values, thereby leaving the companies flexibility and permitting them to gradually adapt their structures. The industry also had two other needs to protect. The first was that of avoiding an excessive difference between Italian legislation and European legislation. In 1992–93, it was more or less known that in the year 2000, the percentage volume of benzene permitted would be brought down to 1 per cent. Therefore, there was the possibility that Italy would be regulated by a law that imposed this standard from 1992, seven or eight years before other countries, with the consequence of creating competition problems on a European scale. The second aspect was that related to the aromatics. If these had been limited in that period, there would have been serious problems for the industry in terms of gasoline formulation. This is a parameter that the industry has always worked on and through research it has been concluded that, in terms of curbing emissions, its reduction would not be particularly relevant in contributing to environmental protection. As it is a very limiting parameter in terms of the formulation of the petrol and thus its production, the agreements sought to manage the problem of aromatics to the best of their ability. This was borne out in the first agreement, which limited aromatics to a value lower than the European average. It was then later decided to improve the aromatic situation without any binding limits until the rest of Europe decided to impose limits. As a result, there is a limit in Italy that is stricter than that which is stipulated by the European Union.

The implementation costs were fully sustained by the sector involved. No compensation or financial assistance was foreseen in the agreements. The oil sector is obviously regarded as a wealthy one, and also a sector which pollutes and, as a consequence, one that must pay for this (Unione Petrolifera, 1999c). No recognition was given to the possibility of companies that might, in fact, have had problems in making technological changes.

3.2 The Content of the Agreements

The first agreement was signed in February 1989 by the Unione Petrolifera, AgipPetroli, the Italian car producers association, the Ministry of the Environment and the Italian Department for Urban Areas. Its main objectives are the following:

- the reduction of the average level of aromatic hydrocarbons in unleaded gasoline in order for it to contain a similar level of pollutants as in other European countries;
- the reduction of the average benzene content within a year in unleaded gasoline by 0.6 per cent with respect to the average content of benzene in the gasoline at that time;
- to respect, as a minimum, the European standard content of benzene for the gasoline sold in Italy, and, at the same time, a commitment for a further maximum level of benzene at 3 per cent of the volume (therefore a stricter limit than in Europe whose limit represents the minimum standard);
- the implementation of a programme that aims at monitoring the environmental performance of Italian gasoline sold by companies committed in the agreement.

In order to evaluate and give an incentive to the better performance of the agreement, in July 1989, an Observatory for the monitoring and control of gasoline quality was instituted. The Observatory included at least one representative of the Ministries involved in the project, though co-ordinated by the Ministry of Industry, and aimed at monitoring:

- the gasoline quality on the basis of the data self-declared by the oil companies every three months;
- the implementation of a two-year research programme on new technologies and the chemical effects of air emissions.

Thus the role of the Observatory was one of monitoring gasoline environmental quality and implementing the research programme on new technologies rather than that of sanctioning.

The agreement was operative as of 90 days after approval of the law and the objective was effective from this date. The programme was implemented within a year.

The second agreement, stipulated in December 1991, followed the implementation of a series of ministerial ordinances for the control of air quality in urban areas. The signatories are the Municipality of Rome, the Unione Petrolifera, the Italian car producers association (ACI). The agreement principally comprised the following elements:

- the definition of deadlines for the average emission limits in the seven urban areas involved in the agreement. The content of benzene was not to exceed the limit of 2.5 per cent of the volume;
- commitment for the diffusion of unleaded gasoline in the urban areas by increasing awareness in the marketing network and thus the supply of those products;
- commitment for the distribution of unleaded gasoline with a low content of benzene and aromatic hydrocarbons and low environmental impact in the seven urban areas involved in the agreement;
- periodic and systematic quality control and monitoring of the unleaded gasoline distributed in the seven urban areas. Comparison, by February 1992, of the benzene content of all other leaded gasoline distributed in Italy and Europe.

This agreement established accurate deadlines: 1 January 1992 for the quality requirements for refinery production, before 1 February 1992 and until 30 April 1992 for the quality of the products sold in the selected urban areas (with substitution of the gasoline stocks).

Finally, the third agreement was signed in October 1992. Industry committed itself to a widening of the activities already under way in the metropolitan areas through an improvement in the quality of petrol products in different regions in order to propose an alternative solution to regulation through the direct definition of a standard for the average benzene content for all gasoline on a national scale. The agreement was signed by the Unione Petrolifera, AgipPetroli, the Ministry of Environment, the Ministry of Industry and the Ministry of Health. This agreement substituted the 1989 agreement.

The commitments in the agreement are the following:

- The reduction of the average content of sulphur in the oil products to 0.2 per cent volume. The reduction was progressive in the different regions and national areas but by 1 October 1994 all oil products sold in Italy were to respect this limit.
- Industry commits itself to limit the average content of benzene for all the gasoline distributed at a national level to 3 per cent volume (for all the gasoline distributed at national level from all the service stations and not only for the unleaded gasoline as in the previous agreements).

The agreement was operational from 1 November 1992. Some benefits were complementary to the agreement. An information dissemination campaign was planned from January to April 1992 in collaboration with the ministries and the oil companies and aimed at the diffusion of products with low environmental impact.

In addition, the partners of the agreement proposed a fiscal differentiation system based on the quality of gasoline to the Government and the Ministry of Finance. If high environmental quality gasoline standards were respected, the Government could implement a sort of fiscal differentiation on the basis of the expected environmental impacts. However, the fiscal differentiation mechanism did not develop and remained a proposal. At present, the Unione Petrolifera is still discussing a possible tax differentiation regarding 'polluting' and 'non-polluting' products with the Ministry of Environment.

It is interesting to note the marketing strategy unilaterally adopted by AgipPetroli in 1992. AgipPetroli introduced a voluntary limit of 1 per cent volume maximum content of benzene for the gasoline sold on the national market, anticipating the law that fixed this limit for 1 July 1999, a limit which may have been influential in the formulation of the legislative standard.

4. ANALYSIS

The objectives of the agreement process were to improve the environmental quality of gasoline without however resorting to the use of a command and control regime which would, in consideration of both uncertainties over the technical feasibility of resolving the problem and standards in other member states, damage the sector in Italy.

The initial negotiations not only succeeded in resulting in an agreement, but also led to an established negotiation process, alternating with the design of successive agreements, over the following three years. The regulator appears to have used the process to evaluate the feasibility of the limits defined in the agreements and later superseded by those achieved by the leading oil company, AgipPetroli, as potential standards for legislative emission limits. Therefore, the agreements have been used as an assessment instrument for the definition of legally binding emission limits and it is possible to affirm that negotiated agreements can be used as effective instruments in substituting command and control policy.

It is true that the real threat motivating the agreements is future legislative compliance; companies understand that the respect of the agreement limits of emission will represent future legislative compliance. It was only later that companies realised that better environmental gasoline quality could be used as a competitive instrument too.

It is clear that the negotiated agreement offered advantages to both parties. This can partially justify the disappointment of the companies when the limits became regulated exclusively by law. The Government was able, due to the power of the oil industry in Italy, to realise the goals it had set out for the environmental problem and the results even went beyond actual existing legislation (the actual average benzene percentage in the gasoline is 0.67 per cent, the legislative limit 1 per cent of the volume). Industry, on the other hand, could make their long-term planning within a stable framework and could choose the most efficient way of dealing with their emissions.

The objectives described in all the agreements can be considered as fulfilled. The data analysed by the Observatory on gasoline quality showed an average content of benzene of 1.3 per cent volume for unleaded gasoline, and 1.4 per cent volume for leaded gasoline in the period considered. The overall benzene emissions, from 1991 to 1995, decreased by 15 per cent. During the last three months of 1996, the average percentage of benzene in gasoline was 1.2 per cent volume.

This outcome has also been obtained as a result of the voluntary commercialisation of gasoline with 1 per cent volume maximum content of benzene. In fact, in 1992 AgipPetroli introduced this voluntary limit for the gasoline sold on the national market, anticipating the law that fixed this limit for 1 July 1999. This nationwide distribution of unleaded gasoline with a maximum benzene content level of 1 per cent thus anticipated deadlines foreseen by both national and European regulations.

The target of a maximum content of 1 per cent, guaranteed at every single outlet in the AgipPetroli chain selling unleaded gasoline, was reached through the determination of the company to develop the quality of its products. This has cost around 600 billion lire in six years of research and modifications to the refining plants. The quality improvements in AgipPetroli gasoline between 1993–96 has led to a reduction of more than 17 per cent in benzene from cars fitted with a catalytic converter, while emissions from vehicles without a converter and using leaded fuel have fallen by more than

20 per cent; emissions from vehicles without a converter but using unleaded fuel have fallen by more than 25 per cent.[2] A conservative estimate puts the reduction in benzene emissions at around 2 500 tons in the period 1993-96, taking into account quality improvements in AgipPetroli gasoline and changes in the pool of vehicles on the roads. A complementary effect has been that there was a shift in gasoline market competition from purely commercial considerations to technological competition, which benefits AgipPetroli and enhances its role as a leader in the improvement of the environment.

These results have been estimated as the best environmental performance on a European level. It has been estimated that the increasing diffusion of catalytic vehicles and the improved quality of fuels will decrease the overall emissions of benzene in Italy by 58 per cent in the year 2000.

Although the Italian oil market distribution is still very static, the environmental agreements allowed for an improvement in the environmental performance, even better than in the other countries in which market forces are stronger. It is possible that such performance can be attributed to the anticipation on the part of the oil companies of future competitiveness in the distribution sector, and, consequently, to a policy regarding market differentiation based on environmental performance.

Learning has undoubtedly taken place through the negotiated agreement process. The regulator, on one hand, and industry, on the other, decided to use voluntary instruments to reach environmental objectives and to overcome the uncertainty related to the definition of emission limits which can be respected feasibly by industry. Here, the negotiated agreements are thus used as instruments to reduce the level of asymmetric information between the signatories: the Government has, through the Observatory instituted by the agreements, the possibility to monitor and control the environmental performance of industry that, on the other hand, can use the agreements to inform the public authorities about the technical limitations of its production processes.

5. CONCLUSION

The concentration of the oil market and the urgency of the environmental problem in some critical urban areas pointed to negotiated agreements as the best instruments to reach significant results in a brief period. The instruments were proposed as a self-regulating solution by which it was possible to respond to industry's immediate negative reaction to the possibility of introducing a command and control regime regarding benzene content in gasoline.

Though the firms identified this voluntary solution as best for improving environmental quality, in a later period, the regulator chose a command and control policy as the optimal instrument for obtaining better environmental performance. The second step was, in fact, the introduction of a set of legislative standards. Even if the main motivation for choosing negotiated agreements was the need to arrive progressively at a standard to be used in future legislation, in this case, negotiated agreements have indeed represented valid and successful instruments for the regulator to assess the feasibility of the limit to be imposed by legislation. By only testing the capacity of the companies to reach the standards, the regulator can impose the same standards on the companies that are followers in the market. Understandably, the companies adhering to the commitments in the agreements demonstrated a certain level of disappointment regarding the intention of the regulator to pursue a command and control policy.

The Agip-Unione Petrolifera negotiated agreements have been revealed as environmentally effective, economically efficient - by allowing the firms some flexibility in timing their investments optimally - and furthermore, able to create new consensus based relationships between key institutional actors and the sector. The actors involved in this case have indicated that they consider it a valid instrument to be used in a policy mix with others and the Unione Petrolifera is currently considering the use of negotiated agreements for other issues.

NOTES

1. International institutions like ACGIH (American Conference of Governmental Industrial Hygienist), IARC, OSHA, NIOSH recognise benzene as a carcinogenic agent.
2. AgipPetroli estimates based on Concawe calculation models for vehicle emissions (Concawe is the oil companies' European organisation for environment, health andsafety).

BIBLIOGRAPHY

AgipPetroli (1999a), *Annual Report 1998*, AgipPetroli Eni Group, Italy
AgipPetroli (1999b), *Environmental Report*, AgipPetroli, Eni Group, Italy
Croci, Edoardo (1998), 'L'evoluzione della normativa italiana sugli accordi volontari', in Paola Amadei, Edoardo Croci and Giulia Pesaro (eds), *Nuovi Strumenti di Politica Ambientale: Gli Accordi Volontari*, Milan: Franco Angeli.
Lewanski, Rodolfo (1997), *Governare l'ambiente,* Bologna: Il Mulino.
Marchetti, Alessandra (1996), 'Climate change politics in Italy', in Tim O' Riordan and Jill Jaeger. (eds), *Politics of Climate Change: a European Perspective*, Global Environmental Change Programme, London and New York: Routledge, pp. 298–329.

Pesaro, Giulia (1999). 'The development of an effective co-operation between public and economic actors in environmental voluntary agreements', paper published at the CAVA Workshop, organised by AKF, Copenhagen, Denmark.

Ramieri, E., Wallace-Jones, J. and Lewanski, R. (1999), 'The process of LA21 implementation in Italy: where will top down meet bottom up?' Draft paper presented at the Conference: Towards a Sustainable Society in the New Millennium, 10–12 June 1999, Umea, Sweden.

Unione Petrolifera (1999a) *Staffetta quotidiana no 56*, Unione Petrolifera, Rome, Italy.

Unione Petrolifera (1999b), *Unione Petrolifera Annual Report 1998*, Unione Petrolifera, Rome, Italy.

Unione Petrolifera (1999c), Interview, *Unione Petrolifera*, Rome, Italy.

Unione Petrolifera (2000a), *Environmental Report 1999*, Unione Petrolifera, Rome, Italy.

Unione Petrolifera (2000b), Unione Petrolifera *Annual Report 1999*, Unione Petrolifera, Rome, Italy.

8. The Eco-Emballages Case Study: Domestic Packaging Waste in France

Franck Aggeri

1. INTRODUCTION

With regard to negotiated agreements, the case of domestic packaging waste is the first one where an open and transparent negotiation, close to the recommendations of the European Commission (COM (96).561), was implemented in France. Indeed, the signing of the decree of 1992 and the creation of the Eco-Emballages consortium was preceded by a phase of consultation and discussion with all the parties concerned, by a large co-operation, reinforced by two reports, and by public debates. This case has been the subject of several reports and studies (see in particular Glachant and Whiston, 1996; Defeuilley et al., 1997; Godard, 1998). But if these studies emphasize the negotiation process which led to the decree of 1992, and the organisation of the Eco-Emballages scheme, they do not focus on the implementation phase for the reason the system was just at its beginnings at the moment these reports were written. The most recent theoretical report carried out by Defeuilley et al. (1997) was rather critical on the Eco-Emballages scheme, putting forward that the results obtained were disappointing (low volumes, insufficient separate collection, pre-eminence of incineration over recycling) and explaining them by the poor level of incentives contained in the agreement, which locked the system in a sub-optimal trajectory.

Taking into account the progress accomplished recently, we will have a more positive evaluation of the French system. First, the environmental performance has improved and is accelerating, in particular, the rate of recycling and the level of separate collection. This environmental performance is still far behind those of northern European countries, but the economic cost of the system is much lower than the German system for instance. Second, thanks to several experiments, there is now a much better knowledge of the technology, of the geographical and social constraints of separate collection and the most cost-efficient organisations to set up according to the different socio-geographical context. In this perspective, the issue of incentives must be put back in a broader framework, taking into account the collective learning processes which have occurred and the issues of co-ordination and monitoring which are central in a context where a multi-actor co-operation process is required. For instance, collective learning processes made it possible in 2000 to change the rules of the Eco-Emballages scheme, especially the aspects relating to incentives, even if these changes could have occurred earlier. The latter point reveals, as we shall see it later in section 4, the contradiction between a consensus-seeking approach which leads to inertia and the need for a stronger monitoring system which would be required to introduce more incentives and limit free-riding. We shall organise these elements according to the following plan: in the second section, after describing the issue to be dealt with, we will present the institutional context in France. In the third section, we will recall the phase of negotiation that led to the signing of the decree of 1992 and the creation of Eco-Emballages. Then, we will present the Eco-Emballages scheme and its principles. In the fourth section, we will evaluate the results obtained eight years after the signing of the decree, by underlining the strong disparities obtained according to the municipalities and recycling channels, and by discussing to what extent results could have improved faster with a more appropriate monitoring system.

2. CONTEXT

2.1 The Domestic Packaging Waste Problem

The production of domestic packaging waste is considerable. Between 1960 and 1990, domestic waste production rose by 64 per cent whilst packaging-waste has more than doubled (Quirion, 1994). The production of domestic waste per inhabitant which was of 220 kg/year in 1960 has reached 450 kg/year (Source: ADEME) in 1998, that is an increase of nearly 25 million tons a year. Among these 25 million tons, the domestic packaging waste production represents approximately 5 million tons (source: ADEME, 2000). In domestic packaging waste all the variety of materials is found: plastics, glass, steel, aluminium, paper, cardboard and so on. This continuous growth has led to a progressive saturation of landfill sites and incinerator capacities. The potential for near saturation of existing capacity treatment is reinforced by the 'NIMBY' (Not In My Back Yard) syndrome whereby local populations are hostile to the location of new landfills or incinerators (Glachant and Whiston, 1996). In

1996, of the 37.2 million tons of domestic and other comparable waste, 58 per cent were landfilled, 29 per cent incinerated (22 per cent with energy recovery) and only 12 per cent recycled or composted (Source: ADEME, 1998). The saturation of landfill and incineration capacities has been a major driving force for public intervention and for the promotion of material recycling.

2.2 The Actors: a Complex Waste Chain

A large number of actors are involved in the packaging waste chain such as material producers, conditioners (packagers), distributors, private individuals, municipalities that collect waste, and all the actors in the valorisation and processing circuit (landfill, incineration, sorting, recycling). At the upper level, we find packaging manufacturers and material producers. They are vertically integrated and specialised by material. At the intermediate level, consumer goods industries use packaging. We will call these firms (Coca Cola, Nestlé, Danone and so on) 'packagers'. At the lower level, the municipalities are responsible for the waste treatment, according to French law. To realise this waste treatment, small and medium size municipalities often co-operate in inter-municipal unions for waste collection (SICTOM in french) or in inter-municipal unions for waste valorisation (SIVOM) in order to obtain economies of scale. These structures, financed by municipal taxes, organise the collection, the sorting and often the incineration of waste. Municipalities may also choose to delegate these activities to specialised waste management companies (generally big companies like Vivendi or Lyonnaise des Eaux). The development of recycling activities has brought new steps and new actors to this waste chain:

1. a prerequisite for recycling is the need for separate collection and the sorting of the different materials to be recycled. This implies specific devices (different garbage cans for the different materials) and new equipment (specific trucks, sorting plants);
2. once the materials are sorted they are oriented towards specialised recycling plants which process them and sell the recycling materials to material producers or packaging manufacturers. The value of these materials is very different according to the kind of material (high value for aluminium, low for glass, cardboard or paper) and to the quality of the raw material, that is, the quality of the sorting activity. The economic balance of these different channels depends on the one hand, on the value of the recycled product and on the other hand, on the complexity, and thus the costs, of waste chain treatment.

Except for glass, the recycling of packaging waste was uncommon ten years ago. There were recycling channels for glass, paper/cardboard, steel or aluminium but these channels did not use packaging waste. There were strong uncertainties about technologies, organisation and costs for separate collection and sorting, as well as for new recycling channels and materials like plastics. Therefore, it was difficult to evaluate the optimal level of environmental targets.

2.3 The Institutional Context in France

2.3.1 The waste legal framework
Facing a growing quantity of waste and the development of uncontrolled landfill, a first law on waste was ratified in 1975 in France. This law defines four basic principles:

1. the law defines the concept of waste treatment which only deals with harmful matter and can be done only in facilities approved by the administration;
2. the law assigns the responsibility and cost of household waste elimination to local authorities and the latter are obliged to provide the population with a household management service;
3. the law creates a national agency (ANRED) in charge of both facilitating treatment and recovery operations;
4. the law recommends the development of prevention and waste valorisation. After the signing of this law, local authorities started to invest in treatment facilities. In the 1970s, the cheapest solutions were chosen, that is controlled landfill and incineration, but prevention and waste valorisation were largely ignored.

The law of 1992 supplements the preceding one, by defining the concept of 'ultimate waste', by specifying the concept of valorisation, by creating a tax on landfill and by creating 'un plan départemental d'élimination des déchets', that is the obligation for administrative 'districts', to define, with all the parties concerned, plans for waste elimination. The decree nr. 96-1008 of November 1996 defines the missions and rules of this plans for waste elimination. In particular, these plans, involving all the parties concerned, have to regulate the incineration, landfill and recycling capacities in each département, to plan new investments, taking into account the needs for the future in terms of waste volumes to be treated and taking into account the decisions and preferences – concerning waste valorisation – made at the municipal level.

At the European level, packaging waste was identified as one of the 'waste streams priorities' in 1989, and a pilot group was set up to prepare a Directive.

At the same time, similar groups were organised in the different member states, like in France or Germany. Concerning waste incineration, it should be remembered that, in the past few years, the legislation has become more and more stringent. At the European level, a Directive for dangerous waste incineration was ratified in 1991, with an amendment in 1996. Another for common waste incineration was ratified in 1998. Severe emission limits for dioxine, NO_x, SO_2 and so on are imposed in these Directives, as well, as the obligation of treating the incineration residues (cinders, ashes). To comply with these regulations, incinerators must have been adapted with important investments for dust and fumes treatment, which contribute to increase the incineration cost. It is against this legislative and regulatory background, that the preparation of the French decree on domestic packaging waste must be interpreted.

3. NEGOTIATION PROCESS

3.1 The European Negotiations

At the EU level, the preparation of the Directive began in 1990. A first draft was issued in 1991. Very ambitious recycling and recovery targets (90 per cent for recovery and 60 per cent for recycling within five years) were set, and the stabilisation of packaging production was targeted. Between 1991 and 1994, an intense negotiation with industrialists and with different EU members took place. An opposition rapidly appeared between northern countries (Germany, Denmark and the Netherlands) which were in favour of ambitious recycling objectives and others, like France and the UK which invoked the uncertainties about technical options and about the economic costs which could be incurred. The Directive adopted in December 1994 was closer to the French position. It ended up with the withdrawal of the waste reduction objective, and defined a valorisation target of 50 per cent to be reached in 2001 of which a recycling target of minimum 15 per cent per material. Contrary to the French decree, which only concerns domestic packaging waste, these targets concern all kinds of packaging waste, including industrial packaging waste.

In the European process, the first mover was Germany. The Federal Minister (M. Töpfer) initiated the process in 1989. In 1990, a first draft was produced including very stringent objectives (80–90 per cent recycling by 1995, excluding incineration, a mandatory returnable system for certain kinds of packaging, an obligation for retailers to take back the packaging placed in the neighbourhood, the obligation for retailers and packagers to undertake recycling). This draft received a very negative reaction from industrialists. Then, retailers and packagers made a counterproposal: the creation of a private consortium (the Duales-System) in charge of collecting fees on new packages, to finance the efforts to reach the objectives of recycling. The Federal Government reacted positively to this proposition and an Ordinance was adopted in 1991.

3.2 The French Negotiation

In contrast to Germany which engaged in a unilateral policy that finally turned out to be a negotiated one with industrialists, French authorities (the Ministry for the Environment) privileged, from the beginning, a more concerted approach with the industrialists and municipalities. This approach was based on two main motives: first a robust compromise would be easier to obtain after real co-operation took place, and second there was a consensus among French authorities and industrialists to reject the German project and to produce as quickly as possible a counter-proposal for the coming European Directive. A major dialogue with the industrial interests and municipalities, was reinforced by the mission that M. Lalonde, Minister for the Environment, gave to M. Beffa and M. Riboud, who were respectively, chairman of Saint-Gobain and BSN. They were asked by M. Lalonde to produce a report explaining the situation and the issues at stake and deriving from it recommendations for public action. M. Lalonde announced a valorisation target (recycling or incineration with energy recovery) of 75 per cent by 2002 for domestic packaging waste. To meet these targets, these reports recommended the creation of a private consortium, run by packagers, to finance, organise and support packaging valorisation. The propositions included in the reports were taken over, with very few modifications, by public authorities in the decree of April 1992.

3.3 The Setting of the Eco-Emballages Scheme

3.3.1 The decree nr. 92-377 of April 1992

The broad outline of the decree was to develop domestic packaging waste valorisation (including material recycling and incineration with energy recovery) and the obligation for packagers to set up, or to delegate to a third party, a system to meet these objectives. It was written that the consortium or firm in charge of these operations had to receive the approval of public authorities for its activity and that precise quantitative targets for valorisation would be defined in the approval. After this decree, an 'arrêté' (decree) of 23 July 1992 created a consultative commission of 33 members including 16 representatives of industrialists (packagers, distributors, conditioners, material producers, recyclers), six of municipalities, three of NGOs, three of consumers and five representatives of public authorities. This commission had to meet at least once a year and was empowered to deliver the permit to the consortium(s), acting as the delegate(s) for packagers. The permit was given for six years at most, and, in exchange, the consortium(s) had to comply with several requirements. These two regulatory texts created the conditions of a co-operation between public authorities, industrialists and municipalities. In this perspective, the creation of a consultative commission marked the beginning of different negotiated agreements (approvals).

3.3.2 The nature of the Eco-Emballages scheme
Following this decree, a private consortium, called Eco-Emballages,[1] which was recommended by the Beffa and Riboud reports, received the approval from public authorities. Created by the initiative of packagers (BSN, Nestlé, Coca Cola and so on), these companies hold 80 per cent of the capital of Eco-Emballages. In the approval, it was written that Eco-Emballages had to meet a 75 per cent valorisation target for domestic packaging waste in 2002. This target only concerns the domestic packaging waste volume contributing to the Eco-Emballages scheme, and not the whole quantity of packaging waste (see section 4). According to this initial agreement, Eco-Emballages had basically four missions to comply with:

1. finance the collection and valorisation of packaging waste undertaken by municipalities;
2. stimulate the development of domestic packaging waste by different means (communication, advertisement);
3. diffuse the minimal technical prescriptions (PTM) of recyclers to the municipalities;
4. guarantee the contracts and outlets between municipalities and recyclers.

The basic idea was, indeed, that the creation of valorisation channels, of sorting sites, and the development of separate collection was going to cost. To ensure this financing mission, Eco-Emballages collects a fee on each new package sold, depending on the volume and the weight of the package. At the beginning, fees were low (EUR cent 0.15/package) and undifferentiated according to the materials, even if these materials had different values for recycling. For instance, the recycling of aluminium cans can be a profitable activity while the recycling of plastics is costly, due to high costs of collection and treatment. According to economic theory, uniform fees do not provide any incentives for packagers since they are not encouraged to select the most 'recyclable' materials, which would make it possible to reduce the pollution at the source. Three explanations can be given for this initial decision:

1. pressure from material producers was important, in particular from those who had large market shares and high recycling costs (plastic producers) while consensus was sought to avoid initial conflicts and free-riding;
2. a progressive take-off was forecasted, which meant that fees should be adjusted progressively;
3. over all, technical and economic uncertainties about technologies (for recycling and collection) and costs made it very risky to impose highly differentiated fees without creating a distortion of competition.

In exchange for the fee, packagers could print a 'green dot' on their packages to show their commitment with respect to the environment. The collected funds were primarily used for financing the efforts of municipalities or delegates (waste management companies). The system rests on several contracts between municipalities and recyclers, in which, municipalities have to meet technical specifications (Minimal Technical Prescriptions) in order to receive subsidies from Eco-Emballages, depending on the type of material and on the volume sorted. Principally, this support is oriented towards operational activities rather than investments. The collected money is also earmarked to support and guarantee the prices of the sorted materials, that is the price to which municipalities sell their collected materials to recyclers. The objective was that this financial support covered the extra costs incurred by municipalities in separate collection, sorting and recycling. At the beginning of the system, the financial support from Eco-Emballages towards municipalities was mainly directed towards pilot site experiments (see next section) which represented 60 per cent of the expenses (12 out of 20 million euro in 1994). With the development of separate collection, the expenses have notably increased (passing from 20 to 125 million Euro between 1994 and 1999) and are now divided as follows: 77 per cent towards separate collection, 10 per cent towards incineration with energy recovery, 9 per cent towards local communication and 4 per cent for others.

The Eco-Emballages scheme is based on incentives. At the packager level, the fee represents, in principle, an incentive to lower the quantity of material used, that is to encourage source reduction. In fact, as Quirion (1994) points out, packagers are not so much sensitive to prices (low elasticity) for two reasons. First, customers are also sensitive to other aspects like marketing, design and utility.[2] Second, costs can be easily recaptured by packagers in the price of final products. In any case, fees have not been, until now, sufficient to encourage prevention. Sometimes, pressures towards recycling have played an important role like in the shift from PVC to PET for plastic water bottles. But this shift is not so much due to economic incentives but to the threat of PVC prohibition. At the municipality level, the financial support given by Eco-Emballages provides an incentive to separate and sort materials. But, as we shall see later, this financial contribution does not always compensate for the investments and operational costs of separate collection. Besides, other factors, like organisational and engineering capabilities of municipalities play also an important motive of involvement in the system. As Glachant and Whiston (1996) point out, one of the originalities of the system lies in the fact that it is managed, not by a fiscal agency, but by a private consortium which is owned by a co-operative group of firms which are in fact tax payers. Thus, the negotiation process has been characterised by a good co-operation between firms and public authorities, even by a degree of voluntarism of firms, especially packagers, who proposed to create Eco-Emballages and to run the system. Two other characteristics are important to stress:

- Complementarity of techniques was also a triggering element of the French system (Defeuilley et al., 1997) in the beginning. In contrast to the German system, no hierarchy was defined for valorisation options in the French one. No specific objective for recycling had been given. In our opinion, this choice is not so much due to a lack of voluntarism but rather to the initial level of uncertainties. In other words, the French position was to keep the different options open rather than taking the risk of engaging in irreversible – a maybe inefficient – technological trajectories. Nevertheless, each material channel set indicative targets for itself in co-operation with Eco-Emballages, according to the technical and economical conditions they were facing. Indicative recycling targets for materials by 2002 were 60–80 per cent for glass, 25–30 per cent for paper-cardboard, 15 per cent for plastics, 50–60 per cent for steel, 35–40 per cent for aluminium.
- Decentralisation of choices is another element to consider. The responsibility for separate collection and sorting remains in the hands of local authorities which decide whether or not to contract with Eco-Emballages, which in turn decides to privilege incineration or recycling (until 1998). This freedom is consistent with the philosophy of a system based on voluntarism and co-operation. Beside the support of Eco-Emballages, it is important to notice that municipalities and recycling companies receive the financial support from ADEME with respect to their investments. This support can go up to 50 per cent for separate collection and 5 per cent for incineration, which is, of course, an incentive to favour recycling over incineration. Other additional support for investments come from the départements or regions. Thus, for new equipment for collection or sorting plants, financial support can reach 80 per cent.

3.4 A Progressive Take-off

3.4.1 An experiment with 40 pilot municipalities

In a perspective of progressive learning, Eco-Emballages and the ADEME launched a call for projects to experiment with different separate collection schemes and sorting technologies in order to learn more about the possibilities and the costs of different solutions, and to identify the best practices. EUR 35 million were spent to finance investments and provide incentives for municipalities. Forty municipalities or groups of municipalities were selected to participate in this programme.

3.4.2 Socio-geographical context

According to Eco-Emballages and ADEME, the choice of technical and organisational solutions to implement depends on the characteristics the municipalities have to face. Three basic situations have come up during the experimental phase: urban, semi-urban and rural areas. Urban areas are characterised by a strong density of population, high-rise housing, by a lack of space (to put waste containers) and a high rate of turnover among the population. In ancient city centres, like Paris, the configuration of buildings is a big problem for undertaking an appropriate separate collection. Semi-urban areas are characterised by a mix of high-rise housing and residential houses, and therefore by differentiated situations with different strategies to implement. Rural areas are characterised by a low density of population, which means higher costs of transportation and collection, and therefore the impossibility of carrying out a door-to-door collection.

In order to have a deeper understanding of these characteristics, we have interviewed two municipalities facing two different contexts: an inter-municipal association in a rural area dedicated to waste management (SICTOM of South Landes) and an urban municipality (Versailles) with a mix of individual houses and high-rise buildings. Three major lessons can be drawn from these two examples.

First, there is no 'one best way' that could be easily duplicated from one municipality to another. Organisational solutions and an economic balance for recycling activities vary depending on local conditions (type of housing, density of population, proximity of recycling plants, homogeneity of population and so on).

Second, implementing a sustainable separate collection system takes a long time (several years), whatever the municipality size, mainly because it requires the involvement of the whole population whose behaviour and ability to comply with technical requirements are quite unpredictable. It means experimenting, a trial and learning process from which the technical and organisational options will be tested on a group of inhabitants, and progressively spread to the municipality. According to the ADEME, the municipalities which tried a quicker implementation did not always succeed because they often faced quality problems (refusals from recyclers), and therefore increasing costs. In particular, if inhabitants have doubts about the system efficiency, then it is difficult in re-establishing the necessary trust vis-à-vis separate collection.

Third, it is important to notice that these two municipalities can be considered as successful cases or 'fast learners'. First of all, contrary to the first municipalities that contracted with Eco-Eballages, the latter ones benefit from past experiences synthesised by the ADEME and Eco-Emballages. In other words, they did not face the same quality problems other municipalities had faced (see next section) with regards to separate collection. Furthermore, thanks to years of communication and debate in the media at both national and local levels, the population knows much better the constraints and interest of separate collection than five years ago.

3.5 First Difficulties and Controversies

3.5.1 Conflicts about technical prescriptions (PTM)

From 1993 on, several conflicts and controversies appeared about the technical prescriptions (PTM). Several municipalities denounced the too high and changing prescriptions imposed by recyclers, which resulted in a high level of waste refusal. They argued that stability was needed to undertake heavy investments in collection and sorting. This claim was taken over by the association of French municipalities (AMF) who threatened to end the contracts with Eco-Emballages. On the other side, recyclers argued that they needed a level of quality compatible with their process. In fact, it seems that the responsibility for the conflict was shared by both parties: on the one hand, municipalities did not have, at the beginning, an efficient organisation to get a good collection and sorting quality. On the other hand, to prevent any drift, recyclers had defined higher standards than what they could actually tolerate. Besides, they were not used to processing domestic waste materials and therefore they adopted a cautious behaviour. As the quality improved and technical progress intervened, technical prescriptions became less stringent. For instance, in 1992, the plastic recycling channel required that corks were removed from the bottles. This prescription was difficult to respect and resulted in conflicts with municipalities. Finally, a technical solution has been found to recycle bottles while keeping the cork on the bottle. Thanks to the mediation of Eco-Emballages and the ADEME, and to the learning of both parties these conflicts rapidly decreased the last few years.

3.5.2 Controversy about incentives

A second controversy occurred about the poor level of incentives. The criticisms were concentrated on two items:

1. The excessive burden resting on municipalities which are not sufficiently supported by Eco-Emballages (the subsidies do not always cover the extra costs incurred by municipalities compared to the scenario without separate collection);
2. The low level of the economic incentives to the various links of the system (an indequate and uniform fee on packages on the one hand, and a too low and undifferentiated support for sorting and separate collection on the other hand) (Defeuilley et al., 1997).

This lack of incentives would explain the weak application of the actors. In particular, since the financial support did not allow extra costs incurred by collection, sorting and recycling to be covered, municipalities had no reason to contract with Eco-Emballages. To sum up this viewpoint, Godard (1998) proposes the notion of 'institutional trajectory'. By 'institutional trajectory', he means that the environmental performance can be explained by the initial level of incentives included in the agreement. In this case, he suggested that environmental targets and incentives were initially very low, due to the 'capture' of public interest by private ones (uniform fees to avoid material competition, no preference for recycling).

3.5.3 The new incentive scheme of 2000

In response to the latter criticism, Eco-Emballages has recently modified (in April 2000) its financial support towards municipalities (the price list for sorted materials) as well as the fees imposed on new packages. Unchanged from 1993, the fees on packages will increase to compensate the growing financial support Eco-Emballages provides to municipalities. The fee will be doubled on average in 2000 (from 0.15 to 0.3 EUR cent/package) and will double again from now to 2002. Furthermore, differentiated fees are now introduced taking into account three factors:

1. the treatment costs of each material;[3]
2. the weight of the package (the lighter the package the higher the fee/kg);
3. the number of packages for a same product (several packages mean higher fees than a single package) and the recyclability of materials.

For instance a plastic bottle in PET, weighing 40 g will have to pay EUR cent 0.4 against EUR cent 0.18 before. Concerning the financial support towards municipalities, the new price list was changed to encourage a quicker implementation of separate collection. In this perspective, only municipalities collecting large waste volumes will receive higher contributions. Thus, the contribution will vary between 230 and 900 EUR/ton for plastics (vs. 230 to 700 Euro/ton in the former agreement), between 3 and 11 EUR/ton for glass (vs. 3 to 7 EUR/ton), between 110 and 300 EUR/ton for paper/cardboard (vs. 110 to 250 EUR/ton), between 230 and 320 EUR/ton for aluminium (vs. 230 EUR/ton), between 45 and 80 EUR/ton for steel (vs. 45 EUR/ton).

3.5.4 Controversy about incineration

Another controversy occurred about the predominance of incineration over recycling. This criticism was based on the statement that *'departmental plans'*, which had the role of regulating the capacities of incineration in the longer term, have led to over-investments in several occasions. D. Voynet, the French minister for the Environment since 1997, denounced this situation. After her declaration, a *'circulaire'* (which has no legal value) was taken in 1998 stipulating that recycling should count for, at least, 50 per cent in the valorisation of municipal waste (packaging and other municipal waste). This controversy does not only concern domestic packaging waste but actually all domestic waste. In fact, as we shall see it later, contrary to domestic waste in general, recycling volumes are higher than incineration volumes for packaging waste. Nevertheless, the risk is that having invested too much in incineration, municipalities would be tempted to give priority to the development of this mode of valorisation in order to pay off the equipment.

3.6 The Improvement of the Environmental Performance

Although conflicts and controversies were important until 1998, the situation has changed since then. First, technical controversies about PTM have almost disappeared. Second, controversies about incentives have decreased with the adoption by Eco-Emballages of a new price list and a more incentive-based fee system. Third, as regards the balance between recycling and incineration, eight *départemental* elimination plans have been adopted in 2000, which respect the new Voynet *'circulaire'*, and twelve more are expected by the end of the year. Nine plans have been rejected and the others are in preparation. A recent assessment of packaging waste by the 'Décision environnement' review of June 2000 confirmed the unanimous recognition of the work and services provided by Eco-Emballages. But, concerning domestic packaging waste, the review also identified three remaining problems to be tackled:

- *The issue of prevention*: the quantity of packaging waste is still increasing. On the one hand, the new fee system should improve the situation but it is important to notice that in 2002, Eco-Emballages will receive EUR 150 million from packaging fees (300 million in 2002) against EUR 1.5 billion in Germany where fees are much higher. On the other hand, reducing pollution at the source also requires providing incentives to inhabitants so that they reduce their waste production. For that purpose, a fiscal reform is required. A first fiscal measure has been taken recently by the Ministry for the Economy to provide incentives to municipalities so that they contract with Eco-Emballages. Thus, municipalities who have contracted will benefit from a VAT of 5.5 per cent on waste transactions instead of the normal rate of 20.6 per cent. The second measure should concern local waste taxation, which is a critical point. Three systems are possible. The first system implies a tax, based on the quantity of waste generated by each family. This system provides incentives but is not redistributive (taxes depend on the waste generated and not on incomes). The second one is a tax, based on the value of the house (with no consideration to the amount of waste generated). This system does not provide incentives but is redistributive. The third one consists of financing waste treatment from the general budget, which causes a total opacity for citizens about waste costs. From an environmental point of view, the first system is the most efficient but it is politically difficult to implement.

- *The optimisation of recycling channels and the development of compost:* to stimulate waste valorisation, the development of material recycling as well as compost for organic waste is required. Glass collection and recycling is already quite high (over 55 per cent), but to increase this figure, door-to-door collection will be required. The potential for plastic recycling is still important (7 per cent only compared to 69 per cent in Germany) and requires an optimisation of separate collection and sorting. Finally, in contrast to Denmark or the Netherlands where organic material composting is a mature technique, volumes are very low in France because the experiments carried out did not reach the quality requirements. Composting is now a priority for the ADEME because it is the most appropriate solution for non-separable waste.

- *Compliance with the future Directive:* The last critical point deals with the effects of the new Directive in preparation for 2001. Eco-Emballages fears that very ambitious recycling targets would disturb the French system and discourage municipalities in their efforts. In effect, to reach recycling targets of a minimum 60 per cent on average, differentiated according to materials, an optimised separate collection will be necessary (which means new investments and organisations for municipalities) as well as increasing costs for packagers and municipalities. These requirements are not necessarily compatible with the municipalities' capabilities (engineering, financial and so on) and could threaten their involvement in the Eco-Emballages scheme. If this Directive is implemented, it can be asked whether the responsibility of municipalities towards packaging waste treatment will still be sustainable, and if not, to what extent this responsibility can be transferred to producers, which would require the modification of the French waste law.

4. ANALYSIS

The problem does not originate from, as often, a lack of data but rather from their abundance, from contradictory and changing signals. The temporal dimension is here essential to the understanding of the co-evolution of the regulatory scheme and the results. In 1996, a research report conducted by Defeuilley et al. (1997) led to severe conclusions about the Eco-Emballages scheme and about its ability to reach environmental targets. Three years after, such a diagnosis is no longer possible since the scheme has proved to be capable of adapting to the problems encountered, as important improvements have been realised during this period. In fact, in order to overcome a too short-sighted view of evaluation it is important to appreciate the specificity of this case and the nature of learning and political processes, which have been taking place since 1993.

4.1 Feasibility

Given the international pressure on domestic waste in general, and on packaging waste in particular, there was no way for public authorities and industrialists and municipalities to escape from a regulation. In these circumstances, reaching a broad consensus through an open negotiation was a deliberate choice from public authorities. It represents a change with traditional 'negotiation processes' characterised by discrete contacts between industrialists, administration and a great opacity. In this new perspective, all the conditions were met to reach an agreement.

4.2 Capability

4.2.1 Specification of the agreement
Target In this case, a quantified target was defined since the beginning, that is to say, a valorisation rate of 75 per cent for packaging waste for 2002. Undoubtedly, this target is ambitious and represents a real improvement with respect to 'business-as-usual'. In effect, before 1992, valorisation rates

remained low for packaging (about 5 per cent in 1989) and improved very slowly, essentially thanks to incineration efforts (a recycling rate of 10 per cent in 1989). To reach this target, industrialists and municipalities could not afford to go on as they used to, and therefore, important efforts of innovation were required to develop new organisations, new technologies for collection, for sorting and for recycling. In this perspective, this case can be classified as an 'innovation oriented agreement' (INOAs) (Aggeri and Hatchuel, 1999, Aggeri, 1999).

Burden sharing The absence of explicit burden-sharing mechanisms is one of the key features of this agreement since no differentiation of efforts or improvements is defined in the French regulation. In particular, targets have not been differentiated according to polluters or to materials. Contrary to the new European Directive projects for 2001, limitations for energy recovery have not been defined either. The initial level of uncertainties and the desire to reach a broad consensus were certainly the two major reasons for not differentiating targets and fees. The first argument (uncertainty) is no longer valid since there are now abundant data about collected quantities and costs. Thanks to this better knowledge of costs and impacts, differentiated fees on new packages have been introduced recently in 2000 by Eco-Emballages. Differentiated targets could be introduced as well.

Monitoring mechanisms Specifying targets and burden-sharing mechanisms requires the implementation of strong monitoring mechanisms to ensure that environmental targets will be met. The design and implementation of monitoring is a key issue for 'innovation oriented agreements'. In effect, if there are initial uncertainties and when the environmental problem involves a multi-actor co-operation process, defining a 'complete' agreement is almost impossible or too risky because consequences are unpredictable. In this context, monitoring means the progressive acquisition of knowledge, in order to be in a position to take additional measures if free-riding or opportunistic behaviour appears (see Aggeri and Hatchuel, 1999). In this perspective, two issues should be distinguished: *co-ordination* on the one hand, and *control* on the other hand. In this case, co-ordination was identified as a major issue because of the multiplicity of actors involved and because stable recycling volumes require to specify 'market rules' (PTM), to guarantee prices and outlets for the different recycling channels. All these co-ordination mechanisms cannot be produced spontaneously by private actors since they require heavy investments and since they cannot be easily appropriated. In other words, they represent 'positive externalities', which benefit all economic actors in the market. In these circumstances, there is a need for public intervention to produce them. In this case, the institutional solution found was to create a private agency (Eco-Emballages) whose compliance with its 'public service mission' is ensured by a consultative commission (see section 2). Until now, Eco-Emballages has provided, with the help of the ADEME, (public environmental agency), an important support (financial, technical expertise, diffusion of information and 'best practices' and so on) towards municipalities and industrialists. According to all actors, this support is considered satisfactory. In fact, the major weakness of the system relates to the capacity of control from public authorities. In effect, the Eco-Emballages scheme has been built on consensus-seeking and democratic control. For instance, the composition and functioning of the consultative commission, which has a key role in the regulation of the system and the control of public interest, illustrates this consensus-seeking attitude. Among its 33 members, all actors are represented (municipalities, public authorities, packagers, materials producers, distributors, Eco-Emballages and so on) but there are only five state representatives representing five ministries with five different conflicting emphases: logic: agriculture, environment, industry, economy and finance, ADEME. In these conditions, reaching a consensus has proved to be difficult, since interests are often contradictory. It has led to a certain dilution of responsibilities, and therefore, to inertia. For instance, fees and price lists per material have been changed only in 2000 although the necessary conditions for change (available knowledge about technical feasibility and costs) probably have been available since 1996 or 1997. Indeed, this commission is only consultative and, in principle, public authorities could have taken other decisions sooner. But, for that purpose, the Ministry for the Environment should have had a stronger leadership over the system and a clearer strategy. Most of all, a strong monitoring does not mean only to create meeting groups and to collect quantitative data but it also requires a prospective vision of forthcoming problems and the elaboration of scenarios in case of non-compliance. In particular, it can be asked whether the functioning of the consultative commission should not be changed, now separate collection and recycling have become effective and accepted by the population, which means that consensus is no longer vital. This diagnosis of the relative eclipse of French authorities towards Eco-Emballages monitoring was moreover the major criticism put forward by a recent and confidential report (2000) of the Conseil Général des Mines (higher officials from the Ministry of Industry) about packaging domestic waste in France.

Additional guarantees and sanctions Concerning guarantees, several modifications have been added to the initial scheme. In particular, as we pointed out, new incentives (fees, price list for sorted materials) have been introduced as well as incentive fiscal measures (VAT, local fiscality).

Concerning sanctions, as the scheme is based on voluntarism, sanctions are not explicitly mentioned.

Contractual forms and general provisions contractual forms have been extensively used in this case. At the upper level, there are contracts between public authorities and Eco-Emballages for each new approval. At the intermediate level, contracts are signed between Eco-Emballages and packagers, and between Eco-Emballages and municipalities to define the mutual commitments of each actor. At the lower level, contracts are used between municipalities and recyclers to ensure outlets for separately collected waste.

4.2.2 Application

Extent The agreement is, in principle, valid for the period up to 2002. In fact, as a new European Directive is in preparation for 2001, it is probable that a new arrangement will be required sooner or later. With regard to its coverage, the existing open agreement, based on voluntarism, has not achieved its initial objective. In effect, about 30 million people effectively participate in separate collection and only one half of the municipalities have contracted with Eco-Emballages. Involving the remaining municipalities will not be easy since a large part of them belong to rural areas which have limited resources, low densities of population, and which are sometimes less aware of this environmental problem. From an economic point of view, it can be asked if involving all municipalities is efficient since marginal costs are higher when dealing with very small municipalities. But, on the other hand, excluding these small municipalities could create local distortions and discourage the efforts of other municipalities in the neighbourhood.

Compliance At the aggregate level, progress is continuous (see Table 8.1 and Figure 8.2) but the capacity of the Eco-Emballages scheme to meet the 75 per cent valorisation target in 2002 is still uncertain. In effect, when extrapolating the tendency, the 75 per cent valorisation target can be met, but it requires that environmental performance increases from 56 per cent in 1999 to 75 per cent in 2002, that is a 34 per cent increase over the next three years. Between 1996 and 1999, the valorisation rate has passed from 41 per cent to 56 per cent, with a 31 per cent improvement in volume (from 1.68 to 2.21 million tons). It will not be easy to maintain this growth rate because the recycling potential of glass, which represents the largest volumes, is almost realised, and also because the most active municipalities are already under contract with Eco-Emballages. Of course, the recent contracts with the remaining large and medium-size cities like Paris, Toulouse or Lyon should improve the situation but it is not sure this will be sufficient. In other words, reaching this performance will either require the development of recycling channels which have low volumes and a large potential (like plastic recycling or composting) or involving the remaining municipalities, in particular in rural areas.

4.3 Impact

4.3.1 Environmental effectiveness

Concerning environmental effectiveness, we shall distinguish results on average and the dispersion of results. The results on average can be assessed at five levels.

The incomes The participation of packagers in Eco-Emballages and the collection of fees are judged satisfactory by Eco-Emballages, which means that the potential has been reached with very few frauds. More than 11 000 firms have joined the Eco-Emballages scheme. The green dot appears on 97 per cent of consumable goods sold in the market. The fee is about EUR cent 0.15 per package in average. Overall incomes have reached EUR 80 million in 1998, and will double with the new fee put into practice from February 2000. This amount should double again in 2002 with the revision of fees.

The expenses For the first time in 1998, the expenses (financial support from Eco-Emballages towards municipalities) exceeded the income, growing from EUR 23 million in 1993 to EUR 120 million in 1998 and EUR 180 million in 1999. This progress is due to the rise of collected and sorted waste which can benefit from the Eco-Emballages support and which increased from 240 000 tons in 1994 to 1.62 million tons in 1999.

The number of municipalities under contract with Eco-Emballages The population under contract with Eco-Emballages is over 40 million in 2000 (32 in 1998, 25 in 1997, 14 in 1994) and more than 10 000 municipalities (over a total of 30 000 in France) have signed with Eco-Emballages.

The modes of valorisation Table 8.1 illustrates the performance of the Eco-Emballages consortium only. The valorisation rate obtained in 1999 (56 per cent) is still far from the target of 75 per cent in 2002 defined in the Eco-Emballages approval. The trend seems a priori insufficient to meet this target in 2002 (see Figure 8.1), and therefore, intensive efforts will be required to accelerate the rate of growth (see previous paragraphs). Projections for 2000, made in tandem by the ADEME and Eco-Emballages, envisage a valorisation rate of 64 per cent. This is based notably on the recent involvement of large municipalities in the system (Paris, Toulouse and so on) who should contribute to the acceleration of the valorised quantities.

The rate of recycling per material Table 8.2 illustrates the heterogeneity of results depending on the type of material. Compared to the recycling targets included in the EU Directive for packaging waste (15 per cent minimum by material to be met in 2001), all materials are above this target except aluminium and plastics. It should be stressed that glass and steel, which obtain the better results, are the oldest channels. In particular, separate collection for glass began long before the creation of Eco-Emballages. Nevertheless the quantities have notably increased since its creation. The very low rate for plastic recycling is due to the difficulties in meeting the technical requirements imposed by recyclers as well as decreasing returns in plastic collection due the variety of plastics. In these conditions, the ADEME considers that recycling is economically viable only for bottles and flasks, which represent one third of packaging plastic waste. When considering this potential, the results obtained are better (approximately 21 per cent are recycled).

Table 8.1   Eco-Emballages environmental performance

	recycling	Energy recovery	Total valorisation	Total waste*	Valorisation rate (%)
1994	239	79	318	4 100*	8
1995	419	284	703	4 100*	17
1996	1 180	501	1 681	4 100*	41
1997	1 334	425	1 759	4 100*	43
1998	1 459	546	2 005	4 050	50
1999	1 624	584	2 208	3 960	56

Note: * Estimation of the quantity of domestic packaging waste in 1997 contributing to Eco-Emballages

Source: Tableau de bord ADEME, June 2000

Table 8.2   Material recycling rates per material in France

	94	95	96	97	98	99(1)	Total(2)*	%recycl. = (1)/(2)
Steel	68	127	146	172	171	163	350	46.5
Aluminium	0	0	1	3	6	4	45	9
Paper-card.	–	24	45	75	122	164	1000	16.5
Plastics	11	12	19	31	40	50	900	5.5
Glass	280	456	1242	1288	1359	1492	2550	58.5
Other	0	3	5	5	5	6	10	60
Total	359	622	1458	1574	1703	1879	4855	39

Note: *: Quantities of material packaging production in 1997 in kilotons

Source: ADEME, June 2000[4]

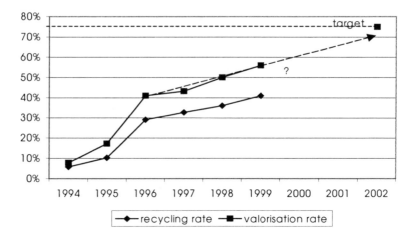

Figure 8.1   Eco-Emballages environmental performance

In February 2000, TN Sofres Consulting (2000) published an interesting comparative cost-benefit study in four EU countries (France, Germany, the Netherlands and the UK). This study is based on environmental performance of 1997 and costs of 1998. Even if assessment methods differ from one country to another, which makes comparison difficult, these figures indicate that France is still far behind Germany or the Netherlands in terms of material recycling, especially as regards paper/cardboard, glass or plastics (compared to Germany). It suggests that the potential for progress is still very important in France.

Table 8.3 Recycling rates (%) per material in France in 1997

	France	Germany	Netherlands	UK
Steel	45	77	70	0
Aluminium	7	63	0	28
Paper-card.	11	91	46	0
Plastics	5	69	0	0
Glass	48	83	84	26

Source: TN Sofres, 2000

Strong disparities among municipalities Another triggering element to consider is the important dispersion of results between municipalities:

1. the dispersion can be measured by the difference between the 20 per cent best municipalities and the results on average. This difference varies from 1 to 1.7 (for glass) to 1 to 3 for papers;
2. differences also appear between materials with high volumes for glass and papers, and low volumes for other packages;
3. 'door to door' separate collection supports higher costs than voluntary collection, obtains higher volumes, especially for paper and cardboard.

To reduce this dispersion, Eco-Emballages and ADEME disseminate, in several documents, the best practices observed on the ground and also provide training services for municipalities. Despite these efforts, there are structural data (like population density, proximity of facilities, ecological awareness of population and so on) which make this dispersion inevitable.

4.3.2 Economic efficiency

Several factors make the evaluation of the economic efficiency very difficult:

1. real prices and costs are unknown because of the multitude of subsidies and financial supports we have already mentioned which are difficult to trace back;
2. costs announced by municipalities are subject to caution since accounting systems are not stabilised and conventions differ from one to another;
3. costs are affected by technological parameters: the mode of collection (door-to-door or voluntary), the size and technology of the incinerator, the existence of sorting plants and so on;
4. costs are affected by geographical parameters: the location of the municipality in rural or urban areas, the density of population, the proximity of recyclers and so on;

5. costs related to packaging waste are difficult to separate from municipal costs because both share equipment and employees;
6. due to learning effects, costs get lower with the experience accumulated, which means that first movers generally bear lower costs than others;
7. institutional variables, like the legal responsibility for waste elimination (resting on municipalities in France, on industrialists in Germany) or the mode of taxation also affect cost comparisons.

In this perspective, it is interesting to notice that the European comparative study we have mentioned earlier (TN Sofres, 2000) does not draw any definitive conclusions about the most efficient systems in Europe because of all these geographical, institutional and social differences. For instance, the Netherlands which combine low costs and a high level of recycling have two major advantages over other European countries: (1) collection and sorting costs are lower because packaging flows are mixed with industrial waste which generates economies of scale; (2) the Netherlands have a high density of population which helps reducing collection costs. Germany combines a good environmental performance (60 per cent waste recycling) with very high costs. For instance, recycling costs (collection, sorting and recycling cost, excluding subsidies, minus the incomes from material sales) are three times higher for glass (82 EUR/ton against 26) or steel (369 versus 89) than in France. In this comparison, France has an intermediate position with a medium environmental and economic performance. The most interesting conclusion of the report for policy makers is that a good environmental performance is not necessarily correlated with higher costs. Another study on cost, was realised, at the French level, by the Sofres institute in October 1998 and ordered by the ADEME and the AMF (association of French municipalities) (see ADEME-AMF, 1998). This study, conducted over a panel of French municipalities, leads to three important conclusions:

1. costs are higher in rural areas than in urban areas (90 to 120 EUR/ton vs 140 to 280 EUR/ton);
2. costs of collection, sorting and recycling (including financial supports) are not higher than costs of incineration (between 70 and 100 EUR/ton);
3. the implementation of separate collection causes municipalities extra costs between 5 and 10 EUR/habitant/year.

Three comments can be derived from this report. The first one is the confirmation that local conditions (density of population and type of housing) have a direct and important impact on costs. The second one relates to an important change. Whereas the Defeuilley report had pointed out the predominance of incineration over recycling, this study indicates that there is no longer a cost advantage when choosing incineration. In fact, this evolution was predictable and is due to the tightening of regulations on incineration which have increased costs 20–30 per cent since 1997. Since there is no reason to think this tendency could change in the future, it is to be expected that incineration costs will go on rising. The third comment concerns the extra costs incurred by municipalities when engaging in separate collection. A main objective for Eco-Emballages was to cover the extra costs municipalities would have to face. What this study confirms is that the financial support is not sufficient even if extra costs are limited.

4.4 Resource Development

In this case, resource development and collective learning processes are key issues. In an initial context characterised by a high level of uncertainties (which we could describe as 'shared uncertainties'), several innovations have been undertaken with regards to technology and organisation of a new economy of recycling. New relations between actors (municipalities, ADEME, Eco-Emballages, recyclers, waste management companies, packagers and so on) have been established to create the conditions for better co-ordination. An interesting indicator of this resource development is the important dispersion of results, which reveals differentiated learning processes. In this perspective, experiments were necessary to organise what we call the *'learning of complexity'*, that is, all the specificities (local conditions, social behaviours, geographical context, municipality size and competence and so on) which make that a particular solution which works somewhere does not work elsewhere, and therefore should be adapted.

In fact, and this is an essential point, if an essential progress has been achieved since 1992, it relates primarily to the knowledge of this *'entrepreneurial chain'* which allows, now, the identification of robust technological and organisational trajectories. Indeed, it arises from the many experiments led initially with pilot municipalities, that neither a too – selective separate selection nor a too – coarse one is a viable solution. In the first case, because of high requirements requested from users, volumes are too small. In the other case, important volumes are obtained but with a too–low quality. The solutions that give the best results today are situated between these two options. It consisted in carrying out an average separate sorting, from three or four categories (glass, newspapers and the remainder), according to the characteristics of the geographical area (level of density and type of housing) on more or less door-to-door collection (versus voluntary collection). This type of scenario gives the best performance in terms of quantities and costs. This process of innovation also requires a ceaseless work of qualification and 're-qualification' (Barbier and Larédo, 1997). Qualification is the process by which technical specifications to the various links of the chain are progressively refined, in order to offer, in the end, products (incinerated or recycled) that satisfy the quality requirements imposed by recyclers and that can be marketed.

5. CONCLUSION

In this report, we have tried to draw the picture of the Eco-Emballages scheme, its history, its progresses and the remaining difficulties that have to be overcome. Contrary to the CFC case where innovation proceeded mainly within the firms, with limited interactions between firms (primarily limited to common tests of toxicology and common research on the negotiable instruments of CFC on ozone), we are here in the case of a complex entrepreneurial chain, made of multiple interactions, where the need for co-ordination is considerable. This is a point that has probably not sufficiently been underlined and taken into account by researchers. In this collective innovation process, Eco-Emballages plays a key role in the co-ordination of actors: 'standard contracts setting' between the various links of the chain, diffusion of technical specifications, guarantee for recycling prices and the organisation of the economic transactions between actors, diffusion of best practices, collection of data, financial and engineering support towards municipalities and so on. In other words, without this infrastructure, indispensable for the working of the market, the deployment of an economy of recycling would be impossible. In this context, the evaluation that can be made in 2000 is very different from that of 1996. It means that in such a complex case, time is a key parameter. It is central because the experiment, which includes learning by trial and error, is a long and chaotic process, involving thousands of municipalities, with different sizes and economic resources, millions of people with different social profiles and habits. This kind of process has nothing to do with a traditional environmental policy towards a limited number of firms. Taking into account these elements, the evaluation of the Eco-Emballages can be considered as globally positive: on the one hand, environmental performance has improved (the 1994 Directive targets are already met and 2002 French targets should be met) while controversies and conflicts among stakeholders have progressively disappeared. This is not the case in Germany where there are growing debates about the increasing cost of the Duales system. The two major criticisms concern the lack of incentives and the lack of monitoring from public authorities, both being linked together. Of course, economic incentives play undoubtedly a key role since separate collection and recycling induce extra costs for municipalities despite the Eco-Emballages support. Furthermore, it is necessary to indicate, by a price signal, recycling of various materials, that is more or less difficulty (what the economists call the 'internalisation of negative externalities'). But the issue is not so much to wonder what are the optimal incentives, but rather to wonder what are the necessary knowledge and resources required to design adequate incentives.

Thus, in a context of strong 'shared uncertainties' (Aggeri, 1999), incentives do not come first; they can be designed once the stakes, the technological limits, the costs have become clearer. In other words, in 1992, knowing very little, it was difficult to design appropriate incentives. From 1996, knowing much more, it is possible to introduce more adapted ones. In our opinion, the main obstacle to a quicker take-off, does not lie in a so-called sub-optimal 'institutional framework' (see Godard, 1998) but rather in a lack of monitoring from public authorities. As we mentioned earlier, the development of the Eco-Emballages scheme required stronger efforts (incentives and/or sanctions) towards the municipalities that have not yet contracted with Eco-Emballages on the one hand, and towards packagers and material producers that have not carried out efforts to reduce packaging at the source, on the other hand. These two aspects cannot be managed by Eco-Emballages itself, which represents the packagers' interests, and cannot be both 'judge and judged'. Therefore, apart from the commission whose role is only consultative, a stronger control from public authorities is required in order to guarantee that the public interest is preserved.

NOTES

1. Another consortium, called Adelphe, also received an approval but their field of intervention is limited to wine bottles valorisation, that is to low volumes. In this study we will only focus on Eco-Emballages.
2. The example of Pampryl bottles (orange juice) is a good illustration. These bottles imported from the USA, are made of PAN, a plastic material which is not recyclable. Despite its non-recyclability, this bottle received a 'packaging oscar' in 1997 and was put on the market in Europe.
3. The net cost is equal to: collection and sorting costs – price paid by recyclers.
4. According to the ADEME, these figures should be interpreted carefully. There are still many uncertainties on the definition of domestic packaging waste and therefore on quantities, because it is difficult to distinguish in practice what is domestic packaging waste stricto sensu from other domestic waste which is collected at the same time.

BIBLIOGRAPHY

ADEME – AMF (1998), *Analyse des coûts de gestion des déchets municipaux (Cost analysis of municipal waste management)*. Report for the ADEME. Paris: ADEME publication.
ADEME, (2000), *Tableau de bord déchets d'emballages ménagers (Figures on domestic packaging waste)*. Paris: ADEME publication.

Aggeri F. (1999), *Environmental policies and innovation. A knowledge-based perspective on co-operative approaches.* Research Policy, **28**, 699-717.

Aggeri, F. and Hatchuel, A. (1999), 'A dynamic model of environmental policy. The case of innovation-oriented agreements'. in C. Carraro and F. Lévêque (eds) *Voluntary approaches in Environmental Policy,* Kluwer Academic Publishers, pp. 151–87.

Barbier, R. and Larédo, P. (1997), *L'internalisation des déchets. Le modèle de la communauté urbaine de Lille (Waste management process. The example of the urban community of Lille).* Collection poche environnement. Paris: Economica

Defeuilley, C., Lupton S. and Serret, Y. (1997), 'The French household waste regime', report for DGXI, European Commission, Paris: CIRED.

Decision Environnement review n° 64, 76, 77, 80, 83, 87.

European Commission (1996), Communication from the Commission to the European parliament on environmental agreements. COM.96.(561). Final, November 27.

Glachant, M. and Whiston, T. (1996). 'Voluntary agreements between industry and governments'. In *Environmental Policy in Europe - Industry, Competition and the Policy Process,* Cheltenham: Edward Elgar, pp.45–61.

Godard, O. (1998). 'Concertation et incitations efficaces, deux dispositifs incompatibles? Une analyse à partir du dispositif de gestion des déchets d'emballage en France'. *(Cooperation and incentives: two incompatible targets? An analysis of the French domestic waste management system).* Paris: Communication aux Journées de l'Association Française de Science Economique.

Molina M.J. and Rowland S. (1974) 'Stratospheric sink for chlorofluoromethanes: chlorine atom-catalyzed destruction of ozone'. In: *Nature,* **249**, 810–812.

Quirion, P. (1994). *La gestion des déchets d'emballage ménagers en France et en Allemagne : éléments d'évaluation économique. (Domestic waste management in France and in Germany: an economic evaluation).* Paris: Mémoire de DEA Paris I Panthéon Sorbonne.

TN Sofres consulting (2000), *Cost-efficiency of packaging recovery systems: the case of France, Germany, the Netherlands, and the United Kingdom,* Report for DG XI, European Commission publication, Brussels: February, 151 p.

9. The UK Farm Films Producers Group

Roger Salmons

1. INTRODUCTION

At the end of 1994 seventeen suppliers of polyethylene silage film agreed to set up the Farm Films Producers Group (FFPG), to operate a non profit-making scheme to collect and recycle waste film from farms on the UK mainland. It started operating at the beginning of April 1995. Each of the participants contributed to the cost of the scheme by paying an Environmental Protection Contribution of £100 per tonne on all sales of silage film to UK customers. The scheme provided free collection of waste film from farmers via a pre-existing network of local collection agents, who compacted and bailed the waste film for transportation to a plant in Scotland for cleaning and reprocessing.

Two overseas suppliers declined to join the group, enabling them to undercut the prices of the participants. This resulted in a destabilisation of the market, and by March 1996 companies started to leave the FFPG. The Packaging and Industrial Films Association (PIFA) – who had been instrumental in setting up the scheme – made repeated requests to the Government for them to introduce supporting legislation to force participation by all suppliers, but this was not forthcoming. At the end of March 1997 operation of the scheme was suspended.

The FFPG is an example of a voluntary collective action (where the participants share the cost of a scheme). Since the UK Government was not directly involved in the process, and was not a party to the final agreement regarding the setting up of the company, one might be tempted to classify the FFPG as unilateral commitment.[1] However, the initiative was prompted by a letter from the Secretary of State for the Environment to the leading producers of silage films, and was encouraged by the Government (which was kept informed of progress). Furthermore, the implicit threat of legislation – whether or not it was actually intended – provided the key motivation for the companies involved to reach an agreement. Consequently, it seems reasonable to classify the FFPG as a voluntary agreement.

2. CONTEXT

By the mid 1990s annual sales of polyethylene silage films to UK farmers amounted to approximately 20 000 tonnes, with consumption growing at around 5 per cent per annum reflecting the underlying growth in on-farm silage production (see Figure 9.1). Three different types of film products can be used in the production of silage – stretch film, sheets, and bags; with the choice of production technology being determined largely by the size of the farm, and hence the quantity of silage produced. Silage sheets are used to line mechanical silage clamps, which entail capital investment. This is only viable for larger producers, and smaller farms are much more likely to use stretch film to bail the silage. In terms of tonnage, stretch film is by far the largest segment, accounting for around 65 per cent of the total market, with sheets accounting for around 33 per cent, and bags for only 2 per cent.

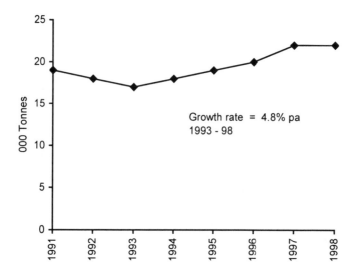

Source: Applied Market Information Ltd. Published in the Annual Report
1998 of the Packaging and Industrial Films Association (PIFA).

Figure 9.1   UK market for polyethylene silage film

Waste silage film is an important issue for farmers. Excluding organic waste (for example manure, slurry, silage effluent, crop residues and so on), plastic films and packaging is one of the largest categories of agricultural waste. However, in terms of the overall waste stream it is not a significant issue. For example, silage film represents 2.2 per cent of total polyethylene film consumption (c.1 million tonnes), and only 0.2 per cent of total packaging waste (c.10 million tonnes).[2]

Agricultural waste is not a 'controlled waste' – that is there is no obligation on local authorities to collect it from farmers. Furthermore, the agricultural sector is not (currently) covered by waste management controls, which means that there is no legal 'duty of care', or requirement for a waste management licence. Farmers have a number of options for disposing of waste silage film. They can take it to a landfill site, although landfill sites may refuse to accept the waste film if it is contaminated. Alternatively, they can pay a commercial waste contractor to remove the waste film and dispose of it for them. However, in practice most farmers either bury or burn the waste film in situ, despite the latter being against the Best Practice Guidance issued by the Ministry of Agriculture, Farming and Fisheries. If they burn or bury waste, farmers are obliged to contact the Environment Agency and their local Environmental Health Department to discuss compliance with relevant codes of practice and legislation, but in practice it is highly unlikely that all will do so.

Polyethylene silage film is non-toxic, stable and is unaffected by water. Therefore it does not produce any leachates when it is buried in the ground, although it does take a long time to biodegrade. The burning of waste film in open fires produces emissions of carbon dioxide, plus certain volatile organic compounds and polycyclic aromatic hydrocarbons (PAHs) due to incomplete combustion – but does not release any dioxins. Even if all waste film were to be burned the resultant CO_2 emissions would account for less than 0.01 per cent of total UK emissions (and less than 0.2 per cent of emissions from agriculture, forestry and land use); emissions of benzo(a)pyrene – used as the main 'marker' for PAHs – would account for less 0.005 per cent of total UK emissions. Of course, concentrations of these pollutants will be much higher in the immediate vicinity of the fires, and consequently there may be limited health impacts on farm workers.

Thus while the disposal of waste silage films may be an issue for farmers, it has minimal impact on the overall waste management picture, and disposal in situ does not appear to create significant environmental problems in terms of water or air pollution. The main environmental problem is likely to be visual pollution due to incomplete or ineffective disposal – particularly for farms located in National Parks. This may help to explain the difference between the perceptions of the Government and the industry about the significance of the issue. The Government does not appear to view waste farm plastics as a major environmental problem, believing that '[regulation] would be a disproportionate response ... to the limited size of the problem'.[3]

In contrast, in its 1998 Annual Report, PIFA describes the problem of agricultural waste plastics' recovery as being 'high profile'.

In order to appreciate the motivations for setting up the FFPG, and the reasons for its subsequent demise, it is necessary to understand the changes in the policy climate that were occurring in the early 1990s, and the influence of the parallel debate that was unfolding on the issue of waste packaging. The first half of the decade saw a dramatic change in the way waste was to be managed and – more importantly – to the underlying policy framework. The process started with the publication of the 1990 White Paper *This Common Inheritance* and the resultant 1990 Environmental Protection Act; was further developed by the Government's 1994 *Sustainable Development* strategy document; and culminated in the passing of the 1995 Environment Act. During this time, waste management was transformed from a largely technical issue to a mainstream political issue that was central to the overall environmental/economic debate (Porter, 1998).

Particularly significant were the developments in Government waste policy. The 1990 White Paper was the first time that recycling had been explicitly included as one of the Government's priorities, and a target of recycling 25 per cent of all household waste by the year 2000 was set. By the time that the *Sustainable Development* strategy document was published in 1994, the Government's waste policy was based on a hierarchy of waste management options – reduction, reuse, recovery, disposal – with the express aim of moving practices up the hierarchy.

Two other principles were also emerging during this period, which would underpin waste policy. The first was a preference to proceed by voluntary means wherever possible (in keeping with the prevailing philosophy of deregulation). The second was that each waste management option should bear its full cost – including any environmental costs, and that those costs should be borne by the polluter (that is the polluter pays principle). These two principles were brought together in July 1993 when the Government announced the introduction of *producer responsibility* for six priority waste streams.[4] Under this initiative, the relevant business sectors were charged with the responsibility of developing and implementing voluntary plans to increase substantially the amount of waste recovered for beneficial use. The Government viewed this as a key element of their policy, particularly for implementing the prospective EC Directive on Packaging and Packaging Waste.

The discussions about the formation of the FFPG took place against the backdrop of the debate (both in the UK and in Europe) about waste packaging and the appropriate policy measures that should be introduced to increase recycling and recovery rates – in particular the emerging principle of producer responsibility. There was never any suggestion that polyethylene films used for farm silage production would be included within the scope of any measures introduced to deal with waste packaging. However, many of the companies producing silage films (and the industry association, PIFA) were involved in the discussions about packaging. Also, farm films were relevant to the issue of protecting the recycling infrastructure for plastics, which became intertwined with the packaging debate in 1993. Consequently, the progress of the packaging debate is likely to have had a major influence over the attitudes of the companies involved in the formation and operation of the FFPG. The events in 1993 provide an important insight into the motivations for the setting up of the FFPG scheme, while those of 1994–95 sow the seeds for its collapse in 1996–97.

By 1993, discussions over the introduction of a voluntary initiative on packaging waste had failed to produce any concrete proposals, and the nascent UK recycling infrastructure was under threat from imports of subsidised materials from Germany – particularly in the case of plastics. In July 1993, the Secretary of State for the Environment invited 28 companies involved in the packaging chain to set up Producer Responsibility Industry Group (PRG) to develop a plan by Christmas 1993 for introducing producer responsibility, with the threat of legislation if a plan was not forthcoming. At the same time he asked the PRG to produce a plan by October 1993 of immediate actions to safeguard the recycling infrastructure for plastics, and for paper and board. This initiative was significant for two reasons. First, it raised the spectre of the legislation. Second, it broadened the debate from packaging to the protection and development of the recycling infrastructure in general. This had the effect of linking the debate about the future of the Second Life Plastics (see page 205) to the debate about packaging, and by inference to the threat of legislation. Thus when the Secretary of State wrote to silage film producers in October 1993 encouraging them to support Second Life Plastics, and saying that he would call them in for a meeting if they did not, this was interpreted as an implicit threat that legislation would be introduced. Based on the experience of the German Packaging Ordinance, industry believed that any such legislation would impose significant costs on them.

By the end of the following year however, it was becoming clear that the Government was unlikely to introduce any legislation on this issue. In January 1994, the PRG produced its draft producer responsibility plan for packaging, in which it rejected the idea of purely voluntary action and called on the Government 'to provide the legislative backing to enforce compliance by all members of the packaging chain' (that is to address the problem of free-riding). Nine months later the Government reluctantly 'accepted in principle the force of the argument put forward by industry in favour of underpinning legislation at the earliest opportunity'.[5] However, it took eight months for them to publish a consultation paper on the issue, and it was only after further widespread negotiations with industry that the draft packaging waste regulations were finally published in July 1996. If the Government was so reluctant to introduce legislation on packaging, it was hardly credible that they would do so for waste silage films.

Box 9.1 Chronology of the Packaging and Farm Films initiatives

1991	April	• German Packaging Ordinance passed
1993	July	• Secretary of State invites 28 companies involved in the packaging chain to set up Producer Responsibility Industry Group (PRG) to develop a plan by Christmas 1993 for introducing producer responsibility, with threat of legislation if plan not forthcoming.
		• Secretary of State also asks for a plan by October 1993 of immediate actions to safeguard the recycling infrastructure for plastics, and for paper and board, threatened by subsidised German imports.
	August	• European Commission publishes revised draft of proposal for Directive on packaging
	September	• British Polythene Industries plc writes to Secretary of State threatening to shut down Second Life Plastics, and switch to cheaper German imports, unless they receive financial support from other suppliers.
	October	• Secretary of State writes to suppliers of agricultural films encouraging them to support Second Life Plastics, saying that he will call them to a meeting if this is not forthcoming.
		• PIFA initiate discussions among all companies supplying silage film to the UK market.
	November	• PRG produces plan to protect recycling infrastructure, but does not fully protect Second Life Plastics – saying only that it will probably continue
	December	• Agricultural films included in the general discussion of plastic packaging recycling within the PRG

1994	January	• PRG produce draft producer responsibility plan, rejecting purely voluntary action and calling on the Government 'to provide the legislative backing to enforce compliance by all members of the packaging chain'
	March	• Agreement in principle from all silage film suppliers to support Second Life Plastics
	September	• Government (reluctantly) 'accepted in principle the force of the argument put forward by industry in favour of underpinning legislation at the earliest opportunity'.
	December	• EC Directive on packaging and packaging waste comes into force
		• FFPG Ltd incorporated with two initial members
1995	March	• FFPG collection scheme launched, with seventeen members
	May	• Government publishes consultation paper setting out options for imposing a legal obligation on businesses in the packaging chain
	August	• Environment Act 1995 passed – included enabling legislation for the introduction of producer responsibility initiatives, but no specific legislative backing for packaging recovery
1996	March	• First companies leave FFPG
	July	• Government publishes draft packaging waste regulations
1997	March	• FFPG suspends operations in the United Kingdom
		• Government introduces Producer Responsibility Obligations (Packaging Waste) Regulations 1997
1998	October	• Government publishes consultation paper on Options for tackling the problem of waste non-packaging farm plastics. Announces extension of waste management controls to agriculture, but rejects extension of producer responsibility legislation to farm films as being disproportionate.

3. NEGOTIATION PROCESS

In 1990 Anaplast Ltd – a subsidiary of British Polythene Industries plc (BPI) – had launched *Second Life Plastics* to collect and recycle waste agricultural polyethylene films. Under the scheme, farmers could call a central Freephone number to arrange collection by a local agent, who would compact and bail the waste film.[6] When the agent had collected 18 tonnes, he would request a pick-up by Second Life Plastics, and the waste film was transported to the Anaplast plant at Dumfries in Scotland where it was cleaned and reprocessed.

The reprocessing plant represented an investment in excess of £1.5 million by BPI, and had sufficient capacity to reprocess 4 500 tonnes per annum. In 1991 (the first full year of its operation) the scheme received 13 000 telephone calls, and 3 750 tonnes of polyethylene films were collected.[7] Agents were paid £80 per tonne, and the total collection cost was around £120–130 per tonne. This was approximately double the cost of better quality waste (that is lower levels of contamination) that could be imported from Germany at that time. At this level of cost the scheme was loss making, with little prospect of breaking even. BPI attempted to enlist the support of other companies in the industry to share the financial burden, but without success.

By September 1993, BPI were no longer prepared to shoulder the burden, and they wrote to the Secretary of State for the Environment, threatening to shut down the UK collection operation and switch to cheaper German imports unless they received financial support from other suppliers. This prompted the Minister to write to all the major producers of silage film, encouraging them to support Second Life Plastics, and threatening to call them in for a meeting if this support was not forthcoming. As a result of this letter, the Packaging and Industrial Films Association (PIFA) initiated a series of meetings to discuss the issue, and to agree a collective response.

All domestic and overseas producers and importers were encouraged to participate in the discussions, irrespective of whether they were members of PIFA or not.[8] The Government did not participate in the discussions, but was kept informed of progress. The National Farmers Union (NFU) and the UK Agricultural Supply Trades Association (UKASTA) were involved during the later stages. Discussions were conducted at a senior management level, reflecting the fact that this was seen as a major commercial issue rather than an environmental issue. Initially, consideration was given to the inclusion of all farm plastics in the scheme (including containers, twine and so on). However, there were too many interests for progress to be made, and it was only when the scope was narrowed to silage films that it was possible to reach an agreement.

PIFA – in particular its Chief Executive, Jim Pugh – performed an important role in the process, acting as an advocate for collective action; persuading the companies of the potential importance of the issue; providing funds for legal fees; and proposing solutions. Two silage film producers – Anaplast Ltd (the company that had operated Second Life Plastics) and Bonar Polythene Films Ltd – took the lead in supporting the initiative, and were the two initial signatories at time of incorporation in December 1994. In addition, a number of outside organisations encouraged and supported the initiative. Two major polymer suppliers – BP Chemicals and Dow Chemicals – provided initial funding and facilities for meetings, while the support of UKASTA and of the NFU was instrumental in reaching the final agreement.

At the start of the process there was little enthusiasm for a collective response. The other suppliers took the view that the financial viability of Second Life Plastics was BPI's problem, and did not concern them. However, PIFA convinced them that there was a potential common problem (that is imposition of costly regulation) that required a collective response. Initial meetings were marked by mutual suspicion; there was no history of communication and co-operation, plus the companies were aggressive market competitors. However, attitudes were gradually transformed over the course of the meetings as the issues were discussed and everyone was able to make an input to the process.

Within a few months, a consensus was reached that best way forward was through voluntary collective action, and also that the product should bear the cost of its own recovery. In March 1994 the Chief Executive of PIFA, Jim Pugh announced that there had been agreement in principle to support Second Life Plastics.[9] However, there were still a number of concerns that had to be overcome. Some of the companies were part of larger groups (for example BPI plc) that were also engaged in the parallel negotiations over shared responsibility in relation to packaging, and they did not want to agree anything that might compromise the position of the converters in these negotiations. There was also a concern that it would not be possible to pass on the additional costs down the supply chain, and that the converters would end up footing the bill. The deadlock on this issue was broken by the proposal by PIFA of an Environmental Protection Contribution. This was perceived as providing a mechanism by which the cost could be passed on successfully to the farmers.

Box 9.2 Packaging and Industrial Films Association (PIFA)

PIFA represents the interests of manufacturers and converters of all forms of plastic films and film products in the UK. It has around 120 member companies, and 37 associate members including major polymer producers (Annual Report 1998).

While membership of PIFA is useful to companies, it is not a commercial necessity. This is reflected in the fact that not all companies in the industry are members – for example less than half of the producers/importers of silage films are members of PIFA. A consequence of this is that PIFA can only act as an advocate for particular policies and actions, and attempt to influence the behaviour of companies through persuasion. It has no power to force participation and/or compliance with particular policies.

The Association has well-established links with Government departments. The 1998 Annual Report highlights the 'privileged relationship that PIFA enjoys with the officers from both the DETR and the DTI', and notes that '[PIFA has] direct channels into several Government departments and [has] worked hard to win the confidence of Ministers and Officials'. It has also developed links with the waste industry and with Local Authorities.

PIFA published its first environmental policy statement in 1991. The latest version of statement (Issue 4; November 1997) contains a commitment by PIFA to promote the re-use, recovery and recycling of waste film wherever environmentally beneficial and economically feasible.

While it was undoubtedly true that there was a desire – at least on the part of PIFA – for the industry to act (and be seen to act) in an environmentally responsible way, the main motivation for supporting the collective scheme was the fear of costly legislation.[10] As has been noted above, the early 1990s saw a number of initiatives that had raised the profile of waste management as a political issue. While these initiatives all contributed to a general 'climate of fear' in industry, it was the announcement by the Secretary of State for the Environment in July 1993 that was the critical factor. Frustrated by the failure of the packaging industry to produce a credible voluntary initiative, the Minister threatened to introduce legislation if a satisfactory plan for the introduction of producer responsibility was not forthcoming by the end of the year. While this statement did not apply to farm films, the companies interpreted the Minister's subsequent threat to call them to a meeting if they did not support Second Life Plastics as an implicit threat that the Government might consider legislation in this area as well.

Based on the experiences of the German Packaging Ordinance (even though it did not cover farms films either), the companies believed that the cost of any legislation might be as high as £400 per tonne, that is approximately four times greater than their operating margin. If they were to attempt to pass on a cost of this magnitude in the price of the film, then a large number of farmers would switch to using silage clamps (an alternative capital intensive production technology) with catastrophic consequences for the stretch film market. By the end of 1994 the threat of legislation was no longer very credible, if indeed it ever had been. However, by this stage the discussions about the setting up of a collective scheme had gained their own momentum, with the FFPG being incorporated in law in December.

The final outcome of the discussions was an agreement to set up the Farm Films Producers Group (FFPG). This was incorporated as limited company at the end of 1994, to operate a non profit-making scheme to recover used plastic silage film from farms on the UK mainland, and to dispose of this waste via recycling (or via incineration with energy recovery). It started operating at the beginning of April 1995, by which time there were nine full members and eight associate members. Two overseas companies declined to join the scheme – Aspla (Spain) and AEP Industries (USA).

A Liaison and Monitoring Committee was established, which included representatives from the NFU, UKASTA, the British Agricultural and Garden Machinery Association, the Department of the Environment, and the Ministry of Agriculture Fisheries and Food. The role of the Committee was to disseminate information about the scheme's progress to agricultural merchants and farmers; to provide feedback from these groups on the operation of the scheme; and to provide guidance on further developments and extensions of the scheme.

FFPG took on the existing collection network of Second Life Plastics, which was bought from Anaplast Ltd for a nominal sum (£1). The existing management continued to be employed by Anaplast Ltd, although an additional administrator was employed directly by FFPG.[11] Farmers did not have to register with the scheme, and could call a Freephone number whenever they wanted to arrange for a collection (as had been the case under Second Life Plastics). Since it was not practical to impose any restriction on the brand of film that would be collected from farmers, the scheme would also collect film produced by non-FFPG companies.

The cost of collecting the waste silage film would be financed through the imposition of a levy (the Environmental Protection Contribution) on all member companies, at the rate of £100 per tonne on all silage film sold in England, Scotland and Wales. A major accountancy firm was appointed as the independent administrator of the scheme. It would receive confidential quarterly sales returns from the members, and invoice them accordingly. It also had the power to audit individual returns.

The concept of the Environmental Protection Contribution was submitted to the UK Office of Fair Trading and to the Competition Directorate of the European Commission (entailing legal fees of around £70 000). It received 'negative' clearance – which meant that while the scheme could be challenged in the courts, the participants would not be faced with the risk of a retrospective prosecution for collusion if it was found to be anti-competitive. However, companies were not allowed to show the Environmental Protection Contribution as separate line item on the invoice – only to state that it was included in the total price.

In addition to providing a (perceived) mechanism for passing on the additional cost, the Environmental Protection Contribution also represented an attempt to differentiate the products of member companies from those of the non-participants. However, because the FFPG would collect any brand of film (irrespective of whether it was manufactured by a member company, or not), the differentiated product did not offer any real additional benefit to the farmer.

4. ANALYSIS

4.1 Specification

The aims of the FFPG were clearly defined in its Memorandum of Association, that is

> *To promote, facilitate, develop and operate any non-profit making scheme for the collection and beneficial recovery or disposal of waste films and products with similar characteristics (including without limitation polyethylene and polypropylene films, sheet, bags, covers, linings, bindings and twines) sold for use in agriculture or horticulture within England, Scotland and Wales and, if thought appropriate, Northern Ireland.*

There was no specified objective for the amount of plastic that would be recycled under the scheme – it was intended that the scale of collections would respond to the level of demand for the service from farmers. However, for planning purposes, it was forecast that collections would increase to around 10 000 tonnes (dirty[12]) by the third year of operation, that is 1997–98. Since the level of the Environmental Protection Contribution (that is £100 per tonne) was based on this forecast, it seems reasonable to interpret it as an implicit objective.[13]

Collections at this level would have represented a recovery rate of around 25 per cent – based on a contamination level of 50 per cent and a market size of 20 000 tonnes per annum. This is less ambitious than the target recovery rate of the EU Packaging Directive (that is 50–65 per cent by 2001 across all packaging materials), but is consistent with the Directive's objective of recycling between 25 per cent and 45 per cent of all packaging waste, with a minimum recycling rate of 15 per cent for each material.

Determining a realistic 'business-as-usual' counterfactual is always difficult, but it does not seem plausible that there would have been any significant collections of silage film from UK farmers in the absence of the FFPG scheme – at least for a number of years. Second Life Plastics had stopped collecting waste silage films in 1994, with the reprocessing plant switching to imported feedstock – as it did again after the suspension of the FFPG scheme in 1997. It seems highly unlikely that collections would have been resumed in the absence of an agreement. While a new initiative was launched in Wales in 1999, this collects only around 1 000 tonnes per year,[14] much less than the amount envisaged by the FFPG.

Given the expected volume of collections, the implementation mechanism was credible. FFPG inherited the collection network that had been used successfully by Second Life Plastics. While the throughput handled by this system had been only been around 4 000 tonnes per annum, it would have been relatively easy to expand capacity – by adding new collection agents, or increasing the frequency of collections from the agents – to meet the forecast increase in volumes. The cost efficiency of the FFPG scheme is somewhat less clear. The use of the local agent network to consolidate collections meant that the total collection cost per tonne (that is the agent fee plus the transport cost per tonne) was relatively low. Furthermore, the fact that the levy was collected from only a small number of converters at the start of the supply chain ensured that administration costs of the scheme were also low. However, the resultant lack of any incentive for farmers to minimise the contamination levels of the waste film would have increased the total tonnage that was collected, and hence increased the total transport costs. In the absence of any direct financial incentive, the scheme relied on the exhortation of farmers to minimise contamination levels, and on the local collection agents to refuse waste that was highly contaminated. However, the agents had no incentive to do this, as they were paid per tonne of waste collected including contaminants.

While it is undoubtedly true that it would have been more costly to collect payments from a large number of farmers than from a small number of converters, it is questionable whether the additional costs would have outweighed the benefits of reduced contamination. Indeed it is interesting to note that in the recently launched collection scheme in Wales, farmers are charged directly – an annual fee of £27.50 for the first 700kg and £40.50 per tonne thereafter.   Of course a direct charging scheme is easier (and less costly) to administer in a small region with a tightly knit farming community, than on a national scale.   Nonetheless, it seems plausible that the total operating costs could have been lower if a collection charge had been imposed directly on farmers, rather than indirectly via the levy imposed on the converters.

There were adequate internal systems for monitoring the amount of waste collected/reprocessed, and the sales of member companies (in order to calculate burden-sharing payments). Because the FFPG was set up as a legal company, it had to keep proper financial records and supporting documentation – including details of the amount of waste collected and the material recovered. However, there was no requirement for the company accounts to be audited, and the tonnage figures were not reported publicly. The calculation of each member's payment into the scheme relied on the self-reporting of sales to the independent administrator, who would then raise an invoice for the appropriate amount. Consequently, there was an incentive for companies to under-report their sales, in order to reduce the amount that they must pay.   To combat this tendency, the administrator was authorised to conduct audits of individual company returns in order to verify their accuracy.

As was noted above, the proposal for introducing the Environmental Protection Contribution received 'negative clearance' from the competition authorities in the UK and in Brussels. Membership of the FFPG was not compulsory, and there was no penalty for remaining outside the scheme. Unfortunately, due to the nature of the market for silage films, companies that remained outside the scheme could gain significant benefits in terms of increased market share (and hence profits), at the expense of the participating companies.[15] Without the inclusion of an explicit 'trigger' mechanism in the agreement, free-riding – and the resultant distortion of the market – was inevitable.[16]

4.2 Implementation

The scheme was launched at the end of March 1995. At this time it had 17 members. By the end of its first year of operation however, companies had already started to leave the scheme, and by the end of January 1997 only four full members remained. The scheme was kept going with deferred income from 1995–96 and support fund contributions – in the hope that the Government would introduce legislative backing. However, when it became clear that this would not be forthcoming, the scheme was suspended in the UK at the end of March 1997. Around 5 000 tonnes of waste film (including contaminants) was collected in each year. This was broadly in-line with FFPG expectations for the first year, but below expectations for the second.

Table 9.1 provides a summary of the financial data for the two years of the scheme's operation. It is based on information provided in the annual accounts, and information provided by former FFPG management, although some of the figures (marked '?') have had to be estimated. During 1995–96, Environmental Protection Contributions were paid on less than 60 per cent of market sales. This is lower than would have been expected, given that the combined market share of member companies was around 90 per cent. However, it can be explained by the fact that the launch of the scheme coincided with the start of the peak selling-in period to the merchants (for example April – June). This meant that it was relatively easy for sales to be brought forward in order to avoid imposition of the Environmental Protection Contribution. The revenue figure implies that around 5 000–6 000 tonnes of sales were brought forward in this way.

Table 9.1   Financial and operating data of the farm films scheme 1995-97

Year ended		31 March 1996	31 March 1997	Total
Gross revenue	£ 000	1 186	264	1 450
less sales of recovered materials	£ 000	(?) 115	115	
EPC revenue	£ 000	1 071	149	
Implied EPC liable sales	000 tonnes	10 710	< 1 490	
% of total market sales		56%	< 7.5%	
Administration expenses	£ 000	841	550	1 391
Less set up costs	£ 000	(?) 140		
Operating costs	£ 000	701	550	1 251
Waste film collected (dirty)	000 tonnes	5 000	5 000	10 000
Cost per tonne		£140	£110	£125

While some sales were brought forward to avoid the Environmental Protection Contribution, there was no time for the two non-participants to exploit their cost advantage. It was not until the spring of 1996 that there was an opportunity for price under-cutting by these companies to have significant impact on the market. Almost immediately, companies started to leave the scheme. Two companies were removed as members of the FFPG by special resolution on 17 March 1996 because they 'ceased to fulfil the qualifications of membership'. A further five companies were removed from the register of members by special resolution on 25 June 1996 'on account of their withdrawal from the company'.

4.3 Environmental Impact

The scheme had minimal environmental impact. 10 000 tonnes of dirty waste film were collected from farms during the two years of the scheme's operation, and approximately 5 000 tonnes of plastic was recovered (that is 12.5 per cent recycling rate). As discussed above, this represents an insignificant fraction of the waste stream, and the resultant reduction of in situ disposal would have had a negligible impact on water and air quality.

4.4 Resource Development

The discussions during 1994 that led to the setting up of the FFPG established new communication channels between the companies in the sector. Previously, the senior management of the different companies had not had occasion to interact directly with one another. The process also established a degree of goodwill between the member companies, which has continued since the collapse of the scheme in the UK. The same companies are involved in a similar collection scheme in Eire, and in a new, extended Farm Plastics Group in the United Kingdom.

The process resulted in some changes to the attitudes and perceptions of the senior management in the companies concerned. It caused them to accept that there was a potential problem that needed to be addressed, and to recognise the benefits of working together. However, there is no evidence to suggest that it resulted in a change to the individual companies' awareness of, and attitudes towards, environmental problems in general. The sector association (PIFA) was already environmentally aware, having had an environmental policy since the early 1990s.

With regard to learning, the process resulted in an improved understanding of the size of the UK market for silage films (that is total tonnage). To a certain extent the experience of the FFPG has also resulted in policy learning. The industry now understands the difficulties associated with a collective scheme of this type, and the need for backing legislation to prevent free-riding. However, this lesson does not appear to have been taken on board by the Government, which – while recognising the issue of free-riding – continues to hope that a purely voluntary scheme along the lines of the FFPG will be resurrected in the future.[17]   Interestingly, the recently launched collection scheme in Wales is based on direct payments by farmers, thus avoiding the problem of free-riding.

There was little impact on the relations between the industry and the Government, which is not surprising given that the Government was not directly involved in the process. The relationship between PIFA and the Government was already good. If anything, the refusal of the Government to provide the necessary backing legislation for the scheme has caused frustration on the industry side.

5. CONCLUSION

The FFPG agreement is interesting for a number of reasons. First, it provides a good example of voluntary collective action to produce a public good (that is avoidance of legislation) with free-riding by some of the beneficiaries. Second, it demonstrates the importance of a credible alternative instrument; not only to the feasibility of a voluntary agreement, but also to its continued operation. Third, it shows how the process can be influenced by events in a related policy area (that is packaging waste).

There are many positive aspects to the FFPG agreement. As a legally constituted limited company, the general aims and rules of membership were clearly defined. The implicit objective for the amount of waste that would be collected and recycled compared favourably with the material specific minimum recycling rate in the EU Packaging Directive, and represented a meaningful improvement over the realistic counterfactual. The implementation mechanism − based on an existing network of local collection agents − was credible and capable of coping with the expected volumes. The imposition of the levy on a small number of 'up-stream' converters minimised administration costs, although the consequent lack of any incentive for farmers to minimise contamination levels is likely to have resulted in higher transportation costs than if farmers had been charged directly for collections. It should also be recognised that the discussions that led to the setting up of the FFPG resulted in an enhancement of the policy resource base. In particular, new communication channels were established between the participants, and a degree of goodwill was established that has continued since the collapse of the scheme.

On the negative side however, the implementation of the agreement, and the environmental impacts were both poor. At the first sign that they might not be able to pass on the cost of the Environmental Protection Contribution − or might lose market share if they did − companies started to leave the FFPG, and after only two years the scheme was suspended. Ironically, at the same time the FFPG started operating in Eire, where the government had introduced legislative backing. Even during the two years of its operation the environmental impacts of the scheme were minimal. The quantity of film collected from farmers represented an insignificant fraction of the total waste stream, and the resultant reduction of in situ disposal would have had negligible impact on water and air quality.

It is tempting to blame the free-riding of the two non-participants for the early termination of the scheme. However, this would be an over-simplification. While it is true that the actions of these companies served to destabilise the market in early 1996, it was not the free-riding per se that led to the collapse of the FFPG. As long as there was a credible threat of alternative regulation, the FFPG could have been sustained, even with some free-riders. Of course, the free-riding would have had implications for the fairness of the scheme, and for overall economic efficiency, but it would not have affected its viability or its environmental effectiveness. However, once this threat was no longer credible – as was the case by late 1995 – the viability of the scheme was fatally undermined. This important point is clearly illustrated by a simple example.

Figure 9.2 shows the Nash Equilibria (shaded) of a two-player simultaneous participation game where the values in the cells represent the profits of the two firms. When there is a credible threat of high cost regulation, one firm participates (that is pays for the scheme) while the other free-rides. However, once the threat diminishes, neither firm chooses to participate and the scheme collapses.

In conclusion, while the FFPG was in many ways well specified, and the process that led to its formation has had some lasting benefits in terms of resource development, its premature demise and negligible environmental impact mean that it must be judged a failure. However, this was in large part due to the refusal of the UK Government to introduce any backing legislation for the scheme, and to the receding threat of alternative legislation if it failed.

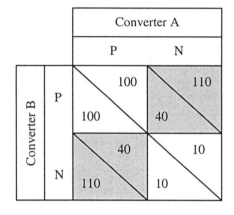

Credible threat/high cost

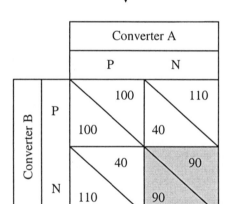

Non-credible threat/low cost

Figure 9.2   Simple participation game

NOTES

1. Borkey et al (1999) classify voluntary approaches into three broad types: unilateral commitments by industry; public voluntary programmes which firms can choose to join; negotiated agreements between industry and Government.
2. Sources: *Waste Strategy 2000 for England and Wales*, Department of the Environment, Transport and the Regions, May 2000 (Cm 4693-2); Applied Market Information Ltd, published in the Annual Report 1998 of the Packaging and Industrial Films Association (PIFA).
3. *Options for tackling the problem of waste non-packaging farm plastics: a consultation paper*, Department of the Environment, Transport and the Regions, October 1998.
4. The six priority waste streams were packaging, newspapers, tyres, batteries, vehicles, and electronic equipment.
5. Joint statement issued by the Secretary of State for the Environment, and the President of the Board of Trade after a meeting with representatives of the PRG on 28 September 1994.
6. A network of 30 local collection agents was set up across the UK to collect waste films from farmers. All of the agents were certified (that is insured, drivers inoculated against tetanus, vehicles disinfected and so on), and had local knowledge and established working relationships with farmers.
7. Source: 'Recycling farm plastics', article by J. R. H. Sale of British Polythene Industries PLC in *Plasticulture*, No. 97 - 1993/1.
8. In the 1995 there were 19 companies producing film products (that is converters) - nine of which were overseas companies selling through UK distributors.
9. *ENDS Report*, No. 230, March 1994
10. The Association's environmental policy statement (published in 1991) had advocated the recycling of materials wherever economically feasible and environmentally beneficial, and stated that PIFA would encourage the more efficient collection of waste film. It was therefore keen to ensure the continuing operation of Second Life Plastics.
11. Anaplast Ltd were paid £125 132 in 1996/97 for the provision of management services and facilities.
12. Waste silage film can be highly contaminated with water, soil, silage and other organic matter. The term 'clean tonnes' refers to the net amount of plastic film recovered, while the term 'dirty tonnes' refers to the gross amount collected, including the contaminants.
13. At the time of the negotiations, it was believed that the market size for silage films was around 15 000 tonnes per annum. On the assumption that FFPG members accounted for around 90 per cent of the market, and that collection costs were around £130 per tonne (dirty), a levy of £100 per tonne of sales would be sufficient to finance collections of 10 000 tonnes per annum (dirty).
14. *ENDS Report*, No. 304, May 2000, page 20.
15. The market for stretch film can be characterised by a 'location model' of monopolistic competition with a fixed number of firms. The firms' products are differentiated in product characteristic space on the basis of technical performance (for example strength, weight and so on), with mechanical silage clamps providing an alternative production technology that places a ceiling on the price that can be charged (Salop, 1979).
16. An agreement of this type can be thought of as a dynamic cost-sharing game, in which at each stage of the game, firms simultaneously decide whether to contribute. It is possible to show that full participation (that is no free-riding) can be enforced by the use of a 'trigger' strategy under which firms revert to a mixed strategy if any firm fails to participate in the scheme at any stage (Salmons, 2001).
17. *Options for tackling the problem of waste non-packaging farm plastics: a consultation paper*, Department of the Environment, Transport and the Regions, October 1998.

REFERENCES

Borkey, P., Glachant, M. and Lévêque, F. (1999), *Voluntary Approaches for Environmental Policy: An Assessment*, Paris: OECD.

Porter, M. (1998), 'Waste management', in Lowe, P. and Ward, S. (eds), *British Environmental Policy and Europe: Politics and Policy in Transition*, London: Routledge, pp 195–213.

Salmons, R. (2001), 'Voluntary collective action: is free-riding inevitable?', *CSERGE Working Paper*, University College London, forthcoming.

Salop, S. C. (1979), 'Monopolistic Competition with Outside Goods', *Bell Journal of Economics*, **10** (1), 141–56.

10. The Disposal of White and Brown Goods in the Netherlands

Hans Th. A. Bressers, Ellis Immerzeel and Josee J. Ligteringen

1. INTRODUCTION

In an attempt to reduce waste and to close material life cycles, the Dutch Environment Ministry made an attempt to sign a covenant with the producers and importers of household appliances (the so-called white and brown goods). The negotiations started in 1992 and involved all stakeholders: representatives of the producers and importers, the government (state, provincial and local), the processing industry, the retailers and the environmental organisations. Some of the issues could not be solved, however, and the discussions did not result in a covenant. From 1994 on, government started to prepare for regulation on the matter. Finally, in 1998 the white and brown goods disposal order was published. The Order sets out the producers' responsibility regarding the disposal of white and brown goods. After publication of the Order the sector started to develop a plan for the disposal and processing of white and brown goods. Discussions with local authorities resulted in a logistic system for the collection and disposal of the goods. The system became operational as of 1 January 1999 and seems to be working reasonably well. In the meantime the sector embraced the system, even to the point that its chairman (Coops, 2000) now presents it as a product of responsible self-regulation and co-operation with government, in an article that is introduced as dealing with 'the success of an environmental covenant'.

The truth is that, despite lengthy negotiations, the government was not able to sign a covenant with the white and brown goods sector. The disposal of white and brown goods had to be settled by means of regulation: the White and Brown Goods Disposal Order. In the context of the NEAPOL project (Negotiated Environmental Agreements: Policy Lessons to be Learned from a Comparative Case study), this chapter aims to explain the unsuccessful negotiations, looking at the economic-institutional context within which the covenant was negotiated.

Section 2 describes the setting in which the covenant was negotiated: Section 2.1 describes the development of the covenant as an instrument in Dutch environmental policy. Section 2.2 gives a general survey of the waste problem and describes the Dutch government's and the European authorities' waste policy in respect of white and brown goods. Section 2.3 describes the specifics of the white and brown goods sector.

Section 3 describes the negotiations on a covenant (section 3.1); the drafting of the regulation when it became clear that a covenant was not feasible (section 3.2); and the white and brown goods disposal order (section 3.3).

The case is analysed in section 4: the results of the negotiation process are analysed in terms of two relevant criteria of performance – feasibility, and resource development. Finally, concluding remarks and an explanation why a covenant was not feasible in this case are given in section 5.

2. CONTEXT

2.1 Covenants as a Policy Instrument in Dutch Environmental Policy

In the Netherlands more than 100 covenants have been signed between the Dutch government and private actors. Over the years, the covenant has become a well-known and widely-used instrument in Dutch environmental policy. Experience with the instrument has led to its further development. The first environmental covenants were introduced in the second half of the 1980s (Glasbergen, 1998). These initial covenants concerned only one issue; they were agreed between the Environment Ministry and a single actor (a company or branch organisation). The covenant instrument fitted in with the idea of 'internalisation', the idea that an industry has to accept its responsibility and deal with its own problems (Suurland, 1994). Within this setting, the government signed many covenants, gradually dealing with more complex sectors of industry.

A key term during the 1990s was the so-called target group policy (Bressers and Klok, 1996). The goal of the Dutch government was to achieve a more integrated environmental policy. This target group policy was officially announced in the first National Environmental Policy Plan (NEPP, 1989) and the NEPP-plus (1990). A fundamental principle underlying this approach is that the responsibility for achieving the environmental targets lies primarily with the target group. In the notes that specified the target group policy, 13 branches of trade were selected for the introduction of negotiated agreements. The covenants had now become multiple issue agreements involving a number of actors! The branches of trade involved contain 12 000 companies that have more than five employees. Together they are supposed to be responsible for more than 90 per cent of the industrial environmental burden in the Netherlands (Klok and Kuks, 1994). It was planned for these agreements to be concluded by the end of 1992. However, the signing of the agreements was delayed, except for three branches of trade. By the end of 1997, nine of the selected branches of trade had concluded a negotiated agreement.

2.2 Waste Policy

In the 1970s the Netherlands experienced an increasing shortage of space for the disposal of waste, influenced by a steep rise in waste production, together with a threatened exhaustion of raw materials, which led to increasing attention being paid to the re-use and recycling of discarded products. During the 1980s, the harmful effects of materials were increasingly the subject of discussions between politicians and civil servants.

On the basis of historical sales figures, it has been estimated that the quantity of scrap white and brown goods will increase from 126.5 kiloton in 1992 to roughly 185 kiloton in 2005 (Novem/RIVM, 1997). But it is not only the quantity of scrap white and brown goods that is seen as a problem; the composition, too, is problematic. Consider, for instance, the use of CFC as coolant and in the manufacture of insulation for refrigerators and freezers.

A serious attempt by the central government to facilitate re-use and recycling, particularly in the white and brown goods sector, originated in 1989 in the National Environmental Policy Plan (NEPP). In this Plan, sustainable development was to be given form by, among other things, 'closing the materials cycle in the raw materials – production process – product – waste chain, together with the associated emissions'.

To this end, challenging and progressive standards were to be set, 'together with the business community, as far as possible' (NEPP, 1989). Furthermore, the NEPP announced the setting up of collection mechanisms for waste streams, such as refrigerators (inter alia in connection with the retrieval of CFCs), electronic and electrical equipment.

In 1990 the Environment Minister sent a letter to the Lower House in which he announced a reorientation of the waste policy. In the Minister's view, the producer and the importer should gain responsibility for their products in the disposal phase.

In the first half of 1993, the Environmental Plan 1994–1997 (NEPP, 1993) announced that a General Administrative Order in respect of the retrieval and re-processing of refrigerators and televisions was in preparation, and that discussions were being held with the industry in respect of its further development. It was expected that the implementation plan would be ready in the second half of 1993.

At the end of 1993 the Second National Environmental Policy Plan appeared (NEPP, 1993). As one of the central themes of disposal policy, it named the further detailing of the producers' responsibility for products in the discard phase.

A year later, in the Environmental Programme 1995–1998 (TK, 1994–95), an announcement was made of a General Administrative Order, in preparation for mid-1995. According to the Long-term Plan, the Order was to contain an obligation on producers and importers to take back their own products, together with a re-processing regulation. Furthermore, it was announced that regular discussions would be held between the parties involved. The implementation plan was practically complete. The cabinet opted specifically for an 'integral chain' approach by seeking to prevent the existence of waste (prevention), and the leak-proof disposal[1] of unavoidable waste. One of the important premises here is the producers' responsibility for their products at the disposal stage.

Box 10.1 White and brown goods

Since 1989, white and brown goods were singled out as a special (waste) category. In the context of attempts to reduce waste and the recycling of materials, the Environment Ministry attempted in 1992 to agree on a covenant with the producers and suppliers of white and brown goods concerning the disposal of their products. In the remainder of this chapter we consider this to be the first phase of discussions about the disposal of white and brown goods. The threat of a General Administrative Order (GAO) was retained; the threat of legislation was supposed to put the actors under pressure to gain agreement. A twin-track policy was pursued: the covenant and the legislation were prepared simultaneously. The point here is that, in the absence of such a threat, there may well have been no negotiations at all. An intense process of negotiation (1992–94) was conducted between all the members of the target group, the government, and third parties. The goal of the process was not achieved; a covenant was not signed. In a second phase (1994–96), the government drafted a GAO: the White and Brown Goods Disposal Order. This Order went into force on 1 January 1999. As a way out, the Order offered participation in a covenant with the Ministry of the Environment. Producers and suppliers were held responsible for the disposal of their products in the discard phase, unless they collaborated with the government in the execution of a covenant.

If we follow the general policy trend, we see that the initial consensus approach to the producers' responsibility for products in the disposal phase grew slowly into the implementation of legislative regulation. However, the possibility of a voluntary agreement was also kept open, virtually throughout this period.

2.3 European Regulation

During most of the period of the negotiations European regulation has been in preparation. On 9 October 1997 the EU's Environment Directorate published a working paper on the issue that was aiming to result in a proposal for a European directive (Directive on waste from electronics and electronic equipment). The directive is in line with the Dutch policy regarding the disposal of white and brown goods as eventually was laid down in the Dutch White and Brown Goods Disposal Order.

2.4 The White and Brown Goods Sector

The white and brown goods sector includes the following product groups:[2]

1. White goods: household appliances such as freezers, refrigerators, and so on;
2. Brown goods: electronic appliances for households such as televisions; video recorders and so on.

There are only a few white goods producers in the Netherlands (Atag, Pelgrim, Schurink). The major producers of white goods are mainly to be found in Germany, Sweden, Italy, the United Kingdom, Spain and France. In other words, most white goods are imported into the Netherlands. The representative body of the white goods sector is the co-operative of producers and importers, united in the Association of Suppliers of Domestic Equipment in the Netherlands (Vlehan). Approximately 30 businesses are incorporated into Vlehan which is about 60 per cent of the group's total membership (mostly white goods importers, of which there are about 50 in the Netherlands). In the negotiations around the covenant and the later regulation, Vlehan was acting as a representative of the producers and importers of white goods, and conducted negotiations in their name.

Philips and Sony have approximately the same market share and dictate the position within the brown goods sector. It is important to note that the profit margins in the electronics sector were under considerable pressure at the time the policy was being framed (Van de Blaak, 1996). In 1992, Philips, a major producer in the Netherlands, suffered a loss of approximately 2 billion guilders. The body representing the producers and importers of brown goods is FIAR: the Union of Manufacturers, Importers and Agents in the electronics area (brown goods), whose membership includes a number of major producers: Philips, Sony and JVC. FIAR has 35 members. Philips has a big influence on the decisions made by FIAR (Gemeentereiniging en Afvalmanagement, 4/97).

We assume that representative organisations in general well represent the general interests of their membership. This assumption is based on Sabatier and McLaughlin (1990). But that is not enough to fulfil the role as a representative in negotiations. The degree to which a representative organisation is actually able to represent its membership can furthermore be derived from the degree to which the organisation is in a position to mobilise the resources of its membership in specific processes. Not merely in the sense of supporting protest activities, but also in the sense of contributing to a change of the target group's behaviour along the lines envisioned by the policy maker.

Vlehan's representation of the producers and importers in the negotiations appears at first glance to be beyond dispute. At every meeting of Vlehan's management, their representative informed the board membership of the progress. Up to a point, the target group's members extended a mandate to the Vlehan board. The individual members did not get involved with the decision making, allowing Vlehan to negotiate on their behalf. At the end of the first phase of the policy formation process (in 1994), however, a number of the companies that co-operated in Vlehan were warned off by their German parent companies, since their co-operation would only be forthcoming if a single collection and processing system were to be adopted (similar to a German system). At this point, Vlehan withdrew (temporarily) from the negotiations, as some of its members had demanded. This incident shows that there were clear limits to the degree that the Vlehan could tie its members to obligations agreed upon with the negotiating partner.

The brown goods sector was represented by FIAR during the negotiations about the covenant. As Vlehan, FIAR had a mandate from its members to negotiate with the government. Philips – being the largest Dutch brown goods producer – had a great influence on the strategy played by the FIAR. Also, Philips kept direct relations/contacts with the Ministry of Economics regarding the issue of disposal of white and brown goods.

The white and brown goods sector is a very heterogeneous sector that includes a wide range of products and many international affiliations and therefore also a wide range of interests. During the process differences in opinion arose between the sectors, as well as within the sectors! Nevertheless, throughout the process, Vlehan and FIAR were more or less on the same side. Together the two trade associations initiated the Appareturn project to gain an insight into collection numbers and costs of disposal and processing of white and brown goods.

3. NEGOTIATION PROCESS

In order to reconstruct the way that the white and brown goods disposal order was introduced, use has been made of relevant policy documents, such as White Papers, memoranda, and notes from the Ministry of Public Housing, Physical Planning and Environment and the Ministry of Economic Affairs. Information was also drawn from other sources, such as newspaper and magazine articles from the period in which the Order developed. Above all, interviews were held with experts who were involved in the policy-making process leading to the Order. In the reconstruction of the background history of the white and brown goods disposal order, use has also been made of the work by Megens (1996) and Ligteringen (1999). After reconstructing the history of development, experts in the field were asked to comment on the reconstruction.

3.1 Negotiations for a Covenant

In global terms, we can divide the process of the creation of the white and brown goods disposal order into two phases (Megens, 1996). The phases differ in terms of the actors involved and the degree of interaction between these actors. The high point, in terms of the number of actors and the degree of interaction, occurred in the first phase of the policy formation process. During this phase negotiations took place in order to come to an agreement (or covenant). The first phase (1992–94) is characterised by the existence of a structural discussion between the actors, centred on the disposal of white and brown goods. In 1994, negotiations about a covenant ended. In the second phase (1994–96) the white and brown goods disposal order was drafted.

3.1.1 Actors involved from 1992 to 1994

In the first phase a great deal of discussion went on between the parties involved. On the side of the government and its policy formation the actors were the Ministry of Housing, Physical Planning and Environment (VROM: full title of the Environment Ministry) and, in a later phase, the Ministry of Economic Affairs. On the side of the target group, major actors are the Association of Suppliers of Domestic Equipment in the Netherlands (Vlehan) and the Manufacturers, Importers and Agents in the electronic area (FIAR). Further, in regard to the collection of white and brown goods, we can distinguish the retail trade; represented by the Union of Electrotechnical Businesses (Uneto) and the Netherlands Retail Trades Council (RND), which represents the chain stores. Further, with regard to collection, we encounter the Netherlands Local Government Union (VNG) and the Interprovincial Consultancy Organ (IPO). The following actors are involved from the (re-)processing sector: The Federation for the Re-extraction of Raw Materials (FHG), the Association of Waste Processors (VVAV) and the Recycling Business Information Foundation (BVK, later represented by the Society of Recycling Businesses in the Netherlands, BKN).

Table 10.1 Parties involved in the structural discussions around the creation of the white and brown goods disposal order

Government policy formation	Target group	Collection	Processing	Consumers/ General public
Ministry VROM	Association of Suppliers of Domestic Equipment in the Netherlands (Vlehan)	Union of Electrotechnical Businesses (Uneto)	Federation for the Re-extraction of Raw Materials (FHG)	Consumers Union (CB)
Ministry of Economic Affairs	Manufacturers, Importers and Agents in the electronic area (FIAR)	Netherlands Retail Trades Council (RND)	Association of Waste Processors (VVAV)	Nature and Environment Foundation (SNM)
		Netherlands Local Government Union (VNG)	Recycling Business Information Foundation (BVK, BKN from 1995)	Environmental Defence Union (VMD)
		Interprovincial Consultancy Organ (IPO)		

Finally, on behalf of the interests of the general public and the environment, the principal actors are the Consumers Union (CB), the Nature and Environment Foundation (SNM), and the Environmental Defence Union (VMD). These actors are also involved with each other outside the structural discussions on the disposal of white and brown goods. Maybe not in the broad context that we see here, but together in varying compositions. Table 10.1 summarises those involved in the structural discussions.

3.1.2 Negotiations for a covenant: 1992 –94

In April 1992, Minister Alders (Environment) revealed his plans to have the purchaser of refrigerators and freezers pay a contribution of a few tens of guilders towards the disposal of the equipment. This was done during the opening of Coolrec, a factory in the Netherlands for the environmentally responsible dismantling of cooling equipment for reuse. The disposal method that Coolrec used at that time cost more than it yielded. The money needed to bridge this gap was to come from the local authorities' waste disposal charges. Minister Alders sought to change that. In order that the polluter pays, he stated in 1992 that he was to send a Bill to the Lower House to institute a disposal charge. He planned to introduce the charge in 1994.

As has been described above, the Environment Ministry's general policy line is in the first instance to sign a covenant with producers, governing their responsibility for their own products in the discard phase. It was this that led the Ministry to set up discussions, to be held at four-monthly intervals, in which all those involved could negotiate on the content of this covenant.

The Department of Domestic Waste, part of the Waste Directorate in the Environment Ministry, commenced its White and Brown Goods project in 1992. In the context of this project, the Ministry took the initiative to conduct regular discussions (every four months) with the main parties involved in the disposal of white and brown goods. The Ministry sent invitations to the parties involved and chaired the meetings. An external consultancy bureau was brought in by the Ministry to support the project. Respondents from the organisations that were present during these meetings characterised the gatherings as a circus event because so many organisations participated in the meetings; just stating their opinions and not really responding to each other's arguments.

3.1.3 The allocation of disposal costs

Major differences of opinion arose during the structural discussions between the discussion partners. Sometimes difference occurred between the trade organisations of the white and brown good sector on one side and the Ministry of Environment on the other. But differences also arose between the trade associations Vlehan and FIAR and conflicts occurred even within the associations. The main reason for these 'internal' conflicts was a difference in interests between the sectors, which include a huge range of various product groups.

The most important point of dispute concerned the introduction of a charge to cover the costs of disposal. While nearly all those involved were agreed on the preference for a disposal charge – on different grounds, incidentally – in advance (on purchase), FIAR and later Vlehan, too, were against it. Vlehan and FIAR were afraid that the disposal charge would increase prices, thus harming the producers' competitiveness against foreign imports. Both organisations emphasised that, if consumers and retailers were to start purchasing goods from the surrounding countries, this would have a negative effect on employment in the Netherlands. Vlehan and FIAR thus expressed a preference for waiting for European regulation before introducing a disposal charge in the Netherlands. A speedy conclusion to the negotiation process was thus not in the interests of Vlehan and FIAR. The two organisations (certainly FIAR) appeared to be bent on delaying the process. Various other actors, including the Environment Ministry, however, were set on a very rapid introduction of the producers' responsibility. This led Vlehan and FIAR into opposition, mainly with the Environment Ministry. In the meantime, the Environmental Management Act was amended in order to provide a legislative context for a possible disposal charge.

In March 1994 it appeared that Minister Alders had reached an agreement with the white goods importers that the retrieval and re-use of the equipment they supplied should be made compulsory from June 1995. The costs of dismantling could be passed on to the consumers. The first plan was to introduce a charge to cover these costs, which was to increase gradually from ten to about 65 guilders for each appliance over several years. The rate at which the charge was to increase depended on whether a similar charge would be introduced in surrounding countries. Initially, the costs of disposal would largely be borne by the local authorities, but they would shift gradually in the direction of the producers. For white goods it was agreed that, from mid-1995, the retail traders would immediately take back old equipment when they delivered the newly purchased item. In the meantime, the white goods sector would set up an organisation to regulate the disposal of the equipment they had taken back. The VNG agreed that the local authorities would process equipment that was retrieved but not replaced.

The agreement was ready for signature in June 1994. It was at this moment that Vlehan declared that it could no longer support the plan. In fact, Vlehan's membership had withdrawn the organisation from the negotiations. A number of companies that collaborated in Vlehan were warned off by their German parent companies. These parent companies in Germany wished only to co-operate in the case that a single collection and re-processing system was opted for (similar to a German system). At that time it appeared that the German government would not opt for a disposal charge, but rather for a contribution on payment, which meant that the Dutch situation would differ from the German one. Vlehan therefore withdrew from the negotiations, but stated that it was still prepared to discuss matters with government and the other parties involved.

Furthermore, the Netherlands Retail Trades Council at that point objected to collection via the retail trade. In a letter to the Environment Minister, the Council set down its arguments as lack of space, possible costs, and hygiene problems. Uneto did not agree with the Council, incidentally. Uneto believed that the retail trade should indeed assume its responsibility for the environment by exchanging new equipment for old.

3.1.4 The scope of producers' responsibility

Another point on which the opinions of the different actors came to diverge was the degree of responsibility that the producers should be allocated. The Environment Ministry wished to have the producers accept a wide area of responsibility, making them responsible for the entire disposal of white and brown goods. This meant that the producers would not only be financially responsible for the processing of white and brown goods, but also for their collection. The view of the consumer and environmental organisations was also that the responsibility for the complete disposal of white and brown goods lay with the producers. The Netherlands Retail Trades Council (RND) also recognised the producers' responsibility, but objected to the collection of the products by the retail trade. Uneto's standpoint on collection was somewhat milder: there were possibilities for collection by the retail trade.

Vlehan, however, was of the opinion that the government had been allocated the legal responsibility for discarded products, including white goods, and should accept it. Also, in view of the high processing costs, Vlehan considered that the producers only had a responsibility for collection. In regard to collection, Vlehan was afraid that too few discarded white goods would be collected in practice to allow them to be processed at reasonable cost. Vlehan's opinion, furthermore, was that the producers should not bear the costs of collection. If it were the case that producers were allocated the responsibility for collection, then the costs would have to be covered by a disposal charge, levied on consumers either at the time of purchase or disposal of the white and brown goods.

If, however, a general responsibility for disposal were to be allocated, then Vlehan's view was that there could be no question of responsibility for equipment that had come onto the market prior to the regulation. According to Vlehan, second-hand shops were selling extremely old equipment that contained large quantities of harmful substances. Processing such equipment would involve excessively high costs.

Neither did FIAR accept complete producer responsibility. Partial responsibility was negotiable. In this option, FIAR took on the responsibility for the design and production process. At the time this policy was being framed, the economic situation in the electronics sector was very poor. The introduction of complete producer responsibility would involve major financial consequences.

Especially if the processing costs were to be incorporated into the sales price, the consequences for the competitiveness against foreign businesses might be very serious.

These differences of opinion between the Environment Ministry, Vlehan and FIAR peaked in 1993, when the Economic Affairs Ministry became involved in the discussions, in an intermediary function, as it were. The Ministry is also formally involved in the disposal of white and brown goods, insofar as the competitiveness of the white and brown goods sector is involved. Formally speaking, then, the Ministry also plays a part in respect of the possible disposal charge for such goods.

At this point the Environment Ministry, possibly under the influence of the Ministry of Economic Affairs, proposed that Vlehan/FIAR should have a role in directing the disposal. To this end, Vlehan/FIAR itself should propose a disposal plan. At that point, the Environment Ministry had allocated responsibility for collection jointly to the local authorities and the retail trade. However, the local authorities and the retail traders did not agree with the director's role to be played by Vlehan. They foresaw problems with Vlehan's involvement with their own part of the disposal – the collection of white goods. At this point the Ministries of the Environment and Economic Affairs, on one side, were in conflict with the local authorities and the retail trade on the other.

When it appeared that Vlehan's plans for the co-ordination of the disposal of white goods did not fulfil the expectations of the Ministries of the Environment and Economic Affairs, the difference of opinion slowly spread to all the actors involved. The Ministries regarded the achievement of a covenant within a reasonable time as no longer feasible. As a result, the structural discussions were terminated.

3.2 Drafting the Regulation (1994–96)

As the structural discussions between the actors in the network foundered in 1994, the Ministries of the Environment and Economic Affairs decided to prepare for legislation. The Environment Ministry actually had a draft General Administrative Order ready in the first half of 1994. This went far further than the final General Administrative Order, as presented in 1996. Officials from both Ministries had been in contact on this matter. Since the Ministries could not form a common position at the official level, the draft Order was discussed at the Ministerial level. The Ministers decided to leave the issue open for a new cabinet.

A new cabinet assumed office. The Ministers of the Environment and Economic Affairs offered the producers a last chance to come up with their own plans for the disposal of white and brown goods. The plans would have to be submitted before the end of 1995, or else it was threatened that an Order would be in place in the course of 1996.

The actors that we have seen in the previous phase no longer appear in the same composition in the negotiations in the present phase. Two networks can be distinguished in the negotiation that was conducted in this phase of the policy formation. In the first place, there were repeated discussions on the disposal of white and brown goods between the Ministries of the Environment and Economic Affairs, and Vlehan and FIAR. Outside this process, the Ministries contacted Vlehan and FIAR separately on other matters. In this phase the other actors initially had no contact with each other on the disposal of white and brown goods. In a later stage of this phase of policy formation (1996), discussions were held between VNG, NVRD, HBD, the Consumers Union, the Nature and Environment Foundation (SNM), the Environmental Defence Union (VMD), Uneto and, later, BKN on the disposal of white goods. These discussions were intended to influence the content of the Order, which had by then been announced.

When it appeared that, in view of the wide differences of opinion, a covenant was scarcely feasible within a reasonable time, the Ministry of the Environment initiated preparations for legal regulation. Many of the actors involved in the first phase were looking forward to legislation with pleasure, in view of the long-drawn-out negotiating process. It was mainly the Consumers Union, the environmental organisations and the retail trade that found that the process had gone on long enough; they wanted a speedy regulation of the producers' responsibility for white and brown goods. The various actors were in large measure unanimous about a policy instrument in the form of legal regulation. Only Vlehan and FIAR did not fit in with these unified objectives, since they rejected any form of producer responsibility, other than in a European context.

One point on which there was still a difference of opinion between the actors related to the content of the General Administrative Order in preparation. The Environment Ministry, which had in the first instance declared itself to be in favour of the incorporation of environmental criteria[3] in the regulation, now abandoned these demands for the reason that the Ministry – as the other parties – did not have any insight into collection numbers. A number of organisations (with HBD as the principal and co-ordinating actor) acquainted the Economic Affairs Minister with their concerns on this point, among others, in June 1996. In a letter, HBD, Uneto, RND, CB, SNM, NVRD, VNG and VMD emphasised the importance of a rapid introduction of a far-reaching producer responsibility, together with the incorporation of environmental criteria into the plans. The letter went on to emphasise that there was a wide area of support for the environmentally responsible disposal of white goods.

In 1995 Vlehan and FIAR started a pilot collection project, called Appareturn (Apparetour in Dutch), in the Eindhoven area. The project was supported by financial contributions from the Ministries of the Environment and Economic Affairs, among others. The project was to give the sector a better insight into costs of disposal and the degree to which obsolete equipment could actually be reused. Furthermore, Vlehan and FIAR wanted to see whether collection projects would deliver sufficient equipment, after German pilot projects had appeared to show that little used equipment was being returned. They wanted to wait for the pilot project's results before negotiating with the Ministries about a national introduction. According to the agreement with the Ministries, the pilot project was to run to the end of 1996. Neither of the Ministries agreed to this, however. In June 1995, the Ministries of the Environment and Economic Affairs wrote a letter to the producers and importers co-operating in Vlehan, informing them that they had to present a declaration of intent before 1 July, in which they were to make clear their views on product disposal.

Thereafter, before 1 November of the same year, they were to come up with concrete solutions. While a declaration of intent was in fact signed, the 1 November ultimatum passed without the submission of any concrete plans for the regulation of retrieval and re-processing. The producers and importers finally submitted their plans at the end of 1995. At first sight, Minister De Boer (Environment) regarded the plans as acceptable: 'They offer sufficient perspective to be incorporated into legislative regulation.'

The RND reacted to the plans of Vlehan and FIAR with disappointment. In RND's view, the proposals to the Ministry embraced only a very limited form of producer responsibility. In the main, it was the responsibilities of the other actors, such as the retail trade, that was set out. The Council informed Vlehan that the key role in the area of physical collection is reserved for the local authorities, in the context of their legal responsibility to take care of consumer waste. The retail trade was prepared to assume a number of tasks within such a physical structure, if that were to lead to discarded white goods being disposed of in an environmentally unobjectionable manner (RND, 1996).

After further study of the plans submitted in December 1995, the Environment Ministry sent a letter to the suppliers in April 1996, in which it indicated that 'the plans as submitted, in particular as these concern consumer goods, do not yet offer sufficient perspectives for the realisation of an adequate disposal structure. This has led to the Ministers', ..., decision to adopt legislation. This legislation will be very limited in scope, leaving as much room as possible for self-regulation.' The letter furthermore made it clear that the producers and importers of white goods would be allocated a directing function (via their branch organisations) for the creation of a disposal structure. 'Producers and importers shall agree with other involved parties on their role.'

In the interim, the Eindhoven pilot project was still running. The environmental movement stated that the meagre results of the pilot project (in their view) suited the producers. As a counter-activity, the Environmental

Defence Union (VMD) organised a collection, to last for three days at the end of 1996. According to the Union's figures, this three-day campaign resulted in an equal quantity of equipment being collected as the Appareturn project had managed in eight months.

The policy forming actors in the process leading to the white and brown goods disposal order were the Ministries of the Environment and Economic Affairs. The actors attempted to formulate a joint policy on the disposal of white and brown goods. The policy's target group is formed by the producers and importers of white and brown goods in the Netherlands. In the policy formation process surrounding the disposal of white goods, Vlehan and FIAR represented the target group. During the first phase in the formation of the policy, these organisations also participated in the structural discussions organised by the Environment Ministry. Other participants in these discussions were the representatives of lower tiers of government (IPO and VNG) and the Dutch retail trade (Uneto and RND), in connection with the collection; representatives of the waste processing sector (FHG, VVAV, BVK); and the Consumers Union and environmental organisations (SNM and VMD) as representatives of consumer and environmental interests. Major conflicts arose during the negotiations on a covenant regarding the disposal of white and brown goods. The Ministry of Economic Affairs was in an intermediary position and did not agree with the 'full' producer responsibility proposed by the Environment Ministry and others. The trade associations were reluctant to take responsibility for the waste products: they did not consider this to be their problem. Within the sector, too, also major differences in opinion existed regarding the disposal issue. The fact that the brown goods sector in particular, had great difficulties at that time due to poor economic performance in the sector and severe competition also created an atmosphere that was not ideal for concluding an agreement. Clearly, the trade associations operated a strategy of delay: keeping discussions going and not taking decisions; wanting to wait for the results of the Appareturn project; and wanting to wait for European regulation. A single, uniform European regulation was attractive to them because (1) this would avoid distortion of competition in Europe and (2) this would create one uniform disposal system in Europe for the producers, instead of having to adapt to different systems in different countries. At the same time, the sector did not participate heavily in European forums to influence European policy making. It seems that the forthcoming EU regulation was used in discussions to delay decision taking.

In the second phase of the policy formation process, Vlehan and FIAR were also involved in negotiations with the policy makers, in a small circle. The other actors played a less important role in this phase. They stated their objections and interests to the policy makers. Now the policy makers – the Ministries of Environment and Economic Affairs – were on the same side, having the same goal: establishing a system for the disposal and processing of white and brown goods.

3.3 Outcome: the White and Brown Goods Disposal Order

The draft General Administrative Order – the White and brown goods disposal order as drafted by the Ministries of Environment and Economic Affairs in the course of 1996 – is an outline regulation. The final order was published on 21 April 1998. The main elements of the Order are the following:

- Producers and importers of white and brown goods are responsible for the disposal and processing of white and brown goods. Therefore they have to set up a disposal structure that is leak-tight, and organise an environmentally friendly processing of these goods.
- A prohibition (ban) on incineration or dumping of white and brown goods.
- A prohibition on the trade in freezers that contain CFCs.
- The retailer has to take in the old product from the consumers free of charge when a new product is bought (old for new system). The retailer can bring the old products to the local authorities or give it to the producers/importers.
- The municipality has to collect the white and brown goods separately. And they have to take in the old products from the retailers without charging them for this service (which is normally the case when it concerns industrial waste). In addition, the municipalities are responsible for the collection and processing of old products where the producer/importer no longer exists.

The producers and importers of white and brown goods had to inform the Minister how they intended to fulfil their obligations concerning the disposal of the goods before 1 September 1998. The Order offers three ways to do this:

- The producers and importers can make individual plans (an individual announcement to the Minister).
- The producers and importers can make a joint plan (a collective announcement).
- They can close a covenant with the government that then discharges them from the obligations in the Order.

It is striking that the order still offered the option for a covenant although this is no longer a real advantage (neither for the government nor for the sector) since the order requires the same elements as a collective or individual announcement. There is a difference in a regulatory sense: a covenant makes all partners responsible for the implementation; the Order holds the government responsible for the implementation. According to a respondent in the Environment Ministry, the option has been included under pressure of the Ministry of Economic Affairs, which wanted to keep the option of a covenant open.

The sector did not make use of the covenant option. FIAR and the Vlehan submitted a joint plan – a collective announcement – before the deadline was passed. The plan was in large part based on the experience with the Appareturn pilot project in Eindhoven. The plan described the disposal structure for white and brown goods and included among others:

- Collection scheme for the appliances
- Percentages for re-use of products and materials
- Finance system
- Monitoring system for the disposal structure.

The FIAR and Vlehan together include about 80 per cent of the total market of the producers and importers of white and brown goods. Those that are not member of Vlehan or FIAR can join this collective initiative.

The Dutch government approved the plans submitted by Vlehan and FIAR. However, this did not mean that the removal and processing of disposed white and brown goods was effective. For the system to become operational, an agreement had to be reached between the other players in this field: most importantly, the local authorities who – on basis of the Order – are responsible for those appliances that have been brought on the market by producers and importers that are no longer active ('orphan equipment', as it is called). In addition, the industry and the local authorities had to come to an agreement on the logistical system. The cost item (who pays for what) in particular made the discussions difficult.

The producers and importers of white (Vlehan) and brown (FIAR) goods created a new organisation – the NVMP[4] – that was made responsible for organising the disposal and processing of white and brown goods. The local authorities were represented by the NVRD.[5] The discussions regarding the collection of white and brown goods took place between the NVMP and the NVRD.

One month before the system was to come into effect (1 January 1999) an agreement was reached between the NVMP and the NVRD. It was decided to use existing regional stations (the so-called ROS, Regionaal Overslag Station in Dutch) as the central point for handing over the disposed white and brown goods to the industry. At the ROS, of which there are 50 spread out over the Netherlands, the appliances coming from the consumers and the retail sector will be collected and divided into different product groups. The NVMP will take care of the goods from the ROS onwards. The NVMP will pay the ROS a handling fee.

To finance the whole system, the consumers pay a separate sum (a so-called 'disposal contribution', 'verwijderingsbijdrage' in Dutch) that is added to the price of the product. The amounts have been set for each product type separately and are based on the expected costs of processing. The retailers have to administer this amount separately so that it can be transferred to a fund that will be used to pay the costs of collection and processing.

The Dutch government decided to lay down the producer's responsibility in a general order after it became clear that a covenant was not feasible. The order determines the general responsibilities of the various players in this field. The industry is given the task of setting up a system for collection and processing of the disposed white and brown goods. The sector organisations – Vlehan and FIAR – set up a separate organisation (NVMP) that developed a plan for collection and processing. The plans were sent to the government before the deadline had passed and were approved by the authorities. Now a new round of discussions started between the actors which play a role in the collection system and which had to co-ordinate their actions: the local authorities, the retailers and the producers and importers. The RVND (on behalf of the local authorities) and the NVMP reached an agreement on logistics and costs in December 1998. On 1 January 1999 the collection and processing of disposed white and brown goods went into effect. Respondents at the Ministries of Environment and Economic Affairs state that they are satisfied with the final outcome: a collective disposal system in which local authorities, the retail trade and the producers co-operate. Due to the short preparation period (an agreement was reached between RNVD and NVMP in December), the implementation of the system showed some initial deficiencies but is now working reasonably well. The sector has even become proud of it, even to the point that its chairman (Coops, 2000) is presenting it as a product of responsible self-regulation and co-operation with government, in an article that is introduced as dealing with 'the success of an environmental covenant'.

4. ANALYSIS

Since the negotiations did not result in an agreement it is only possible to look at part of the performance of the covenant. Taking our theoretical framework as a starting point, we can conclude that we can only assess the feasibility and the resource development aspect of the performance.

4.1 Feasibility

Although initially all actors preferred to sign a covenant, in the end a covenant was not feasible mainly due to opposing objectives and a lack of willingness to compromise. As we have seen, the primary objective of both the Ministries of Environment and of Economic Affairs was an extension of producer responsibility (although the Environment Ministry wanted to go further in this respect than the Ministry of Economic Affairs), whereby the costs of disposal would have to be born by the producers. They may pass these costs on to the consumer.

Insofar as the disposal of white goods did not fall to the account of the suppliers, and thus did not necessitate the introduction of a nation-wide price increase, the sector (producers/importers) was prepared to negotiate on the disposal of white goods.[6] While they were willing to consider disposal, and seek to contribute to a solution, the sector wished to avoid incurring the costs. The position of the sector was also determined by their foreign offices: the sector in the Netherlands consists mainly of importers, the producers are located outside the Netherlands. These foreign producers were kept informed of the negotiations and also had an influence on the position that the Vlehan took in the negotiations. When, during the negotiations on a possible covenant, the conflicting views of the sector and the policy makers collided, the sector withdrew (temporarily) from the negotiations.

Apart from objectives concerning the content of the measures, we also have to consider here the various objectives concerning the process. The Ministry of the Environment and the other actors were concerned that the producers' responsibility should not be postponed but introduced as quickly as possible. Vlehan and FIAR, however, were bent on delaying the introduction of national regulation. Such a delay would give Vlehan/FIAR the advantage that a regulation might possibly be introduced at the European level, or that one might come into view.

The resulting situation consists of a failed attempt to sign a covenant and later on a regulation that, however, still has some remaining elements that make negotiation-based elaboration possible. All in all we assess the performance as 'non-feasible'.

4.2 Capability, Impact and Resource Development

Since no covenant was signed in the end, we cannot assess its capability and impact. The negotiations did not result in a covenant. However, as we have seen, the negotiations continued in a somewhat smaller group. The subject was the same: the disposal of white and brown goods. The instrument was different: not a covenant but regulation. It might be interesting to see if and how the negotiations on a covenant strengthen or weakened the resource base for the further discussions on the regulation.

The development of the resource base can be looked at from three perspectives:

- *Learning:* During the negotiations many questions and issues came up regarding the disposal and processing of white and brown goods. An answer was not always available. Some of the issues were: the extent of the producer responsibility; question of how to finance the system; question of how to deal with the equipment of a producer/importer no longer operating in the market. In this context, the negotiations provided a forum for discussing these issues and learning about possible solutions.
- *Building relationships*: The first phase of the negotiations (1992–94) involved many organisations. In interviews, participants referred to these meetings as 'circus events' and complained that the meetings were too big to be productive. On the one hand, the meetings established communication lines between all those having a stake in the issue. On the other hand one can question the quality of these relations. The discussions taking place in smaller circles involving the ministries and trade associations had more impact on building relationships.
- *Improving general awareness and attitudes*: Interviews with and articles by representatives of the two key organisations, Vlehan and FIAR, clearly show that the sector was not prepared to take responsibility for their products in the final, disposal phase. In interviews (Milieumagazine 12-98, Magazine Recycling Benelux no. 1-1999) Vlehan still argued that the disposal and processing of consumer goods is a responsibility of the (local) authorities and not a responsibility of the sector. At the same time, the sector – once the regulation was published in April 1998 – took up the implementation in a progressive way. In October 2000 an interview with the chair of Vlehan was published in a trade journal. The journalist's introduction suggested that it was a successful covenant and the interviewee suggests that it was the product of co-operative negotiations with the Ministry; presents it as obvious that the sector feels itself responsible for a well functioning system and proudly claims that the 'Dutch approach' has been influential in shaping the European regulation (Coops, 2000).

5. CONCLUSION

Since 1989, white and brown goods have been singled out as a special (waste) category in Dutch environmental policy. In the context of attempts to reduce waste and to encourage the recycling of materials, the Environment Ministry attempted in 1992 to negotiate a covenant with the producers and suppliers of white and brown goods concerning the disposal of their products. An intense process of negotiation (1992–94) was conducted between all the members of the target group, the government, and third parties. The goal of the process was not achieved; a covenant was not signed. In a second phase (1994–96), the government drafted a GAO: the white and brown goods disposal order. This Order went into force on 1 January 1999. The sector has set up a system for the disposal of white and brown goods in co-operation with the local authorities.

Several factors explain why a covenant was not feasible in this case of the disposal of white and brown goods. Of the hypotheses with which this study started out, two were rejected on the basis of the case analysis.

The *competition hypothesis* seems to suppose another context than that of a complete sector negotiating with government, leaving no consumer choice to evade possibly bad environmental behaviour within the domestic market.

In the case of the *instrumental hypothesis* the relationship with this case is somewhat mixed. Although the threat of alternative policy instruments, namely regulation, was present, this did not push the negotiations towards a covenant. The explanation lies in the position of the Dutch government during the negotiations and in the fact that regulation was in preparation at another policy level, the European level. This 'alternative policy instrument' did not act as a threat, but rather as a sign of hope for the sector negotiators, making then prone to delay rather than accept any agreement. So it is difficult to say to what extent the hypothesis failed or is confirmed in this case.

Two other hypotheses about the explanation of the feasibility of a negotiated agreement in this case were supported by the case description.

The policy hypothesis stresses the importance of a climate of consensus-seeking and mutual trust. In this case, the lack of a real climate of consensus-seeking and joint problem-solving during the negotiations has played an important role in the outcome that a covenant was not feasible. The case supports the hypothesis.

The *sectoral hypothesis* is also confirmed. Within the sector differences in opinion existed on the issues discussed, since the interests of the sectors differed, due to heterogeneity. The power of the representative associations over their members was limited. Their mandate to compromise with government on behalf of the sector was restricted, partly due to the involvement of the foreign producers.

Partly as a background for these conclusions and partly as additional explanations, the following observations deserve mention here.

First, a *joint problem perception* on the basis of which a sense and acceptance of inevitability could rise, was absent in this case. The producers and importers of white and brown goods did not consider the waste coming from 'their' goods as their problem. The authorities in the Netherlands had always been responsible for the disposal of household waste and this was not to change, in their view. They certainly did not agree with the principle of producer responsibility that was a key issue in the discussions.

Second, the sector did not see these negotiations as possibly leading to new *joint business opportunities*. Instead they saw such opportunities as better warranted by a European regulation that would place them in the same position as their international competitors, but also as their foreign parent companies. Instead of looking for compromises or solutions to the problems, the sector operated a strategy of delay, arguing that they wanted to wait for European regulation on the matter.

Third, though the negotiations failed, nevertheless some positive learning occurred, making the drafting of formal regulation thereafter more feasible. In that sense the negotiations have had an important *information resource building* function.

Fourth, when the sector was forced by regulation to take its responsibility, it not only did so, but even tried to present its efforts as belonging to the main stream of Dutch co-operative, covenant-based policy implementation. The relationship with European regulation also seems to be turned around. The Dutch approach is claimed to have had a big impact on the formulation of the European regulation.

NOTES

1. Leak-proof disposal comprises both reuse and environmentally responsible disposal.
2. In this chapter we do not include the so-called grey goods: the information and communication technology that includes printers, copiers, computers and so on. These grey goods are included in the Decree.
3. Such as collection percentages, percentages for the reuse of products and materials, and the processing of waste streams.
4. NVMP: the Dutch Association for Disposal of Metal Electronic Appliances.
5. Branch organisation of the waste collection departments of the local authorities.
6. The financial problem involves in particular the disposal of the (obsolete) CFC-containing refrigerators and freezers.

BIBLIOGRAPHY

Blaak, M. van de (1996), *Witgoed, bruingoed: eind goed al goed? Evaluatie van het project 'wit- en bruingoed' van het ministerie van VROM*, doctoral thesis, Katholieke Universiteit Nijmegen.

Bressers, J.Th.A. and P-J. Klok (1996),'Ontwikkelingen in het Nederlandse milieubeleid', *Beleidswetenschap*, 1, pp. 445–60.

Coops, R. (2000), Het succes van de verwijderingsbijdrage, *ROM Magazine*, 10, pp. 7–8.

Glasbergen, P. (1998), 'Partnership as a learning process, environmental covenants in the Netherlands', in P. Glasbergen (ed.), *Co-operative Environmental Governance, Public-Private Agreements as a Policy Strategy*, Dordrecht: Kluwer Academic Publishers, pp. 133–56.

Magazine Recycling Benelux (1999), 'Inzameling en verwerking van wit-en bruingoed van start', 1999 1.

Klok, P-J., and S.M.M Kuks (1994), 'Het doelgroepen beleid,' P. Glasbergen (ed.) *Milieubeleid: Een beleidswetenschappelijke inleiding,*, The Hague:VUGA Uitgeverij, Den Haag, pp. 79–96.

Ligteringen J.J. (1999), *The Feasibility of Dutch Environmental Policy Instruments*, Enschede: Twente University Press.

Megens, W.A.J. (1996), *Toetsing van het netwerk-instrumentenmodel, een toetsing van de empirische houdbaarheid van het netwerkinstrumentenmodel voor wat betreft de case 'verwijdering van afgedankte witgoedproducten'*, Enschede: University of Twente, CSTM.

NEPP (1989), Tweede Kamer der Staten-Generaal, *Nationaal Milieubeleidsplan* (NMP), TK 1988-1989, 21137, nr. 1–2, Den Haag.

NEPP-plus (1990), Tweede Kamer der Staten-Generaal, *Nationaal Milieubeleidsplan plus* (NMP+), TK 1989-1990, 21137, nr. 20-21, Den Haag.

NEPP-2 (1993) Tweede Kamer der Staten-Generaal, *Nationaal Milieubeleidsplan-2* (NMP-2), TK 1993-1994a, 23560, nrs 1–2, Den Haag.

Novem/RIVM (1997), *Hergebruik van wit- en bruin goed*, Delft: November 1997.

RND (1996), Raad Nederlandse Detailhandel, Jaarverslag 1995, Zoetermeer: RND.

Sabatier, P.A. and S.M. McLaughlin (1990), 'Belief congruence between interest-group leaders and members: an empirical analysis of three theories and a suggested synthesis', *Journal of Politics*, **52** (3), 914–35.

Suurland, J. (1994) 'Voluntary agreements with industry: the case of Dutch covenants', *European Environment*, **4** (4), 3–7.

Tweede Kamer der Staten-Generaal, *Milieuprogramma 1995-1998*, 1994-1995, 24525, no.1–2, Den Haag.

Tweede Kamer der Staten-Generaal, *Nationaal Milieubeleidsplan-3* (NMP-3), 1997–1998, Den Haag.

'Verwijdering wit- en bruingoed' (1998), in *Milieumagazine*, **9** (12), Samson H.D. Tjeenk Willink, Alphen aan de Rijn.

11. The Energy Efficiency Agreement with the UK Chemical Industries Association

Roger Salmons

1. INTRODUCTION

On 18 November 1997, following eighteen months of negotiations, the UK Chemical Industries Association (CIA) and Secretary of State for the Environment, Transport and the Regions signed an agreement on energy efficiency improvement. The objective of the agreement was to reduce the aggregate specific energy consumption of the UK chemical industry by 20 per cent from its 1990 level by the year 2005.[1]

The agreement was due to run until 2005. However, in March 1999 the Chancellor of the Exchequer announced the Government's intention to introduce a Climate Change Levy on industrial energy consumption with '. . . significantly lower rates for those energy intensive sectors that agree targets for improving energy efficiency which meet the Government's criteria.'[2] Negotiations started immediately on a new agreement with revised targets and conditions, and this came into force on 1 April 2001 when the Climate Change Levy was introduced, at which point the original 1997 agreement ceased to apply.

The 1997 energy efficiency agreement is a voluntary agreement. It is not binding on either side, and there are no penalties for non-compliance – nor are there any rewards for compliance. The negotiations between the two sides were more in the nature of discussions than bargaining – although there were some issues that needed to be resolved. This is in sharp contrast to the serious bargaining over the negotiated agreement under the Climate Change Levy, which is legally binding and where the penalties for non-compliance are substantial (that is loss of tax exemption). The voluntary nature of the agreement is important, because it imposed a ceiling on the level of ambition that could be expected.

The agreement represented a new manifestation of the long tradition of co-operation and voluntary action in UK environmental policy. It built on – and brought together – two existing energy efficiency initiatives: the Government's Energy Efficiency Best Practice Programme which provided support and advice to industry; and the CIA's unilateral commitment on Responsible Care which included a significant energy component. As such, it should be seen as a means of improving the leverage of these programmes, rather than as a completely new, alternative policy approach.

2. CONTEXT

The agreement addresses an issue – industrial energy efficiency – that is highly relevant to the attainment of the Government's climate change policy objectives. The UK Government has two policy objectives. First, it has a legally binding commitment under the Kyoto protocol to reduce total greenhouse gas emissions by 12.5 per cent below 1990 levels by 2008–2012; which implies a target of 185 MtC. Second, it has an internal target of a 20 per cent reduction in carbon dioxide emissions (CO_2) by 2010, again versus a 1990 baseline; which implies a target of 134 MtC. Emissions forecasts for 2010 (see Table 11.1) suggest that planned measures will be sufficient to achieve the Kyoto target, but additional reductions of around 22 MtC will be required to meet internal targets for CO_2. If industry is to make a proportionate contribution to these additional reductions, then a 12–13 per cent improvement in energy efficiency will be needed, over and above any improvements that are already built into the projection.

In 1997 the CIA estimated that energy consumption by its members was responsible for CO_2 emissions totalling 6.8 MtC, which represented around 11 per cent of emissions from the entire business sector.[3] Therefore an effective agreement (that is one that delivered a substantial improvement over business-as-usual) would make a valuable contribution to the attainment of the Government's climate change policy objectives.

Throughout most of the 1990s the UK Government's policy on industrial energy efficiency focused on the provision of support and advice, and the encouragement of voluntary action by industry. This strategy was underpinned by three principle initiatives. The *Energy Efficiency Best Practice Programme* was launched in 1989 with the aim of stimulating the take-up of energy efficient good practice throughout the economy. The programme's industrial component publishes 'benchmarking information' which companies can use to assess their relative performance, and provides detailed information about proven energy efficiency measures. It also undertakes the evaluation of new energy efficiency measures, and provides limited financial support for basic R&D into potential energy efficiency measures.

Table 11.1   Forecast greenhouse gas emissions by end-use sector

Sector		1990 Baseline	2010 Projection
Business	CO_2	66.9	57.3
	GHG	90.5	65.6
Transport	CO_2	39.1	46.0
	GHG	39.6	48.2
Domestic	CO_2	42.7	38.5
	GHG	46.6	41.2
Agriculture	CO_2	10.3	7.4
	GHG	24.8	20.4
Public Sector	CO_2	9.0	7.2
	GHG	10.0	7.9
Total	CO_2	168.0	156.3
	GHG	211.7	183.3

Source: Climate Change: Draft UK Programme, Department of the Environment, Transport and the Regions, February 2000.

The *Making a Corporate Commitment Campaign* was launched in 1991, with the aim of increasing the priority that businesses gave to energy efficiency. Companies that signed up to this public voluntary scheme[4] were asked to assign board level responsibility for developing and reassessing energy efficiency strategy, to set performance improvement targets, and to ensure that plans are considered regularly at board level. These initiatives were supplemented by the *Energy Management Assistance Scheme*, which ran from 1992 to 1996, and provided financial assistance to small and medium sized enterprises (SMEs) to enable them to obtain consultancy advice on the design and implementation of energy efficiency projects. It was replaced in 1996 by the *Small Company Environmental and Energy Management Scheme*, which was itself incorporated into the Energy Efficiency Best Practice Programme in December 1998.

The last two years of the decade saw the initial steps towards the introduction of economic incentives. In 1998, Lord Marshall was asked to evaluate the use of economic instruments to improve industrial energy efficiency. Following the publication of his report in November 1998, the March 1999 Budget Statement included a commitment to introduce a *Climate Change Levy* in 2001, with provision for energy intensive sectors to gain partial exemption by entering into negotiated agreements with the Government.

The CIA and Department of the Environment (DETR)[5] shared some common motivations for entering into an agreement. Both were looking for ways to provide greater focus for their respective energy efficiency programmes, and both were interested in evaluating the practicalities and potential impacts of a voluntary agreement. As part of the evolution of its Energy Efficiency Best Practice Programme, the Government wanted to place a greater emphasis on specific sector activities, and it believed that a long-term agreement with a quantified target would provide a good focal point for these activities. It was felt that this would improve the effectiveness of the programme's expenditure. This view was mirrored at the CIA, which was looking for a vehicle that it could use to raise the profile of energy efficiency within its membership, and to act as a focal point for the re-launch of its Responsible Energy programme. In doing so, it hoped to convince outside stakeholders that the industry was taking a responsible attitude towards the issue of greenhouse gas emissions.

The Government had been impressed with the results that had been achieved by agreements in the Netherlands, and the 1994 *Sustainable Development* strategy document had already recognised that there might be a role for voluntary agreements within UK environmental policy. However, the document had also identified a need for further work on the scope of agreements, and how they could be negotiated, implemented and enforced. A pilot agreement with the chemicals industry would therefore provide a valuable learning experience regarding their potential as a policy tool. The UK chemicals industry was also well aware of the experience in the Netherlands, and the potential advantages that an agreement might provide. The chemical industry is highly international, and several major UK companies have operations, or sister companies, based in the Netherlands. Indeed, some are owned – either wholly or partly – by Dutch parent companies.

For its part, the CIA also hoped that an agreement would allow it to ward off the introduction of a carbon-energy tax, or at least ensure exemption for their members. Interest in the use of voluntary agreements on energy efficiency first arose after the publication of proposals by the European Commission in September 1991 for a combined carbon-energy tax. In March 1992 the Confederation of British Industry told the House of Lords Select Committee on the European Communities' inquiry into the tax proposal that '[energy intensive sectors] stand ready to negotiate voluntary agreements with the Commission to limit emissions in return for reduced exposure to the proposed tax'. By the time that the Draft Directive was finalised in May 1992, it included provisions for tax relief for energy intensive industries that were prepared to 'give national public authorities firm commitments to reduce their CO_2 emissions or their energy consumption'.

Although this initiative was abandoned in December 1994, following opposition from the United Kingdom, the concept of a carbon-energy tax did not disappear off the political agenda. In May 1995 the Commission proposed a new framework that would allow member states to introduce national carbon-energy taxes on a discretionary basis, but with aim of moving towards harmonisation some time after 2000. Again these proposals left open the possibility of tax exemptions for energy intensive industries that entered into negotiated agreements. Furthermore, the merits of a tax continued to be actively promoted by environmental groups. Thus, although the UK government showed little interest in pursuing the idea of a carbon-energy tax at that time, it was always likely to return to the agenda at some point in the future.

In response to the Commission's proposals, the chemical industries' European federation (CEFIC) launched its voluntary energy efficiency programme (VEEP) in 1992. The stated objective of this unilateral commitment was to reduce specific energy consumption by 15 per cent between 1990 and 2000, on the condition that EC dropped its proposals for the tax. In June 1996, CEFIC extended the commitment through to the year 2005 and amended the target to a 20 per cent improvement in energy efficiency (versus 1990), although again this was conditional on the Commission not resurrecting its proposals. VEEP had two important influences on the magnitude of the target that was to be included in the final agreement. First, the investigations undertaken by the CIA before they endorsed the CEFIC target had convinced them that a 20 per cent improvement in energy efficiency was achievable. Consequently, they were already comfortable with this figure. Second, it established a 'going rate' for energy efficiency improvements that could be delivered by a voluntary agreement. In effect it also probably placed an upper limit on the target that the CIA would be willing to agree, as a more ambitious improvement target would have tended to undermine the credibility of the CEFIC programme.[6]

3. NEGOTIATION PROCESS

In 1995 the DETR, the Department of Trade and Industry (DTI), the CIA, and several leading chemical companies entered into a 'sector dialogue' with the aim of identifying long-term environmental issues that might have an impact on the international competitiveness of the sector. This generated a number of specific follow-up actions, including a commitment by the CIA to consider whether aggregate sector targets were feasible and whether such targets could form the basis of voluntary agreements.

While this dialogue helped to set the scene for the negotiations that were to start in the following year, it was the work that the Energy Technology Support Unit (ETSU) was doing with the CIA to re-launch its Responsible Energy programme that provided the specific impetus for an agreement on energy efficiency. The CIA had already recognised the desirability of having a quantified target for the improvement in energy efficiency, and ETSU raised the idea of a voluntary agreement with the Government. By May 1996, the CIA and DETR had agreed in principle to explore the practicalities of an agreement, and at the re-launch meeting for the Responsible Energy programme the Junior Environment Minister announced that the two sides were to start discussions.

Box 11.1   The Chemical Industries Association

The Chemical Industries Association (CIA) is the main representative body for the UK chemicals sector. While it has fewer than 200 member companies (that is only around 5 per cent of the sector total), the membership is heavily weighted towards large companies, and basic chemicals production. As a result it accounts for approximately 50 per cent of sector employment, 66 per cent of sector capital spending and turnover, and 85 per cent of sector energy consumption.

Its Responsible Care programme was launched in 1989 (the Responsible Energy component was launched in 1991–92, and re-launched in 1996), and all companies are required to sign up to a set of Guiding Principles as a condition of membership. The CIA publishes an annual Health, Safety and Environment report (UK Indicators of Performance) which includes aggregate performance data on energy consumption and energy efficiency.

Policy is determined by the Council – comprising around 40 member companies, and is implemented by a full-time executive staff. The Association has no powers to enforce compliance with policy decisions; relying instead on a combination of support, benchmarking and peer pressure to achieve compliance.

The CIA has always had strong links with Government departments – particularly the Department of Trade and Industry, which is the sponsoring department for the sector. In the early–mid 1990s it started to develop closer links with the Department of the Environment – a process that was formalised by the 'sector dialogue' in 1995.

The negotiations were conducted between officials from the Energy, Environment and Waste Directorate of DETR, staff members from the CIA, and three CIA member companies – ICI, BP Chemicals and Rhône-Poulenc – who were there to represent the membership.[7] In addition, representatives from the UK Environment Agency and the DTI attended the early meetings as observers. ETSU were instrumental in progressing the negotiations – acting as a facilitator, arranging meetings, writing minutes and drafting the agreement document. It also played an important role in the design of various aspects of the agreement. Formal meetings were held every couple of months, which were attended by all parties. In addition, ETSU had ongoing bilateral contacts with the individual parties to discuss specific issues, and to keep the process moving.

Both the CIA and DETR were positively pre-disposed towards the idea of an agreement, and both were keen that the negotiations should reach a successful conclusion. However, each side had certain reservations that instilled a degree of caution. The CIA had two main concerns. First, it was worried that an agreement might impose a potential constraint on the growth of the sector. This concern is somewhat surprising, given that the agreement relates to relative energy consumption (that is per tonne of output) rather than absolute energy consumption, and suggests a degree of misunderstanding. However, these fears were allayed after a meeting with the Dutch Environment Ministry and NOVEM[8] in November 1996.

Second, it was concerned about the possible interaction of an agreement with the EU Directive on integrated pollution prevention and control (IPPC). The Directive, which was adopted in September 1996, required that (inter alia) operating permits must contain measures to ensure that certain basic principles are met, including the efficient use of energy.[9] When fully implemented, the Directive will apply to over 300 plants in the chemicals sector; the large majority of which are operated by CIA members. Consequently, the CIA wanted to ensure that any agreement would not impose a double burden on these companies.

For their part, DETR officials were cautious regarding the political acceptance of any final agreement. The negotiations had been started against a backdrop of political uncertainty about the future of the incumbent Conservative government, and about the attitude of a new Labour administration towards agreements as a policy instrument. The uncertainties continued after the Labour Party's election victory in May 1997 as decisions were put on hold while a thorough policy review was undertaken. Despite a supportive speech by the new Parliamentary Under–Secretary of State at a CIA press event in June 1997, there was a degree of discomfort among some ministers over the use of voluntary agreements as a policy instrument, reflecting a suspicion that they let industry off the hook.

This unease may explain the hiatus after June 1997, even though all of the major points of principle had by then been agreed. However, by November there was a sudden urgency on the part of the Government to sign the agreement, as any lingering reservations were outweighed by a desire to be able to 'put something on the table' at the Kyoto conference.

The negotiations revolved around five main issues, although only the first three of these were at all contentious. The first related to the appropriate definition of energy consumption – the CIA wanted continuity with historical practice, while DETR wanted to extend the definition to include all relevant energy sources. Closely related to this was the issue of how individual data should be aggregated in order to ensure that the performance measure identified real changes in energy efficiency rather than the effects of changes in the output mix. In the end it was agreed that the definition of energy consumption should be broadened to include the energy content of waste streams combusted on site and imported steam, and that aggregate performance would be calculated by dividing aggregate energy consumption by aggregate output. While this was the simplest approach, it meant that the measure would not exclude the effects of changes in the relative output levels of the various sub-sectors.

As has been noted above, one of the main motivations for the CIA entering into the negotiations was a desire to extract a promise from the Government that its members would be exempted from any future carbon-energy tax. However, this was not acceptable to the DETR, which was adamant that it wanted to keep open all of its policy options for the future. The issue remained on the agenda for the first nine months of the negotiations (and several drafts of the agreement) before the CIA reluctantly accepted that the Government was not going yield on this issue.

If the CIA was not to get its desired tax exemption, then it wanted the Government to fund a consultancy support programme aimed at its small and medium sized members, to help them improve their energy efficiency. Analysis by the CIA had shown that its members' sites could be divided into three groups: a small group of high energy users accounting for 80 per cent of total energy consumption; a relative large group of mid-range energy users accounting for 19 per cent of consumption; and a slightly smaller group of low energy users accounting for the remainder.[10] On the assumption that energy efficiency was already likely to be a priority for the high energy-use group, the mid-range users were identified as being critical to the achievement of further significant improvements. The DETR was happy to accept this, as the money would come from within the existing budget of the Energy Efficiency Best Practice Programme. Thus while the CIA members would get a larger share of the programme's resources, it would not require any additional expenditure by the Government.

In return DETR wanted some assurance that the CIA membership would deliver the desired improvement in energy efficiency. However, while the CIA was willing to commit itself to encourage and support its members in delivering the objective, and to promote their co-operation with the Government, it was reluctant to undertake any firm commitments on behalf of its members.[11] The only commitment that it was willing to make on their behalf was that they would supply the necessary information on energy consumption and product output to allow performance to be monitored.

Interestingly, the need for a rigorous monitoring and verification mechanism was not a major issue, nor was the magnitude of the improvement target. The CIA wanted strong monitoring and verification procedures to enhance the credibility to its Responsible Care programme. While some work was required on the detailed design of the mechanism (which was largely undertaken by ETSU), the main issue relating to monitoring was over who should bear the cost.

With regard to the objective, the CIA offered a 20 per cent improvement in energy efficiency by the year 2005 (compared to a base year of 1990), which was equal to the revised objective that was included in the CEFIC unilateral commitment. The investigations that it had conducted before signing up to the CEFIC commitment meant that it was confident that an improvement of this magnitude could be achieved. Indeed by the time the negotiations started, CIA performance data showed that their members had already made a 10 per cent improvement in energy efficiency. However, the Government were sceptical about the methodology that had been used to calculate this figure and – based on an analysis conducted by ETSU – it believed that 20 per cent represented a reasonable target. Speaking at a CIA press event at the end of June 1997 (that is after 12 months of negotiations), the Junior Environment Minister stated that '[The objective] would, according to our initial assessment, require the take-up by CIA members of all cost effective energy efficiency measures. If further evaluations bear this out, this target would not be a soft option, and a negotiated agreement might offer the most efficient way forward for all concerned.'[12]

It should be noted that, given the voluntary nature of the agreement, the Government did not believe that it was reasonable to expect the CIA to agree to an objective that would require going beyond the introduction of all cost effective measures. As such, both sides saw the agreement as a way of encouraging firms to reduce energy inefficiencies, rather than as a vehicle for delivering fundamental changes in the energy intensity of the chemical industries.

After eighteen months of negotiations, the final agreement was signed on 18 November 1997. An important feature of the agreement was the commitment by the Government to provide additional support to small and medium sized members of the CIA. Under this programme, 150 sites would be offered a visit by an energy consultant who would provide a detailed written report on the site's performance and make recommendations of measures to improve energy efficiency. The total cost of this programme amounted to around £750 000 across three years (that is £5 000 per site),[13] which represented approximately 2 per cent of the total budget for the Energy Efficiency Best Practice Programme, and around 90 per cent of the direct expenditure on the chemicals sector. The support programme was to be reinforced by a series of promotional workshops arranged by the CIA, which would publicise the generic findings of the visits and disseminate best practice.

Box 11.2 The contents of the agreement

In addition to specifying the objective of a 20 per cent improvement in energy efficiency by 2005 (compared to 1990), the agreement set out a number of commitments by both DETR and the CIA. For its part, the DETR committed:

- to continue to support the chemical industries through its Energy Efficiency Best Practice Programme;
- to provide additional support, mainly to small and medium sized members of the CIA, in the form of free on-site audits to help achieve energy efficiency improvements;
- to provide a guidance leaflet for companies in the chemical industries, describing the agreement and providing advice on how the necessary data should be produced;
- to provide independent verification of the industries' performance in achieving the objectives of the agreement, based on data supplied by the CIA.

For its part the CIA committed:

- to encourage its members to ensure that the objectives of the agreement are met in an ordered and timely manner, by offering the services of CIA staff to advise on the best way forward;
- to provide help and encouragement for members to set individual targets for energy efficiency improvements that are consistent with the overall objective;
- to promote members' co-operation with the Government to provide data to enable the agreement to be monitored effectively;
- to advocate best practice, emphasising the support available, and to liaise with DETR to direct resources to companies requiring assistance.

The only direct obligation on CIA members is for them to provide energy consumption and product output data to the CIA, to allow the calculation of aggregate specific energy consumption.

The agreement identified a number of specific milestones, both in relation to performance and in relation to the support programme. A quarter of the sites eligible for consultancy support would be visited during the first year of the agreement, 40 per cent in the second year, and the remainder in the third year. Promotional workshops would be organised by the CIA in the first, second and fourth years of the agreement.

The agreement was not binding on either party, and it contained no sanctions for non-compliance. However, neither were there any rewards for compliance. Indeed, it explicitly allowed the Secretary of State to pursue other policy measures to improve energy efficiency and achieve carbon savings, even if performance was on track to meet the objective.

4. ANALYSIS

4.1 Specification

The environmental performance objective of the agreement was well defined and quantified, and the base year for the comparison was stipulated – that is 'To reduce the specific energy consumption of the chemical industry by 20 per cent of the 1990 level by the year 2005'. Furthermore, the agreement clarified the meaning of specific energy consumption, and addressed the issue of the windfall efficiency gains that had arisen from the restructuring of the energy supply industry. However, the broadening of the definition of energy consumption meant that there was no accurate information on energy consumption for the 1990 reference value. The agreement did not contain any explicit, quantified intermediate milestones, but these were implicit in the inclusion of a provision to compare annual performance against a smoothly declining (that is linear) trend line to the 2005 target.

While the objective of the agreement was clearly and unambiguously defined, doubts were expressed at the time as to whether it represented a genuine improvement in energy efficiency compared to business-as-usual. For example, one assessment commented that 'On the face of it, the target is not very demanding at all. According to CIA data, its members' energy consumption per tonne of product declined by 14 per cent between 1990 and 1996 ... Under the agreement, they will need to make further reductions over the next eight years at only one-third of the average annual rate achieved up to 1996.'[14]

Like many other countries, the United Kingdom has extensive official data on industrial energy consumption – published in the annual *Digest of United Kingdom Energy Statistics* (DUKES). However, it is unusual in that its also has independently produced projections of future trends in specific energy consumption (SEC) under a three different scenarios. These projections provide a basis for constructing a realistic counterfactual that can be used to assess the objective, although they require careful interpretation.

Box 11.3   Projected trends in specific energy consumption

Every year, ETSU publish a report for DETR which includes projections of specific energy consumption (SEC) for each industrial sector under three different scenarios. [a]

The *'Business As Usual'* (BAU) scenario reflects a situation where there are no major changes to the economic and regulatory environment in which industry operates. As such, it should be considered as a base reference scenario rather than a realistic counterfactual. It assumes that Government support programmes continue unchanged, and that general economic conditions and energy prices remain at prevailing levels.

The *'All Cost Effective'* (ACE) scenario assumes the rapid uptake of all 'no regrets' measures, that is those measure that satisfy normal investment criteria. A distinction is made between retrofit measures and major new plant installations, with different payback criteria being applied to each. It is assumed that retrofit measures are implemented immediately, but that major investments occur over a period of time as part of the normal plant replacement cycle. As such, this scenario represents the optimal cost-minimising trajectory starting from the actual non-optimal position in the base year.

The *'All Technically Possible'* (ATP) scenario assumes the instantaneous introduction of the most energy efficient technologies currently available irrespective of the cost, and that all production processes are optimised solely with respect to energy efficiency. No consideration is given to the impact on profits, or on the availability of capital. As such it should not be considered as a meaningful forecast, but rather as a benchmark showing the technological limit for improvements in energy efficiency.

It is useful to interpret the ACE projection in terms of a *'Gap Closure'* between the BAU trend and a potential ACE trend-line. The latter is a hypothetical construct which assumes that all cost efficient measures are introduced immediately rather than following the natural plant replacement cycle, and that future improvements occur at the same exogenous rate as under BAU projection. As such, it is analogous to the ATP projection, providing a benchmark of the economic limit for improvement in energy efficiency. [b]

---

a   *Industrial Sector Carbon Dioxide Emissions: Projections and Indicators for the UK, 1990–2020.* April 1999 (ref: EPSC 20616001/Z/1), ETSU, Harwell.
b.   Analysis of the ETSU projections for the chemicals sector, implies that the long term BAU trend reduction in specific energy consumption is around 0.4 per cent points per annum, and that the magnitude of the potential BAU–ACE gap is

around 8 per cent points.   Consequently, the projection under the ACE scenario for the chemicals sector represents a BAU–ACE gap closure of 60 per cent after 5 years; 75 per cent after 10 years; 85 per cent after 15 years; and 97 per cent after 25 years.

Figure 11.1a shows the official data for SEC up to 1997 (1995 was the latest available data at the start of the negotiations), together with the ETSU projections under the three scenarios up to 2005.   Compared to these projections, the 20 per cent target appears to represent a meaningful improvement versus business-as-usual, lying half way between the projected outcomes under the ACE and the ATP scenarios.

However, as can be seen in Figure 11.1b, by 1996 CIA members had already reported a 14 per cent reduction in specific energy consumption compared to 1990 – an improvement not expected under the ACE scenario until the year 2003.[15]   As the above quotation noted, this meant that the 20 per cent target would require annual improvements in energy efficiency over the period 1997–2005 that were much smaller than those achieved over the previous seven years.   On that basis the objective does not appear to be very challenging at all.

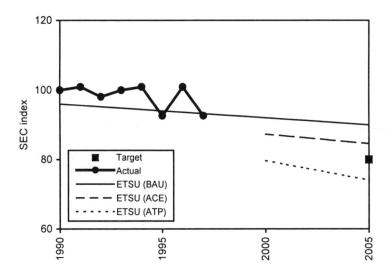

Figure 11.1a   Specific energy consumption, ETSU/DUKES data

Source: ETSU/DUKES

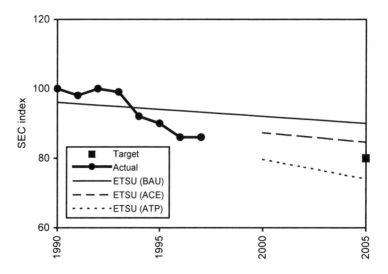

Figure 11.1b   Specific energy consumption, CIA data

Source: CIA

There are a number of potential factors that could explain the difference between the energy efficiency performance calculated by ETSU using the DUKES data, and that reported by the CIA. However, two would appear to be particularly significant. The CIA membership is more heavily weighted towards basic chemicals than the sector as a whole (basic chemicals account for approximately 80% of total CIA tonnage, as opposed to around 60% for the sector). Therefore, unless basic chemicals and speciality chemicals had exhibited the same rate of improvement in energy efficiency, one would expect there to have been a divergence between the aggregate CIA performance and that of the sector as a whole. Econometric analysis of disaggregated performance data provided by the CIA for 1990-97 (see Table 11.2) shows that when changes in production levels are controlled for, there was a marked difference between the underlying trends for two sub-sectors. While specific energy consumption had been declining at 2.4% points per annum for basic chemicals, it had actually been increasing at around 0.9% points per annum for speciality chemicals.

Table 11.2   Econometric analysis of CIA performance data 1990–97

Regression coefficients (t statistic)	Basic chemicals	Speciality chemicals
Production index	−0.62 (5.0)	−0.96 (6.3)
Year (1990 = 0)	−2.37 (12.1)	+0.85 (2.6)

Applying the CIA weightings to the two trend coefficients gives an aggregate trend reduction of 1.7 per cent points per annum. When the estimated sector weights are used, the aggregate trend reduction is much lower, at only 1.1 per cent points per annum. While this is closer to the official figure (corrected for changes in the level of production), it is clear that composition effects do not explain all of the difference between the two sets of figures. A full explanation requires an understanding of the relative performance of CIA member companies compared to the industry average.

To the extent that the CIA's Responsible Energy programme had raised the awareness of energy efficiency among its members, one would expect them to have out-performed non-members over the first half of the decade. Combining the trend values estimated from the CIA data with ETSU's gap closure assumptions, it is possible to adjust the BAU and ACE projections to reflect the CIA weighting of basic and speciality chemicals. These adjusted projections are shown in Figure 11.2 (at constant 1990 production levels), together with the aggregate trend-line for the CIA membership, that is minus 1.7 per cent points per annum.

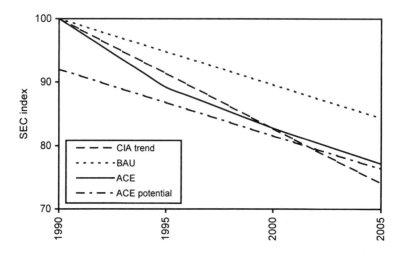

Figure 11.2   Adjusted SEC projections

For the period 1990–97 the CIA trend-line lies between the BAU and ACE projections – which seems entirely plausible – and by 1997 the CIA members had achieved a 60 per cent gap closure. Specific energy consumption is now projected to decline to 84.5 by the year 2005 under the BAU scenario and to 77.5 under the ACE scenario (representing an 85 per cent gap closure). On the basis of these adjusted projections, the 20 per cent improvement target for 2005 represents no more than a maintenance of the 60 per cent gap closure already achieved by 1997 – that is it represents the BAU trend from 1997 onwards. However, Figure 11.2 also shows that it would not have been reasonable to simply extrapolate the CIA trend-line out to the year 2005, as this would have taken it below the adjusted ACE projection (that is it would have required CIA members to voluntarily undertake unprofitable measures).

If one assumes that the best the CIA members could have achieved by 2005 would have been an 80 per cent gap closure, then this suggests that a reasonable value for the SEC index under the counterfactual lies in the range 78–80. On this basis, the 20 per cent objective does not appear to represent a real improvement, or at best – given the uncertainties over the projections – it represents only a small improvement over the counterfactual. However, given the voluntary nature of the agreement, this analysis would suggest that the scope for setting a higher target was limited (that is the maximum feasible target would have been around 22–23 per cent). A corollary of this analysis is that the maximum real improvement in energy efficiency that a purely voluntary agreement could be expected to deliver is also limited – lying in the range 1.5 – 3.5 per cent.

The agreement made no attempt to allocate the collective 20 per cent improvement target to individual member companies. The CIA believed that the target could be achieved through the monitoring of member companies' actions and performance; the provision of encouragement and support from the centre; and peer pressure to discourage free-riding by individual companies. However, if the above assessment of the target is correct (that is that it will require less than 100 per cent implementation of all cost-effective measures), then it is likely that such a combination of actions would be sufficient to ensure its achievement.

The CIA had planned to review progress in 2000 (that is five years before end of agreement) in order to identify the need for any additional action. However, this review was overtaken by the negotiation of the new agreement linked to the Climate Change Levy. The intention had been to identify 'laggards' by comparing member companies' scores on an Energy Management Matrix[16] together with their individual year-on-year performance trends, and by following up those companies that had received visits from the energy consultants to see whether they had acted on the recommendations. Attention – in the form of additional support and encouragement – would then be focused on these companies. The rationale for this approach was that these firms were likely to have the largest potential for cost-efficient improvements in energy efficiency. Again, given the assessment of the target, this approach should – in theory – lead to a relatively cost-efficient outcome (that is ex post cost-efficiency).

The agreement defined a highly credible control system, with monitoring based on a combination of self-reporting and independent verification. All member companies were required to make annual returns to the CIA for each of their sites, detailing energy consumption – broken down by fuel type – and production in tonnes. The data would be reviewed and audited by an independent consultant – appointed and paid for by DETR, with site visits being undertaken for a 5 per cent stratified random sample of returns to check the accuracy of the information that had been provided. The calculation of the aggregate specific energy consumption index figure would then verified by DETR, and the aggregate performance data published in the CIA's annual *Indicators of Performance* report. There is an annual review of performance against a smoothly declining trend by a small review group comprising representatives from DETR, ETSU, CIA, and two member companies. If necessary, the agreement contains an explicit provision for the re-negotiation of targets and/or the level of Government support.

The agreement did not contain an explicit statement with respect to learning. However, the programme of consultancy visits targeted at the 'mid-range' energy-users defined a number of implicit learning objectives in relation to the reduction of information asymmetries regarding the potential for energy efficiency improvements.   These related both to asymmetries between firms (for example about available technologies), and to asymmetries between the industry and the Government (for example about the potential scale and cost of further improvements). The programme that underpinned these objectives was well defined and credible. The agreement set out clearly how the sites would be selected; provided a detailed brief for the work that the consultants would undertake for each site; and specified how (and to whom) the findings would be communicated. It also placed a joint responsibility on the CIA and DETR to summarise and publicise generic messages from these visits on an annual basis.

4.2 Implementation

The agreement came into force on 18 November 1997, and performance indicators for 1997 were published in June 1998. Although these indicators related to the period immediately preceding the signing of the agreement, the data collection occurred after it had come into effect. The first annual review took place in December 1998, at which progress was deemed to be satisfactory. Performance indicators for 1998 were published in December 1999. Returns detailing energy consumption and production levels for 1998 were received from 92.9 per cent of manufacturing sites. This represented a slight improvement over the previous year's figures of 91.2 per cent, but was still some way short of the 100 per cent coverage committed by the CIA.

ETSU was appointed as the independent auditor, and during the first year of the agreement 15 sites were visited to verify the accuracy of their returns for 1997. These audits discovered a number of errors in the reporting of energy consumption, particularly in relation to net steam used. Surprisingly perhaps, the errors resulted in energy consumption being overstated by 3.8 per cent (Morrell and Ward, 1999). As a result, in December 1998 the CIA wrote to all member companies recommending minimum procedures for energy data collection based on the best practice that had been observed during site visits, and five of the original sample sites were revisited during 1999 to check the effectiveness of these new procedures. Despite this however, the CIA reported that there were still some problems with the 1998 returns.[17]

The support and dissemination programme was rolled out successfully, with ETSU being given responsibility for co-ordinating the programme and appointing energy consultants to undertake the site visits.   Forty sites received a visit in 1998, and potential energy savings of around 7 per cent were identified, with more than half of these savings requiring only modest investment. When the impact of new CHP installations was included, the magnitude of the potential savings rose to over 15 per cent (Morrell and Ward, 1999). The CIA ran energy efficiency seminars in February 1998 and March 1999, which included best-practice feedback from the consultancy visits. In addition, specific case studies were used to demonstrate energy efficiency improvements that could be achieved from a range of different initiatives. These seminars were not restricted to CIA members, but were open to all companies in the industry.[18]

At the time of writing, performance data is only available up until 1998 (that is the first full year of the agreement). Consequently, it is difficult to assess whether the agreement has had any impact on the underlying trend in energy efficiency. Specific energy consumption in 1997 was unchanged compared to 1996, while in 1998 it fell by 0.8 per cent points. However, over these two years aggregate production fell by 4 per cent, which (ceteris paribus) would have been expected to increase specific energy consumption by around 3 per cent points (see Table 11.2). This implies an underlying improvement in energy efficiency of almost 4 points across the two years, which is broadly in-line with the performance trend over the 1990–97 period.

Figures 11.3 and 11.4 compare the actual SEC index figures for the two sub-sectors with the figures predicted by the model that was estimated from the 1990–97 performance data, together with the 90 per cent confidence interval for the predicted values. While the actual and predicted figures for 1998 are very close for the basic chemicals sub-sector, there is some suggestion of an improvement in energy efficiency for speciality chemicals, although the difference between the actual and predicted figures is not statistically significant. However, this picture is consistent with what one would expect to occur under the agreement, given the preponderance of SMEs in the speciality sub-sector. Thus, while it would be premature to conclude that the agreement is definitely having a positive impact on energy efficiency (versus the trend), the initial signs are encouraging.

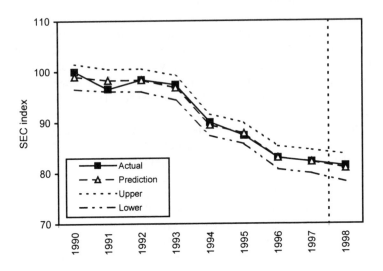

Figure 11.3   Actual versus predicted SEC: basic chemicals

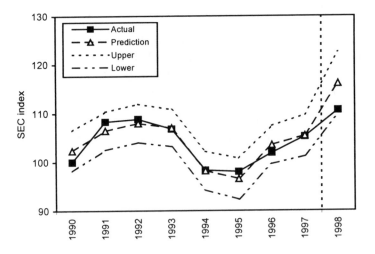

Figure 11.4   Actual versus predicted SEC: specialty chemicals

4.3 Environmental Impact

After only two years of operation, it is too early to conduct a full ex post analysis of the environmental impact of the agreement. However, based on the information provided by the consultancy visits in the first year, it is possible to provide an ex ante assessment of the magnitude of the impact that the agreement would have made in 2005 if it had been allowed to run its full course.

In order to assess the likely impact of the agreement it is necessary to isolate those components that are incremental – that is would not have happened anyway. To this end, Table 11.3 summarises the main factors driving further improvements in energy efficiency under two alternative scenarios. The first represents the situation with the agreement, while the second provides a reasonable view of what would have happened if it had not been signed. In both cases, only those regulatory changes that were known at the time the agreement was signed have been included.

Table 11.3   Factors driving energy efficiency improvements

With agreement	Without agreement (counterfactual)
IPPC Directive	IPPC Directive
Responsible Energy	Responsible Energy
EEBPP	EEBPP
20% improvement target	20% improvement target
Monitoring and reporting	Monitoring and reporting
Independent verification	
Consultancy support	
Best practice feedback	

The most important factors are common to both scenarios – that is the implementation of the IPPC Directive by 2007, and the continuation of the Energy Efficiency Best Practice Programme (EEBPP) and the CIA's Responsible Energy programme. It is also highly likely that the CIA would have introduced their own 20 per cent target for improvement in energy efficiency (that is the target in CEFIC's unilateral commitment), and that monitoring and reporting would have continued to improve – at least in terms of coverage. This leaves three elements of the agreement that can be considered as being incremental – independent verification of performance data; consultancy support to SMEs; and best-practice feedback.

Given the targeting of the consultancy support and the orientation of the best practice feedback seminars, it is likely that the main beneficiaries of these incremental elements will be the mid-range energy users. If the 40 sites visited in the first year of the agreement are representative, then it does not seem unreasonable to expect that the consultancy support programme could result in an overall improvement in energy efficiency of between 5–10 per cent compared to the counterfactual for this group. Assuming that the agreement has no incremental impact on high and low energy users, this implies that it will lead to an improvement in aggregate energy efficiency of between 1.0–1.9 per cent. If one assumes that under the counterfactual energy efficiency would have improved by 20 per cent, this implies that the reduction in specific energy consumption (versus 1990) will be between 20.8 –21.5 per cent under the agreement.

In order to estimate the impact of the improvement in energy efficiency on the emissions of CO_2 in 2005 it is necessary to make some assumption about the level of output in that year. For its calculations, ETSU assumed a 23.6 per cent growth in output for the chemical sector between 1990 and 2005. However, given that output in 1998 was at the same level as 1990, this seems overly optimistic. Consequently, the impact on CO_2 emissions has been calculated under two alternative scenarios (see Table 11.4). The first scenario combines the high estimate for improved energy efficiency with the ETSU growth assumption; while the second uses the low estimate and assumes that output in 2005 is only 5 per cent higher than in 1990.

Assuming that there is no change to the average fuel mix (so that changes in emissions are proportional to changes in energy consumption), the estimated reductions in CO_2 emissions under the two scenarios are 150 KtC and 70 KtC respectively. It seems reasonable to interpret these figures as upper and lower bounds for the likely impact of the agreement. This range is somewhat lower than the Government's expectation at the time the agreement was signed, which were that it would yield an incremental reduction in CO_2 emissions of between 150–245 KtC.[19]

Table 11.4   Calculation of impact on CO_2 emissions in 2005

	SEC Index	Prod Index	Energy Index	CO_2 (ktC)
High scenario				
1997 (actual)	85.8	102.2	87.8	6 820
2005 (without agreement)	80.0	123.6	98.9	7 680
2005 (with agreement)	78.5	123.6	97.0	7 530
Incremental				150
Low scenario				
1997 (actual)	85.8	102.2	87.8	6 820
2005 (without agreement)	80.0	105.0	84.0	6 520
2005 (with agreement)	79.0	105.0	83.0	6 450
Incremental				70

4.4 Policy Resource Development

The negotiation and the implementation of the agreement had a positive impact on the policy resource base. Both the CIA and DETR believe that the discussions resulted in a strengthening of the relationship between the two. The process also helped to establish a high level of trust in ETSU as an independent facilitator, particularly on the part of the CIA. Finally, the discussions resulted in an improved mutual understanding of some of the technical issues involved in the measurement of energy efficiency.

The implementation of the agreement has provided a number of informational benefits. The increase in the percentage of CIA sites providing annual returns and the independent verification process has led to an improvement in the quality of the performance data that is reported – although there are still some problems. The returns themselves have provided the CIA with valuable information on the extent of CHP, giving them a better understanding of the contribution that this had made to past improvements in energy efficiency, and of its future potential. Finally, the dissemination of 'best practice' through the consultancy visits and annual workshops has reduced the level of information asymmetries between companies within the sector.

Both the CIA and DETR believe that these benefits have proved helpful during the negotiations for the new agreement under the Climate Change Levy. In particular DETR claims that the negotiations with the CIA have been more open than with other sectors, and that the CIA have been more forthcoming with constructive ideas to address problems. However, even with these advantages, the new negotiations between the two sides have proved much more difficult and involved than those required for the original agreement. In large part this was due to the fundamental differences between a purely voluntary agreement and a legally binding negotiated agreement where the penalties for non-compliance are substantial (that is the loss of tax exemption). However, a need to maintain a high degree of consistency in the structure of the Climate Change Levy agreements across a number of different sectors, has also probably prevented the improved relationship between the CIA and DETR from being exploited to the full.

5. CONCLUSION

Compared to many voluntary agreements, the agreement between the CIA and the DETR is relatively well specified. The environmental performance objective is clearly defined and quantified, and there are implicit objectives with respect to learning. Given the level of the target, the implementation mechanism is adequate and is likely to result in a relatively cost–efficient allocation of effort. The monitoring system is highly credible, based on a combination of self-reporting and independent verification, and there is a formal review mechanism.

The agreement was fully implemented, and the milestones that were set for the first two years were achieved. The percentage of manufacturing sites providing annual returns increased, although it was still some way short of the 100 per cent coverage that was committed by the CIA. There is some evidence to suggest that there may have been of an improvement in energy efficiency (versus business-as-usual) during the first year of the agreement for speciality chemicals.

In terms of its environmental effectiveness however, the picture is less positive. The preceding analysis suggests that the 20 per cent improvement objective does not require the implementation of all cost-effective improvement measures, nor does it represent a significant improvement over a realistic counterfactual. While the findings of the first year's consultancy visits suggest that the objective is likely to be over-achieved, the magnitude of the incremental reduction in annual CO_2 emissions by the final year of the agreement is unlikely to exceed 150 KtC. This is significantly less than the reduction that will be needed from the sector if the Government is to meet its internal policy objective of a 20 per cent reduction in emissions by 2010.

An interesting aspect of the agreement is the apparent contradiction between the relatively modest level of its ambition and the sophistication of its specification. There are several explanations for this. First, the progress that was already being made under the CIA's Responsible Energy initiative meant that the scope for additional improvements under a purely voluntary agreement was limited. Second, the CIA's desire to improve the credibility of its actions with outside stakeholders meant that it was important to them that the agreement be well specified and for there to be independent verification of performance. However, the most significant explanation relates to policy learning. Both sides saw the agreement as an initial step in an ongoing process – as an experiment that would lay the foundations for future negotiated agreements. Consequently the agreement specification was viewed as providing a prototype that could be used in other situations, and with other (more stringent) targets. This is implicit in the wording of the agreement, which includes a provision for the re-negotiation of targets and support, and which states that 'both partners expect that substantially greater resources will be needed to promote energy efficiency and targets beyond this first agreement.'

If it is judged on this basis – that is, as a transition step from a unilateral commitment (Responsible Care) towards a more ambitious, binding negotiated agreement – then the agreement should be regarded as a qualified success.

NOTES

1. Specific energy consumption is defined as primary energy consumption per tonne of output.
2. Economic and Fiscal Strategy Report, HM Treasury, March 1999.
3. UK Indicators of Performance 1990–97, Chemical Industries Association.
4. Borkey et al. (1999) classify voluntary approaches into three broad categories: unilateral commitments, public voluntary schemes, and negotiated agreements.
5. In June 1997 – that is during the course of the negotiations – the Department of the Environment was amalgamated with the Department of Transport to form the Department of the Environment, Transport and the Regions. For simplicity, the acronym DETR is used to refer to both the amalgamated Department and the original Department of the Environment.
6. Although it should be noted that the Dutch Government's 1993 agreement on energy efficiency with its chemicals sector stipulates a 20 per cent improvement by the year 2000 compared to 1989, which is more stringent than the original CEFIC target.
7. The CIA set up a steering group – comprising members of its Business and Trade Board and its Chemical Industry Safety, Health and Environment Council (CISHEC) – to direct its negotiating team. However, the final agreement required ratification by its full

Council, although this was facilitated by the participation of the three member companies in the negotiations.

8.   The Netherlands Organisation for Energy and the Environment (NOVEM) is the equivalent of ETSU.

9.   The IPPC Directive was required to be transposed into national law by the end of October 1999, and applied to all new plants (and those undergoing major changes) from that date, with existing plants being phased-in by 2007 at the latest.

10.   See appendix 1 of the agreement.

11.   *ENDS Report*, No. 259, August 1996

12.   Extracts of the speech are reproduced in the CIA's newsletter for the Responsible Care programme – *Responsible Care Reports*, Issue 14 July 1997.

13.   Personal communication from ETSU.

14.   *ENDS Report*, No 274 November 1997.

15.   *UK Indicators of Performance, 1990–96*, Chemical Industries Association.

16.   The Energy Management Matrix was developed initially by BRESCU in relation to the energy efficiency of buildings. It was modified for the chemicals sector by ETSU as part of the re-launch of the CIA's Responsible Energy programme. The matrix provides an explicit framework within which a company can be scored (from 0 to 5) in terms of six key factors that underpin energy efficiency, that is policy; organisation; training; performance measurement; communication; investment.

17   Verbal communication.

18.   Around 150 companies attended the seminar in February 1998, and around 100 attended the seminar in March 1999.

19.   *ENDS Report*, No. 274, November 1997.

REFERENCES

Borkey, P., Glachant, M. and Leveque, F. (1999), *Voluntary Approaches for Environmental Policy: An Assessment*, Paris, OECD

Morrell, M. and Ward, J. (1999), 'Energy Efficiency Agreement Delivers Significant Savings for Chemical Industries', *Energy and Environmental Management*, Department of the Environment, Transport and the Regions, March/April 1999.

12. Dutch Covenant Regulating the Reduction of Sulphur Dioxide and Nitrogen Oxide Emissions by the Power Generation Industry

Ellis Immerzeel

1. INTRODUCTION

In 1990, the power generation industry, the Dutch Environment Ministry, and the provinces signed a covenant on the reduction of sulphur dioxide and nitrogen oxides emissions by the power generation industry. Emissions of sulphur dioxide (SO_2) and nitrogen oxides (NO_x) are a major cause of acidification, a problem that has adverse effects on the environment and materials such as buildings. In the Netherlands, acidification has resulted in a significant degradation of the forests.

The Dutch government therefore formulated an acidification policy, which has been part of the national environmental policy plans since 1989. The targets include maximum levels of emissions of SO_2, NO_x and NH_3 (ammonia) for the relevant sectors. Targets have also been set for the power generation industry to reduce the emissions of SO_2 and NO_x to be achieved by the implementation of an agreement. This agreement – the covenant concerning the reduction of sulphur dioxide- and nitrogen oxide emissions by the power generation industry – is the focus of this chapter.

The covenant covers the period 1990 to 2000. Even before this period had expired it became clear that the targets – the stipulated emission reductions of SO_2 and NO_x – had been achieved by the sector. The covenant is a success. In the context of the NEAPOL project, this chapter aims to explore the overall performance of the agreement in terms of feasibility, capability, impact and resource development. The explanation of the success of the covenant will only be discussed briefly since a more extensive analysis can be found later in this book.

2. CONTEXT

2.1 Covenants as a Policy Instrument in Dutch Environmental Policy

The covenant concerning the reduction of SO_2 and NO_x was one of the earlier environmental policy covenants in the Netherlands.

The first environmental covenants were introduced in the second half of the 1980s. These initial covenants concerned only one issue, they were signed by the Environment Ministry and a single actor (a company or branch organisation) and had mostly a symbolic function. In fact, these covenants were also called 'gentlemen's agreements' since their legal status – enforceability – was not clear. Discussions on the legal status of the covenant as a policy instrument thereafter came to occupy a dominant position. The question was how a covenant, which is a contract under civil law, relates to regulations under public law (environmental legislation). The outcome of these discussions was basically that a covenant is a voluntary agreement that cannot contradict the system of public law. It is possible to use a covenant to anticipate regulations that have not yet been formulated, and it is also possible to use a covenant to supplement existing regulation, but a covenant can never replace something that has already been established in public law. At the same time, the covenant instrument fits with the idea of 'internalisation', the idea that industry has to accept its responsibility and deal with its own problems.

Within this setting, the government signed many covenants, among them the covenant regulating the reduction of SO_2 and NO_x emissions by the power generation industry (June 1990). This covenant is closely linked to the (already existing) regulatory system.

Although this covenant is still a single issue – single actor covenant, covenants are also signed with more complex sectors of industry. In the years that followed, the government was to sign many more covenants with Dutch industry as part of its so-called target group policy.

2.2 Acidification: the Problem

Acidification is the result of atmospheric pollution by (directly or indirectly) acidifying components – *sulphur dioxide* (SO_2), *nitrogen oxides* (NO_x), and *ammonia* (NH_3). When excessive quantities of these substances deposit on the ground or water, adverse effects ensue. For instance, certain kinds of fish are directly affected if the acidity of lakes and streams increases. In soils, excess acidity harms micro-organisms, influences the supply of nutrients and can mobilise (toxic) metals such as aluminium. Over the longer term this can have an impact on the quality of groundwater stocks and the health of plants and trees. Besides these effects on the environment, acidification also degrades materials such as buildings (National Environmental Policy Plan 3, 1998). The anthropogenic emission of sulphur and nitrogen oxides is closely related to the combustion of fossil fuels.

In 1997, the major contributors to acid deposition were foreign countries (45 per cent) and the Dutch agricultural sector (34 per cent). The agricultural sector (NH_3) and the transport sector (NO_x) are the most problematic sectors. The modern power generation industry was in 1997 responsible for only 1 per cent of the total acid deposition in the Netherlands (RIVM, 1998). Table 12.1 shows that in the past the sector made a significant contribution to the total SO_2 and NO_x emissions in the Netherlands.

Table 12.1 Emissions per target group

	1985	1990	1995	2000 (expected)
NO_x (kilotons)				
Consumers	26	21	22	21
Traffic	335	351	314	261
Agriculture	6	10	15	27
Industry	84	76	65	69
Services	14	11	12	17
Power generation	88	81	57	37
Refineries	20	19	18	15
Other	7	5	3	3
Total	580	574	506	450
SO_2 (kilotons)				
Traffic	23	27	31	22
Industry	68	50	31	24
Power generation	67	48	17	13
Refineries	87	70	59	33
Waste disposal	3	3	1	1
Other	8	5	4	1
Total	256	203	143	94

Source: Dougle and Kroon, 1998, p. 45

2.3 The Power Generation Industry

The Dutch electricity system developed out of small-scale municipal electricity companies, established in the first decades of this century. Technology improvements guided the electrification of the country, headed by SEP[1] the grid co-ordinator since 1949. Between 1950 and 1989, electricity generation and distribution was well organised in small-scale monopolies, with clearly defined positions and legally authorised tasks reflecting the public utility character of electricity supply and the company's public service obligations. Until 1989 the system was publicly owned and public service oriented in its operation and performance (Arentsen et al., 1997).

The years 1985–98 mark a period of institutional instability in the Dutch electricity system, due to several tensions in the system and the emerging debate on the liberalisation of the European electricity market. Before 1985, generation, transport and distribution was integrated in 14 larger generation/distribution companies, each holding leading market positions, ten of them with provincial ownership structures and regionally based, and four with municipal ownership structures, operating in the urban areas in the western part of the country. A debate, started in 1985, reinforced the need to improve the efficiency of electricity supply by concentration. Distribution and generation were de-integrated and mergers reduced the number of generation companies to four.[2]

In 1990, the year in which the covenant was signed, the Electricity Act of 1989 governed the legal structure of the Dutch electricity system. Table 12.2 displays the major features of the value chain of electricity as it was legally structured by this Electricity Act.

Table 12.2 clearly illustrates the distinction between production and distribution of electricity and the dominant position of SEP in generation and high-voltage transmission. SEP also held a de facto monopoly in the import and export of electricity. The actual functioning of the Dutch electricity system is illustrated in Figure 12.1.

SEP was organised as a limited liability company formed under private law, having the four regionally based generation companies, EPON, UNA, EZH and EPZ, as its shareholders. In the 1989 Electricity Act SEP was re-established as a co-ordinating agency to safeguard efficiency in the production and high-voltage transmission of electricity. SEP developed a system of technical dispatch, allowing only the most efficient power plants to be connected to the grid, in combination with a system of nationally pooled prices. SEP co-ordinated the production by the four generation companies and it actually dominated generation and transmission in the Netherlands. SEP became the dominant player in the electricity system, deciding on imports, investments, transmission costs and electricity prices.

Table 12.2   Electricity Act of 1989

Value chain	Electricity Act 1989
Generation	Long-term strategic and operational planning by SEP
	Central economic and technical dispatch by SEP
Transport/Services	De facto SEP monopoly
	Technical dispatch by SEP, from 1989 on also economic dispatch
	Internal rules of the electricity industry
Distribution	Geographic monopoly distribution company
Wholesale	De facto SEP monopoly on import and export[3]
Retailing	Not operational, integrated with distribution
Products and services	No (commercial) services allowed in combination with electricity supply

The Act demands an administrative and financial unbundling of generation, trade and supply on the one hand and transmission and distribution on the other. Access to the grid is arranged as regulated TPA and the market will be liberalised stepwise: beginning in 1999 (650 giant consumers, consuming more than 2 megawatt, representing 34 per cent of the market), next in 2002 (some 56 000 small industrial consumers up to 3x80 ampere, representing 27 per cent of the market) and finally in 2007 (some 6.7 million households, representing 39 per cent of the market). The Act became operative in 1999 and from that time on competition was launched in the Dutch electricity market.

As a consequence, SEP will be dismantled to continue under the name TenneT as the national transmission company in charge of the high-voltage transport of electricity. The four producers no longer co-ordinate their generation activities as in the pre-1998 period by technical dispatch and national price pooling. By the end of 1999, two of the four generation companies were in the process of being taken over by foreign companies.

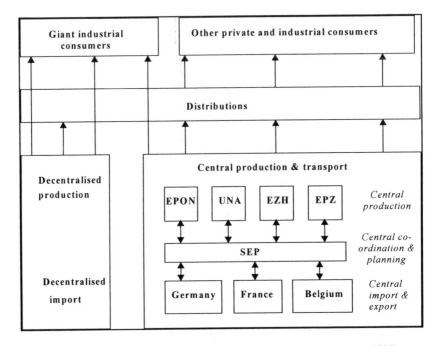

Figure 12.1   The organisation of the Dutch electricity system up to 1995

Source: Arentsen et al., 1997, p. 169

2.4 The Dutch Acidification Policy

The problem of acidification came onto the Dutch policy agenda in 1983: a call was made for extensive research on acidification and its effects on the environment. This was mainly due to reports from Germany regarding serious damage to domestic forests. The report on the problem of acidification (Notitie inzake de problematiek van de verzuring) was published in 1984. An extensive research programme on acidification was set up following this report (Additioneel Programma Verzuringsonderzoek), which was to last until 1994. The interim outcomes of this extensive research formed the basis for the acidification policy of the Dutch government. The policy is formulated in the Acidification Abatement Plan (Bestrijdingsplan Verzuring, 1988–89) and the National Environmental Policy Plans (NEPPs).

2.4.1 Goals
The first National Environmental Policy Plan (NEPP-1, 1989) includes objectives to combat the acidification problem. The objectives are formulated

in terms of deposition levels to be reached in the coming years by the different sector/industries that contribute to the problem. Six months after the NEPP, the NEPP-Plus was published: the objectives regarding the acidification problem were tightened up (partly based on commitments made by the industry, in particular the power generators!). The overall objective was to reach a maximum deposition level of 2 400 acid equivalents (including sulphur dioxide, nitrogen oxide and ammonia) in the year 2000 (65 per cent reduction in deposition compared to 1985 levels), and a maximum deposition level of 1 400 acid equivalents in the year 2010 (80 per cent reduction in deposition compared to 1985). To achieve these objectives, the emissions of acidifying substances of various industries in the Netherlands as well as emissions abroad (since these are imported into the Netherlands) would have to decrease significantly. The power generation industry in the Netherlands is set the following targets in NEPP-Plus:

- Sulphur dioxide: maximum of 18 kilotons emission per year in the year 2000 (SO_2 emissions in 1985 were 65 kilotons)
- Nitrogen oxide: maximum of 30 kilotons emission per year in the year 2000 (NO_x emission in 1985 were 82 kilotons)

These objectives reappeared in subsequent national environmental policy plans, NEPP-2 (1993) and NEPP-3 (1998).

2.4.2 Policy instruments

Since April 1987, the emissions of the power generating industry in the Netherlands have been regulated via the Decree on Emission Requirements for Combustion Installations (Besluit emissie-eisen stookinstallaties, BEES).

BEES-A (1987) focuses on large installations for which the provinces act as the responsible authorities (granting the permit). BEES-B (1990) focuses on installations in companies; here the local authority grants the permit. Both Decrees involve emission requirements for SO_2 and NO_x from combustion installations. Requirements differ for various types of combustion plants (gas, coal, and so on) and also for existing or new plants and small or larger installations. BEES leaves it up to the sector to choose the best technology to meet the requirements. BEES implements the EU directive on large combustion plants of November 1988 (88/609/EEG).

BEES-A is especially relevant for the power generating industry and it provides the legal framework for the Dutch government's combating of SO_2 and NO_x emissions from electricity generation. The emission requirements in BEES have also been tightened up a few times over the years in order to comply with the EU directive.

Besides regulation, a more voluntary approach was followed in 1990 when a *covenant* was signed between the power generation industry and the Dutch government (the national government and the provincial authorities). The covenant includes targets for reducing the emissions of sulphur dioxide and nitrogen oxides by the power generation industry and covers the period from 1990 to 2000. These targets correspond with the targets laid down in NEPP-plus. The covenant gives the sector the freedom to determine the most cost-effective way and the set of measures to achieve the targets.

In the Netherlands the covenant – or negotiated agreement – is used in combination with the licensing system included in regulation. In this case, too, the covenant is combined with the permit system included in the Decree on Emission Requirements for Combustion Installations (BEES). In practice this means that the permit system will be maintained, and will take the agreements laid down in the covenant into account. This happens in two ways:

1. After signature of the covenant, the BEES regulation was revised in accordance with the agreement. For example, in the covenant it was agreed that existing plants will not be faced with more stringent emission requirements and that stricter emission requirements will be in place for new plants. This has been included in the regulation.
2. The covenant committed the sector to draw up a Plan of Action to explain how the sector is planning to meet the targets. The Plan of Action includes a survey of measures to be taken at the individual plants. These measures will be part of the plants' permit applications and in this way the measures could be included in the permit granted by the Province.

2.4.3 Results

The overall acidification policy had mixed results: The NEPP-2 (1993) stated that the total acid deposition target of 2 400 total acid equivalents/ha for the year 2000 and 1 400 by the year 2010 would not be achieved with the current policy. Indications are that the total acid deposition in the year 2000 will reach 2 600 acid equivalents. Foreign countries play an important role in this setback (NEPP-2, 1993). Also, in subsequent years, data show that the targets set for 2000 and 2010 will not be achieved with current policy. The main bottlenecks are the emissions of nitrogen oxides (traffic) and ammonia (agriculture). The emissions of sulphur dioxide have been reduced significantly and are in line with the policy objectives. In the NEPP-3 (1998) the Dutch government decided to continue implementing the policy that was set out in earlier plans; to defer the targets set for NO_x and NH_3 emission reductions to 2005; and to assess the feasibility of the total deposition objectives by the end of the period covered by the NEPP-3.

The power generation industry is making good progress with reducing its SO_2 and NO_x emissions.[4] The sector's SO_2 emissions in 1994 were 17.8 kilotons, which is already below the 18 kilotons target for the year 2000. The NO_x emissions were 53.4 kilotons and this is in line with the target that was set at 55 kilotons for 1994. The sector's SO_2 emissions in 1997 were 12.4 kilotons; NO_x emissions in 1997 were 35.2 kilotons (source: Progress Report N.V. Samenwerkende electriciteitsproductiebedrijven, November 1998a).

2.4.4 Outlook

Up to the end of the plan period (2002) the policy will be maintained, which means regulation via the Decree on Emission Requirements for Combustion Installations (BEES) and implementation of the agreements laid down in the covenant of 1990.

It is not yet clear how the future will look beyond 2000–2002. The Dutch government aims to set new, stricter targets for SO_2 and NO_x emission reductions for the sector for the year 2010. For the sector, however, the future is unclear due to the liberalisation of the electricity market. This changes the context for discussions about reducing SO_2 and NO_x emissions. The discussion focuses on NO_x: a new approach is being tried out by the government, the idea being that extensive investments need to be made in order to reduce NO_x emissions. Cost-efficiency is important in achieving these reductions. Therefore the government has chosen the option of cost spreading (in Dutch: kostenverevening): a single NO_x target is set for the refineries, industry and energy companies. The industries themselves can decide where it is most cost efficient to realise the emission reduction.

3. NEGOTIATION PROCESS

3.1 Negotiations on the Covenant

The negotiations on a possible covenant started at the beginning of 1989. Discussions between the power generation sector and the government regarding SO_2 emission reduction, however, had started as early as the seventies. SEP had always been interested in agreeing on a 'bubble' or an overall emission ceiling for the sector so that they would no longer be confronted with arbitrary decisions by provincial authorities. An overall trend towards decentralisation meant that these discussions never led to an agreement on an emission ceiling for the whole sector.

In 1987 the Decree on Emission Requirements for Combustion Installations (BEES) was announced, regulating the emissions of the power generation industry in the Netherlands. BEES provides the legal framework for combating the SO_2 and NO_x emissions coming from electricity generation.

In 1989 representatives of the Environment Ministry, SEP and the provinces (represented by their association IPO) started discussions on a ceiling for SO_2 and NO_x emissions for the entire power generation sector. Draft proposals for the covenant were discussed in meetings (February and March 1989) between representatives of SEP, Environment Ministry and IPO. The Ministry chaired these meetings. The discussions focused on elements of the covenant:

- The Environment Ministry and IPO wished to include a target for SO_2/NO_x emission in the year 1994. Initially SEP opposed to this.
- SEP would have liked to have had a representative of the Ministry of Economic Affairs (EZ) in the covenants commission. VROM and IPO did not agree.
- SEP objected to the arrangement that the covenants commission could terminate the covenant if the agreements could not result in the emission reduction for 2000.

However, the most import difference of opinion between SEP and IPO/Environment Ministry was on the emission reduction targets for SO_2 and NO_x to be set for the year 2000. In the discussions IPO and VROM stuck to the targets of a maximum of 25 million kg SO_2 emission in the year 2000 and a maximum of 30 million kg NO_x emission in the year 2000 (these numbers are usually referred to as 25/30 SO_2/NO_x). SEP held out for targets of 30 million kg SO_2 emission in 2000 and 40 million kg emission in 2000. The Dutch government based its numbers on two policy documents that were in preparation during that period, namely the Acidification Abatement Plan (in Dutch: Bestrijdingsplan Verzuring) and the first National Environmental Policy Plan (NEPP). The negotiations for the covenant were not completed when the NEPP was published. The NEPP included a maximum of 30/40 SO_2/NO_x for 2000. However, based on insights gathered during the preparation of the Acidification Abatement Plan the Dutch government was convinced that the 25/30 targets for SO_2/NO_x were realistic. SEP argued that these stricter targets did not leave enough room to implement the emission reductions in a cost-effective manner. In a meeting on 29 June 1989 this difference of opinion regarding the targets for SO_2 and NO_x emission reduction resulted in the termination of the discussions: SEP withdrew from the negotiations.

The government now started to prepare the revision of the existing regulation for SO_2 and NO_x emissions by the power generation industry, the

Decree on Emission Requirements for Combustion Installations (BEES): stricter emission requirements would be included for all installations.

The ministry stopped work on the regulation when, at the beginning of 1990 (10 January), a meeting was again arranged between SEP, the Environment Ministry and IPO, this time at the request of SEP. Since their last meeting (29 June 1989), a new Cabinet had assumed office and the National Environmental Policy Plan had been revised to the NEPP-Plus: the acidification targets had been tightened up. According to an expert at SEP, SEP postponed the negotiations exactly for the reason that the Cabinet fell: 'SEP could not do business with a government that lacked political legitimacy.' In any case, SEP returned to the negotiation table. In this second round of discussions a compromise was very soon found between the negotiation partners. The stricter emission targets (aimed for by the Dutch government) were agreed, but some allowed flexibility for the sector in reaching those targets: a maximum of 18 kilotons SO_2 emission in the year 2000 (with a margin of 4 and 3 kilotons in case of equipment malfunction) and a maximum of 30 kilotons NO_x emission in the year 2000 plus 5 kilotons for implementing co-generation (which will be explained further in the next section). These targets correspond with the policy set out in the NEPP-plus.

The provinces had representatives at the negotiations who reported back to the Interprovincial Consultancy Organ (IPO). At the beginning of the process the position of the provinces was one of doubt: as the licensing authority for the electricity producers they were not convinced of the (environmental) benefits that the covenant would bring: whether the SO_2 and NO_x emission reductions agreed upon in the covenant would actually be higher than by implementing the BEES regulation. At the same time they found it difficult to predict future (technological) developments and to make a sensible estimation of emissions. In addition, the provinces had no clear view at that time on how the covenant would work in practice, nor what role the provinces would retain. Furthermore, the instrument of a covenant was new to the provinces. They learned how to negotiate during the discussions. In the meetings the provinces and the Environment Ministry were on the same side and discussed their positions before going into the meetings with SEP. In the second round of discussions the provinces made a case for realising a regional diffusion of the emission reductions by the power generators. This was agreed by SEP, in a rider added as a letter to the covenant.

In the end, the Environment Ministry and SEP were both very satisfied with the outcome of the negotiations. Respondents from both organisations consider it to be a win–win situation: the Environment Ministry had the sector's commitment to achieve a significant reduction of SO_2 and NO_x emissions. At the same time, SEP had the freedom to implement the agreement in the most cost-effective way since the focus was on aggregate levels (maximum emission levels for the whole sector, not for individual plants). The provinces were happy with the success of the negotiations in which they had played a role, but were more sceptical about the added value of the covenant compared to regulation.

3.2 Contents of the Covenant

3.2.1 Commitments
The specific objectives for 2000 laid down in the covenant are a maximum of 18 kilotons SO_2 emission, and a maximum of 30 kilotons NO_x emission. To be able to proceed with the co-generation of electricity, SEP is allowed to exceed the NO_x ceiling by a maximum of 5 kilotons per year (article 3). In case the desulphurisation equipment in coal fired electricity plants should malfunction, and the plant is within legal limits, the emission ceiling can be raised by 4 kilotons SO_2. This corrected ceiling can be exceeded by 3 million tons once every three years (article 4).

SEP committed itself to developing a Plan of Action within six months after concluding the covenant (article 7 of the covenant). This plan gives a detailed overview of how SEP intended to achieve the reduced emission levels. SEP could do this because of its special position within the sector: it has a co-ordinating role regarding production as well as the cost pooling system.

The covenant states that the Environment Minister would take the agreement into account when developing further regulation on the matter (article 5). This is a reference to BEES, which would be revised just after the agreement: existing plants would not be confronted with stricter emission requirements. Stricter emission levels would be in place for new plants. The provinces, who are the licensing authority, agreed to operate in line with the provisions of the covenant and the Plan of Action.

3.2.2 Monitoring
The covenant obliges SEP to write a progress report every two years. A commission is established with representation of the involved parties (Environment Ministry, Provinces and SEP). The Ministry of Economic Affairs is allocated a position in the Commission as observer. The task of the commission is to guide the implementation of the covenant, evaluate the progress reports and serve as a discussion forum in case conflicts should arise.

3.2.3 Legal framework
The legal framework is formed by the Air Pollution Act, in particular by the Decree on Emission Levels of Combustion Plants (BEES). BEES sets down specific permitted maximum emission levels for combustion plants for which

the provinces provide permits to the companies. After the signing of the agreement, BEES will be revised in concordance with the provisions of the agreement.

The covenant does not formulate individual emission requirements for the individual plants. The Plan of Action that SEP needed to make to implement the covenant, however, did specify the measures that were planned for individual installations in order to reduce the emissions. Accordingly, this has been translated into the individual permits for the plants.

3.3 Implementing the Covenant

The implementation of the covenant by SEP is proceeding very well. Within six months SEP presented its Plan of Action, which was approved by the Commission. The basis of the Plan is cost effectiveness. SEP operated (and still operates) a counting programme which includes all the combustion plants. This programme is used to implement the cost pooling mechanism that involves production costs of all companies. It was used to define the most cost-effective measures. SEP started with a scenario – setting out the trend to 2000 – in which no extra measures were taken. This scenario gave an insight into how many extra measures were needed to achieve the emission reductions. SEP asked the companies to propose projects for decreasing the emissions of SO_2 and NO_x. A selection was made by SEP, after which the companies made more detailed cost estimates. This was an interactive process between the companies and SEP that was possible because of the openness of information exchange. In the end, some 70 measures were selected for implementation and included in the Plan of Action. The reason that SEP was able to develop the Plan of Action in the most cost-effective way was the existence of the cost pooling mechanism.

The sector adopted three basic measures to achieve the SO_2 emission reductions (Themadocument verzuring 1998):

1. The older coal-fired plants without desulphurisation were taken out of service.
2. The other coal-fired plants have been equipped with flue gas desulphurisation installations. Moreover, the desulphurisation installations have improved, so that desulphurisation percentages are reached that exceed 90 per cent.
3. Coal containing less sulphur is used.

To combat the NO_x emissions, some of the old coal-fired plants have been replaced by gas-fired installations. Other measures include the installation of certain technologies such as the Selective Catalytic Reduction (SCR)/Denox or High temperature NO_x Reduction.

From 1990 on, SEP reported every two years to the Commission on the progress made in reducing SO_2 and NO_x emissions and provided an overview of further plans until the year 2000. According to all respondents (from SEP, Environment Ministry and the provinces) these meetings were always very satisfactory. Sometimes the Plan of Action had to be modified because some techniques or technologies did not perform as expected. SEP had to introduce other measures in order to reduce the SO_2 and NO_x emissions. The most important means by which SEP fulfilled the emission requirements were the closure of coal-fired power plants that had no abatement equipment; equipping other plants with flue gas desulphurisation installations (to reduce SO_2 emissions) and/or SCR (to reduce NO_x emissions). Furthermore, coal was used that contained less sulphur.

The progress reports show the reductions in SO_2 and NO_x emissions by the power generation sector, see Table 12.3.

Table 12.3   Emission of SO_2 and NO_x by the power generating industry

Emissions	SO_2	NO_x
1990	44 815	72 474
1991	34 551	68 207
1992	28 753	65 475
1993	22 080	58 543
1994	17 846	53 426
1995	16 180	48 880
1996	18 693	42 630
1997	12 446	35 174
2000 (target)	18 000	30 000

Source: Progress Reports Covenant, SEP

3.4 Follow-up Discussions

A new round of discussions between SEP and the Environment Ministry has taken place to explore the grounds for a new covenant, setting targets beyond 2000. They agreed that – as long as there is no follow-up covenant – the current agreement should remain valid. A covenant nowadays will have to be negotiated with the individual electricity producing companies, since SEP will cease to exist in its current form. However, as it looks now, a joint agreement on NO_x emission reduction may be more feasible, including three sectors: the industry, refineries and the electricity producers on NO_x emission reduction. The basis for such an agreement is cost spreading.

4. ANALYSIS

4.1 The Performance of the Covenant

'Within the government, this covenant is seen as a success story' an expert of the Environment Ministry stated. He is referring to the targets for SO_2 and NO_x emission reduction that are included in the covenant. So far, the emission reductions are in line with (or even ahead of) the timetable.

Our theoretical framework provides an extensive evaluation framework in which the success (or not) of a negotiated agreement is not only related to the question whether the targets have been reached: performance, the dependent variable here, is made up of more aspects that are linked to various stages in the policy process: feasibility; capability, impact and resource development.

4.1.1 Feasibility
The negotiations resulted in a covenant and therefore a covenant was feasible. The initiative to start the negotiations came from the Dutch government in the context of its overall acidification policy. The power generation industry, represented by SEP, was willing to negotiate with the government. It was very clear that the alternative to the covenant was that the emission reductions would be imposed via regulation. The Environment Ministry intended to tighten up the regulations, which would mean that all combustion plants would need extra equipment to reduce SO_2 and NO_x emissions. SEP foresaw enormous investments and wanted the freedom to achieve the targets in the most cost-effective way possible. The Environment Ministry aimed for the commitment of the sector because they expected more success in reducing SO_2 and NO_x than demanding it via regulation. The third party in the negotiations, the provinces, represented by the IPO, hesitated, but were convinced by the Environment Ministry of the benefits of this approach. One can speak of a clear win–win situation since both parties had a clear interest in coming to an agreement.

4.1.2 Capability
The covenant has proved to be eminently capable of achieving the targets set: a ceiling on emissions of SO_2 and NO_x by the electricity producers in the year 2000. In between, targets being set for 1994. The covenant includes a clear set of targets that can easily be monitored. Also, the commitments for each partner laid down in the covenant are clear and easy to check.

The covenant does not explicitly include a burden-sharing mechanism since such a mechanism already exists in the sector: it is the responsibility of SEP to achieve the targets for the sector as a whole. Herein lies the main advantage and reason for SEP's signature of the covenant in the first place: they have the opportunity to achieve the targets in the most cost-effective way. SEP was also very much in a position to do so: it had central co-ordination tasks regarding the generation of electricity by the four producers and price setting. The covenant obliged SEP to develop a detailed Plan of Action within six months after concluding the agreement: the Plan of Action needed to include an overview of how the sector was going to achieve the targets, and an overview of the emission targets for each combustion plant.

As mentioned earlier, monitoring is one of the strong aspects of this covenant. Based on the Plan of Action, the producers knew exactly what their targets were: the covenant states that these targets are included in the permit that the provinces grant to the producers. Each electricity producer needs to report every year to the province and SEP on the emission of SO_2 and NO_x. In addition, the covenant commits SEP to report every two years to the covenant commission, which had been established especially to guide the implementation of the covenant.

In case problems or conflicts occur in the implementation, the covenant installs a commission to serve as a kind of discussion forum that ultimately can decide that the covenant should be terminated. In more individual cases, the province, which is the licensing authority for the combustion plants, can decide to take measures in a case where the plant is not complying with the provisions of the covenant.

Therefore the covenant is in theory is eminently capable of achieving the targets. This has also been the case in practice. SEP co-ordinates the implementation of the covenant. It drew up a Plan of Action for the sector that was approved by the commission. A progress report is published every two years.

4.1.3 Impact

The environmental impact or effectiveness of the covenant is the reduced SO_2 and NO_x emissions from the combustion plants. As we have seen, the SO_2 and NO_x emissions have been reduced significantly.

To achieve the reductions in SO_2 emission, the sector took the following measures:

1. closure of coal-fired plants having no abatement technology;
2. new coal-fired plants with abatement technology;
3. fuel substitution;
4. changes in the type of coal used (the percentage of sulphur in the coal);

5.   improvement of the abatement equipment.

To reduce NO$_x$ emissions, some of the old coal-fired plants have been replaced by gas installations, and some plants installed denox installations.

The SO$_2$ emission reductions were achieved within a few years. A large part of the reductions were realised by the closure of old coal-fired plants having no abatement technology. These plants were scheduled for closure because of their age and impending (BEES) regulation. The covenant might have speeded up this process a little. Furthermore, the sector made some improvements in the desulphurisation equipment over the years. At the same time, however, the sector started to use coals that contain more sulphur instead of less (Lulofs, 1999). One may question the extent to which the reductions of SO$_2$ emissions by the power generating industry are due to the covenant. There is no easy answer to this. What would have happened if there had been no covenant and normal practice were to have continued, complying with the BEES regulation? It seems that the effect of the covenant is clearly visible at a macro level where the reductions of SO$_2$ and NO$_x$ emissions are guaranteed by the sector. At a micro level, however, higher emissions can sometimes occur.

The covenant offered SEP the opportunity to achieve the targets at sector level in the most cost-effective way. The covenant did not add anything to the emission requirements for individual power plants, only an aggregate emission ceiling was agreed upon. SEP used the existing cost pooling mechanism to implement the covenant. Although no financial assessment has been made regarding the costs that were involved in implementing the covenant, it can be assumed that implementation took place in an efficient manner.[5]

4.1.4 Resource development

When the covenant was signed in 1990, it was not very clear what technical developments would occur. SEP had been experimenting with some new techniques and, in that sense, the covenant has stimulated learning about technical options to reduce SO$_2$ and NO$_x$ emissions by combustion plants in a cost-effective way. On the other hand, no new innovative technologies have been developed during the last ten years. There was no reason to since it was very clear at the beginning of the process that the sector would achieve the targets. Thus, the incentive was missing. The flue gas desulphurisation installations have improved over the years.

The people working within the power generating companies are enthusiastic about the covenant. For the government, in many respects this covenant was a kind of pilot project to try out the instrument of negotiated agreement. In that sense, the covenant performed very well, getting everyone (business and regional and state authorities) enthusiastically involved about this way of working together and learning how to work together in a different relationship.

In terms of relationships, the covenant has without doubt been very rewarding. Relationships have been built and trust and respect between the partners has grown over the years. However, it is difficult to see what this will mean for the future since the electricity market is now changing from a monopolistic market to a competitive one. The electricity companies will operate as businesses in an open and competitive market which will surely change their agenda. Prices and thus production costs will become more important. SEP will be dismantled as the organisation co-ordinating production and will continue under the new name TenneT, as the national transmission organisation.

The conclusion is that the performance of the covenant has been good: the covenant was feasible because all partners saw an advantage in signing an agreement together; the covenant was capable since it included a clear set of targets, a burden-sharing mechanism and a monitoring system. Its effectiveness is good insofar as the targets for SO_2 and NO_x emission reduction have been achieved. However, it is questionable to what extent the reductions can be ascribed to the efficacy of the covenant. It can be assumed that the agreement has been very efficient due to the cost pooling mechanism within the sector. Finally, the covenant developed its resource base mainly in terms of relationship building and learning about working in the setting of a covenant.

5. CONCLUSION

In 1990, one of the major contributors to the acidification problem in the Netherlands was the power generation industry. The Dutch government formulated an acidification policy in which targets for emission reduction were set for the relevant sectors, including the power generation sector. After one year of negotiations, the Dutch Environment Ministry, the provinces and SEP (representing the sector) signed a covenant on the reduction of emissions of sulphur dioxide and nitrogen oxides. Almost ten years later, the covenant has proved to be a success: the emission targets have been realised within the agreed timeframe.

In exploring possible explanations of the success of this covenant, the hypotheses of the NEAPOL project proved to be helpful and provided an insight into those conditions that explain the performance of this covenant:

1. trust, respect for each other's positions in the negotiations and the recognition of a possible win–win situation *(policy hypothesis)*;
2. the fact that regulation was a real alternative to the negotiated agreement gave an extra incentive to the negotiations *(instrumental hypothesis)*;
3. for the government it was very easy to discuss and make agreements with the sector: SEP was a powerful association that was able to speak for its members during the negotiations. The role/position of the SEP and the structure of the sector and electricity market in the Netherlands during the 1990s made it possible that the covenant was implemented successfully in a cost-effective way *(sectoral hypothesis)*.

The presence of these factors provided a fruitful setting for negotiating and implementing the covenant. The covenant's success – the achievement of its emission reduction targets – has also in large measure been due to the contents of the covenant itself (which in itself is an outcome of the negotiation process and thus an aspect of performance, namely capability): it included a clear set of targets, a timetable and provisions for monitoring and reporting.

NOTES

1. SEP stands for *Samenwerkende ElektriciteitsProduktiebedrijven* [Cooperating Electricity Production Companies].
2. The initiative to separate generation from distribution was actually taken by the Dutch government of that time. For a more detailed description of the debate see Arentsen et al., 1997.
3. The Electricity Act 1989 did allow for direct import of electricity by giant consumers, but the costs on transport were high, leaving SEP in a de facto monopoly position.
4. In 1995, Minister de Boer (Environment) reported to parliament that the implementation of the covenant with the electricity sector was progressing according to the agreement: the SO_2 and NO_x emission reductions would be achieved in time (Milieu Management, January 1995, number 1).
5. No financial review of the costs incurred by the sector in implementing the covenant was available. Respondents at SEP estimated that the total costs were about $500 million to reduce the emission levels of SO_2 and NO_x. They also estimated that if the same reductions were to have to be achieved by regulation, costs would have increased by a factor of two.

BIBLIOGRAPHY

Arentsen, M.J., R.W. Künneke and H.C. Moll, (1997), 'The Dutch electricity reform': reorganization by negotiation, in A. Midtun (ed.), *Electricity systems in transition*, Elsevier.

Biekart, Jan Willem (1992), *Uitvoering van het NMP door de doelgroep Energie*, september 1992, report SNM-MB 92/2, Utrecht: Stichting Natuur en Milieu.

P.G. Dougle and P. Kroon (1998), *Evaluatie Verzuring in het NMP3: Verzuringsbeleid op de lange baan?*, achtergrondstudie 003, The Hague: Vromraad.

Pieter Glasbergen (1998), 'Partnership as a Learning Process: Environmental convenants' in the Netherlands, in P. Glasbergen (ed.), *Co-operative Environmental Governance: Public-Private Agreements as a Policy Strategy*, Dodrecht: Kluwer Academic Publishers.

Lulofs, K.R.D. (1999), 'Implementing 88/609/EEC in the Netherlands: A case study on the environmental effectiveness, allocative efficiency, productive efficiency and administrative costs, report, first draft, May 1999, Enschede: University of Twente, CSTM.

National Institute of Public Health and the Environment (RIVM) (1998), *Environmental Balance Sheet 1997*, http://www.milieubalans.rivm.nl.

N.V. Samenwerkende elektriciteitsproduktiebedrijven (1991), *Plan van aanpak ter uitvoering van het convenant over de bestrijding van SO2 en NOx*, Arnhem: SEP N.V.

N.V. Samenwerkende elektriciteitsproductiebedrijven (1992), *1ᵉ voortgangsrapportage betreffende de bestrijding van SO2 en NOx emissies van elektriciteitsproductiebedrijven in de jaren 1990 en 1991 in het kader van het convenant*, Arnhem: SEP N.V.

N.V. Samenwerkende elektriciteitsproductiebedrijven (1994), *2e voortgangsrapportage betreffende de bestrijding van SO2 en NOx emissies van elektriciteitsproductiebedrijven in de jaren 1992 en 1993 in het kader van het convenant*, Arnhem: SEP N.V.

N.V. Samenwerkende elektriciteitsproductiebedrijven (1997), *3e voortgangsrapportage betreffende de bestrijding van SO2 en NOx emissies van elektriciteitsproductiebedrijven in de jaren 1994 en 1995 in het kader van het convenant*, Arnhem: SEP N.V.

N.V.Samenwerkende elektriciteitsproductiebedrijven (1998a), *4e voortgangsrapportage betreffende de bestrijding van SO2 en NOx emissies van elektriciteitsproductiebedrijven in de jaren 1996 en 1997 in het kader van het convenant*, Arnhem: SEP N.V.

N.V. Samenwerkende elektriciteitsproduktiebedrijven (1998b), A*nnual Report 1997*, Arnhem: SEP N.V.

Suurland, J. (1994), 'Voluntary agreements with industry: the case of Dutch covenants', in *European Environment*, vol. **4** (4), 3–7.

Ministerie VROM (1998), Themadocument Verzuring 1998: Stand van zaken verzuringsbeleid 1998; *Effecten, huidige doelstellingen en resultaten*, report Publikatiereeks Lucht en Energie, nr. 128, Den Haag: Ministerie van VROM.

Tweede Kamer der Staten-Generaal, *Bestrijdingsplan Verzuring [Abatement Plan Acidification]*, TK 1988-1989, 18225, nr. 31, The Hague.

Tweede Kamer der Staten-Generaal, *Nationaal Milieubeleidsplan* (NMP) [National Environmental Policy Plan, NEPP-1] TK 1988-1989, 21137, nr. 1-2, The Hague.

Tweede Kamer der Staten-Generaal, *Nationaal Milieubeleidsplan-plus* (NMP+) [National Environmental Policy Plan-Plus, NEPP-Plus] TK 1989-1990a, 21137, no. 20-21, The Hague.

Tweede Kamer der Staten-Generaal, *Nationaal Milieubeleidsplan-2* (NMP-2) [National Environmental Policy Plan 2, NEPP-2] TK 1993-1994a, 23560, nrs 1-2, The Hague.

Tweede Kamer der Staten-Generaal, *Nationaal Milieubeleidsplan-3* (NMP-3) [National Environmental Policy Plan 3, NEPP-3] TK 1997-1998, The Hague.

13. The Belgian Electricity Agreement

Marc De Clercq, Steven Baeke and Akim Seyad

1. INTRODUCTION

On 18 October 1991, the national and regional authorities, on the one hand, and the electricity producers ELECTRABEL and SPE, on the other, signed an environmental agreement concerning the reduction of SO_2 and NO_x emissions of their power stations until 2003. The agreement applies to all Belgian combustion power plants. It does not include foreign plants fully owned by Electrabel or SPE or installations wherein they participate.

Before this agreement, SO_2 and NO_x emissions from the ESI (electricity supply industry) were regulated by environmental legislation through exploitation permits. The emission targets in these permits were based upon the following international agreements:

- Helsinki Protocol: signed in 1985, aims at a reduction of SO_2 emissions of 30 per cent to be achieved by 1993 compared with 1980;
- Sofia Protocol: signed in 1988, aims at a reduction of NO_x emissions to their 1987 levels in 1994;
- Oslo Protocol: signed in 1994, Belgium committed itself by signing this Protocol, to reduce the acidic emissions by 2000 with 70 per cent relative to 1980;
- Large Combustion Plants Directive (24 November 1988, Directive 88/609/ EEC, Belgium aims at a NO_x reduction of 40 per cent and SO_2 reduction of 70 per cent in 2003 in reference to 1980).

In 1989, an assessment of the Belgian environmental situation with respect to SO_2 and NO_x emissions revealed, considering the growing energy needs in Belgium and the investment plans of the ESI, a continuous rise of the SO_2 and NO_x emissions and an equal rise in acidification. It also revealed the need for strong public intervention to attain the targets, defined in the international agreements and the European Directive. The intention was to redirect the ESI towards a reduction of their SO_2 and NO_x emissions and towards the use of alternative energy sources.

At the same time the Belgian ESI concluded that although they had achieved a considerable reduction of SO_2 and NO_x emissions through the intensified use of nuclear power, they expected these emissions to rise in the following years. The emissions were bound to increase due to a growing demand for electricity and due to the end of the nuclear investment programme of the ESI. In view of the above assessment, the ESI feared government intervention through regulation. The ESI acknowledged the fact that measures were to be taken in order to guarantee the attainment of SO_2 and NO_x reduction objectives. However, these measures had to be economically feasible, especially considering the fact that many power plants were almost completely depreciated and not fit for expensive end of pipe solutions.

2. CONTEXT

2.1 Acidification: the Problem

Just like other human activities, the production of electricity in Belgium has an important impact on the environment. The environmental impact starts with the use of non-renewable natural resources (gas, oil and coal). During the production of electricity, CO_2- (greenhouse effect), NO_x- and SO_2- (acidification) emissions are released into the air. Especially for Belgium, there is also the problem of the nuclear waste generated in the two nuclear reactor parks of Doel (near the Dutch border) and Tihange (near the French border). However, only relevant for this case are NO_x and SO_2 emissions causing acidification. Acidification is a complicated problem. Caused by air pollution, acid rain's spread and damage it involves weather, chemistry, soil, and the life cycles of plants and animals on the land and from acid rain in the water.

2.1.1 Contribution of the Belgian ESI to acidification
Figure 13.1 indicates the importance of different energy sources in the production of electricity.

Uranium is used in nuclear power stations, which generate more than 50 per cent of Belgium's electricity. Gas and coal account for about 40 per cent of electricity generated. Renewable forms of energy, such as water and wind, are used whenever possible.

Acidification is primarily caused by ESI through coal- and oil-fired generation, which generates emissions of NO_x- and SO_2, particles, toxins, and incompletely-burnt hydrocarbons. Also the combustion of natural gas causes NO_x emissions, though in general natural gas emits less NO_x per unit of electricity than oil or coal. An important amount of atmospheric emissions is thus generated each year by Belgian power stations. Table 13.1 shows the evolution of SO_2 and NO_x emissions by power stations in Belgium.

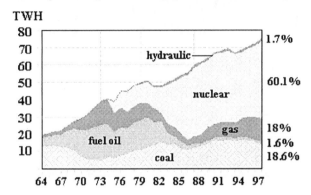

Source: Electrabel, 1998

Figure 13.1   Development of energy sources used in power stations in Belgium

Table 13.1   Evolution of SO_2- and NO_x-emissions by Electrabel and SPE

Year	SO_2 emissions		NO_x emissions	
	Tons	%	Tons	%
1980	351 643	100	87 010	100
1985	124 712	35.5	46 153	53.0
1990	94 381	26.8	59 183	68.0
1991	89 357	25.4	58 817	67.6
1992	82 487	23.5	56 605	65.1
1993	77 973	22.1	53 748	61.8
1994	78 225	22.2	56 737	65.2
1995	77 447	22.0	53 412	61.4
1996	68 781	19.6	50 623	58.2
1997	60 911	17.3	44 925	51.6
1998	61 235	17.4	46 834	53.8

Source: Electrabel, 1999

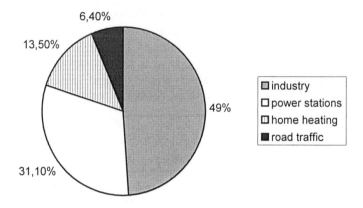

Source: VMM, 1998

Figure 13.2   Emission of sulphur dioxide (SO₂): various sources

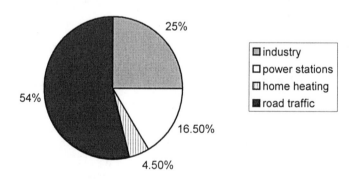

Source: VMM, 1998

Figure 13.3   Emission of nitrogen oxides (NOₓ): various sources

Not only the ESI is responsible for the emission of SO_2 and NO_x. Many other industries as well, emit in the air. However Figures 13.2 and 13.3 make it clear that the electricity supply industry is responsible for an important part of both the SO_2 and NO_x emissions in Belgium.

2.1.2 Technical or economic solutions for the environmental problem

The technical solutions towards the environmental problem of the ESI are guided by the BAT principle, laid down in the European Directive of September 1996 (96/61/EEC). The solutions can be found in primary NO_x measures and secondary exhaust fume purification techniques.

Primary NO_x measures aim at reducing the generation of NO_x. Over the last decade Laborelec, the Belgian Laboratory of the Electricity Industry, has developed a very important know-how with respect to the main parameters that determine the oxidation reaction of nitrogen. This know-how, by means of newly developed techniques, is used in several power stations, in order to limit the production of NO_x during the combustion process. The most important technical adaptations are amongst others the installation of 'low NO_x burners' and 'Over Fire Air (OFA)'-, 'Burner Out of Service (BOOS)- and 'Reburning' techniques.

Secondary exhaust fume purification techniques wash the sulphur out of the smoke before it goes up to the smokestacks. Scrubbers remove sulphur from the smoke by spraying a mixture of water and powdered limestone into the smokestack. The mixture traps the sulphur before it can escape into the air above.

2.2 Institutional Context and Public Environmental Policy

2.2.1 Institutional and legislative arrangements with respect to air management

In 1964 the national Law on Air Pollution established the legal framework for minimising air pollution through the control of emissions and the setting of ambient air quality standards. This national law has since been complemented by a range of decrees in each of the regions and has also been amended to incorporate the various European Directives on ambient air quality and emissions from stationary and mobile sources.

Federal administrations The federal government has responsibility for all matters that, for technical and economic reasons, require uniform treatment at the national level. Hence control of air pollution from mobile sources is a federal responsibility and EU regulations on fuel quality are implemented through federal regulations issued by the Energy Administration in the Ministry of Economic Affairs. Other air pollution issues are the responsibility of the regions. The gendarmerie, part of the Ministry of Internal Affairs, has local environmental responsibilities as part of its basic police functions (for example, control of illegal emissions).

Flemish administrations   In Flanders, the Department of the Environment and Infrastructure has the mission of improving the environment, protecting the architectural and ecological heritage, carrying out spatial planning and formulating policy concerning traffic and transport. This department has six administrations, one of which, the Administration for Environment, Nature, Land and Water Management (AMINAL) is the environmental agency with responsibilities for policy, planning, licensing and inspection in the areas of water management, land use, forestry and nature conservation (including air pollution issues).

The Flemish Environment Agency (VMM) is responsible for air quality monitoring networks and emission inventories and co-operates with AMINAL in policy implementation.

Walloon administrations   The Ministry of the Walloon Region includes the Directorate-General of Natural Resources and the Environment (DGRNE) which comprises five divisions. The Division for Pollution Prevention and Soil Management is responsible for air pollution issues. DGRNE publishes an annual report on the state of the Walloon environment.

Brussels-Capital administrations   The Brussels Institute for Environmental Management (IBGE/BIM) deals with most environmental issues in the Brussels-Capital Region. The Institute carries out investigations and planning and formulates environmental regulations. It is also responsible for issuing and enforcing discharge and emission permits for classified installations.

Standards and regulations   The ambient air standards adopted by the three regions are based on the various EU Directives. To communicate general information about ambient air quality to the public, an indicator has been developed; a scale of ten is used to represent air quality based on measurements of SO_2, NO_2 and O_3 concentrations.

In Flanders the regulations set general and sectoral BAT-based emission limits, depending on the type of installation. In Wallonia and Brussels-Capital there is a case-by-case approach based on internal guidelines. In the three regions, issuing permits for air emissions is part of the licensing of classified processes and installations. Permits are generally based on the above mentioned emission limits, but stricter limits can be imposed where required by local conditions. Permits stipulate the method of monitoring and the required monitoring frequency. Permit holders can engage an expert to monitor compliance with permit conditions or can carry out the monitoring themselves in accordance with a method approved by an expert.

Inspection and enforcement systems have been strengthened in all three regions. The regional inspection agencies also train municipalities to carry out inspections.

2.2.2 Emission inventories

Since 1993, Flanders has maintained a compulsory emission inventory (comprising 45 substances) to which all firms whose emissions exceed a certain threshold must contribute information. In the precious decade, a similar inventory had already been operated on a voluntary basis. Emissions generated by households, transport, agriculture and nature are calculated yearly. Public access is granted under EU rules.

In Wallonia, about 200–300 firms contribute data to a similar inventory (comprising 27 substances) that is still voluntary. The Brussels-Capital system is also voluntary and emissions data are organised on the basis of a geographic grid with cells of 250 m^2.

2.2.3 Specific acidification policies

Belgian emissions of SO_x amounted to 828 kilotons in 1980; between 1990 and 1996 they decreased by 25 per cent from 322 to 240 kilotons. Industrial combustion and electricity generation account for the largest share of emissions and emission reductions from these sources were responsible for most of the total decrease.

NO_x emissions were 442 kilotons in 1980 and 334 kilotons in 1996. Transport accounted for 54 per cent, industrial combustion for 21 per cent and electricity generation for 16 per cent.

The relative contribution of the various sources has changed considerably since acidification first became an issue in Belgium. The substantial reduction in sulphur emissions from industry and from electricity generation in the first half of the 1980s has been followed by large increases in NO_x and ammonia emissions from road transport and from animal husbandry activities.

Belgium is both a source of transfrontier air pollution and is exposed to it due to emissions of SO_2 and NO_x in Europe and of NH_3 in the Netherlands. Belgium is nevertheless a net exporter of acidifying substances. In Table 13.2 you can find (in 100 tons) how much of the acid deposition in 1996 in Belgium and in foreign countries is caused by foreign countries or Belgium.

Table 13.2   Acid deposition in 1996 in Belgium and foreign countries caused by foreign countries or Belgium

Country of origin or receiving country	In Belgium		From Belgium	
	SO_x	NO_x	SO_x	NO_x
Belgium	89	42	89	42
France	88	52	131	102
Germany	121	62	134	116
Luxembourg	1	1	3	2
The Netherlands	22	30	55	24
UK	57	42	40	31
Other EU Countries	23	16	32	45
Other OECD Countries	34	8	30	42
Others (incl. sea)	84	47	373	365
Total	519	300	887	769

Source: UN-ECE, 1997

The total deposition in 1997, compared to 1990, decreased by 17 per cent, against the proposed 39 per cent for 2002.

Especially during the period 1960–75 there was a strong increase in the emissions of acid substances. In this period there was a much higher SO_2 concentration, especially in urban and industrial surroundings. Since 1980 the Flemish Region is registering all acid emissions in the region and the authorities have done important efforts to reduce the acid emissions in Flanders.

Figure 13.4 gives an overview of the average acid deposition in the Flemish Region for the period 1980–96. Since the beginning of the 1990s, ammonium is the most important acid substance and is responsible for the largest contribution to acidification in Flanders. In 1996, the NH_x deposition amounted for 1 849 (45 per cent), the SO_x for 1 437 (35 per cent) and NO_x for 802 (20 per cent) acid equivalents/hectare/year.

Figure 13.5 shows the contribution of the different target groups in the acid deposition in Flanders in 1994. 58 per cent of the SO_x depositions is import from foreign emissions. The electricity supply industry is responsible for 26 per cent of the Flemish share of the SO_x depositions.

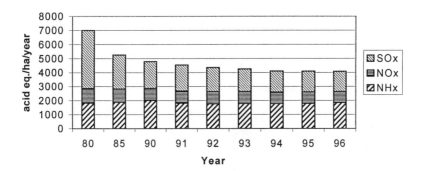

Source: VMM, 1998

Figure 13.4   The average acid deposition in the Flemish Region for the period 1980–96

Of 1994 NO$_x$ depositions 70 per cent were imported from abroad. The electricity supply industry is responsible for 12 per cent of the Flemish share of the NO$_x$ depositions.

SO$_x$

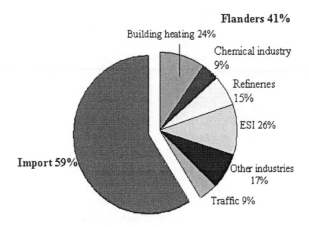

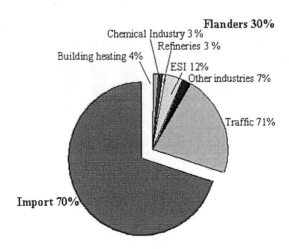

Source: VMM, 1998

*Figure 13.5   The contribution of the different target groups in the acid
deposition in Flanders in 1994*

In 1980 the electricity producing industry was responsible for 40 per cent
of the total potential of acid emissions in Flanders. Its share decreased,
especially during the period 1980–85 and for the moment the industry is
responsible for 18 per cent of the total potential of acid emissions in Flanders.

The Flemish Environmental Policy Plan (1997 – 2001) defines broadly the
Flemish environmental policy for the following 20 years and defines what the
Flemish Government wants to realise in the next five years.

Acidification is included in this Environmental Policy Plan as one of the
13 environmental themes that needs special attention of the Flemish
authorities.

The current situation with respect to this problem is the following:

- Because of the transboundary atmospheric transport of acidifying
  elements, acidification is an international problem.
- The total acid deposition in 1990 was 4 763 acid equivalents/ha. 39
  per cent of this deposition was caused by emissions of SO_2, NO_x
  caused 23 per cent. 60 per cent of these SO_2 emissions and 72 per cent
  of these NO_x emissions came from abroad. In 1996, 53 per cent of the

acidifying depositions in Flanders came from outside the Flemish Region. On the other hand one has to say that Flanders is a net exporter of acidifying substances.

- Total potential of acid emissions in Flanders decreased from 24 000 million acid equivalents in 1980 to almost 12 500 million in 1997. This decrease was almost completely realised in the period 1980 – 85. One can also detect a shift in the relative share of SO_2 and NO_x: from 67 per cent and 18 per cent to 38 per cent and 30 per cent. The small decrease during the period 1990–97 is caused by the decreasing SO_2 emissions from industry.
- Belgium has committed itself to comply with several international agreements to reduce acid emissions:

  — Sofia Protocol (stabilisation of NO_x emissions in 1994 relative to 1987);
  — Helsinki Declaration (NOx reduction of 30 per cent in 1998 relative to 1980);
  — Oslo Protocol (Belgium committed itself to a reduction of SO_2 of 70 per cent in 2000, 72 per cent in 2005 and 74 per cent in 2010, relative to 1980).

- The Flemish Region already imposes emission reduction for acid substances on companies by means of limiting values in the permit system (VLAREM II).
- During the timeframe of this policy plan (1997 – 2001), the Flemish Government wants to achieve the following goals: reduction of the total acidifying deposition by 39 per cent in 2002 compared to 1990 (this would mean 2 900 acid equivalents/ha per year)

Tables 13.3 and 13.4 give a clear picture of the different categories of polluters and their contribution to the acid deposition in Flanders and the goals for 2002.

Table 13.3   SO₂ and NOₓ deposition in Flanders: reality and goals

SO_2*	1990		2002	
	Flanders	Foreign Countries	Flanders	Foreign Countries
Industry	542	964	225	533
Households	152	98	106	56
Traffic	50	53	20	33
Total	**744**	**1 115**	**351**	**622**
NO_x*				
Industry	73	276	45	188
Households	14	44	12	30
Traffic	228	474	153	331
Total	**315**	**794**	**210**	**549**

Note: *: in acid equivalents/ha/year

Source: VMM, 1997

The Flemish strategy to achieve these goals:

- Since acidification is an international problem, the Flemish Region wants to co-operate on international level to develop international agreements on emission reductions.
- Flanders has developed the following policy for emission reductions that must lead to a total reduction of acid emissions of 46 per cent.

Table 13.4 SO₂ and NOₓ deposition in Flanders: distribution

SO_2 in tons/year (and % compared to 1990)	1990	2002
Industry	188 368 (100)	78 100 (41)
Of which the electricity industry	*71 926 (100)*	*23 600 (33)*
Households	23 599 (100)	16 519 (70)
Traffic	7 748 (100)	3 021 (39)
Total	219 715 (100)	97 640 (44)
NO_x in tons/year (and % compared to 1990)	1990	2002
Industry	81 759 (100)	49 855 (61)
Of which the electricity industry	*46 462 (100)*	*21 700 (47)*
Households	6 707 (100)	6 036 (90)
Traffic	105 326 (100)	70 568 (67)
Total	193 792 (100)	126 459 (65)

Source: VMM, 1997

With respect to the electricity industry, the Flemish Environmental Policy Plan (MINA Plan) identifies the Negotiated Agreement (of 1991) and the planned investments of the sector, as the main elements to achieve these goals. The Flemish Government expects however that the actions developed in the Flemish policy with respect to the reductions of CO_2 emissions will also contribute to the reduction of the acidic emissions.

The Flemish Government is also planning to develop a network to continuously measure the depositions. This network should enable the authorities to control the evolution of the acid deposition.

No estimation has been made yet of the costs needed to counteract the effects of acidification in Flanders. It is known however that Flanders spends approximately BEF 1 billion on the restoration of buildings damaged by acidification.

2.3 The Belgian Electricity Supply Industry

2.3.1 Market structure of the Belgian electricity supply industry
A legal framework, formalised in 1925, which granted municipalities the right to determine how electricity supply would be met in their area, modelled the economic context of the electricity supply industry.

The industry was also shaped by the dominating influence in the Belgian economy of industrial holding companies, such as Société Générale de Belgique (SGB) and Bruxelles Lambert, which has ensured a major role for privately-owned production companies in the sector. The mixture of predominantly privately-owned producers and publicly-owned or controlled distributors have continued ever since.

There was pressure to bring the sector into public ownership in the 1950s on the grounds that the development of the ESI was an essential prerequisite for post-war reconstruction and was best guaranteed by state control.

However, this was resisted and the industry was subjected to an institutionalised form of regulation and scrutiny with the establishment of a control committee in 1955 to regulate prices and investments and in 1964 it became the Comité de Control de l'Electricité et du Gaz (CCEG).

The Belgian energy sector in general and the electricity sector in particular have undergone drastic changes in the last few years. In 1990, the three remaining private producers, Ebes, Intercom and Unerg, merged into one private company, Electrabel.

According to the Government, the objectives of the merger were to create an entity better able to resist possible take-over bids and with a better competitive position in the emerging European single energy market.

Although electricity production is unrestricted in Belgium, this merger resulted in a quasi-private monopoly for Electrabel.

Following an agreement concluded in 1981, confirmed by a protocol in 1990, Electrabel and the small public producer SPE concluded a major convention in 1995.

Since the agreement in 1981, SPE has joined the three private producers in organising a modern central dispatch system for merit order loading of all their plants and in specific organisations, among others for:

- investment planning, tariff and general policy in a common board of directors (BCEO);
- central dispatch of the power system in the Centre for Production and Transport of Electricity (CPTE);
- research in Laborelec.

Since 1995, the new structure of the electricity sector is shown in Figure 13.6.

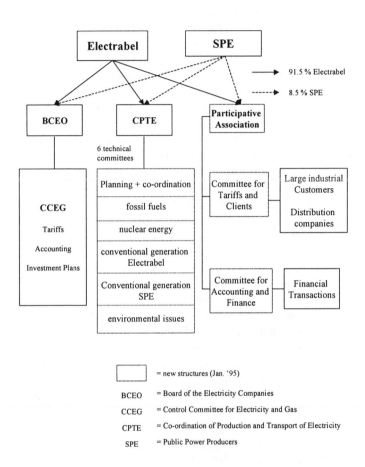

Source: Verbruggen, A., 1998

Figure 13.6 The new structure of the electricity sector in Belgium

The significant degree of cross-ownership in the industry – together with a high degree of vertical and horizontal integration and a mixture of formal and informal relationships among production, transmission, and distribution companies – has produced a centralised and monopolistic power sector. Competition is carefully avoided, the barriers for new generators to enter the market are relatively high and consumers' choices are limited. It comes as no surprise that electricity tariffs in Belgium are among the highest in Europe.

In the past, long-term contracts with a duration of 20 to 30 years were signed between Electrabel and municipalities in order to settle the distribution of power in certain areas. In 1995 Electrabel started the realisation of a plan to renegotiate these contracts and to extend their lifetime with a period of 18 years. This would have meant that certain contracts would be extended to the legal maximum of 30 years. Electrabel also wanted the municipalities to become shareholders in Electrabel by taking over 5 per cent of the Electrabel shares from Tractebel. Along the contract renewal move, Electrabel and Intermixt founded a new organisation on 13 December 1995, the 'vzw Committee Intermixt/Electrabel'. This Committee will shadow the functioning of the CCEG and has a mission to increase the understanding between Electrabel and the mixed intermunicipal companies.

There was however strong opposition against this contract renewal, arguing that these third generation contracts were set up to protect Electrabel against competition and to guarantee its monopoly profits in the future. Also the European Commission has opposed the new contracts. The stipulations of the contract conflicted with Art. 85 and 86 of the European Treaty on Competition. The EC objected strongly to the protection of the domestic market against other producers and/or suppliers, to the 18 years-term of the contracts and to the participation of the municipalities in Electrabel's shares. In response to the amendments asked by the EC, Electrabel only proposed to reduce the term of the contracts to 15 years. Lengthy negotiations followed between the EC and Electrabel. Finally in April 1997 Electrabel-Intermixt and the EC came to an agreement. The EC accepted the term of 15 years. However after 10 years, in 2006, other electricity producers are allowed to supply 25 per cent of the electricity demand of the mixed intercommunal companies. The year 2006 is also the deadline for the EU-Directive on the liberalisation of the internal electricity market for consumers with at least a demand of 9 megawatt per hour. In 2011 municipalities are completely free to leave the Mixed Intercommunal Company and to choose their own supplier. Also the 5 per cent shares in Electrabel held by the municipalities will end in 2011.

Some actors in society argue that through this move, Electrabel has been able to extend its monopoly position into the twenty-first century and to anticipate the liberalisation of the electricity market imposed by the EU. According to them, the events of the last years confirm the strategic, political and organisational strength of Electrabel in the Belgian market and the weakness of public authorities and of regulatory control.

2.3.2 Public regulation of the Belgian electricity sector

The ESI is regulated by Government through the Control Committee for Electricity and Gas (CCEG) and the National Energy Committee. The basic framework was set up in the 1950s and expanded by the 1980–81 reforms.

The Control Committee is a typically Belgian institution involving members from employer organisations and trade unions, whose representatives are carefully balanced between linguistic (Flemish and Walloon) and political (Christian Democrat and Socialist) interests. This committee controls the gas and electricity producers and transporters (Electrabel and SPE) and the distribution organisations (Intermixt and Interregies). The social partners carry out the control, while the government has only a limited observatory role.

In practice the CCEG has very limited resources, works with a small secretariat and is housed in Tracebel-Electrabel office buildings. Unlike the US public utility commissions, but like most European regulators, the permanent staff of the committee is minimal. As a result, the committee has rather limited competencies, namely monitoring cost price trends and profitability, and giving recommendations on the organisation of the sector, investment plans and tariffs.

However, the committee is only advisory and the government can, on the basis of broader considerations of national interest, ignore its recommendations.

There exists no formal, legal restriction on the production or sale of electricity, though the conditions of sale have to be negotiated. Price regulation is basically carried out on rate-of-return basis. There is a single set of tariffs, which apply nationwide regardless of distributor. The regulatory procedure is that the utilities submit their financial results to the committee's accountants who assess their costs. Prices are set according to a formula agreed by the committee on the basis of this analysis. This formula includes terms to cover all the major costs including fuel, labour and financing. Indices for movements in each of these terms are derived and consumer processes are adjusted on a monthly basis. This formula is generally valid for a number of years until there is a significant change in the structure of the generating stock, for example, the commissioning of a nuclear power plant.

Investment regulation is somewhat more complex. The CGEE is required to submit a ten-year investment plan to the Control Committee and the National Energy Committee detailing investments in new plants, major investments in existing plants (for example conversion to coal-firing), plants to be decommissioned and major transmission network investments. These are backed up by electricity demand forecasts. In the first years of operation of this procedure (from 1980 onwards), the CGEE submitted its investment plan annually (1981–83) but in recent years, only two investment plans have been drawn up – in 1985 and 1988. The Control Committee and the National Energy Committee each have 30 days to express their opinions on the plan and if at the end of this period the government has not voiced any opposition to it, the plan is accepted.

At a parliamentary level, there is no standing committee on energy although there are occasional ad hoc research committees. The standing committee on industry and the economy does carry out inquiries on electricity but these are infrequent and there is little accumulated expertise. The volatile nature of Belgian politics means that the role of parliament is greater than in other countries and that debates can influence the broad parameters of policy accordingly. Thus, energy policy in the early 1980s was determined mainly by a series of parliamentary debates.

2.3.3 Environmental policy of the electricity supply industry

Electrabel has long been geared to the future. For years now the company has executed action plans focusing on the environment and RUE (rational use of energy). Electrabel's efforts can be summed up in a single sentence: generate more efficiently, not just more; consume more efficiently, not just more.

The environment, like the rational use of energy, is part of Electrabel's corporate philosophy. Electrabel has long been committed to the environment, and it is still determined today to meet its commitments. Some examples of the environmental commitments are:

Reduction of atmospheric emissions Electrabel is committed to combating atmospheric emissions. In 1991 it signed an agreement to this effect with the federal and regional authorities. Not only is it upholding its commitments, but the results have exceeded the targets set. Despite greater output by fossil fuel-fired power stations, emissions of acid substances into the atmosphere remain well below European target values.

Sulphur dioxide (SO_2) emissions have fallen thanks to:

- the more widespread use of natural gas and other low-sulphur fuels and
- higher energy yields from generation units (STAG, co-generation).

In future, flue gases from modern conventional units will be desulphurized.

Nitrogen oxide (NO_x) emissions have fallen as a result of special combustion technologies. In future, catalytic converters will be used to denitrify flue gases from modern conventional units.

By the same token, it should not be forgotten that Belgian nuclear power stations (responsible for 60 per cent of the electricity production) make a considerable contribution toward limiting carbon dioxide (CO_2) emissions, which are partly responsible for the greenhouse effect. Major efforts are being made to reduce the output of radioactive waste. Over a ten-year period, while nuclear generation remained virtually unchanged, the volume of radioactive waste fell by 50 per cent.

Renewable energy sources: hydroelectric power, photovoltaic cells, wind power Renewable forms of energy are used wherever possible (see Figure 13.7), but their use is limited in Belgium due to unsuitable and uncertain geographical and climate conditions.

⬚ Photovoltalc conversion   solar energy

⬚ Hydroelectric Total capacity: approx. 100 MW

■ Wind farms Total capacity: approx. 4MW

Source: Electrabel, 1999

Figure 13.7   Renewable energy sources connected to the network

Electrabel makes the best possible use of available hydroelectric facilities. It currently has 11 run-of-river power stations, which have a total installed capacity of 27 megawatt and account for around 0.3 per cent of annual electricity generation. Electricity generators have assured the Walloon regional authorities that they will help with the installation of new hydroelectric units when the dams on the upper Meuse are renovated. The Coo pumped-storage power station (1 100 megawatt) is also counted as a hydroelectric unit, although in actual fact this is not a form of renewable energy. During periods of low consumption the electricity generated by other stations is used to pump water from the lower reservoir to an upper reservoir. During consumption peaks, the water's potential energy can be released and used to drive water turbines coupled to generators. As a result, there is no need to start up additional generation units.

Belgium does not really have a suitable climate for wind energy. Electrabel is, however, a member of the consortium that submitted the EURE-Wind project to the European Union authorities. The project aims to study the feasibility of a large wind farm (100 megawatt covering one or more sites in Europe).

The technological development of the photovoltaic conversion of solar energy into electricity looks very promising. Early photovoltaic cells had yields of just 10 per cent. Today's versions have upped this figure to between 14 and 16 per cent. The high cost of manufacturing cells is clearly proving to be an obstacle to the use of solar power, although a number of experimental sites are currently testing its potential.

3. NEGOTIATION PROCESS

In 1989 the ESI concluded that although there had achieved a considerable reduction of SO_2 and NO_x emissions through the intensified use of nuclear power, they expected these emissions to rise in the following years. The growing demand for electricity in the following years and the end of the nuclear investment programme of the ESI were the most important factors to explain this increase.

The ESI feared government intervention through regulation. Although the ESI acknowledged the fact that measures had to be taken in order to guarantee the attainment of SO_2 and NO_x reduction objectives, they wanted these measures to be economically feasible, especially considering the fact that many power plants were written off and not fit for expensive end-of-pipe solutions. The ESI came up with an (dis-)investment programme, which guaranteed a gradual reduction of SO_2 and NO_x emissions through:

- shutting down old power stations;
- co-generation (jointly producing electricity and heat);
- STAGs (combined-cycle steam and gas turbines);
- reduction of fuel sulphur level;
- general prevention measures.

The ESI considered negotiated agreements best fit to create a stable legal framework wherein the above investment programme could be realised. Therefore they started informal and open talks with the cabinet of the Flemish Ministry of the Environment. The cabinet was also found for the idea of using a negotiated agreement inspired by the positive experience in the Dutch ESI and by the bubble concept included in the European Directive 88/609/EEC. During the negotiation rounds, both parties interchanged information and gradually came to a draft agreement. After one year the ESI and the cabinet of the Flemish Minister of the Environment were close to signing the agreement. At that point the Flemish authorities involved also the Federal, Walloon and Brussels Authorities in the negotiations.

The Negotiated Agreement was finally signed on 18 October 1991 between the Belgian State, the Brussels region, the Flemish region and the Walloon region on the one hand, and Electrabel and SPE on the other hand. The main goal of this negotiated agreement is to reduce the SO_2- and NO_x-emissions, generated by the installations of the electricity producers mentioned above, up until 2003.

The negotiated agreement will automatically end on 31 December 2003. However both parties have agreed to start the negotiations of a new agreement starting from 1 January 2004 as of 2001.

The obligations for the electricity producers can be divided into general obligations falling within the bounds of their environmental policy, and specific obligations with regard to overall reductions of their SO_2- and NO_x-emissions.

The general obligations can be summed up as follows:

- power stations must be supplied exclusively with fuel having a low sulphur content (max. 1 per cent);
- measures must be implemented to limit the amount of NO_x emitted by combustion. Such measures are decided within the framework of a study programme entitled 'NO_x control' launched in April 1989 by Laborelec (National Laboratory of Electricity Producers);
- equipment for continuously measuring SO_2- and NO_x- emissions must be installed on all large generation units;
- a specific research project in the area of fuel gas cleaning (desulphurisation prototype) must be continued.

Lastly, it is stipulated that the electricity producers shall participate in governmental development programmes aimed at disseminating environmental technologies in Belgium and abroad, especially in Eastern Europe.

Besides these general obligations, the electricity producers undertake to reduce total SO_2 and NO_x emissions from current and future power plants. These emission reductions shall be expressed in the form of a comparison with the emissions from 1980, the year taken as a reference year in accordance with the EEC decision on this matter. The SO_2-emissions for 1980 were 351 643 tons, the NO_x-emissions amounted up to 87 010 tons.

Table 13.5   Targets for the SO_2 and NO_x- emissions

	1993	-70%
SO_2	1998	-75%, with a target value of −77.5%
	2003	-80%, with a target value of −85%
	1993	−30%
NO_x	1998	−40%
	2003	−40%, with a target value of −45%

The targets set in the agreement were based on the European Directive (bubble principle) and on simulations by the ESI based on the actual situation and future developments with respect to SO_2 and NO_x emissions. The actual emissions are corrected in function of the in- or decreasing use of co-generation and nuclear power according to a formula included in the agreement.

The obligations incumbent upon the authorities concern maximum emissions standards for SO_2 and NO_x that may be applied to existing and new generation units, either via legislation or within the framework of operating licences.

The authorities undertake not to impose standards on the combustion units concerned, which are more stringent than those applicable at the time the environmental agreement is signed. Failing that, the agreement shall specify the standards accepted by both parties.

The agreement also stipulates that the authorities may be exempted from these principles in the event that an EU directive is passed which is more restrictive than the provisions laid down in the environmental agreement.

The electricity producers have to draw up a detailed annual report of their SO_2 and NO_x emissions and the authorities shall be provided with all information needed to make an appropriate inspection.

A follow-up Commission was installed. The majority of its members are representatives of the authorities and it is chaired by one of these representatives. This follow-up Commission has the task of ensuring the correct execution of the negotiated agreement and to submit reports to this effect.

4. ANALYSIS

4.1 Performance of the agreement

Electrabel, committed by the negotiated agreement of 1991 to combating atmospheric emissions, is not only upholding its commitments, but the results have exceeded the targets set. Despite greater output by fossil fuel-fired power stations, emissions of acid substances into the atmosphere remain well below European target values.

Sulphur dioxide (SO_2) emissions have fallen (see Figure 13.8) thanks to:

- the more widespread use of natural gas and other low-sulphur fuels;
- higher energy yields from generation units (STAG, co-generation).

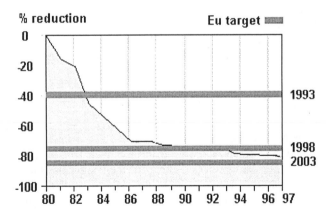

Source: Electrabel, 1998

Figure 13.8   Emissions of SO$_2$ by power stations in Belgium: reduction since 1980

In the future, flue gases from modern conventional units will be desulphurized in order to further reduce the atmospheric emissions.

Nitrogen oxide (NO_x) emissions have fallen as a result of special combustion technologies (see Figure 13.9). In future, catalytic converters will be used to denitrify flue gases from modern conventional units.

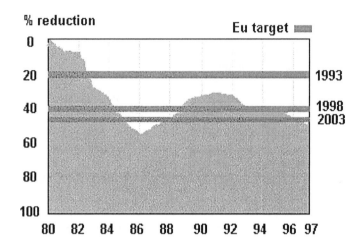

Source: Electrabel, 1998

Figure 13.9   Emissions of NO_x by power stations in Belgium: reduction since 1980

4.2 Monitoring Issues

4.2.1 At agreement level
The Negotiated Agreement foresaw in the establishment of a Surveillance Commission, composed of representatives of the Authorities and of the two Electricity Generators: Electrabel and SPE. The Surveillance Commission has the task of monitoring the execution of the content of the agreement, and in particular:

- take into consideration the reporting and the controls conducted by the electricity generators;
- compare, in 1994 and 1999, the emission reductions achieved with the obligations of the electricity generators and report thereon;
- compare every two years beginning in 1992, the emission reductions achieved in the previous year with the reductions to be achieved in the

following reference year and report the measures that are planned by the electricity generators for the emission reductions provided for the following reference year;

- compare annually the emission prescriptions with the obligations of the authorities in this regard and report thereon.

4.2.2 At corporate level

Electrabel and SPE measure on a regularly basis a number of environmental parameters for air, water, soil and noise. They also are developing new methods for measuring and predicting the environmental impact of power stations.

The emissions of SO_2 and NO_x are measured and monitored continuously in all power stations producing at least 300 megawatt. Specific software is developed for power stations that use fossil fuels (the 'Ecovision' system) that is able to manage the most important environmental parameters of a power station. This 'Ecovision' system automatically processes the registered data, what allows adapting the combustion process immediately as a function of the environmental impact.

In order to guarantee the accuracy and the reliability of the emission measurements, Laborelec frequently evaluates the measurement equipment used. At the same time Laborelec is doing continuously research to find the most appropriate measurement techniques for emissions.

Since 1972 the Belgian authorities have installed a measurement network all over the country that continuously observes the air. Electrabel and SPE also have installed a measurement network that continuously registers the concentrations of SO_2 and NO_x in the neighbourhood of power stations. The network of Electrabel and SPE consists of 16 measurement units. These units are integrated in the measurement network of the VMM (Vlaamse Milieumaatschappij) that observes the air quality in the Flemish Region. Electrabel and SPE have signed a co-operation agreement with VMM on the integration of both measuring networks and the exchange of data. In this regard, Electrabel and SPE have bought six new NO_x-measurement appliances in order to extend the measurement network of the authorities.

If (at a certain moment) two emission units in a certain zone (the Flemish region is divided in six zones) register an amount of SO_2 that is higher than $250 \ \mu g/m^3$, then Electrabel and SPE are obliged to adapt their combustion process in order to decrease the amount of SO_2 in the air (for example by using fuel that contains less sulphur).

A similar co-operation on the registration of emissions exists with the Walloon authorities for the Walloon Region.

5. CONCLUSION

Belgium has a long tradition of political consensus seeking and joint problem solving in the electricity market. This was an important factor in the decision to use a negotiated agreement instead of other instruments to solve the emission problem.

The ESI and the public authorities have a tradition of negotiating with each other through many committees. These experiences have made it easier to negotiate the agreement in a professional matter.

It can be assumed that compliance with a negotiated agreement is better guaranteed if there is a stick behind the door. In other words when there is a real and credible thread for the private sector that, in case of non-attainment of the goals, the government will use other policy instruments. It is difficult to judge ex post whether such a credible threat existed at the moment of negotiation and during the lifespan of the agreement. Nevertheless it is remarkable that this negotiated agreement explicitly states that the government can make an end to the agreement if the private sector does not fulfil the goals. In that case the government can use alternative regulations.

Another important feature of this agreement is that only a small group of negotiators were involved in the electricity covenant, namely the three Regions, Electrabel and SPE. This considerably simplified the negotiation process. Moreover, one actor, namely Electrabel, heavily dominates the electricity sector. This situation almost completely took away the risk of free-riders, which could jeopardise the realisation of the goals in the negotiated agreement.

BIBLIOGRAPHY

Bulteel, P, Malengreaux, J., et al., (1996), 'Environment Specific Committee Group of Experts: Environmental Policies for Electricity Supply Undertakings', Report

Cuijpers, C. and Proost, S., 1994, 'Energie en Milieu in het Federaal België:Historiek en Toekomstverkenning', paper, KULeuven.

De Clercq, M. (1998), 'Success Determining Factors for Negotiated Agreements: A Comparative Case Study of the Belgian Electricity Supply Industry and the Packaging Sector' in *Environmental Agreements, Public–Private Co-operation as a Policy Strategy*, Glasbergen: Kluwer Academic Press.

Electrabel (1995), 'Sectoriële overeenkomst over de vermindering van de SO2 en NOx-emissies afkomstig van de installaties voor electriciteitsproductie', *Verslag van de electriciteitsproducenten,* Brussels

Electrabel (1998), 'Annual Report 1997', Brussels.

Electrabel (1998), 'Environmental Report 1997', Brussels.

Electrabel (1999), 'Environmental Report 1998', Brussels.

Eurelectric (1997), 'Position paper on the Commission Communication on Environmental Agreements'.

IEA (1993), 'Electricity Info 1993', Paris.

IEA (1993), 'Energy Policies of IEA countries', Paris.

Van Hoorick, G. and Lambert, C., 1995, 'Het decreet betreffende Milieubeleidsovereenkomsten', in *Tijdschrift voor Milieurecht.*

Van Woensel, T. and Verbruggen, A, (1998), 'Eindrapport 1998: MIRA-S, Electriciteitsproductie', *Studiecentrum Technologie, Energie en Milieu,* UFSIA

Verbruggen, A., (1998), 'Naar een open electriciteitssector in België', *Studiecentrum Technologie, Energie en Milieu,* UFSIA.

Verbruggen, A., (1998), 'Electricity Sector Restructuring in Belgium', in *Electricity in Europe in the 21ᵗ Century: What performances and what game rules?* , UFSIA, STEM paper.

VMM (Vlaamse Milieumaatschappij) (1997), 'MINA-plan 2', Garant Uitgevers NV, Leuven.

VMM (Vlaamse Milieumaatschappij) (1998), 'MIRA-T 1998', Garant Uitgevers NV, Leuven.

Winsemius, P.(1992), 'Environmental Contracts and Covenants: New Instruments for a Realistic Environmental Policy?'in *Environmental Contracts and Covenants: New Instruments for a Realistic Environmental Policy?*, Rotterdam.

14. The Province Of Vicenza Negotiated Agreements[1]

Jane Wallace-Jones

1. INTRODUCTION

The negotiated agreements and ensuing Protocol of Intent were drawn up respectively in 1997 and 1998. They were part of a more extensive process promoted by the Vicentine Provincial Authorities – an Observatory – which aimed at bringing local actors together in order to gain a greater understanding of the widespread environmental problems linked to local industrial activity and furthermore, to solve or at least limit them through the use of environmental management systems and cleaner technology. A concerted effort by provincial authorities, local industrial associations and the Chamber of Commerce, which permitted access into firms for the purpose of the research, resulted in the publication of specific information regarding the use of environmental management systems and cleaner technology in different industrial sectors in the Province. The agreements were envisioned as 'vehicles' for the planned dissemination of the information thus far consolidated, in addition to foreseeing specific new directions for research and local applications. The goals of the agreement were multiple: to initiate new experiments concerning technological solutions to environmental problems in the tanning process; to set up an environmental innovation service; to ensure the dissemination of the information regarding environmental management systems in firms. The process was regarded as successful in so far as agreements were undersigned. However, actual uptake of the ideas regarding the use of cleaner technology and environmental management systems at firm level and, therefore, apparent environmental effectiveness of the agreement is lacking.

The context in which these agreements were promoted is rather particular: very little was known by the authorities about the nature or extent of these environmental problems, the production processes in a number of small firms in many sectors and thus the suitable means for and costs of pollution abatement. The case displays some striking characteristics which may prove partially explanatory to the poor environmental effectiveness of the agreement: some weakness in the contents of the agreement; the potential fragility of a local agreement as compared to one signed at the national level; the importance of political momentum in keeping the agreement process in evolution.

2. CONTEXT

2.1 The Environmental Problems Targeted

The Province of Vicenza is 2 722 km^2 and is found in the north-east of Italy in the Veneto region. In the Province of Vicenza, and the Veneto region as a whole, industry has rapidly spread over the last 40 years, resulting in industrial and residential settlement patterns referred to as the urbanised countryside. It has a population of over 747 000 and 73 004 firms (including agricultural practices), which are largely of the small-medium dimension. The main industrial sectors are metallurgy and mechanics (36 per cent of provincial employment), textiles and clothing (23 per cent), gold-smithy (7 per cent), wood and furniture (5.5 per cent), tanning (6 per cent) and others (22.5 per cent). Unemployment is low, about 3–4 per cent for the whole Province.

Much of Italian industry in the north-east has characteristically evolved in districts. These are defined as 'local territorial areas characterised by high concentrations of small firms, and refer specifically to the relationship between the presence of firms and the resident population, as well as the industrial specialisation of the whole of the firms' (Regione del Veneto, 1997). The Veneto region is one of the regions with the highest concentration of districts as about 34 (17.1 per cent of the total number of districts identified in Italy) are located here. In the Province of Vicenza, the main districts are that of tanning and marble working in Arzignano, electro-mechanics in Montecchio Maggiore, textiles and mechanics in the Alto Vicentino, ceramics and furniture in Bassano, gold smithery in Vicenza. Much of the collateral industries, such as mechanics, are specialised in the construction of machinery for the production processes of the other industries.

In spite of the economic growth in the area, the industry in the Province of Vicenza is characterised by specific problems such as: underdeveloped internationalisation; a frequent under-capitalisation of the small and medium enterprises, a training policy which does not respond to the needs of the area; a lack of adequate service structures for research into innovation, above all aimed at opening up opportunities on the market. However, the ex-director of the Provincial Department for the Environment, wrote that 'the greatest problem in this area is that of the gap between economic growth and territorial sustainability. This has two consequences, the apparent inadequacy of the existing mobility infrastructure as well as an increase in environmental degradation, in the excessive use of soil, the poor water quality, the vulnerability of the natural resources, the air pollution, the difficulty in waste disposal' (Poletto, 1997).

The environmental problems that the negotiated agreements, and the whole process in which they are embedded, aim to deal with, are the problems of: waste resulting from local industrial activities in terms of its minimisation, simplification of its disposal and/or its recovery; pollution of freshwater resulting from the aqueous discharge from production processes and the atmospheric pollution resulting from emissions.

This very generalised description and the diffuse nature of these problems directly reflect the fact that the Provincial Authorities lacked hard knowledge at the beginning of the process (considered as the beginning of the Observatory in 1995). The Provincial Authorities knew what the overall problem was – increasing degradation of the water, air and soil quality, they knew what the general cause was – the industries, and they knew that it was necessary to take steps regarding pollution prevention. However, they lacked emission data, information on the exact type of production processes employed and thus information on the opportunities available either through the introduction of new technologies or different management for cost-efficient ways to improve the environmental quality of the area. The environmental problems and thus their eventual solution were, moreover, examined from the perspective of how *small* firms could contribute to this process.

The work of the Observatory involved case studies of local small firms in different sectors, which eventually led to the publication of sector specific manuals aimed at fostering the introduction of environmental management systems.

2.2 A Focus on the Arzignano-Chiampo Tanning District

The following focuses specifically on the Arzignano-Chiampo tanning district for a number of reasons. First, because the Arzignano-Chiampo tanning district came under scrutiny during the Observatory through the experiments carried out concerning sludge treatment, as well as later in the negotiated agreement which regarded research into the replacement of solvent-based varnishes in the refining phase with water-based varnishes. Second, a study by Michieli (1999) based on interviews with 55 firms, gives an insight into the relationship between industrial activities and the environment in the Province of Vicenza through an in-depth survey of the tanning district's environmental problems and, above all, the way in which they are managed and viewed by the firms. Furthermore, there is continued interest in the potential use of negotiated agreements to tackle the environmental problems of the area.

In the 1800s, leather tanning in the area was still a service activity to the local farming community. Arzignano became progressively famous for the silk industry until after the Second World War when the district began tanning on an industrial scale in the wake of increased pressure on the silk industry caused by demand for synthetic fibres. Michieli (1999) notes the conditions which permitted the expansion of tanning as the patrimony of technical knowledge, the vast quantities of water, the availability of factory workers; the small amount of initial capital necessary.

The number of tanning firms in the area rose from 15 in 1951 to 70 in 1960 (Michieli, 1999). In the 1980s the district's structure was transformed by the crisis that hit the sector. A large number of medium-large tanning firms were bought by families who them formed groups which controlled 50 per cent of local production. However, the sector still remains dominated by the presence of small and medium sized firms. The Industrial Association's 1994 data shows that 370 of the firms in the district carry out either the entire technological tanning cycle or one/some of the phases while the other firms carry out collateral activities.

The firms in the Arzignano-Chiampo area show a strong propensity for export, 69.1 per cent of those interviewed by Michieli have relations with the foreign market. At present the Italian tanning industry represents about 60 per cent of the European market (which is the main market for the sector) and 12.5 per cent of the global market (Michieli, 1999).

The tanning process is composed of three main phases. The first involves the removal of hair from the hides and preparation for tanning. The second is the tanning process itself, carried out in the majority of cases with the addition of chromium salts, further tanning with tannins and the dying of the leather and the addition of oils. The refining phase involves the protection of the leather from external agents usually by spraying.

The entire production process has the following main environmental impacts: consumption of large quantities of water; sludge (considered special waste) disposal; discharge of process water containing chromium, sulphates, chlorides and nitrates; emission of hydrogen sulphide (the area is often permeated with the smell of rotten eggs); emissions of volatile organic compounds during the phase of leather finishing.

To give an idea of the quantity of waste generated, 100 kg of bovine hide generates (adapted from Michieli, 1999):

- 3 500–8 000 litres of aqueous discharges (when chrome is used);
- 10–20 kg (dry weight) sludge;
- 15–20 kg (dry weight) solid residues (tanned and not tanned);
- 1–2 kg atmospheric emissions.

Up until the middle of the 1970s the firms did not have monitoring or pollution abatement systems. There were, therefore, notable problems caused to both local inhabitants and agricultural activities in the vicinity. With the emanation of the Merli law (law 319/76) aimed at establishing control of water pollution, the municipalities of the Valley equipped themselves with water treatment plants run by consortia. One is in Arzignano and serves 336 industrial users, 160 of which are involved partially or fully in the technological phases of the tanning cycle while the rest are involved in leather refining. On average, it daily treats 25 000m^3 of wastewater which generates 200–220 tons of sludge. Since beginning operations the Arzignano consortium has already filled six legal landfills with an average capacity of 25 000 tons and a new one has recently been prepared. The second consortium at Montebello Vicentino treats 9 140 m^3 of water a day (Michieli, 1999).

At the end of the 1970s when the consortia were constituted, the tanning firms applied to use the water treatment services and fixed the maximum quantity of waste water which they would be able to use. Today, the firms water treatment capacity remains as established, thus creating a limit to the production capacity of the firms. Furthermore, the creation of new tanning firms at full cycle is no longer possible because of the lack of available water treatment quotas. The implications of this rigid system has meant that large firms have remained large whilst small ones have remained such that they do not manage to reach the critical size necessary for achieving internal economies of scale. New firms in the district carry out parts of the production process not involving the use of water while others do not have any production processes but rather buy and sell raw hides and market the final product.

It was found (Michieli, 1999) that few pollution prevention initiatives have been undertaken specifically by the firms, leaving innovation in tanning techniques with the chemical industry and research on more efficient water treatment methods to the consortia. In the district, the protection of natural resources has taken place principally through technical means at the process and product level through experimentation with cleaner technologies which permit pollution levels to be lowered in a way which respects the standards imposed by the Province of Vicenza.

In fact, CO.VI.AM., the Vicentine Tanning Consortium (the tanning section of the Industrial Association of the Province of Vicenza), which was set up in 1993 and has a membership of 60 firms has been promoting research and experimenting with clean technology. Three initiatives were promoted with the regional authorities and the financial assistance of EU 'LIFE' projects. These dealt with the substitution of sulphides in the hair removing process via chemical or enzymatic methods, the substitution of spraying in the refining process with a rolling method, the treatment of desalination water with electrochemical systems for the reduction of sulphides and the recovery of chlorides and sulphates. CO.VI.AM. then turned its attention to the problem of emissions and carried out a series of studies aimed at the use of water-based chemical substances capable of preventing the emission of VOCs. However, it was found that many of the firm-oriented initiatives have been limited to experimentation, as it has been shown that they are unable to resolve the environmental problems and at the same time guarantee the same quality of final product. An example of this is the new techniques related to water-based refining products.

Michieli's analysis also portrays a clear picture of the firms' attitude to environmental variables. In terms of pollution prevention technology, 7.27 per cent of the firms interviewed have a chemical–physical pre-treatment plant which separates polluting substances out as sludge which is pressed and disposed and water treated by the consortia. 92.73 per cent of the firms have abatement technology for atmospheric emissions and the large majority of firms carry out refining using the spraying rather than the rolling method, though the latter is said to be becoming more well known. When asked to prioritise, 89.09 per cent of firms believe that atmospheric emissions are the greatest environmental problems followed by that of wastewater. Of firms contacted, 61.82 per cent declared to not have adopted any internal environmental policy (those that have are medium–large firms) and most have chosen to look to cleaner technology in order to reduce environmental impact as opposed to environmental management systems. Of the firms interviewed, 18.18 per cent made environment related investments.

When asked to name who the firms feel pressure from concerning environmental issues, 78.18 per cent feel pressure from the local authorities, 5.45 per cent from shareholders and 16.36 per cent responded that they do not feel *any* pressure regarding environmental problems.

In response to the question made to gauge the extent of environmental initiatives in the district, 78.18 per cent of firms said that that they had never been part of initiatives such as the experimental LIFE projects. The environment could be considered a strategic variable according to 65.45 per cent of the firms, but mainly because it is a limit to production which has to be respected.

Michieli also asked if firms felt there was an eventual necessity to form consortia in order to manage problems or activities related to the environment. In spite of the inherently co-operative nature of the economic activities in the district, 83.64 per cent of firms believe this is not necessary. Those who do believe it is necessary, argue that it would lead to better management of the water treatment plants in the local authorities control, to better management of the consortia and to the possibility of putting more pressure on the local authorities.

2.3 The Instruments Chosen to Tackle the Problem

The Observatory and the agreement focused largely on the development and dissemination of information regarding the application of environmental management systems (EMS) and the introduction of cleaner technology in firms.

The fact that the authorities chose to combine such an instrument-based approach with of a punctual problem-based approach (experiments and research for certain environmental impacts regarding specific industrial activities) merits comment. As had already been said, the regulatory bodies and those responsible for environmental control aimed at the improvement of environmental performance of firms (and consequent reduction in pollution), while, however, in this instance, lacking complete information on individual firm activities and impacts. In light of this, the choice of strategy, encouraging the adoption of EMSs and the introduction of cleaner technologies, were considered to be able to reduce the asymmetry in information by encouraging the voluntary dissemination of information on environmental performance on the part of firms, thus seeking to overcome the limitations in the controlling bodies' ability to enforce regulation. In addition, the aim was to promote (at least implicitly) the continuous improvement of environmental performance and encourage a change in the relationship between firms and public authorities from conflict to co-operation.

It may, however, have been to soon for such an innovative approach to environmental problems and the results of a recent survey shed some light on the use of these EMSs in firms in the north-east of Italy and thus the context in which the negotiated agreements were placed. This survey focused on the diffusion of environmental management in firms in the Veneto, Friuli-Venezia-Giulia and Trentino Alto Adige Regions. The study notes that although the firms have carried out a number of different measures aimed at mitigating the environmental impacts (which mainly correspond to legal obligations), they are still in a preliminary phase with regard to structured and formalised environmental management systems (Borghini and Cibin, 1999). The study shows that the consideration or application of an environmental management system is taking place in the larger firms (those with more than 500 employees).

This is, perhaps, better understood when examined in the wider content of environmental management systems in Italy. In Italy, EMAS (1836/93/EEC) became operational rather late and the first Italian site was registered in December 1997. In fact, even though Decree nr. 413 establishing the Comitato per l'Ecolabel e l'Ecoaudit (Committee for Ecolabel and EMAS), acting both as Competent Body and Accreditation Body for EMAS was issued on 5 May 1995, the committee only became operational in February 1997. The Committee is divided into two sections: one section called 'EMAS Italia' and the other one called 'Ecolabel'. The first section acts both as a competent body and an accreditation body for EMAS, while the latter corresponds to the competent body for Regulation 880/92. The Committee approved the registration procedures for EMAS sites in November 1997 and the accreditation procedures for environmental verifiers as organisations in September 1997, while individual verifiers have been able to register since June 1998. In accreditation the Committee is supported by SINCERT, which is an accreditation body for ISO 9 000 as well as for ISO 14 000.

So far, the success of EMAS has been rather limited in Italy (29 registered sites, in September 2000), particularly when compared to the success of ISO 14001. One of the causes of the slow diffusion of EMAS in Italy is actually thought to be public administration's low awareness of this instrument and as a consequence in the future the Committee intends to promote EMAS among the public bodies. ANPA, the national environmental agency which provides technical support to the committee has launched a project with the regional agencies for the environment (ARPA) and the industrial associations which foresees an articulated network for both the dissemination of information on EMAS and EMSs in general. The network also seeks to gather information on local firm experiences and the identification of specific instruments that can be adopted by public authorities to further facilitate and provide incentives for EMS adoption. Some Italian regions are already trying to promote EMAS by introducing regional laws for financing firms willing to implement it. In addition, the Italian Parliament is discussing a law which aims at simplifying the authorisation procedures for EMAS registered sites.

3. NEGOTIATION PROCESS

3.1 The Evolution of Co-operative Relationships: the Creation of the Observatory

In 1995, Vicenza provincial authorities set up the 'Observatory for the ecological conversion of industrial activities'. This was created as a facility for discussion and negotiation between the public sector and the local industrial system and thus, among the different actors involved in managing local environmental problems. It aimed at improving the impact of industrial activities on the environment through negotiating and consensus between the parties (Giannandrea,1996). Its objectives were to introduce environmental management systems, activate integrated environmental management systems in districts or industrial areas, experiment with innovative technology for environmental protection, define specific areas according to their environmental quality (with the possibility of environmental certification of areas) and improve communication between firms and citizens (Poletto, 1997).

The local actors who participated were representatives of the Chamber of Commerce, the local industrial associations, environmental associations, the trade unions and the local health units (USL). The Observatory had a scientific committee that consisted of a team of technical experts from, or nominated by, the different participating institutions.

As far as the provincial authorities were concerned, the Observatory was an opportunity to overcome the conflictual relationships characterising the management of local environmental problems (Vicenza Province, 1999). It was furthermore, an opportunity for the authorities to learn about and monitor environmental problems, to not only have a theoretical understanding of them, but also to gain real on-site experience (API, 1999). It should be noted that little on-site verification of emissions had been previously carried out and was most definitely unwelcome from the firms themselves.

The operational activities derived from the setting up of the Observatory were firstly the creation of a permanent forum for consultation and negotiation between the various subjects directly involved in the issues related to firms and the environment. This forum was foreseen to lead to the stipulation of negotiated agreements based on the proposals.

The provincial authorities, or rather their appointed environmental consultants, with the co-operation of the industrial associations, carried out a series of 44 case studies of small and medium firms from different sectors in the area. These aimed at determining the possible application of environmental management systems in accordance with the EMAS regulations. The final result was the publication of sector-specific manuals which contain a series of guidelines for first, the application of EMAS as a strategy for pollution prevention and second, technical documents which assist firms in applying an environmental management system as well as in the introduction of cleaner technologies. Manuals were published for firms of medium dimension, the marble working sector, swine butchering, the goldsmith sector, vehicle maintenance and repair, ceramics, textiles, graphics and printing, wood and the metallurgy and mechanic industry (Vicenza Province, 1996).

In addition, the Observatory focused on research into the use of 'cleaner' technologies in the Vicentine area with the greater aim of disseminating information on the experience already gained, of favouring the diffusion and transfer of innovative technology, of setting up a database on the technological opportunities for reducing pollution. The research carried out in 1996 revealed the finding of 56 types of 'cleaner' technology in 67 different sites (Poletto, 1997). Specific research dealing with special waste had the overall objective of guiding industrial associations and firms on the possible managerial or technological solutions to reduce the quantity of waste produced, the simplification of its recycling and/or recovery. The provincial authorities stressed that the intent was not that of proposing the technological solutions themselves, but to stimulate an assessment of best solutions, in terms of both technical and economic feasibility, with the aid of some of the operators from these sectors. The study analysed the technological and production problems of the following four sectors: marble working (marble cuttings and filings); foundry (slag, sludge and dust); disused tyres; the tanning industry (sludge from the purification process).

Out of all of these studies, further steps were envisaged for the tanning industry and particularly for marble. The results of the study carried out on waste in the marble sector concluded that there is indeed both a high degree of compatibility in composition between the waste derived from the cutting of marble and the raw materials used in the production of cement and that furthermore, the local cement industry would be capable of handling the quantities of marble filings and pieces generated locally. The greatest technological obstacle to the reuse of waste in cement production is the degree of material humidity, which is acceptable up to 25–30 per cent or must undergo mechanical dehydration. The economic analysis revealed that the introduction of mechanical dehydration technology in the larger firms would have an economic gain which goes beyond that of the recovery of filings in the cement industry and thus the avoidance of their disposal in the landfill. The calculations show that the larger firms would be able to amortise the costs of mechanical dehydration equipment in five years through the recycling of the filings in the cement industry (Giannandrea, 1996).

The agreements described below and the other agreements which were planned yet never concluded, were foreseen amongst the objectives of the Observatory, and thus similarly, brought about on the instigation of the provincial authorities. Their stipulation appears to mark the advent of a new phase in the Observatory's work; that of disseminating and thus processing the knowledge collected prior to that moment, in addition to carrying out pilot projects.

3.2 The Agreements

In July 1997, two framework agreements were signed.[2] The initiative was promoted by the Vicenza Provincial Authorities. The slight difference in content is that the former agreement includes specific provisions for the promotion of environmental management systems in accordance with EMAS regulations, while the latter foresees the promotion of environmental management systems without any specification of EMAS. The provincial authorities (1999) have said that this is due to the difficulties in the application of EMAS to small enterprises.

The premise of the agreements first of all stresses the provincial authorities' intention to bring their policy in line with European Union policies with regards to the environment by specifically orienting it to promote clean technologies and to encourage the widespread use of environmental management systems. Furthermore, it states that they are responding to the call in the EU Fifth Action Programme for the integration of other instruments aimed at the reduction of the environmental impact of industry, particularly those based on increasing firm responsibility and voluntary approaches, with those of command and control. In addition, the premise delineates the responsibilities, which the Chamber of Commerce and the Vicenza industrial associations have in the protection and management of the environment and in internalising environmental variables into firm strategies.

3.3 The Commitments

The agreements foresaw commitments to disseminate the technical manuals, guidelines and case studies prepared during the Observatory, through the use of seminars or any other instruments considered suitable in the Vicenza Province. In addition, they foresaw ensuring the availability of information and technical consulting for the firms regarding technological innovation and environmental management systems through the industrial associations and in particular through the creation of an Environmental Innovation Service. The signatories furthermore committed themselves to execute the

Observatory initiatives regarding the experiments for marble filings and the sludge derived from the tanning process, and to promote feasibility studies for the introduction of clean technologies as well as for the adoption of environmental management systems. Lastly, the commitment was made to improve technical knowledge at the tanning firms in order to arrive in the shortest time possible at a Protocol of Intent for the reduction on a voluntary basis of the volatile organic compounds in the Arzignano industrial district.

There were additional and more general commitments. The Province committed itself to set up the opportunity for consultation between the Provincial Co-ordinating Committee and the industrial associations in order to co-ordinate the inspection activities of the Veneto Agency for Environmental Protection and Prevention (ARPAV) with regards to the pollution prevention initiatives and those of environmental restoration promoted by the Observatory or carried out by the firms. The signatories also agreed that this agreement would be implemented by specific Protocols of Intent which would be separately approved by the various interested actors.

3.4 Agreement Implementation: Obstacles and Achievements

The stipulation of the agreements provoked questions about the fragility of a negotiated agreement regarding the degree to which it is rooted in a political or administrative process and furthermore, whether this fragility is exacerbated by being stipulated at a local rather than national level.

In August 1997, the month after signing the agreements, elections were held for the provincial council. It appears that the change in council led to a change in the dynamics of the Observatory and of the negotiated agreement, and there is evidence to suggest that this is due to the loss of the initiative's 'champion', that is, the figure in the provincial authorities who had largely stimulated the Observatory and the negotiated agreements. Although the provincial authorities' obligations concerning studies continued to be carried out by the internal technicians, and the other signatories fulfilled their obligations, the whole process seems to have been low on the new political agenda. In view of the fact that the agreement lacked provisions for monitoring or revision, political momentum may have been able to protect the agreement by ensuring the processing of the results of studies and stimulating further work. In short, it appears that the evolution of the work of the Observatory and negotiated agreements was brought to a halt.

The following describes the extent to which each of the obligations in the agreement were fulfilled. In May 1998, a Protocol of Intent was signed by the Province of Vicenza, the Chamber of Commerce, the Vicentine Industrial Association and the Artisan Association. Its objectives concern the implementation of certain provisions made in the previous agreement. These are, first, the institution of the 'Technological Innovation Service' aimed at supplying information to the firms on both clean technologies and the introduction of environmental management systems (either ISO 14 000 or EMAS) in addition to the possibility of obtaining environmental quality product labels. The service-specific tasks are detailed, which not only include the dissemination of the manuals and case studies produced by the Observatory along with information on clean technologies most appropriate to the Vicentine industrial situation, but also the organisation of seminars and further studies. It also stipulates the absence of obligations for firms in making use of the service.

It furthermore specifies the roles of the provincial authorities, the Chamber of Commerce and the industrial associations. The provincial authorities have the obligations to provide the technical information on clean technologies; to supply the software for the use and to update this technical information; to make the manuals resulting from the Observatory available, to promote the service and to sponsor related conferences and information dissemination initiatives. The Chamber of Commerce is committed to make the data relevant to the functioning of this service available. The industrial associations host the Environmental Innovation Service and thus have the obligation of promoting clean technologies and information on environmental management systems through it to the firms.

The agreements also stipulate that the service will also publicise the availability of funding to firms. The provincial authorities and the industrial associations have the responsibility of identifying access to funds and financial instruments which can be useful to the firms. There is a further stipulation that the information diffused concerning technological intervention will take quality and safety issues into consideration.

The Environmental Innovation Service was set up by the Vicentine Industrial Association and the Vicentine Artisan Association with the technical support of the consultants, Ambiente Italia and Arianna s.r.l. It was closed in November 1998. There was a distinct lack of quantitative data concerning the extent to which firms made use of this service, though an interview with the provincial authorities suggested that the response was poor. In retrospect, the provincial authorities suggested that the lack of success of this initiative was possibly caused by the fact that it was seen as a service which doubled the consulting services already provided by the industrial associations. They also made the criticism that technologies were promoted as innovative solutions to problems in a specific sector, and that their inter-sectoral transferability was not adequately dealt with. In addition it was felt that the technologies promoted as innovative were not continuously updated and therefore two years later could no longer be considered as such.

Regarding the dissemination of information, during the autumn of 1998, seminars was carried out regarding the manuals for environmental management systems and technological innovation. Participation of either firm owners or for the larger firms, the safety officer, has been reported as being very poor (Vicenza Province, 1999).

The provincial authorities made funds available for the 50 per cent co-financing of feasibility studies for environmental management systems or clean technologies in firms but the initiative was abandoned because only one firm applied.

Three separate studies were carried out regarding technical intervention in the Arzignano-Chiampo area. These had the following objectives: to experiment with different raw materials; to update data from this first study and to generate other data (such as the type/amount of emissions resulting from a certain type/amount of raw materials); to develop technology to be applied at the beginning of the process and the technical and economic assessment of the containment system at the end of the process.

However, no protocol of intent was drawn up as these studies were unable to give conclusive results regarding the next steps to be taken.

4. ANALYSIS

The Observatory which preceded the 1997 negotiated agreement is distinctly innovation oriented: it aims at 'learning about the problem(s) and identifying new technologies'. The negotiated agreement signed in 1997 and the ensuing protocol of intent aim at promoting the continued research for appropriate managerial and technological solutions to the environmental problems identified, but also at encouraging the use and implementation of the knowledge acquired during the Observatory. Thus they are innovation oriented and additionally seek to promote implementation, although no target objective is specified.

The Observatory and the negotiations were successful in the sense that they did indeed result in the signing of the agreement by the provincial authorities, the Chamber of Commerce and the industrial associations. However, it is difficult to see why the signatories would not have signed the agreement. In exchange for facilitating the provincial authorities through their existing communication channels with firms (the provincial authorities are allowed to 'make use of' an existing relationship of trust which the industrial associations have with the firms) the industrial associations gain a role in decision making and research and information financed by the provincial authorities. An incentive for the provincial authorities is to gain access to firms and thus to information while the increasing importance of environmental policy on the regulator's agenda implies that industrial associations have no choice but to recognise that the environment is a variable to be considered and thus give an incentive to their members to do the same.

The explicit policy objectives of the negotiated agreement are never expressed in terms of quantitative targets. The only protocol of intent, the implementation agreement which delineated the roles and responsibilities concerning the Environmental Innovation Service did not even specify any particular monitoring strategy which would have permitted the utility of the service to be understood. Both the agreement in 1997 and the protocol of intent clearly define the parties, their respective obligations and terms. However, they do not stipulate the duration of the agreement or specify conditions under which it can be revised or terminated. There is no monitoring mechanism provided for nor provision for making information on the performance of the agreement available to the public.

Although the loss of political momentum in the Vicentine negotiated agreement process may well have negatively influenced the taking of further steps, it could be said that the agreements were not structured in a way which protected the process against obstacles of this nature.

The agreements appear to have two types of implicit goals. The first involves a change in the nature of the environmental policy process from that of 'command and control' to making local actors responsible and a collective approach to knowledge sharing and problem solving. The second is that of bringing about an improvement in environmental quality as a direct result of the introduction of environmental management systems and 'clean' technologies in local industry. With regard to stimulating collective responsibility for these environmental problems and their solution, although the commitments undertaken by the Vicentine industrial associations can be read as indicative of their willingness to take on a responsible role, the process in Vicenza never put the individual firms' potential commitment or opposition to these principles to the test. The lack of monitoring makes it difficult to say conclusively if the second of these implicit goals has or has not been reached. However, as pointed out earlier, evidence suggests that this goal has not been achieved, either as a direct result of the agreement or through other mechanisms.

As noted above, one of the implicit objectives of the Observatory and negotiated agreement was to evoke a social change through making actors responsible and a collective approach to knowledge sharing and problem solving regarding the relationship between industry and environmental quality in the Province of Vicenza. However, it can be hypothesised that the full extent of the social impact desired extended beyond that of the industrial associations' commitment to the process to include changes in the firm's approach. The industrial associations' signing of the agreement and fulfilment of their commitments can be taken as indicative of their assumption of this responsibility while there is little evidence of any cultural change on the firms' part in terms of taking responsibility for environmental problems beyond the co-operation of the firms in the case studies carried out during the Observatory.

Some of the results of Michieli's survey, which specifically regarded the tanning industry, bear witness to the firms' lack of involvement in the process. He found that none of the firms interviewed have ever stipulated a negotiated agreement and only 27.28 per cent consider the instrument useful for co-operation between private and public sector. Most important, only 21.82 per cent of firms interviewed had heard of the existence of the agreement central to this study, while even fewer knew what the contents were. Those who knew what the agreements were, largely indicated that they felt they were destined to stay on paper, unrealistic and difficult to achieve.

The ultimate practical aim of both the Observatory and the agreement is to increase the use of environmental management systems and the introduction of pollution prevention technology in firms. There is evidence that the agreements have not been particularly successful. Only one firm applied for the financing for an environmental management system feasibility study made available by the provincial authorities. The environmental impacts of the agreements are rather limited. The only clearly visible impacts are that of the knowledge gained through the studies carried out on atmospheric emissions in the tanning industry, the experiments carried out in the marble sector and sludge in the tanning process.

The provincial authorities and the Chamber of Commerce bore the costs of the studies carried out in the Observatory as well as the costs of the Environmental Innovation Service as foreseen by the negotiated agreement. The provincial authorities would have borne greater costs if any firms had applied for the co-financed feasibility study funding which they made available but this was not the case. The firms would have had to provide the other 50 per cent of the feasibility study and thus it appears that this was too high a cost (or the co-financing offered too small an incentive) for the firms to bear in relation to their interest in introducing environmental management systems or cleaner technologies. The industrial associations did not have additional costs as they communicated with the firms through the channels that were already established.

The negotiated agreement can be seen as part of a wider process undertaken by the Province of Vicenza and the industrial associations. It places emphasis on learning and on the fostering of an approach of joint responsibility for the understanding and solution of environmental problems. The Observatory sought to reduce shared uncertainties through the studies carried out concerning the pollution prevention technologies and the generation of the sector-specific manuals for environmental management systems. The agreements' objectives were to both reduce the shared uncertainties concerning specific issues through research based learning and furthermore, to disseminate the knowledge gathered during the Observatory. Thus learning could take place by first grouping local actors and experts together in the Observatory to facilitate learning from each other (generation of information), second, by allowing the Observatory participants to learn about production processes, the nature of the environmental problems and the actual abatement costs by gaining access to the firms (generation of information). The knowledge acquired during the Observatory and the research foreseen by the agreement are then processed and disseminated to the firms (dissemination of information to firms thus giving them an opportunity to learn).

There is evidence that learning did, in fact, take place with regard to the first two points. There is little or no evidence to suggest that the third point stimulated learning.

The provincial authorities originally initiated the process of which the negotiated agreement is a part, with the aim of changing what has been described as a conflictual relationship in the management of environmental problems related to industrial activities. It has, however, also been said that this collective approach originally aroused some suspicion, particularly in firms, and was somewhat relegated to being part of a 'green politics' approach (Vicenza Province, 1999). Interviews with some of the actors (Vicenza Province, 1999; API, 1999) reveal that most of the Observatory members already had long-established working relationships, though not specifically concerning the problem dealt with in the Observatory and agreements, they also say that their relationship was not particularly altered by this process. However, interviews have also revealed that the actors involved in the Observatory and the agreement view the process and the instruments very positively. There are currently other provincial Observatory initiatives in process concerning clean technology and furthermore, ARPAV and local authorities are in the process of negotiating an agreement that specifically concerns the Arzignano-Chiampo tanning district. Both the provincial authorities and ARPAV have commented on the fact that in 1995, competent bodies had difficulty entering the firms to obtain the data needed, and were at times accompanied by the police in order to gain access. ARPAV believes that access to data, and moreover, the firms' voluntary provision of data in the implementation of this agreement will be greatly facilitated by the fact that the firms have started providing information (ARPAV, 1999), whether the firms' willingness to do so is as a result of resignation to the idea of increased trust in the authorities or of learning, remains unclear.

More recently, there is increasing evidence that the provincial authorities intend to pursue, albeit with different instruments, similar objectives. The authorities are currently seeking to establish simplified authorisation procedures for firms with ISO 14 001 or EMAS as an incentive. They are furthermore planning to hold courses on environmental management systems and initiate a dialogue with the regional authorities about eventual funding for firms who want to adopt such systems.

It is also interesting to note that in terms of absolute numbers, there are currently more firms in the Province of Vicenza with ISO 14 001 and EMAS than there are in other provinces in the region. It is impossible to attribute this directly to the negotiate agreements and thus to consider it as an 'impact', but it may well be attributed to learning.

5. CONCLUSION

In spite of the emerging mistrust on the part of the firms for instruments of this type, the Province of Vicenza is considering their use for different sectors and environmental problems. The approach this time appears to be one of specific problem targeting with specific instruments as opposed to the heterogeneous, across the board approach which has been witnessed in the above-described agreement. Furthermore, there is a distinct interest in Italy in dealing with the interconnected and collective nature of the environmental problems in a geographic district, which is homogeneous in terms of its economic activity. This has brought the focus on the potential offered by more innovative instruments such as tradable pollution permits and quotas, environmental reporting at the area level, and the use of negotiated agreements as the vehicle for their implementation.

NOTES

1.   The case study in the chapter was developed during the period 1998 to 2000 and thus contains data and observations related to the situation at that time.
2.   The agreements were basically the same, except one was signed by the Vicenza provincial authorities, the Vicentine Chamber of Commerce, the Vicentine Artisan Association and the Vicentine Industrial Association whereas the other was signed by the Vicentine provincial authorities, the Vicentine Chamber of Commerce, the Vicentine Artisan Association and the Vicentine Association for Small and Medium Enterprises (API).

REFERENCES

API (1999), *Interview with API*, Vicenza, Italy.

ARPAV (1999), *Interview with ARPAV*, Padova, Italy.
Borghini, Stefania and Cibin, Mara (1999), *Indagine sulla Gestione Ambientale d'impresa nel Veneto, Friuli Giulia e Trentino Alto Adige,* Venice: Fondazione Eni Enrico Mattei.
Croci, Edoardo *(1998),* 'L'Evoluzione della Normativa Italiana sugli Accordi Volontari' in Paola Amadei, Edoardo Croci and Giulia Pesaro (eds), *Nuovi Strumenti di Politica Ambientale: gli Accordi Volontari,* Milan: Franco Angeli.
Giannandrea, Giovanni (1996), *Studio e Promozione di Iniziative per la Diminuzione dei Rifiuti Speciali,* Final Report, Vicenza: Dipartimento Ambiente, Amministrazione Provinciale di Vicenza.
Michieli, Filippo (1999), 'Lo Sviluppo Sostenibile nel Distretto Industriale del Valchiampo attraverso l'Analisi degli Strumenti di Politica Ambientale', Tesi di laurea,Venice, Italy: Facoltà di Economià, Università Ca Foscari di Venezia.
Poletto, L. (1997), *'Pubblico e privato a scuola di ecologia',* Imprese Ambiente 8/97.
Regione del Veneto (1997), *Studio per Individuazione di Distretti Industriali nel Veneto,* Venice: Osservatorio Regionale del Mercato del Lavoro e della Professionalità, Giunta Regionale del Veneto.
Vicenza Province (1999), *Interview with Vicenza Province*, Vicenza, Italy.

PART THREE

Bringing Theory and Practice Together: an
Evaluation of the Studied Agreements

15. Comparative Evaluation of the Case Studies

Marc De Clercq, André Suck, Bart Ameels and Roger Salmons

1. INTRODUCTION

1.1 The Different Research Phases of the Study

The aim of this study is a comparative evaluation of 12 individual case studies. During the theoretical phase of this, a theoretical framework was designed, based on the existing literature on voluntary agreements. This framework led to the postulation of four hypotheses concerning the influence of the socio-economic context on the performance of negotiated agreements (see the previous chapters). To provide for data for this comparative analysis, the following 12 European negotiated agreements were selected (Table 15.1).

Each agreement was analysed following a common case study design, in order to be able to extract as much comparative data as possible. This descriptive phase resulted in 12 cases, each containing the elements needed to perform the cross-case comparison.

Consequently, the aims of the cross-case comparison are to:

- analyse and compare the performance of the different agreements studied;
- analyse and compare the socio-economic context wherein each agreement existed;
- analyse and compare the influence of the socio-economic context on the performance of negotiated agreements.

Table 15.1   The selected negotiated environmental agreements

Abbreviation	Country	Description of the agreement
GBAT	Germany	Agreement to reduce the mercury-content in batteries and to collect used batteries separately.
GELV	Germany	Agreement to maximise the recycling rate of end-of-life vehicles.
FCFC	France	Agreement to eliminate the use of CFCs in the industry.
FECO	France	Agreement upon the collection and recycling of packaging waste, to maximise the valorisation rate.
BBAT	Belgium	Agreement upon the private separate collection and recycling of used batteries.
BELE	Belgium	Agreement to reduce the emission of SO_2 and NO_x in power plants.
DSO2	The Netherlands	Agreement upon the reduction of the SO_2-emission of power plants
DWHI	The Netherlands	Agreement upon the take-back of worn household appliances by their producers ('white and brown goods').
IVIC	Italy	Regional agreement upon the improvement of the environmental quality in the province of Vicenza.
IAGI	Italy	Agreement upon the improvement of gasoline quality
EFAR	UK	Agreement upon the collection from farms of waste plastic films used in the production ('farm films')
EEFF	UK	Agreement to improve the energy efficiency in the chemical industry.

1.2 The Central Research Question

The central question of this research project is the following: 'Which specific characteristics of negotiated agreements and which factors within the institutional-economic context wherein a negotiated agreement is used, influence the performance of this negotiated agreement?'

Based on theoretical insights gained during the theoretical phase, four hypotheses were postulated regarding the relation between the elements that constitute the institutional-economic context and the performance of the negotiated agreement.

- *Policy hypothesis*: The fact that the public environmental policy evolves in a tradition and in a climate of consensus seeking, joint problem solving, mutual respect and trust is a crucial positive factor for the performance of negotiated agreements.

- *Instrumental hypothesis*: The fact that the public policy makers show readiness to use alternative policy instruments, as a stick behind the door to deal with the environmental problems, in case the negotiated agreement fails, is a crucial positive factor for the performance of negotiated agreements.
- *Sectoral hypothesis*: The fact that the industry sector involved is homogeneous, has a small number of players and is dominated by one or two players, or has a powerful industry association that can speak for all its members, is a crucial positive factor for the performance of negotiated agreements.
- *Competition hypothesis*: The fact that firms can gain competitive advantages by co-operating in the negotiation and by compliance of a negotiated agreement, is a crucial positive factor for the performance of negotiated agreements, due to the consumer pressure.

To test these hypotheses, we first have to assess the performance or success of the negotiated agreements studied. We will do this by using the performance indicators set out in Chapter 2, Section 6.

Second, we need to assess to what extent the conditions of each of the four hypotheses complied with the situation of each particular case. When we can make an assessment on the success of the NA, and on the presence of the conditions in the hypotheses, we can examine whether there is in fact a relationship between the institutional-economic context wherein a NA is used and the performance of that NA (Figure 15.1).

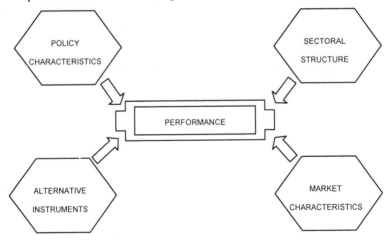

Figure 15.1   The performance of negotiated agreements and the socio-economic context

2. THEORETICAL ASSESSMENT OF THE PERFORMANCE OF A NEGOTIATED AGREEMENT

The central question in this part is: *'How can the performance or successfulness of a negotiated agreement be measured?'* The answer to this question is not simple, because the definition of 'performance' can vary. We will try to measure the performance of a negotiated agreement, using four evaluation dimensions, mentioned in the theoretical part, and already discussed in the case studies:

1. feasibility;
2. capability, further divided into two aspects: specification and application;
3. impact, and;
4. resource development.

In fact, we argue that these dimensions will allow us to evaluate the performance of the negotiated agreements. First of all, we will take a closer look at the meaning of these four dimensions.

2.1 Feasibility

'Feasibility' addresses the question whether the negotiation process did result in the signing of the agreement. Since the dimension 'feasibility' is of a binary nature, it does not give us a lot of useful information on the degree of performance or successfulness of the (feasible or unfeasible) agreement. When it appears that an agreement was not feasible, it will not be applied and will therefore have no environmental or economic impact. However there might have been negotiations between the different parties before it became clear the agreement was not feasible. These negotiations may influence the resource base (the relations between the parties, the trust or mutual respect, the reduction of information asymmetries between the private sector and the authorities, learning…) in a positive way.

2.2 Capability

'Capability' has two aspects: the first relates to the specification of the agreement in terms of its consistency (or 'fit') with the underlying policy objectives, and its compatibility with national and international law on trade and competition. The second relates to the application of the agreement in practice, and the extent to which this reinforces, or erodes, the original agreement.

2.2.1 Specification

The specification of an agreement can be assessed under three separate headings (Table 15.2).

Table 15.2 The sub-dimensions of the dimension 'specification'

Environmental Performance
How is the environmental target defined?
What mechanism will be used to achieve it?
Is there an adequate control system?
Learning
What is the learning objective?
How will this objective be realised?
Is there an adequate co-ordination system?
Economic Efficiency
How will burden-sharing be achieved?
How will free-riding be dealt with?
How are any competitive distortions addressed?

If every single one of those elements is clearly present in the specification of an agreement, the agreement is being considered to be well specified.

Most agreements will have both an environmental performance objective and a learning objective, although the latter may not be identified explicitly. The potential for learning is a feature that distinguishes negotiated agreements from other policy instruments. Of course, the two objectives may be closely linked, particularly if learning is a prerequisite for improved environmental performance (learning – in the form of reduced information asymmetries – may also improve the cost-efficiency of the agreement). However, the relative emphasis is likely to vary from case to case, with some agreements placing much greater emphasis on environmental performance, while others focus more on learning.

2.2.2 Application

The application of the agreement refers to the compliance of the parties with respect to the targets and obligations specified in the agreement (Table 15.3). A distinction between the 'targets' and the 'obligations' should be made: a good performance on the environmental targets defined in the agreement can influence the environment, while the performance on the other obligations (such as reporting, control, monitoring...) can for example, influence the cost-effectiveness and the (policy) resource base, and not the environment.

Table 15.3 The sub-dimensions of the dimension 'application'

Environmental targets
Other obligations
Concerning cost-efficiency
Concerning resource development
Concerning competition

2.3 Impact

The dimension 'impact' does not only concern the environmental effectiveness of the agreement, but also incorporates the economic impacts of the performance (Table 15.4). Consequently, the total impact of an agreement, as we define it, consists of:

- an environmental impact, not only taking into consideration whether the parties have fulfilled the prescribed targets, but also whether achieving of those targets has led to an actual improvement over the business-as-usual scenario;
- an economic impact, taking into consideration any impacts on cost-efficiency and competition.

Table 15.4 The sub-dimensions of the dimension 'impact'

Environmental impact
Is there an improvement over the business-as-usual scenario?
Cost-Efficiency
Are the private costs low and efficiently shared?
Are the administration costs low?
Competition
How is free-riding being dealt with?

We can assume that the impact on those three elements will also depend on the way in which these topics were included in the specification of the agreement.

2.4 Resource Development

Finally, 'resource development' refers on the one hand to the improvements in the policy resource base resulting from negotiating and implementing the agreement. The relations between the policy makers and the private actors can be tightened, the attitudes and goodwill of both parties towards each other can be strengthened or the relations between different private actors can improve through negotiations prior to a possible agreement or through the monitoring or control obligations of both parties. On the other hand, the existence of a negotiated agreement can lead to more productive relationships in terms of product or process innovations. Innovation-oriented agreements often include the setting up of a technology pass-through, the commitment to work together to stimulate innovation and so on.

2.5 Interrelationships between the Different Dimensions and Implications

After explaining the meaning of the four dimensions, it should be clear that measuring the performance of any agreement will depend heavily on which dimensions will be taken into account. Several options are possible here.

One could take into account only the specification of a negotiated agreement, arguing that, when an agreement is well specified, with quantified targets, clearly defined burden-sharing and learning mechanisms, the chance that it will be successful increases. This approach is however questionable: although a good specification is an important precondition, it is no guarantee for a good performance.

Another interpretation of the performance of an agreement could be to take into account only the degree of application of the agreement: an agreement would then be considered successful when the targets defined in the agreement are reached. This is a rather narrow interpretation on 'performance', since the targets mentioned in the agreement can be (lower than) business-as-usual targets. Moreover, this interpretation requires a good specification of the agreement: the targets and milestones have to be quantified. If there are no targets specified, how will the performance then be measured?

Another option is to consider only the impact of the agreement: did the existence of the agreement lead to a substantial environmental impact, without leading to substantial economic disadvantages for the stakeholders? This seems to be a valid reasoning, since the impact of the agreement is what is important in the end. But this approach also is problematic: often, it will be difficult to determine whether an environmental or economic impact is solely due to the existence of the agreement, let alone to measure that impact. For example, is the substantial reduction in SO_2 and NO_x emissions in Belgium in the recent years only due to the existence of the negotiated agreements with the power plants, or is this evolution merely the consequence of technological progress and existing legislation or initiatives at the European level? What is the contribution of the agreement to the reduction in these emissions?

Combining the above two approaches (measuring application and impact) will probably result in more detailed and nuanced results: the question on whether the agreement's targets are reached, is combined with the question on whether the reaching of the targets has had an environmental and/or economic impact. However, in this case, we do not take into account the development of the resource base, which is a feature important for negotiated agreements.

This reasoning leads us to conclude that the four evaluation dimensions all play a certain, but different role in the performance of a negotiated agreement. It is not recommendable to look only at one or two of the four dimensions (for example application or impact).

If, on the other hand we take into account all four dimensions in measuring the performance of a negotiated agreement, we cannot treat them as independent and additive pieces of the 'performance total'. Often there will be an interaction between them, although this is not necessarily the case. For example, the fact that an agreement has a good application with respect to its environmental target does not evidently mean that there will be an actual impact on the environment, or that the agreement is cost-efficient. On the other hand, an agreement with a good environmental and economic impact, but with an insufficient resource development, can be considered inferior to an agreement with the same impacts but with a better development of the resource base.

In addition, the impact and the resource development are sometimes difficult to measure. An agreement can contribute to the environmental quality, though the precise extent of this contribution is difficult to assess. Also the resource base is influenced by different factors. Therefore, it is difficult to determine what the precise contribution of each factor is. Figure 15.2 below explains visually what relations can exist between the different dimensions of an agreement.

The specification can influence the application, the impact and the resource development. The influence on the application is direct (1), while the influence on impact is both direct (3) and indirect (2): clear targets, burden-sharing mechanisms, and clauses to prohibit free-riding affect the application of the agreement (1), which in turn has a positive influence on the environmental and economic impact (3). The direct influence on impact (2) refers to the ambition of the targets: if these are set too low, the specification of the agreement directly influences the possible impact, no matter if the application is in accordance with these targets. The specification can also influence the resource base through different channels. The resource development can be indirectly influenced through the inclusion in the agreement of clauses to promote technological research among the subscribers, clauses that set regular meeting dates between policy makers and private parties,... if of course what is specified is applied in practice (1 and 5). The resource development is directly influenced by the specification in the sense that a well specified agreement will mostly be the consequence of fruitful negotiations, during which the resource base can be influenced positively (4). We have to mention however that the influence on resource development of both specification and application could be rather small, given the fact that most agreements are primarily aimed at implementation rather than innovation and resource development.

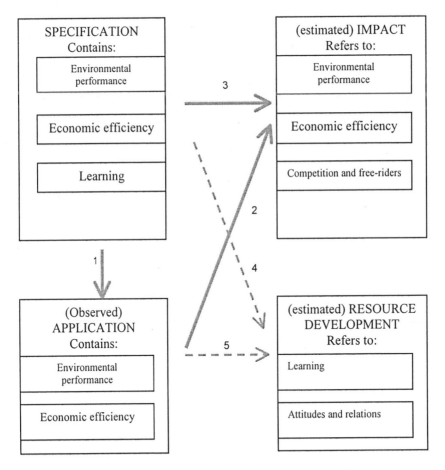

Figure 15.2 The dimension 'specification' as a precondition for the performance of an agreement

The application of the agreement can have an influence on the impact (2), and is moreover a proxy for the more difficult measurable impact. As stated in the previous point, the application can also influence the resource development.

Finally, we think that the impact of an agreement, will have no effect on the resource development, since the impact is only the final result of the agreement, and the resource base is mainly affected during the negotiation and application phase.

Of the four dimensions, clearly it is the impact and the resource development that in the end will determine the performance of an agreement. The dimension *application* is too narrow as a judgement base, and the dimension *specification* is in fact a precondition for the performance of an agreement. The dimension *application* can however provide for a good estimate of the difficult in measuring the dimensions *impact* and *resource development*. We will therefore define the performance of any agreement to be a mix of the degree of *application, impact and resource development*. This measured performance should show a positive correlation with the degree of *specification*, which is an internal precondition for a good performance (Figure 15.3).

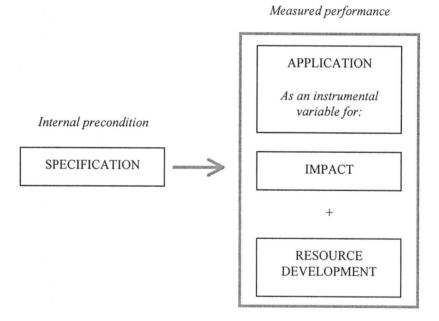

Figure 15.3   The performance of a negotiated agreement

3. APPLICATION OF THE THEORETICAL ASSESSMENT

What we will do now is try to measure all four evaluation dimensions. *Application, impact* and *resource development* will be measured and aggregated to obtain a 'total performance score'. The dimension *'specification'* will be converted into a score to check the validity of this total performance score. If we consider *specification* to be an internal precondition for the performance of a negotiated agreement, there should in fact be a positive relationship between the score for the specification of an agreement and its performance.

More precisely, an agreement with a very low specification score but with a very high performance score could lead us to conclude that our scoring mechanism is not adequate. On the other hand, a high specification score does not have to lead to a high performance score, since we consider that there are socio-economic factors that can influence the performance of an agreement.

The assessment of the different evaluation dimensions is done by means of a grading scale technique. This technique is used to be able to measure the extent of the contribution of each evaluation dimension to the total performance of the agreement. Later we will use the same technique to test a possible correlation of this total performance with the proposed hypotheses. Therefore a whole series of statements has to be assessed for each agreement, by giving them a grade from 1 to 5, showing to what extent the statement is valid.

The individual grades of each statement do not necessarily have to be added to obtain one overall grade for the dimension. They are merely indicators that the respondents can rely on to give an overall score for each dimension. Adding the grades together to obtain a mean for each dimension could be done if each statement (W, X, Y and Z) added an equal part of explanation for the performance of the dimension (F) in question, that is if the statements and the criterion form an additive model (Figure 15.4).

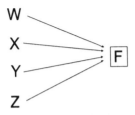

Figure 15.4   An additive model

This is however not always the case. In a particular case e.g., the validity of one statement (W) can be dominant, while the others (X, Y and Z) can help to assess the dimension, but play a clearly inferior role. Adding the scores for these statements together would undervalue the importance of the most important statement (Figure 15.5).

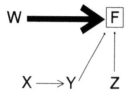

Figure 15.5   A model with one dominant statement

In other cases, some of the statements (W, X) can contain elements that contribute to the idea behind the main statement, while others can be the consequences (Y, Z) of the idea behind the main statement (Figure 15.6).

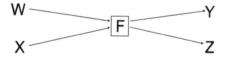

Figure 15.6   A model with contributors and consequences

Finally, the statements can consist of a chain of necessary conditions to assess the idea behind the main statement. We call this a multiplicative model (Figure 15.7).

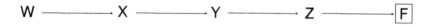

Figure 15.7   A multiplicative model

In the following we will postulate and explain all statements that need to be assessed in order to have a clear view on the performance of an agreement. What contribution each score has for the dimension in question, depends on the particularities of each case and should be judged by the respondents themselves. To avoid a too subjective evaluation, the survey had to be filled in separately by both members of the team that studied a particular case. After that, they compared their answers, discussed dissimilarities and changed certain scores if misunderstandings were clarified, made additional comments and so on, resulting in a definite survey on which the cross-case evaluation is based.

Where necessary, the statements are accompanied by a scoring guide, and some explanatory notes.

3.1 Specification (sp)

We set up ten statements to assess the specification of the agreement, keeping in mind the four headings we mentioned earlier: specification relating to the environmental performance, to the economic efficiency, to competition and free-riding, and to learning. When a statement was considered completely justified, it received a score of 5. When a statement was completely untrue for a certain agreement, it receives a score of 1. Respondents were provided with a scoring guide, and some explanatory notes, which are not included in this book.

a. Environmental performance (ep)

Four statements try to capture how well the agreement is specified with respect to the environmental targets it has to reach.

sp1. The agreement contains a well-defined environmental performance objective (or objectives).
sp2. The objective (or objectives) represents a meaningful improvement in environmental performance.
sp3. The agreement contains a credible mechanism for achieving the environmental performance objective (or objectives).
sp4. The agreement contains a credible system for monitoring performance against the specified objective (or objectives).

Since we believe that the relevance of each of those four statements is of an equal importance, we will take an arithmetic mean of the four statements to arrive at a mean score for the specification regarding the environmental performance.

Score sp/ep = (sp1 + sp2 + sp3 + sp4) / 4

b. Learning (le)

Three statements try to measure to what extent learning is incorporated into the specification of the agreement. First of all, the explicitness of the learning objective is important. Next to this, the learning objective can be reached more easily if there is a mechanism provided in the agreement. Finally, the learning objective is easier to attain when the learning mechanisms can be monitored.

sp5. The agreement contains a clear objective (or objectives) with respect to learning.
sp6. The agreement contains a credible mechanism to support and encourage learning.
sp7. The agreement contains an adequate monitoring system for co-ordinating learning activities.

Again here we believe that these scores for these statements can be added together to become a mean score for the presence of learning in the specification in the agreement.

$$\textbf{Score sp/le} = (\textbf{sp5} + \textbf{sp6} + \textbf{sp7}) / 3$$

c. Economic efficiency (ec)

Here, we take a look at whether the agreement's specification allowed for or stimulated an economically efficient application of the agreement.

sp8. The agreement contains a burden-sharing mechanism that is consistent with a cost-efficient outcome.
sp9. The agreement contains a credible mechanism to prevent free-riding by participants.
sp10. The agreement does not create any barriers to new entrants.

Both free-riding and market distortions can occur during the application of the agreement. For simplicity reasons we will just ad the scores for the three statements together and consider this mean score as the degree of economic efficiency.

$$\textbf{Score sp/ec} = (\textbf{sp8} + \textbf{sp9} + \textbf{sp10}) / 3$$

For a total score on specification, we now take the average of each sub-score for specification. This means that the total score for specification can be calculated as:

Score sp = (Score sp/ep + Score sp/le + Score sp/ec) / 3

3.2 Application (ap)

To assess the performance of an agreement with respect to its application, we make a distinction between the application of the environmental targets defined in the agreement, and the fulfilment of the individual obligations by the parties.

The degree in which the parties reach the prescribed environmental targets is a necessary condition for assessing the environmental performance of the (application of the) agreement. Since it is possible that agreements break down before the intended ending date, we included a statement to take this possibility into account. There is in fact a difference between an agreement that does not break down, but doesn't reach the environmental targets, and an agreement that breaks down for some external reason, but has reached the environmental targets during its existence.

On the other hand, most of the negotiated agreements also contain individual obligations beside the aggregate environmental target(s). These can be monitoring obligations by the authorities, the obligation of the private parties to provide data, the obligation to set up a research programme, etc. The fulfilment of the individual obligations does not directly tell us something about the environmental performance of the agreement, but can tell us something about the economic efficiency of the agreement and the resource development. An agreement where the aggregate target has been met, but where a deficient burden-sharing mechanism led to economic inefficiency, is not as successful as an agreement that reaches the aggregate target due to an efficient burden-sharing mechanism.

ap1. Compliance with (interim) environmental performance targets is good.
ap2. The agreement did not break down or eroded substantially during its intended life span.
ap3. Compliance with the individual obligations is good.

Calculating the total score for application is done in a specific manner. The interpretation of the score for statement ap1 and ap3, depends on whether the agreement broke down or eroded during its existence (statement ap2). We therefore use a multiplicative model. Moreover, we think that the compliance with the environmental targets in most European NAs is more important than the compliance with the individual targets or obligations. We decided to give statement ap1 a weight of 2/3 and statement ap3 a weight of 1/3.

$$\textbf{Score ap = 2/3 . Square root of (ap1 . ap2) +}$$
$$\textbf{1/3 . Square root of (ap3 . ap2)}$$

3.3 Impact (im)

While the assessment of the application of an agreement is limited to explicit and implicit policy objectives, the assessment of the impact of an agreement implies a broader view on the performance of the agreement: next to the environmental impact, also economic efficiency and wider economic impacts, such as competition distortion are taken into account.

a. Environmental performance (ep)
The degree of environmental impact or performance can be measured by only one statement:

im1. There is a significant improvement on the target environmental variable, compared to the business as usual situation.

$$\textbf{Score im/ep = im1}$$

b. Economic efficiency (ec)
Here we try to consider both both parties to the agreement: the private party and the policy maker.

im2. The application of the agreement is cost-efficient with respect to compliance.
im3. The administration cost of the agreement is fairly low.

$$\textbf{Score im/ec = (im2 + im3) / 2}$$

c. Competition (co)
The application of the agreement can cause competition distortions, both between firms inside the agreement or between firms inside and firms outside the agreement. To check for this distortion, the following statement has to be scored.

im4. There is no negative impact on competition due to the application of the agreement.

$$\text{Score im/co} = \text{im4}$$

Since it is difficult to measure the precise contribution of each of those sub-dimensions to the total impact of any agreement, we suppose that they contribute proportionally to the total impact. Therefore, we also make use of the additive model. The total score for impact is then:

$$\text{Score im} = (\text{Score im/ep} + \text{Score im/ec} + \text{Score im/co}) / 3$$

3.4 Resource Development (re)

The enhancement of the policy resource base again is interrelated with the specification, application and impact of the agreement. The policy resource base can be enhanced during each of those phases. In this context, we distinguished three (overlapping) sub-dimensions for resource development: learning, relations between actors and general attitudes. Relations between actors for example can improve through contacts during the specification of the agreement, or through monitoring meetings during the application phase. The impact the agreement has on for example, the economic efficiency can affect the relations between private parties and the authorities with respect to further negotiations and so on.

A very important feature of resource development is its dynamics, as the word 'development' indicates. Relations, learning and attitudes can change over time. It is therefore even more difficult to evaluate it. The statements below all reflect the idea of a certain improvement in relations, learning and attitudes.

A non-successful agreement with respect to the environmental impact or target compliance can still have favourable effects on the resource development.

The degree of resource development is measured by four statements:

re1. The agreement led to an important improvement in the attitudes of the parties concerning environmental issues.
re2. The agreement led to an important improvement in learning.
re3. The learning has led to substantial innovation in policy making in this area.
re4. The agreement led to greater trust and more productive relationships between parties.
re5. The agreement has generated product- or process-related innovations and/or market opportunities.

For the same reason as we took the arithmetic mean to measure the total impact of an agreement, we will do the same here.

$$\text{Score re} = (\text{re1} + \text{re2} + \text{re3} + \text{re4} + \text{re5}) / 5$$

4. MEASURING THE AVERAGE PERFORMANCE OF THE STUDIED AGREEMENTS

After assessing all the statements necessary to measure the performance of agreements, we will now look at all the results of this analysis for each agreement that was studied. To obtain the average performance of each agreement, we have taken the arithmetic mean of the scores on the three dimensions 'application', 'impact' and 'resource development').

$$\text{Performance Score} = [\text{Score ap} + \text{Score im} + \text{Score re}] / 3$$

This calculation leads to the results in Table 15.5.

Table 15.5   The scores for the different dimensions of the studied agreements

	Specification	Application +	Impact +	Resource development	= Average performance
GBAT	2.03	2.09	2.42	3.10	2.54
GELV	3.22	3.67	3.42	3.00	3.36
FCFC	2.17	1.41	2.33	2.20	1.98
FECO	3.72	3.87	3.00	5.00	3.96
BBAT	3.89	4.74	4.42	3.10	4.08
BELE	3.25	5.00	4.50	2.60	4.03
DSO2	3.50	5.00	3.67	2.40	3.69
DWHI	1.00	1.00	1.00	2.60	1.53
IVIC	2.72	1.73	3.00	3.20	2.64
IAGI	3.40	4.91	4.50	3.40	4.27
EFAR	2.67	1.77	2.50	2.40	2.22
EEFF	3.76	5.00	2.92	3.20	3.71

Note: GBAT: German batteries agreement; GELV: German end-of-life vehicles agreement; FCFC: French CFC agreement; FECO: French Eco-Emballages agreement; BBAT: Belgian batteries agreement; BELE: Belgian electricity agreement; DSO2: Dutch SO_2 agreement; DWHI: Dutch white and brown goods agreement; IVIC: Italian Vicenza agreement; IAGI: Italian Agip agreement; EFAR: English farm films agreement; EEFF: English Energy Efficiency agreement.

The ranking of the agreements based on their average performance score is shown in Figure 15.8. Five agreements score well below average: GBAT, IVIC, FCFC, DWHI and EFAR. Three agreements have a score that is near the total average of 3.37 (GELV, EEFF and DSO2). Finally, four agreements score well above the average (FECO, BBAT, BELE and IAGI).

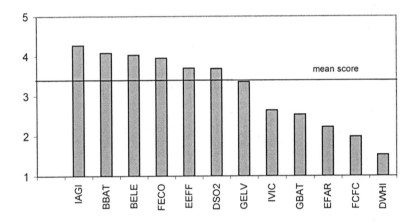

Figure 15.8   The average performance of the studied agreements

4.1   The Specification of an Agreement as the Precondition for its Performance

As we said earlier, the average performance score should reflect the degree of specification. If this is true, we may say that our average performance score is a fairly good approximation of the actual performance of an agreement.

Figure 15.9 clearly shows that there is in fact a positive relationship between the specification of an agreement and its performance. There are no agreements situated in the upper left corner nor in the lower right corner. This shows what we already expected: the degree of specification of an agreement is an important internal precondition for the performance of an agreement.

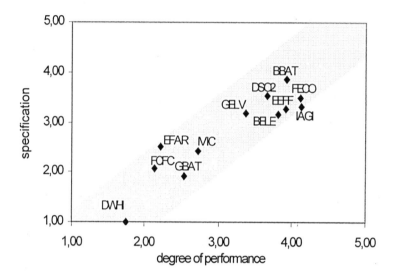

*Figure 15.9   The performance of negotiated agreements and the
specification*

4.2 The Interrelations between the 'Performance' Dimensions

Next to the relation between the specification of an agreement and its average
performance, we have also mentioned that the separate 'performance'
dimensions (application, impact and resource development) can influence
each other. As Figure 15.10 shows, there is primarily a positive relationship
between the application and the impact of a negotiated agreement. This is
rather easy to explain: the impact of an agreement depends on the application
of this agreement. If an agreement is badly applied, chances that there will be
a substantial environmental or economic impact are small. This does not
mean however that a good application of the agreement is a sufficient
precondition for a substantial environmental impact. If the targets are merely
representing a 'business as usual' situation, then a good application of those
'weak' targets will not cause a great deal of impact.

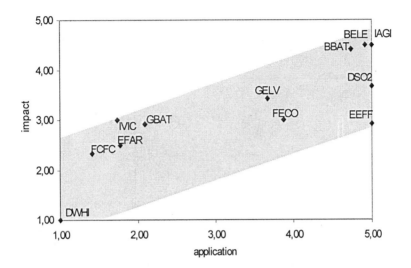

Figure 15.10   The relation between the application and impact of an agreement

Between impact and application on the one hand, and resource development on the other hand, there seems to be no distinct relation (Figure 15.11 and Figure 15.12). This we already presumed earlier.

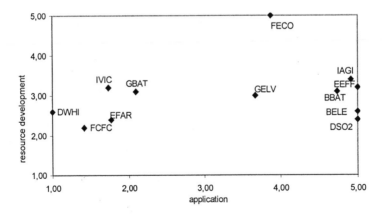

Figure 15.11   The relation between the application and the resource development of an agreement

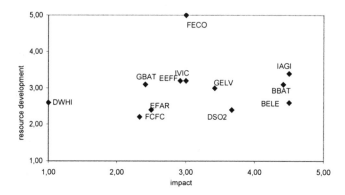

Figure 15.12   The relation between the impact and resource development of an agreement

4.3 The Influence of the Specification on the Separate Performance Dimensions

Next to the question whether the 'performance' dimensions influence each other, we can also analyse how the specification influences these three dimensions separately, rather than the aggregate of them (as in 3.5). The results we obtained can again be explained logically: specification influences the average performance of an agreement primarily through its influence on the application of the agreement. There is a clear positive relationship between specification and application (Figure 15.13). Through the application of the agreement, the specification also influences the impact of an agreement, although here the positive relationship is not as steep as the one before (Figure 15.14). Finally, there seems to be no clear relationship between the specification and the resource development (Figure 15.15). It seems as if statements written in the agreement about learning and resource development have in fact no strong influence on the actual resource development or learning.

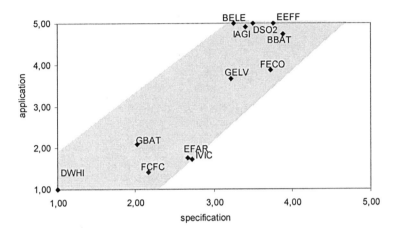

Figure 15.13   The relation between the specification and application of an agreement

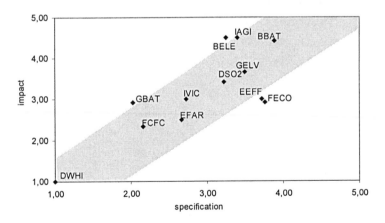

Figure 15.14   The relation between the specification and impact of an agreement

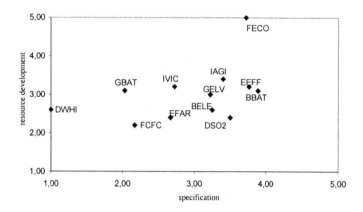

Figure 15.15   The relation between the specification and the resource development of an agreement

In the following, we will try to explain why certain agreements performed well and other badly, using information on the socio-economic context the agreement was reached in. This information is obtained through a survey having a similar structure compared to the one used to obtain information on the performance of the agreements.

5. ASSESSING THE SOCIO-ECONOMIC CONTEXT

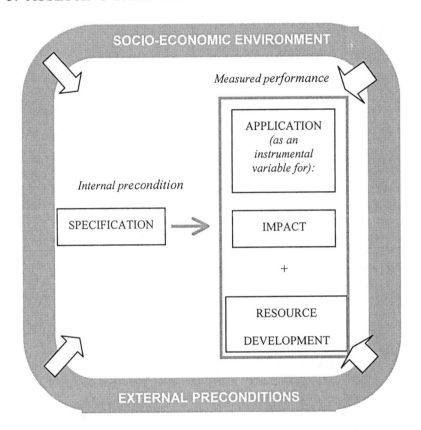

Figure 15.16   *The influence of the socio-economic context on the*
                     performance of agreements

After assessing the performance, the socio-economic context of each agreement is analysed. In our definition, the socio-economic context is an important external precondition for the final outcome of each agreement, just as the specification is an internal precondition (Figure 15.16).

Through four hypotheses, we will consider four different socio-economic aspects and their expected influence on the performance of negotiated agreements. We do not however, deny that there can be other socio-economic impacts besides those included in our hypotheses, that have an influence on the performance.

To gain information on the socio-economic context, we have carried out an analysis, using the same technique as for the performance evaluation. Different statements were judged for each agreement studied, by giving them a 1 to 5 score. Using these scores, we then will try to measure how favourable each of the four socio-economic aspects is with respect to the agreement's performance.

5.1 The Policy Style (po): Is There a Tradition of Consensus-seeking and Joint Problem Solving?

Three statements have to be assessed to be able to gain insight into the policy style in the country of the agreement and to test for the policy hypothesis. The first one considers the general policy style, while the second and third statements focus on respectively, mutual trust and self-responsibility within the sector considered. If all those statements receive a high score, we consider this policy context to be favourable for the performance of the agreement considered.

We have to note that these external factors can change over time. If there are sudden changes in for example, the climate of trust, this should be reflected in the score for the policy hypothesis.

po1. Environmental policy evolves in a tradition of consensus seeking and joint problem solving apart from the conclusion of the agreement.

po2. Apart from the process leading to the conclusion of the agreement, policy making in the area covered by the agreement is characterised by a climate of mutual trust.

po3. Apart from the process leading to the conclusion of the agreement, the private sector(s) covered by the agreement show(s) a clear readiness to self-responsibility with respect to the environmental problem.

The average score for the policy hypothesis is calculated as follows:

$$\text{Score po} = (\text{po1} + \text{po2} + \text{po3}) / 3$$

5.2 The Use of an Alternative Instrument (in): Is There a Stick behind the Door?

This hypothesis concentrates on the readiness of the policy makers to use an alternative instrument in case of non-compliance to the agreement by the private parties. The readiness of the policy makers however has to be combined with the severity of this alternative when applied. When the threat of the alternative instrument is credible, and this instrument has more stringent or costly consequences for the companies involved, they should have a bigger incentive to make the agreement succeed.

in1. The chances that public authorities will use an alternative instrument in case of non-success or non-conclusion of the agreement are high.

in2. If applied, the alternative instrument has more severe consequences for the target group than those resulting from the application of the agreement.

Here, the calculation of the score for the instrumental hypothesis differs from that for the policy hypothesis, since the two statements are not independent from each other (for example the severity of the alternative instrument becomes nearly irrelevant when the chance that this instrument is used is non-existent). We therefore use a multiplicative approach and we will multiply the scores for both statements instead of adding them. By taking the square root of this multiplication, we again obtain a score between 1 and 5.

$$\textbf{Score in = Square root of (in1 . in2)}$$

A high score for IN means that there is in fact a credible and severe alternative instrument present, and this should refrain the companies in the agreement to forsake their duties described in the agreement.

5.3 The Sectoral Structure (se): Is the Sectoral Structure Fit for an Agreement?

The first two statements here reflect the idea that an agreement will have more chance of succeeding if the target group can negotiate as one collective actor and thereby make it easier for the authorities to apply a negotiated agreement approach. The chance that the target group will be able to negotiate as one actor will depend primarily on the existence of a powerful player or association, and on the fact that the private parties belong to the same industrial sector.

Once the agreement is concluded, free-riding can prevent the participants from complying with the targets and obligations of the agreement.

se1. There is already a dominant interest of a major player/a small number of players or a powerful and representative industry association in the area covered by the agreement.

se2. The private parties to the agreement belong to the same industrial sector.

se3. The potential for significant free-riding between the members of the targeted sector covered by the agreement, is low.

Again, in order to obtain a total score for the instrumental hypothesis, we do not merely add the scores for the three statements together. Statement se3 is crucial in our opinion. It could outnumber the positive effects of the features described in the two statements below: even if there is either a dominant major player/a small number of players or a homogeneous sector, the existence of free-riding could break down the agreement. In a situation where there is no free-riding possible, the first two statements can explain the effect of the sectoral structure on the performance of the agreement. For that reason, the average score for the sectoral hypothesis is calculated as follows:

Score se = (Square root of (se1 . se3) + Square root of (se2 . se3))/2

5.4 The Competitive Structure (co): Is There a Competitive Incentive?

The central idea behind this hypothesis is that an agreement will be more feasible when the companies have a certain competitive incentive *vis-à-vis* the other companies in the area covered by the agreement, to distinguish themselves, for example through a green image. A higher participation in the (future) agreement will be more probable if the companies know that:

a. buyers will be able to distinguish which companies are performing environmentally better (by co-operating in the agreement), and;
b. buyers are sensitive to the environmental quality of the products these companies sell. This sensitivity can be the consequence of pressure by green movements, press attention and so on.

co1. Buyers can distinguish the difference in environmental quality performance of the firms in the participating sector(s).
co2. Buyers value environmentally sound products in the area covered by the agreement.

The score for the competition hypothesis is calculated as follows, because the two ideas behind the statements are interrelated:

Score co = Square root of (co1 . co2)

5.5 Evaluating the Socio-economic Environment of the Agreements

Just like we measured the average performance of each agreement, we can now turn to the socio-economic context wherein each agreement was concluded by checking to what extent this context is in accordance with the ideal situation brought forward in the four hypotheses.

Calculating these scores each of the respondents gave, gives us the following results (Table 15.6 and Figures 15.17 to 15.20).

Table 15.6   The scores for the different socio-economic aspects

	Policy hypothesis	Instrumental hypothesis	Sectoral hypothesis	Competition hypothesis
GBAT	2.67	3.24	2.70	2.83
GELV	3.00	3.24	3.30	2.00
FCFC	2.33	1.00	1.73	3.00
FECO	3.00	1.73	2.24	3.87
BBAT	2.17	5.00	3.95	3.46
BELE	3.00	5.00	5.00	1.00
DSO2	4.00	5.00	5.00	1.50
DWHI	1.83	1.87	2.47	3.00
IVIC	1.67	1.00	3.70	1.00
IAGI	1.17	5.00	4.62	3.15
EFAR	3.00	2.12	3.16	3.15
EEFF	3.67	2.96	2.81	2.28

Note: GBAT: German batteries agreement; GELV: German End-of-life vehicles agreement; FCFC: French CFC agreement; FECO: French Eco-Emballages agreement; BBAT: Belgian batteries agreement; BELE: Belgian electricity agreement; DSO2: Dutch SO_2 agreement; DWHI: Dutch white and brown goods agreement; IVIC: Italian Vicenza agreement; IAGI: Italian Agip agreement; EFAR: English farm films agreement; EEFF: English Efficiency agreement.

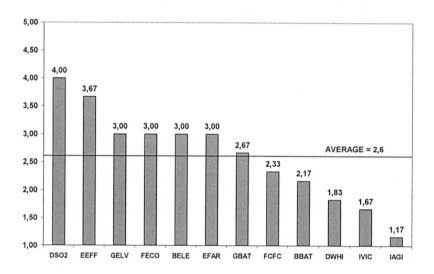

Figure 15.17   The scores for the favourability of the policy climate

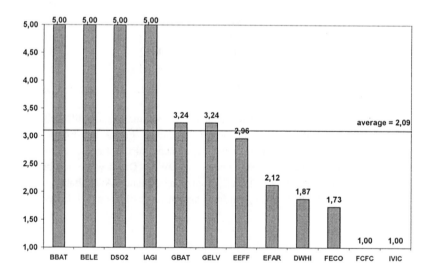

Figure 15.18   The score for the existence of an alternative instrument

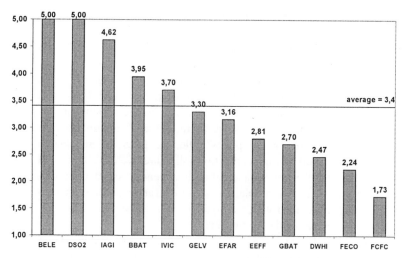

Figure 15.19   The scores for the homogeneity of the sector

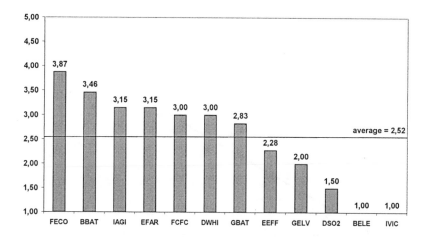

Figure 15.20   The score for the competitive structure of the sector

6. EVALUATING THE HYPOTHESES QUANTITATIVELY

6.1 The Methodological Framework

The survey above allowed us to do a quantitative evaluation of each agreement and of the socio-economic context wherein it was concluded. This quantitative evaluation is based on the scores given by the respondents.

Now that we have an aggregate score for the average performance of each agreement, and a score for the policy style, the threat of an alternative instrument, the sectoral and the competitive structure, we are able to look at the relation between the performance of each agreement and the hypotheses. Does a high score on for example, the sectoral structure, which means that the agreement is concluded within a homogeneous sector, correlate with the success or performance of the agreement?

We can do this for each case study and for each hypothesis. Having a whole series of data, we should be able to represent the validity of each hypothesis graphically as shown in Figure 15.21.

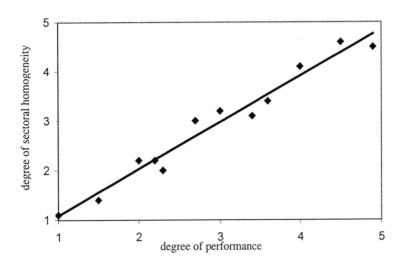

Figure 15.21   An example of a possible outcome

Obtaining for example, this graph for the sectoral hypothesis would mean that this hypothesis is valid in most cases, since we can see a clear positive trendline: agreements concluded with a heterogeneous sector tend to have a low performance, and agreements concluded with a homogeneous sector tend to perform rather well.

6.2 Results

In the following part we will combine the results of the performance of the agreements with the results obtained from the analysis of the socio-economic context wherein these agreements were concluded. We have already mentioned that the aspects of the socio-economic context that we studied, can be a precondition for the performance of negotiated agreements. These aspects will therefore function as independent variables that can explain the dependent variable, that is the performance of an agreement. This will allow us to check the four hypotheses put forward in our theoretical analysis. The (absence of a) relation between the performance and the favourability of the socio-economic context will be represented graphically, for each of the hypotheses postulated.

On these graphical representations, the horizontal axis measures the performance of the agreement, which we calculated above as an average for the scores on application, impact and resource development. The vertical axis represents the different scores on the socio-economic aspect considered.

6.2.1 The policy hypothesis

The fact that the public environmental policy evolves in a tradition and in a climate of consensus seeking, joint problem solving, mutual respect and trust is a crucial positive factor for the performance of negotiated agreements.

Plotting the data gave us the following graphical representation (Figure 15.22). Except for the BBAT and the IAGI agreement, we can see a clear positive relation between the degree of consensus seeking, respect and trust in the policy, and the performance of agreement. Since there are no scatter points in the upper left corner, we can consider this hypothesis as not rejected by our data. Agreements that are situated in the lower right corner, might be agreements that, despite the policy climate, are successful because of other beneficial socio-economic aspects, such as the existence of an alternative threat. We will discuss this possibility later on in this chapter.

It is clear that the policy style is not the only precondition for a successful implementation of environmental agreements. For that reason further, more important features for a successful implementation of environmental measures must exist. Nevertheless it is possible that a consensus-oriented policy climate increases the chances for a good implementation in certain cases.

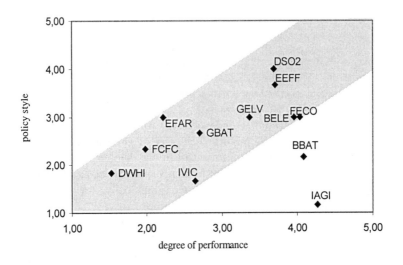

Figure 15.22   The relation between the policy style and the average performance of the studied agreements

6.2.2 The instrumental hypothesis
The fact that the public policy makers show readiness to use alternative policy instruments, as a stick behind the door to deal with the environmental problems, in case the negotiated agreement fails, is a crucial positive factor for the performance of negotiated agreements.

Figure 15.23 shows again a clear positive relationship between performance and the existence of an alternative instrument, next to the absence of agreements in the upper left and lower right corner.

Four agreements were concluded in a context where there was a very strong and severe alternative threat (DSO2, BELE, BBAT and IAGI). All those cases were also evaluated as rather successful ones. These agreements in particular support the validity of the instrumental hypothesis. Besides these successful agreements there are also two cases, which are assessed with the lowest grade possible (1.00). These two cases are the French CFC agreement and the Italian Vicenza agreement. It is again important to notice that the upper left part of the scatter graph remains almost empty. Here, this means that there are no low-performance agreements when a strong alternative threat was present. In the lower right area, we can detect some agreements, which again contribute their high performance to another aspect. We can conclude by saying that, while a strong alternative threat is not necessary, it can clearly contribute to the performance of any agreement.

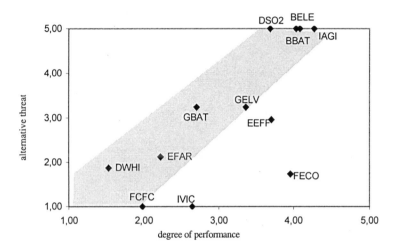

Figure 15.23   The relation between the existence of an alternative threat and the performance of the agreements studied

6.2.3 The sectoral hypothesis
The fact that the industry sector involved is homogeneous, has a small number of players and is dominated by one or two players, or has a powerful industry association that can speak for all its members, is a crucial positive factor for the performance of negotiated agreements.

Again, a positive relationship emerges from Figure 15.24. Only two agreements break this positive trend, that is the British energy efficiency agreement (EEFF) and the French Eco-Emballages agreement (FECO). All other agreements seem to be in line with expectations.

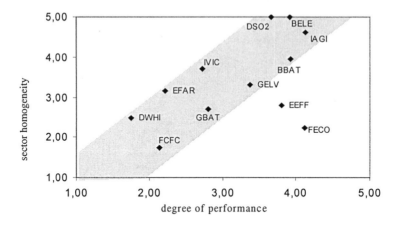

6.2.4 The competition hypothesis

The fact that firms can gain competitive advantages by co-operating in the negotiation and by compliance of a negotiated agreement, is a crucial positive factor for the performance of negotiated agreements, due to the consumer pressure.

Whereas the previous three hypotheses seemed to be confirmed, there is less clarity here: the scatterpoints on Figure 15.25 are dispersed throughout the entire graph. The theoretical idea that firms will be prone to a good environmental performance when there is demand pressure from green consumers is not confirmed by our agreements. On the one hand, we have a few agreements concluded with firms or in sectors where there is demand pressure, that performed badly (DWHI, EFAR, FCFC), and on the other hand, we have agreements with a rather good performance in markets where demand pressure was not strong (DSO2, BELE, EEFF).

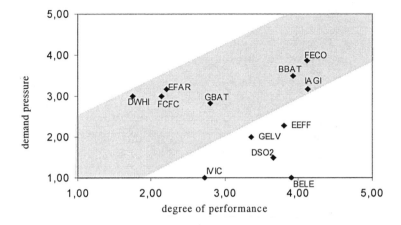

Figure 15.25   The relation between the demand pressure and the average performance of the studied agreements

6.2.5   The influence of the combined socio-economic context on the performance of negotiated agreements

We now have looked at the different hypotheses separately, and we have mentioned already that the absence of a relation between one socio-economic aspect and the performance of an agreement, can be due to the fact that this performance is positively or negatively influenced by another socio-economic aspect, diluting the influence of the first one.

Looking at the different hypotheses together, can bring us more insight in the possible existence of a 'combined (un)favourable socio-economic context'. In Table 15.7 we define the hypotheses to be 'not rejected' for an agreement, when the agreement is situated within the grey area of the above graphs.

Table 15.7   The validity of the different hypotheses for the agreements studied

	Policy hypothesis	Instrumental hypothesis	Sectoral hypothesis	Competition hypothesis
GBAT	✓	✓	✓	✓
GELV	✓	✓	✓	✗
FCFC	✓	✗	✓	✓
FECO	✓	✗	✗	✓
BBAT	✗	✓	✓	✓
BELE	✓	✓	✓	✗
DSO2	✓	✓	✓	✗
DWHI	✓	✓	✓	✓
IVIC	✓	✗	✓	✗
IAGI	✗	✓	✓	✓
EFAR	✓	✓	✓	✓
EEFF	✓	✗	✗	✗

Note: ✓: not rejected, ✗: rejected

The IAGI agreement for example, which is relatively successful in its application and impact, does not support the policy hypothesis. The reason for its performance had to be sought in the existence of a strong alternative threat and in the homogeneous sectoral structure, which made negotiations easy. Therefore, the influence of the rather unfavourable policy climate did not play a major role in the performance of the agreement. We can make an analogue reasoning for, for example, the BBAT agreement.

For the GELV, FCFC, BELE, DSO2, DWHI and the EFAR agreement, the (absence of) demand pressure could not outweigh the influence of the other three socio-economic aspects.

Based on the above argumentation, that the influence of certain socio-economic aspects can be outweighed by the influence of other aspects, we could argue that the 'combined' context (all of the four separately studied aspects together) will provide a favourable or unfavourable climate.

For all agreements, at least two hypotheses are not rejected, except from the IVIC agreement. For nine of the twelve agreements, at least three hypotheses are not rejected. This could lead us to conclude that most of the agreements studied were negotiated and applied within a rather favourable combined socio-economic context or within a rather unfavourable combined socio-economic context, leading to a relative good respectively bad performance.

This leads us to conclude that the favourability of each of the socio-economic aspects we studied is not a necessary condition for the good performance of a negotiated agreement. The socio-economic context does not need to be favourable in all aspects:

- The absence of a good policy climate can be outweighed by the use of a strong and credible alternative instrument.
- An alternative instrument on the other hand might not be necessary if the private parties feel that there is a certain degree of market pressure (from consumers or competitors) to succeed in the agreement.
- The disadvantage of a very heterogeneous sector with very different parties can be minimised by the imposition of a strong alternative instrument, making the incentive for these different parties the same and stimulating co-operation between them.
- There might be no need for an alternative instrument or market pressure, if the private parties and the policy makers already have a very good relation, and if they act as 'gentlemen' towards each other.

7. QUALITATIVE EVALUATION OF THE VALIDITY OF THE HYPOTHESES

Following the quantitative analysis of the different relations between the hypotheses and the individual cases, we will now attempt to draw some more definitive conclusions regarding the validity of the different hypotheses. As the previous discussion made clear, the quantitative results alone provide too little information to assess whether a hypothesis is supported or not. We therefore only evaluated the hypotheses as being 'not rejected' or 'not supported'. Thanks to a further qualititative analysis, we can see more clearly which aspects of the socio-economic context actively contributed to the (non)-performance of an agreement. The fact that a certain aspect does not actively contribute to the (non)performance, does not however mean that the hypothesis in question can be rejected. For example, the absence of an alternative threat in a relatively successful agreement does not reject the instrumental hypothesis. The agreement could have performed as well or better if an alternative threat had been present. Similarly, the fact that a successful agreement was concluded in a homogeneous sector, does not automatically support the sectoral hypothesis. The success of the agreement could be attributed solely to the existence of an alternative threat. Moreover, in some cases, different hypotheses can be clearly supported, while the exact contribution of one socio-economic aspect is more clear than the contribution of other ones.

7.1 The Policy Hypothesis

In the quantitative evaluation, the agreements that most clearly did not reject the policy hypothesis, were the DSO2, the EEFF (both successful agreements) and the DWHI agreement (unsuccessful).

The Dutch SO2 case
In policy making in the Netherlands, one can certainly speak of a tradition of consensus seeking, joint problem solving and mutual respect. The Netherlands are well known for this approach all over the world. Policy makers have experience in working with the instrument of negotiated agreements. More specifically, the relationship between the Dutch government, in particular the Ministry of Environment, and the power generators goes back to the 1970s when the idea of one emission ceiling for the whole sector was discussed. Relationships between the provinces and the power generation companies have existed for longer as a result of the discussions on the permits given by the provinces.

The English energy efficiency case
The evolution of environmental policy in the UK reflects a long tradition of pragmatism, voluntarism, and discretion. Historically, the general policy style has been one of consultative and negotiated consensus, involving close-knit and tightly drawn policy communities with significant industrial representation. However, since the mid-1980s there has been a move towards a more open and independent style of regulation. Also the strong trend towards deregulation of industry – reflecting the dominant neo-liberal political ideology of the 1990s – has provided an important impetus to experiments with new, market-oriented policy tools such as economic instruments and negotiated agreements. The Chemical Industries Association already had well-established relationships with Government departments, and had participated in a sector dialogue with the Government in the year before the negotiations commenced. Furthermore, both sides were positively predisposed towards the idea of an agreement, and both were keen that the negotiations should reach a successful conclusion.

The Dutch white and brown goods case
At a national scale the Netherlands can be considered a consensus-oriented country. Also its policy style and government – private sector interaction often reflect this. On the level of this sector however the interactions between the Ministry of the Environment and the sector had not been very intensive previous to this agreement. So on that level there could have been little opportunity to build a climate of trust and so on.

There seem to be two agreements that do not support this policy hypothesis in the quantitative evaluation: the BBAT and the AGIP agreement. These agreements are both relatively successful, while the policy climate was rather unfavourable.

The Italian AGIP case

Concerning this hypothesis only one case exists which performed relatively well (average performance rate: 4.27) although its policy context was assessed extremely badly. The bad evaluation of the policy hypothesis seems to contradict the qualitative analysis given: several features indicate efforts to realise such a policy approach. In fact, a climate of consensus seeking, joint problem solving and trust was developed during the negotiation process. It must be pointed out that this policy style only developed after the beginning of the negotiations but did not exist before. Before the negotiations the different actors did not have a relationship based on consensus seeking or trust. Since the evaluation survey only took into account the situation that existed before the conclusion of the agreement, the Italian Agip case does not support the validity of the policy hypothesis. It should be taken into consideration that the development of a consensus-oriented policy style through the negotiation might have supported the good performance of this case.

The Belgian battery case

In the Belgian environmental policy a tradition of consensus-seeking, joint problem-solving and climate of trust has only started to emerge in the last few years. For that reason there must have been other reasons driving this agreement to success. Mainly there are two factors which describe the success. One is a very strong stick behind the door. In this case it was the threat to issue an ecotax on batteries. The other factor is the homogeneous structure of the factor: the Belgium battery market is dominated by two producers which, together with the FEE – the Belgian Federation of Electronic Producers – led the negotiations with the ecotax commission.

7.2 The Instrumental Hypothesis

The quantitative evaluation showed that four agreements seem to perform very well, and have a very strong stick behind the door: DSO2, BBAT, BELE and IAGI. One agreement performs rather badly in the absence of such an alternative threat. Does this imply a causal relation between the performance and the (non)existence of this threat?

The Dutch SO2 and NOx case

This agreement is evaluated as a success. It was capable of achieving the defined targets, mainly to reduce SO_2 and NO_x emissions. Although some criticism remains to what degree the reductions achieved are due to the covenant. This issue is difficult to assess, but it must be pointed out that the covenant made the most cost-efficient achievement of the objectives possible. In the Dutch SO_2 and NO_x case a credible threat was clearly present, namely the Decree on Emission Requirements for Combustion Installations (BEES). If the negotiations for an agreement had failed, the government would have revised this ordinance in order to tighten up the emission limits for SO_2 and NO_x. For NO_x it would have meant that the industry branches would have been forced to make expensive investments for technical installations to apply the regulations. While the government started to prepare for a serious revision of the BEES-Ordinance the power generating industry requested the reopening of the discussion for the agreement that later became a success.

The Belgian Electricity case

The agreement concerning the reduction of SO_2 and NO_x emissions to be achieved by the Belgian electricity producers contains an unclear instrumental threat in case the objectives should not be achieved. It explicitly states that the government can make an end to the agreement if the private sector does not succeed in attaining the proposed reduction targets. What the alternative legislation then would be, is however not specified.

The foundation for possible reduction targets is laid down in the Flemish Environmental Policy Plan. During the time frame of this policy plan (1997–2001) the Flemish government wants to reduce the total acidifying deposition by 39 per cent in 2002 compared to 1990. The Flemish government developed the following strategy to attain these objectives: Besides a more intensified international co-operation on this matter these targets should mainly be achieved by the implementation of negotiated agreements and by the investments the electricity sector was supposed to undertake. If the industry would not succeed in achieving the reduction targets one possibility to force them to compliance would have been the tightening up of respective regulations. For example for the Flemish Region this could have meant a stricter regulation in the permission procedure concerning the limit values for emissions (VLAREM II).

The Italian AGIP case

The Italian Agip case, consisting of three negotiated agreements, which were signed to improve the quality of gasoline, represents a successful case. The objectives described in all the agreements can be considered as fulfilled. The content of benzene in gasoline could be decreased to 1.3 per cent of the volume for unleaded gasoline and to 1.4 per cent of the volume for leaded gasoline in the period considered. The improvement of the quality of gasoline was still in progress at that time: during the last three months of 1996, the average percentage of benzene even decreased to 1.2 per cent of the volume.

One reason for this success is the existence of a very efficient alternative threat. In the Italian Agip case the oil industry was in great fear that the government would tighten up legislation on benzene more strictly than in other European countries. In this context the agreements of 1989 and 1991 emerged principally from the sector's consideration to avoid the imposition of much stricter regulation obligating it to a specified 'maximum' content of benzene in fuel and providing for sanctions if these 'maximum' limits were not respected. Already in the beginning of the 1990s it was emerging that in the year 2000 the share of benzene permitted would be reduced to 1 per cent. For that reason the Italian oil industry feared the possibility of being regulated by law imposing this standard in 1992, eight years before other countries would be obliged to realise the reduction objectives. In other words, the Italian oil industry feared market distortions discriminating against them vis-à-vis foreign oil companies, since it would be very expensive to realise the reduction objectives as proposed by different social groups.

The Belgian Battery case

The Belgian Battery case can be evaluated as a success. The capability to achieve its targets has been assessed very well. Concerning its impact it was environmentally effective (it even outnumbered the objectives defined), could be implemented in an economically efficient way (freedom to chose the most cost-efficient path to realise the targets) and finally affected resource development positively.

The Belgian Battery case explains clearly the effects of a credible governmental threat on the outcome of an agreement. In this case the stick was the passing of an ecotax on all sold batteries (16/7/93) which was to come into effect on 1 January 1994. Although there was already a European Directive concerning batteries, the Belgian government intended to subject all sold household batteries to an environmental tax of BEF 20 until a deposit refund system was set up. For that reason the battery industry started negotiations with the ecotax commission even in 1993, trying to find a more appropriate solution. By this, the battery industry tried to avoid the ecotax, first by minimising its application field (to differentiate between labelled and unlabelled batteries), later on by proposing a voluntary scheme organised by the industry.

Although the demand of batteries is relatively price-inelastic, the imposition of an ecotax would have decreased battery sales in Belgium drastically. The reasons for this would on the one hand be the extent of the price increase (30 per cent or BEF 20 on an average price of BEF 60 per battery) and on the other the small amount of used batteries per capita per year: each person consumes on average seven batteries in one year. As a consequence to this consumers would probably buy their yearly stock abroad. For that reason the Belgian battery industry asked for a voluntary agreement. Once the agreement was concluded, the imminent existence of the ecotax forced the battery sector to do everything to comply with the targets in the agreement.

The Dutch white and brown goods case

During the negotiations for a covenant, the stick behind the door was definitely there. The threat of legislation was supposed to put the actors under pressure to gain agreement. And probably it did: in the absence of such a threat, there may well have been no negotiations at all.

But the stick behind the door at least did not push the negotiators far enough to reach a covenant. An important factor here is also the role that the Ministry of Economic Affairs played. This ministry supported a less broad implementation of producers' responsibility and weakened the position of the Ministry for Environment in this question. The government did not strive for a joint solution. For that reason the stick behind the door was not that strong. After it became clear that the sector was not going to sign a covenant or come up with plans for the disposal of goods themselves, the Ministry of Economic Affairs shifted position and worked with the Ministry of Environment on the drafting of a regulation: the *White and Brown Goods Disposal Order*.

It is interesting to pay some attention to the possible explanation for this deviation. Our suggestion is that this case shows a limitation of the hypothesis. The hypothesised relationship considers the logic of the game at one level. What happened here is that the policy process proved to be a multi-level game. The European policy making level interacted here with the national one. The effect of the threat with alternative policy instruments at a national level was fuzzy because of the expectation of a European–wide policy that, for better or worse, in any case would be equal for all countries. This provided a great incentive to delay, rather than proceed with the negotiations and – later – the implementation.

The case shows a – rather slow – race in time of two policy levels, one preferred by the national government (obviously the national level) and the other preferred by the sector (the European level).

Three agreements seemed to reject the importance of an alternative threat.

The Italian Vicenza case

Although this agreement scored high in the performance evaluation, it remains controversial if it can be evaluated as a successful one. A more in-depth study of this agreement shows it performed rather badly. If this case will be assessed as a relatively successful one, one explanation for this outcome may be its limited scope of application. Its total environmental impacts are rather limited. The only clearly visible impact is an increase of knowledge gained through the studies carried out on atmospheric emissions in the tanning industry and the experiments carried out in the marble sector. As a credible threat is missing in this case, the apparent failure of the agreement seems to support the instrumental hypothesis.

The British Energy Efficiency case

In the British Energy Efficiency case, instrumental pressure to conclude a substantial agreement was rather ambiguous. The original interest in the idea of a negotiated agreement can be traced back to 1991 and the publication of the European Commission's proposals for a combined carbon/energy tax. However, by 1995 these proposals had been shelved, and the UK Government showed little interest in the idea of a tax, although a revised proposal was still being promoted by the Commission. Thus while there was no immediate threat of a tax being introduced, it was always likely to return to the political agenda at some point of time in the future. A desire to pre-empt any future tax was one of the main motivations for the Chemical Industries Association entering into the negotiations. However, the Government was not prepared to close off its options for the future, and the final agreement explicitly allows for the introduction of a tax (or other instrument), even if the agreement is successful.

One of the main reasons for the relative success of the agreement is the inclusion of a support programme aimed at SMEs to disseminate best practice in relation to energy management. This programme was financed by the Government, with the funds being reallocated from an existing support programme. Thus – at least to a certain extent – the performance of the agreement can be explained by the presence of a 'carrot' to encourage improvement, rather than a 'stick' to punish failure. It should also be noted that the performance of the agreement is likely to have been affected by its high score in relation to the policy hypothesis (the score for the policy style was 3.67).

The French Eco-Emballages case
The French Eco-Emballages case is a successful one although there was no strong stick behind the door. On the one hand the driving factor for the success of this agreement was its positive influence on the policy resource base. Another explanation for the success of this agreement might be specific features relating to the inclusion into the international market of consumer goods. The French industry was forced to label its products since in Germany and in other countries similar efforts were made to finance the recycling and disposal of packages (for example in Germany: 'Duales System Deutschland'). A further explanation for the success of this agreement, consists in its good competitive structure.

7.3 The Sectoral Hypothesis

Five agreements do not reject the sectoral hypothesis, if we base our decision on the quantitative analysis.

The Dutch SO_2 and NO_x case
The Dutch SO_x and NO_x agreement has been assessed as a successful case. The sectoral context supports this outcome: it was evaluated with the maximum grade possible (5.00). This is a consequence of the fact, that in 1990 the industry sector concluding the agreement was very homogeneous, had only a small number of players (four large producers of energy) and a powerful association (SEP), too. The electricity sector was rather special compared with others: it was a very protected market with a low degree of competition. As a consequence extra costs could easily be included in the prices consumers pay for electricity.

The homogeneous nature of the power generation sector made the various aspects of the agreement relevant to all members. The dominant position of SEP put it into the central position as negotiation partner for the government and increased the 'accessibility' of the sector for a negotiated agreement approach. The fact, that SEP was so powerful to co-ordinate and control the implementation of the agreement played a crucial role for its successful performance.

The Belgian Electricity case
The Belgian Electricity case has been described as a success. This outcome is supported by the maximum grade (5.00) for the sectoral hypothesis. Even if the Belgian electricity sector can be characterised as being very homogeneous during the 1980s, this homogeneity intensified in 1990, when the three remaining private producers (Ebes, Intercom and Unerg) merged into one private company, Electrabel. This merger resulted in a quasi private

monopoly for Electrabel. Electrabel and SPE together have a market share of 96.7 per cent of the total electricity-producing sector.

As a consequence of this only a small group of negotiators were involved in the negotiations for this agreement, namely the three regions, Electrabel and SPE. This considerably simplified the negotiation process. Since mainly one producer, namely Electrabel, dominates the electricity sector the successful implementation of the agreement could not be threatened by free-riders.

The Italian AGIP case

Among other reasons the success of the Italian Agip case can be explained by its performance under the sectoral hypothesis which was the best possible. The main players of the Italian oil market consist of one market leader and eight other smaller operators. With respect to the final product this market has a very homogeneous character. This fact is intensified by the existence of a powerful association in this sector: the Unione Petrolifera. This association represents a well-organised industrial organisation capable of speaking for all of its members. For these reasons the sectoral hypothesis gets the highest scores possible. The case sustains its validity.

The Dutch white and brown goods case

The sector analysed involves many product groups ranging from refrigerators and freezers (white goods) and televisions and video-recorders (the brown goods). The interests of the white and brown goods sector differed on the issues discussed in the context of the covenant. Therefore the sector can be considered to be heterogeneous.

Two organisations, Vlehan and Fiar represented the sector, the producers and importers of white and brown goods. They incorporate most of the sector in the Netherlands and could speak for their members.

The power of the industry associations to represent their members has two sides. On the one hand the legitimacy of the association to present the opinions of the members is at stake. There are not many indications that these organisations were not legitimate in this respect. On the other hand also the power of the associations to make a deal that binds their members to a compromise in which they also have 'to deliver' is of crucial importance in negotiations. Here the forced withdrawal of the association from the negotiations shows that the power of the association over its members has been rather weak.

The French CFC case

Apparently the quantitative results confirm the hypothesis according to which the degree of concentration in a sector affects positively the willingness for signing an agreement. In effect, homogeneous sectors (aerosols, automobiles) seem to have had less difficulties to comply with the agreement than atomistic ones (refrigeration) where free-riding problems have occurred among small firms. However, we have no indications that the negotiations leading to the agreements were more difficult in the more heterogeneous sectors than in the homogeneous sectors. One explanation for this may be the absence of an alternative threat that made most of the possible stakeholders indifferent to the conclusion of an agreement.

The FECO and EEFF agreement are however quite successful, while the sector concluding the agreement was a rather diverse collection of participants. Why did this heterogeneity not affect the good performance of those agreements?

The French Eco-Emballages case

This case is not distinctly successful or unsuccessful. But the performance has been improved recently. The rate of recycling and the development of separate collection are in progress. Furthermore in the meantime a better knowledge of technologies, constraints and most cost-efficient organisation forms for adequate solutions has been generated. A collective learning process has been established improving the policy resource base. For that reason this case can be assessed as a relatively success.

This outcome stands in contrast to the sectoral hypothesis given in this case. The implementation of this agreement took place in a complex network of actors with disparate interests. For that reason this sector must be characterised as being heterogeneous. Since this hypothesis does not account for the relative, other features must have driven it to success. One factor was probably the high competitiveness of the market concerned by the agreement (competition hypothesis!). Due to the international dependencies (import and export of consumer goods) the French industry was forced to sign its products because in Germany and in other countries similar efforts were made to finance the recycling and disposal of packages. In this context the French NA was driven by the developments in Germany and those on the level of EU legislation.

The British Energy Efficiency case

The relatively low score in relation to the sectoral hypothesis for the British energy efficiency case reflects a high *potential* for free-riding within the sector (that is a score of 2.00 for se.3 compared with scores of 5.00 and 3.00 for se.1 and se.2 respectively). However, because the target improvement under the agreement requires only the implementation of cost–effective measures (i.e. those with a commercial payback), the costs imposed on the sector are negligible – and hence free-riding is not an *actual* issue in this case. If however the agreement had imposed significant costs, then one might expect that this potential for free-riding would have had a negative impact on performance.

7.4 The Competition Hypothesis

We can see no clear pattern emerging from the quantitative evaluation. It is therefore difficult to decide which agreement supported this hypothesis and which one did not. We will however look at some agreements where the closeness to the consumer market played a role.

The Belgian electricity case
It should be quite clear that, at the moment of signing the agreement, Electrabel and SPE together had a de facto monopoly on the Belgian electricity producing market. Moreover, demand for electricity is quite inelastic. Interviews with representatives of the industry make it quite clear that consumer pressure hardly played any role in negotiating and signing the agreement.

The Italian Agip case
The sector concerned in this case is close to the final market as it does not only deal with refining but also with the distribution of gasoline. Agip Petroli can, in fact, be seen to make use of this closeness to final markets through their choice to publicise their over-compliance (with respect to the objectives of the negotiated agreements): they differentiate their product by establishing a voluntary limit of a maximum content of benzene at less than 1 per cent for the gasoline sold on the national market.

In concluding that the case sustains this hypothesis, it should be noted that the Unione Petrolifera maintains that the sector has not gained a more positive image with the public through fulfilling the agreement's commitments but rather has gained a more positive image in the eyes of the institutional actors. It would appear here that the consumers put pressure on the institutions to resolve the environmental problems, which then in turn put pressure on the industry.

The Dutch white and brown goods case
The logic of this hypothesis presupposes that consumers have relevant choices when an industry 'misbehaves' in the eyes of the public. In this case – like in other Dutch target group approach cases – the scale of the negotiations is however national, including the importers. That means that consumers do not have meaningful choices when they consider the white and brown goods sector to behave in an irresponsible way. Though this sector is

clearly very close to final markets, we conclude therefore that the hypothesis cannot be applied in this case.

During the negotiations, the sector however argued that the price increase as a result of the disposal system would have a negative impact on their sales since consumers could go to neighbouring countries where there the prices of these goods do not include a fee for disposal. This means actually that the sector suggested another theorem: closeness to consumer markets forces a sector to be critical about costly environmental measures taken in one country because customers can start buying abroad.

The German battery case

In the German battery case the industry was close to consumer markets. The consumer pressure seemed to be high because of the awareness of the environmental problems related to the disposal of batteries. Although the competitive context should be favourable, this is not true in this case: the consumers' behaviour prevented a better performance and implementation of this agreement. Since the establishment of an efficient collection scheme for batteries failed, the adequate preconditions for an efficient recycling were missing. Another factor for the relatively failure of this agreement is the structure of the retail sector which is responsible for the collection of batteries. The structure of this sector can be characterised as being very heterogeneous, ranging from international operating companies to little family owned retail shops. The heterogeneity of the sector set difficult obstacles for the branch to inform each enterprise efficiently about the correct collecting of batteries (only a specific type of batteries - the labelled ones - should be collected). Since this information campaign failed, the efficient implementation of the collection scheme was made impossible. For that reason the sectoral heterogeneity outnumbered the competitive effects of this agreement.

The British energy efficiency case

The British energy case was evaluated as being relatively successful despite the fact that it is not close to the final consumers. With the exception of the soap, perfumes and cosmetics sub-sector, a very high proportion (that is less than 70 per cent) of output goes to intermediate consumption. Consequently, consumer pressure is not very high, and other factors must exist which explain the relative success of the agreement

The main driving force behind the successful performance has been the creation and dissemination of information to SMEs concerning cost-efficient improvements in energy efficiency. This programme of consultancy visits was funded by the Government, and was embedded within existing support programmes (see instrumental hypothesis). The agreement also benefited from a supportive policy framework (see policy hypothesis).

The Dutch electricity case

This case is evaluated as a clear success. The reduction targets for SO_2 and NO_x have been achieved clearly by the power generation industry. Due to the fact that a strong competition in the electricity market of Netherlands does not exist the competition hypothesis does not support the outcome of the agreement. Until recently the electricity market was non-competitive (monopolistic structure) and in addition consumer electricity demand was rather inelastic. For that reason image did not play a role for the electricity producing sector. The link between selling directly to consumers and being dependent on the industry's image with these consumers is not obvious.

This fact leads to the question which other features of the agreement influenced the positive outcome. One reason seemed to be the clear and strong threat to revise the Decree on Emission Requirements for Combustion Installations (BEES) resulting in stricter regulations concerning the emissions for SO_2 and NO_x. For NO_x it would have meant that every plant needed an expensive SCR installation. The threat to impose such cost-intensive regulation forced the Dutch power generation industry to make more cost-effective investments on order to achieve reduction targets. As a large part of the reductions was realised by the closure of old coal-fired plants without abatement technology it remains unclear to what extent these reductions are due to the agreement. The agreement might have speeded up this process a little.

16. General Conclusions and Policy Recommendations

Marc De Clercq and Bart Ameels

1. INTRODUCTION

In the NEAPOL-project we tried in a multidisciplinary way to identify the critical factors leading to success or failure of negotiated agreements. To do this we relied on theoretical analysis as well as on empirical research covering twelve cases from six different European countries. The case studies were carried out according to a common case study design, thus enabling to a greater extent comparative analysis.

In the sample of case studies that were analysed in NEAPOL, one agreement was related to a specific region, five of them were process-related agreements, and six of the agreements covered extended producer responsibilities.

Although the sample was limited by practical and financial considerations the study nevertheless points to a number of important policy considerations. Looked upon from a positive research methodological point of view, their validity of course relates strictly to the cases studied. The sample was indeed restricted to only twelve cases and the choice of the cases studies was guided by a number of practical considerations and accordingly was not done at random:

- There had to be enough information available on them in the public domain.
- The cases had to be significant for the environmental problems they deal with.
- The period during which they had been used should be long enough in order to enable a performance evaluation.
- The sample had to consist of both successful and unsuccessful negotiated agreements.

- The economic context of the different industrial sectors involved had to be diversified enough.
- Overlapping with other European project on negotiated agreements (for example the VIAE project) had to be avoided.

Table 16.1 The different agreements studied

One regional agreement
- Italian regional agreement upon the improvement of the environmental quality in the province of Vicenza

Five process-related agreements
- French agreement to eliminate the use of CFCs in the industry
- Dutch agreement upon the reduction of the SO_2-emission of power plants
- Belgian agreement to reduce the emission of SO_2 and NO_X in power plants
- UK agreement to improve the energy efficiency in the chemical industry
- Italian agreement upon the improvement of gasoline quality

Six agreements covering extended producer responsibility
- German agreement to reduce the heavy metal content in batteries and to collect used batteries separately
- German agreement to maximise the recycling rate of end-of-life vehicles
- French agreement upon the collection and recycling of packaging waste
- Belgian agreement upon the private separate collection and recycling of used batteries
- Dutch agreement upon the take back of worn household appliances by their producers ('white and brown goods')
- UK agreement upon the collection from farms of waste plastic films ('farm films')

In our view, the performance of a negotiated environmental agreement is a mixture of the degree of good application of the agreement, the degree of impact the agreement has on the environment and on the economic efficiency, and the degree of resource development that occurs while negotiating and implementing the agreement. Taking into account only the application of the agreement results in a very narrow definition of performance. Taking into account only the impact of the agreement is a better solution, though the individual impact of an agreement on the environment and on the economic efficiency is difficult to measure. We therefore take into account both the application and the impact, while not minimising the resource development.

The theoretical analysis as well as the empirical research point to a number of internal as well as external factors of good performance or success. Four external preconditions for success were identified:

1. the general policy style: a tradition of consensus seeking and joint problem solving is generally considered to be an enabling factor for the realisation of a successful negotiated agreement;
2. the readiness to use severe alternative instruments in case of non-compliance with the agreement concluded: the stick behind the door;
3. the potential of the sector to negotiate and act as one collective actor due to, for example, the dominance of one major player, the small number of actors concerned, the power of the industry association, the low potential for free-riding, the homogeneity of the actors concerned, etc.
4. the potential for market success triggered off by the implementation of the negotiated agreement (the market 'carrot'). In other words the potential that firms participating in the agreement have to distinguish themselves towards other firms in the sector(s) covered by the agreement by environmentally beneficial behaviour. Putting it differently participating in the (future) agreement can be rewarding in market terms because:

   • potential customers are able to distinguish clearly which companies are performing environmentally better by participating in the agreement;
   • buyers are sensitive to the positive environmental behaviour of firms: their willingness to pay for their products is higher or to the minimum buyers are willing to favour them over substituting products at the same price due to their higher environmental performance.

In the cases we studies we found evidence that at least the three first factors could be important for enabling the success of a negotiated agreement. The evidence for the last factor is less convincing at least for the twelve cases studied, although the theoretical arguments in favour of this fourth factor are robust. It seems at least for the cases considered in NEAPOL that the market incentives for concluding and implementing correctly a negotiated agreement were less important. Indeed of the two fundamental reasons advanced by theoretical analysis for voluntary action – avoiding regulatory pressure and enhancing green reputation – in the cases analysed the second one seemed largely absent.

It should be noted that taken individually each of the factors is not as such a conditio sine qua non for the success of a negotiated agreement. Rather it is the combination of the success factors that is ultimately decisive for the success or non-success of the agreement. This is important because some of the success factors – the sector structure and to a large extent the competitive structure – are independent factors that cannot be manipulated by the government. The other two – the general policy climate and certainly the alternative instrument – however are under the control of the policy maker and can thus be used to create a combination of external factors that constitute a favourable environment for a negotiated agreement.

The questions used in the study to enable the research teams to assess the environment wherein the different negotiated agreements were functioning could be used as a quick checklist to assess whether or not the environment is potentially favourable for the conclusion of a successful negotiated agreement.

Even when the external factors are favourable to the conclusion and the execution of a negotiated agreement, success is by no way automatically guaranteed. Success indeed depends also upon the creation of a number of internal preconditions. They are to a certain extent influenced by the external factors identified above, but the degree of policy freedom in this respect is much larger. In the study, those internal factors of success were captured under the heading of 'specification'. They relate to environmental performance, economic efficiency and learning. Well-specified negotiated agreements are important because they lead to a higher rate of application, more demanding objectives and as such a better impact on the target variables. Our analysis essentially points to the following important elements.

2. WELL-DEFINED ENVIRONMENTAL PERFORMANCE INDICATORS

Successful negotiated agreements are characterised by clearly specified targets that represent a meaningful improvement over the business-as-usual evolution. The targets are quantified and intermediate milestones are identified. The identification of the business-as-usual scenario is often not an easy task but is clearly necessary if one aims at significant progress in environmental performance. Nevertheless it should be pointed out that even if in the end nothing more than business-as-usual is realised the agreement can still be successful in terms of efficiency, because it enables industry to realise the targets in a flexible way, thus decreasing the associated costs.

3. A CREDIBLE AND WELL-SPECIFIED MONITORING MECHANISM

Success clearly depends on monitoring. Thus the creation of a mutually accepted and performing monitoring system is crucial. In the sample we studied, successful NAs were to a large extent NAs where the performance was followed-up by a monitoring mechanism. A number of elements seem important here. First of all, monitoring mechanisms are working better if they are clearly specified and agreed upon by the parties concerned at the start of the agreement. If the monitoring rules still have to be discussed at the moment of evaluation itself the monitoring agreement clearly lacks credibility. Second, monitoring is not only important because it can – potentially at least – be linked to a sanctioning mechanism (cf. the 'stick behind the door' hypothesis), but perhaps even more important because it creates for the parties concerned the social momentum according to which they are positively motivated to prove that their performance is at least sufficient if not exemplary with respect to other parties concerned. Third, a good monitoring mechanism provides credibility also to the outside word. Often it is noted that third parties are critical with respect to the effectiveness of voluntary agreements and do question their usefulness. A reliable monitoring scheme could help convincing them of the opposite. Involving them in the monitoring process could help overcoming those concerns. Fourth, in order to guarantee its objectiveness as well as its social acceptability the autonomy and the independence of the monitoring body should be guaranteed. Fifth, it should be realised that credible monitoring mechanisms demand a significant investment in terms of time, personnel and financial resources. Negotiated agreements are therefore not costless; their administrative feasibility should be judged against the implementation costs of other instruments.

4. A CREDIBLE MECHANISM FOR ACHIEVING THE ENVIRONMENTAL PERFORMANCE OBJECTIVE

Agreements clearly perform better if they do not only state goals but indicate clearly how the participating parties will effectively realise them. The kind of mechanism is of course dependent upon the nature of the goals to be realised. For example with respect to agreements relating to product responsibility often collective action is required. The credibility of such a scheme is undermined if no realistic funding scheme is created. Other potential approaches include the setting of individual performance targets, the provision of encouragement, technical support and advice by either sector associations, public authorities or independent bodies. The capability of the implementation mechanism must be judged in relation to the stringency and the nature of the environmental performance objective.

5. A CREDIBLE MECHANISM FOR PREVENTING FREE-RIDING

A number of agreements studied clearly were performing sub-optimally because their implementation demanded some form of collective action and free-riding occurred. As a result the effectiveness of the agreement is diminished and the erosion of the agreement is stimulated because participants in most cases no longer see the advantage of participating in it. The potential for free-riding of course is dependent partially upon the characteristics of the sector concerned, but it can be positively or negatively influenced by the design of the agreement itself. Prevention of free-riding can be done by the private sector itself (for example through its buying policies) or can rely upon government action (for example fines of taxes in case of non-participation or non-compliance). The strictness of the sanctioning mechanism must be judged against the severity of the consequences of participating in the agreement. It should be realised that 'overkill' measures are seldom politically realistic.

6. THE STIMULATION OF LEARNING PROCESSES

The theoretical analysis as well as the case study analysis pointed to the importance of the so-called resource development: the improvement in the policy resource base resulting from negotiating and implementing the agreement. The theoretical analysis pointed to the fact that voluntary initiatives are especially interesting in situations of shared uncertainty because due to their interesting properties (co-operation, flexibility, revisability) they stimulate learning processes. Learning could relate to the reduction of information asymmetries (for example the dissemination of current best practices, the identification of new technical and managerial solutions, or the generation of new environmental insights). Even if no explicit learning targets are included, the practical implementation of the agreement should favour the development of such collective learning processes. An explicit implementation mechanism stipulating how the learning is expected to occur (for example through co-operative research programmes, or through site visits) is to be provided for. Here also, the effectiveness of the learning process could benefit from a well devised monitoring system that tracks down the learning initiatives taken and the dissemination of the results of these activities. The detailed requirements of a monitoring system will depend upon the nature of the learning objective and the implementation mechanism that is adopted. As learning is a long-term phenomenon and often requires insight into a variety of complex processes, a sufficiently long time horizon for the agreement is to be welcomed as well as stability with respect to the other elements of the regulatory environment.

7.   A BURDEN-SHARING MECHANISM CONSISTENT WITH A COST-EFFICIENT OUTCOME

The burden-sharing mechanism defines who is responsible for achieving the environmental performance objective. In order to limit the total cost of achieving the environmental goals an explicit ex ante burden-sharing mechanism that differentiates between actors in order to reduce the aggregate costs of achievement of the objective is necessary. For an 'individual action' agreement the responsibilities for action and payment coincide: the actors that take the actions effectively have to bear the costs. In this case, burden sharing refers to the apportionment of the general policy goal to the different actors concerned. Those actors that have the lowest marginal costs should do the most efforts to reach the collective target. In other words targets should be differentiated in such a way that marginal costs of action are equalised. In case this allocation conflicts with other political goals additional instruments should be used to compensate for the undesired effects rather than changing the allocation pattern of the efforts themselves. In case collective action is required to reach the goals of the agreement, the cost allocation should reflect the difference in contribution of the actors concerned to the environmental problem that lies at the origin of the negotiated agreement. Particular care should be taken to avoid the situation where in the negotiating or even in the executing phase powerful actors can shift the burden of adaptation to less powerful ones when such a shift is not in line with efficiency considerations.

8. THE IMPORTANCE OF BACK-UP POLICIES

An important factor explaining the success or failure of negotiated agreements is whether or not the different actors considered it in their own interest to join the agreement and faithfully execute it. The objectives pursued through the agreement should be complementary to the business strategies of the participants. Within this perspective private industry will only voluntarily execute certain requirements if the investments that are required are characterised by a positive return on investment. This private business logic limits the applicability of this instruments and leads some scholars and policy makers to conclude that negotiated agreements as all-voluntary initiatives are only effective to pick low-hanging fruits and thus are not suitable instruments in the substantial industrial restructuring processes that are required to achieve sustainable development. One should not forget however, that whether or not a particular environmental investment is characterised by a positive return depends on the economic parameters (the relative prices) that directly or indirectly influence the calculation of the relevant benefits and costs. This points to the importance of incorporating negotiating agreements in a total policy package that aims among other things, to correct relative prices in an environmentally friendly way. Some successful cases clearly pointed to the fact that in the negotiating game preceding the conclusion of the agreement, the fact that the government made a unilateral and drastic first move explained to a large extent, why demanding targets could be set and were realised. This argument pleads in favour of a greater government involvement in the setting of the targets to be reached, while leaving it to the private parties concerned to select the appropriate ways to realise those targets. The greater degree of flexibility obtained in the negotiated agreements in comparison to the regulatory approach enables significant cost savings and as such provides still enough incentive for private industry to participate. More research is needed to investigate the role that negotiated agreements could play as a part of total policy packages and to identify the economic and institutional conditions under which such policy packages (for example the combination of voluntary agreements and environmental taxes, the combination of voluntary agreements and negotiable pollution rights) could be effective.

Index